TOUGH LOVE

D0619936

Edited by Michèle Aina Barale,

Jonathan Goldberg, Michael Moon,

and Eve Kosofsky Sedgwick

TOUGH LOVE

Amazon Encounters in the

English Renaissance

Kathryn Schwarz

Duke University Press

Durham & London 2000

© 2000 Duke University Press
All rights reserved
Printed in the United States
of America on acid-free paper ∞
Designed by Rebecca M. Giménez
Typeset in Monotype Centaur
by Tseng Information Systems
Frontispiece: "*They, best injoy their
Hearts desires, In whom,* Love,
kindles mutuall-fires." George Wither,
"The Third Booke," in *A Collection
of Emblemes, Ancient and Moderne:
Quickened with Metricall Illustrations, both
Morall and Divine* (London, 1635), 178.
Reproduced with permission of the
Houghton Library, Harvard University
Library of Congress Cataloging-
in-Publication Data appear on the
last printed page of this book.

for Cara

Contents

Illustrations

Preface

"Ancient Graves of Armed Women Hint at Amazons."[1] Like its counterparts in the exploration narratives of the sixteenth century, this *New York Times* headline from February 25, 1997, is followed by an account of recent discoveries. In this case the discoveries result from archaeological excavations in the Eurasian steppes: female skeletons, buried with weapons, hint that a culture in which women's bodies were equipped for war might both substantiate and localize one of our most elusive myths. For the *Times* as for early modern explorers, however, material proof is at best dubiously connected to sensational claims; as the article hastens to admit, the women whose graves have been discovered "probably did not quite fit the larger-than-life Amazon image of women who seemed to prefer making war to making love" (B10). The site, according to the article, is far from the geographical areas in which classical histories locate Amazons; few of the skeletons show evidence of wounds received in battle; and the find is less valuable as evidence of actual Amazons than as a foundation for reconsidering the roles of ancient women more generally. Why, then, bring up Amazons at all? Why quote Herodotus on their history in order to point out that these women don't fit? What does it mean to attach a headline proclaiming the discovery of Amazons to an article about discovering something else?

Most obviously, it means that readers of the *Times* are more likely to be interested in Amazons than in more generic women warriors, that an Amazon is more compelling than just any woman with a sword, that Amazons have a particular cachet, and that their discovery is of particular interest. This is true in part because Amazons, for us, are less a presence than a rhetorical move. The term "Amazon" appears in a variety of contemporary contexts, from bad movies to the radical lesbian feminist separatism of the 1970s, and, as this diversity of implicit audiences suggests, it does not mean the same thing to everyone. Its status is at once absolute and oddly contingent; we know what it means, but "we" are difficult to limit or define. Wearing, for example, a shirt that says "Amazon" in a gay pride parade is not the same thing as being featured in a documentary called *Modern Amazons,* which is not the same thing as belonging to a basketball team called The Amazons, which is not the same thing as belonging to a rock group called The Amazons, which is not the same thing as being called an Amazon during a domestic disagreement. In this limited range of examples, the term might mean "lesbian," "feminist," "tall," "loud," or "bitch," and, although it is true that in our cultural lexicon these terms are far from mutually exclusive, they are far from equation as well.

The situation of utterance shifts with each of these examples, but in each, too, the utterance itself reflects a sense that something strange has come close to home. What, then, would it mean to "find" "the Amazons"? It might mean rhetorical crisis, or at least a drastic circumscription of what the term can do. In the early stages of this project, it was suggested to me that the worst thing that could happen would be that moment of discovery, a photo on the cover of *People* magazine, say, with the caption " 'We are lovers, not fighters,' say Amazons." Now (or rather on February 25, 1997) we have moved from that fantasized cover of *People* to an actual page B7 of the Science section of the *New York Times,* and the moment of discovery, of literalization, of a foreclosure of interpretation, has arrived—only to prove to be nothing of the kind. These Amazons, it turns out, are not "really" Amazons at all, although they can tell us something about them. "So Dr. Davis-Kimball is not jumping to any conclusions that these women were indeed the Amazons of legend," John Noble Wilford assures *Times* readers, "only suggesting that they could be contemporaries of the Amazons or that their lives, and those of similar nomadic women who could ride and wield a sword or dagger in combat, may have inspired the legend" (B10). Clearly we are caught here between the usefulness of information and the pleasures of mystery; clearly, too, that "we" is both a transparent and a necessary fiction. Who, after all, wants to know?

I am concerned here with that relation of knowledge to desire, with the tension between "really" and "not really" as it shapes stories about Amazons in the early modern period. These stories waver between triumphant claims of recognition and uncomfortable disclaimers of the fantastic, between the discovery of something new and the rediscovery of what Freud, in his discussion of the uncanny, describes as "something which is secretly familiar, which has undergone repression and then returned from it."[2] Amazon encounters describe both excursions and returns, appearing equally at home in explorers' accounts of the edge of the world and in conduct manuals prescribing domestic conventions. Nor are these contexts distinct; domesticity, when it engages amazonian subjects, is easily estranged from the intent of its production, even as amazonian quests often discover well-worn relations rather than new things. Amazonian narratives negotiate the gap between out there and in here, and disrupt the structuring presumptions of both places. There seems, in early modern English texts, to be infinite pleasure in imagining Amazons, and tremendous uneasiness as well: as an epic battle of the sexes, Amazon myth sets up a story in which patriarchy (usually) wins; but as a reflection of the everyday relations of women and men, it is the story that should not be told. " 'We are lovers, not fighters,' say Amazons." That distinction, at once obvious and misleading, is at the center of this book.

For early modern English texts, Amazons inspire an intensity of fascination and ambivalence akin to, and perhaps productive of, our own. The coincidences of known and unknown territories, of conventional and experimental theories, which characterize geography, gender, literary production, and sovereign authority in this period suggest that strange things might always be found in familiar places, and offer Amazons as a case in point. The tension between not knowing what—if, where—Amazons are and knowing what they mean condenses a larger pattern of friction between the unimaginable and the everyday, engendered, as friction tends to be engendered, not by distance but by proximity. Does Amazon myth, with its odd constructions of gender and power, represent the antithesis of normativity, or play out its logical extremes? At once evading and responding to this question, early modern narratives use "Amazon" not only like but as a theoretical term, a figure that articulates without resolving social and sexual incongruities. For such narratives, as for the *New York Times*, the drive toward discovery is at once powerful and reluctant, the desire to find Amazons abroad balanced and sometimes displaced by the impulse to figure, and to figure out, what they are doing at home.

This book has been shaped by the knowledge, insight, and generosity of its readers; I am particularly grateful to Roland Greene and Barbara Lewalski for their guidance in the early stages. I owe great debts to Marjorie Garber, who from the beginning has given me indispensable advice and support, and to Jonathan Goldberg for his enthusiasm and thoughtful reading. I am very fortunate in my colleagues at Vanderbilt; special thanks to Jay Clayton, Lynn Enterline, Teresa Goddu, Leah Marcus, Mark Schoenfield, and Mark Wollaeger, and to Vereen Bell, who, as department chair, provided help both institutional and personal. I completed the first version of this project in the company of an extraordinary group of women working in early modern studies: Jennifer Carrell, Elizabeth Fowler, Carla Mazzio, Kristen Poole, Katherine Rowe, and Elizabeth Spiller were and continue to be sources of inspiration. My thanks to Anita Barbagallo, Deb Bartle, Lynn Dobrunz, and Julia Garrett for living with me, literally and figuratively, over the years, and to Marvin Taylor for his ever stimulating conversation. I am grateful to my family for their support, and particularly to my mother, Susan Schwarz, who throughout this process has given me unexpected references and good thoughts. Thanks to Rachel Mann for her help as I finished writing, and to Richard Morrison for his help at the beginning of the publication process. Harvard University and the Whiting Foundation provided fellowship aid during the early stages; the University Research Council and the Robert Penn Warren Center for the Humanities, both at Vanderbilt University, provided important support for more recent research.

My deepest thanks to Carolyn Dever, who in all kinds of ways made this happen.

NOTE ON THE TEXT: Chapter 2 of the following discussion appeared in *Shakespeare Quarterly* 49, no. 2 (summer 1998):140–67, and was reprinted in the *1998 Yearbook of Shakespeare Criticism*; it is reprinted here by permission of *Shakespeare Quarterly*. An early version of chapter 3 appeared in *Studies in English Literature* 35, no. 2 (spring 1995): 293–319, under the title "Amazon Reflections in the Jacobean Queen's Masque." Part of chapter 4 appeared in *Historicism, Psychoanalysis, and Early Modern Culture*, ed. Carla Mazzio and Doug Trevor (New York: Routledge, 2000), under the title "Breaking the Mirror Stage"; it is reprinted here by permission of Routledge Press.

NOTE ON CITATION: In citing early modern texts, I have retained their spellings; however, except when quoting from recent editions that retain original appearances, I have modernized typography in several ways. Consonantal *u* and *i* have been revised to *v* and *j*, and vocalic *v* has been revised to *u*; long *s* has been revised to *s*; ligatures of *æ* and *œ* have been expanded to their component letters; *&* and *yᵉ* have been altered to *and* and *the*; where a macron over a vowel indicates the suspension of *m* or *n*, I have supplied the letter.

Introduction

AMAZONS

For since the daies of Adam women were never
so Masculine; Masculine in their genders and whole
generations, from the Mother, to the yongest daughter;
Masculine in Number, from one to multitudes; Masculine in
Case, even from the head to the foot; Masculine in Moode, from
bold speech, to impudent action; and Masculine in Tense: for
(without redresse) they were, are, and will be still most
Masculine, most mankinde, and most monstrous.
—*Hic Mulier: Or, the Man-Woman*

It is a story of rapine and robbery.
—Guy Rothery, *The Amazons*

DEVICES AND DESIRES

This is a book about Amazons and domesticity. It is not, however, a book about the ways in which early modern notions of normative femininity are constituted against the figure of the Amazon; it does not take that figure as the exception that justifies enforcement of the rules. Instead I want to suggest, perhaps somewhat counterintuitively, that stories about Amazons are testing grounds for social conventions, playing out the relationships between homosocial and heterosocial systems of connection that produce an idea of the domestic. At once masculine and female, mistaken for men and looked at as women, Amazons generate desire between men, between women, between women and men. Their constant eroticism precludes hierarchical distinctions between substance and spirit, matter and idea, object and agent, other and self, revealing instead the extent to which identities and relations overlap. And because amazonian doubleness is at once efficient—a convergence of multiple appetites on a single body—and troubling—a reflection of the possibility that roles might shift—the message conveyed is double as well. Early modern stories about Amazon encounters insist on the integrity of categories and hierarchies, taking amazonian domestication as proof that those structures work. But they also reveal concern with the potential fragility of socialized desire, suggesting that there is something risky

Tough Love

about representing its aggressive performance so aggressively *as* a perfor-mance. While watching social logic work, we might always see it break down.

In a sense, I am writing against my epigraphs. In the texts with which I am concerned, Amazons are not only taken up to illustrate the strange-ness of female masculinity, but are implicated in the construction of familiar space. This gives a twist to the "rapine and robbery" of which Rothery accuses Amazons, and which might more obviously apply to the men who attack and exterminate them. Early modern narratives, I argue, are interested less in the Amazons' resistance to patriarchy than in their participation in it. As a strategy of consolidation, the domesti-cation of Amazons subsumes a threat to social order, but it also leaves it there: amazonian wives do not lose the adjective when they acquire the noun, and the spectacle of amazonian domesticity is at least as discon-certing as it is triumphant. I argue throughout this book that the point is not whether Amazons "win" or "lose" in their battles with men, but rather the difficulty of telling the difference, as incorporation into the social makes the line between conquering Amazons and being invaded by them indecipherable. It may seem merely obvious to say that Ama-zons are not good examples of conventionally heterosexual, patriarchally governed, ideologically secure domestic bliss. Again and again, however, early modern texts discover this truth not through its self-evidence, but through trial and a good deal of error. If there is something perverse about imagining Amazons within domestic roles, there is also, appar-ently, something irresistible.

To account for such impulses of imagination, it is worth thinking about the imaginative power of Amazons themselves. The meaning of "Amazon" is constituted out of an inappropriate relationship between sexed bodies and gendered acts, constructing an identity defined by the agency of sexual choice and by a perception of that choice as inher-ently perverse. In this sense, "Amazon" constructs a sexual identity in a way that early modern understandings of heterosexuality (because it is presumed) and homosexuality (because it is presumed invisible) do not. Famously distinguishing between categories of identity and categories of practice, Foucault writes, "As defined by the ancient civil or canoni-cal codes, sodomy was a category of forbidden acts; their perpetrator was nothing more than the juridical subject of them."[1] This distinction shapes readings of early modern same-sex desire; so in *Homosexuality in Renaissance England* Alan Bray warns, "To talk of an individual in this period as being or not being 'a homosexual' is an anachronism and ruinously misleading."[2] The distinction between normative and illicit sexual practices certainly exists in the sixteenth and seventeenth centuries, but a set of such practices does not accumulate to a logic of person in any modern sense. Bray writes, "Outside an immediately sexual context, there was little or no social pressure for someone to define for himself what his sexuality was. And the way homosexuality was conceived of and understood did not encourage him to make that connection had he wished to, which was unlikely" (70). Early modern subjects, reasonably enough, had little motive to invent for themselves identities that invited reprisals; and if in the abstract they invented such identities for others—if there were, as Bray argues, monstrous beings called "sodomites" who synthesized all imaginable threats to a well-ordered society—those others were in practice difficult to find.[3]

It is this condition—"difficult to find"—that makes it possible to identify Amazons in terms of sexual identities. If "sodomite" has a legal meaning, however confused and capacious, to which individuals are subject, the same cannot be said of "Amazon"; there are no "real Amazons" in early modern England to leave a trail in court records. At the same time, the conviction that there might be real Amazons somewhere, if one could only find them, does leave traces in early modern texts. And because Amazons are explicitly fantastic, even in the accounts that take their existence most seriously, they catalyze unexpected ways of thinking about the intersection of the sexual and the social: in placing Amazons at the beginning of time or at the edge of the world, texts open up a space in which identity can be understood differently. Speaking of "sexual identity" implies that sexuality engages, signifies within, and potentially disrupts social roles. Early modern representations of sexual deviance, appearing largely through ellipsis and displacement, often seem opaque in these terms; but the Amazons imagined in this period make sex a public display, from their modified bodies and the bodies of their children to the spectacular nature of their encounters with men. In the fantasies of amazonian domesticity that I consider in this book, sexuality aggressively intervenes in the constitution of social hierarchies and bonds.

In *Gender and the Politics of History*, Joan Wallach Scott writes, "It follows then that gender is the social organization of sexual difference. But this does not mean that gender reflects or implements fixed and natural physical differences between women and men; rather gender is the knowledge that establishes meanings for bodily differences."[4] Amazonian sex, in the sense both of recognizable gender and of sexual acts, disrupts the presumptions of meaning and knowledge. Amazons manipulate sexed bodies by removing a breast in order to use weapons; this not only frustrates expectations of eroticism and nurture, but challenges the convention that weapons define and protect male bodies. As Gail Kern Paster writes, "The Amazons' significance as ambivalently powerful figures of aggressive, self-determining desire is epitomized by their self-mutilation."[5] Amazons choose inappropriate sexual objects: men who are enemies, barbarians, prisoners, or physically maimed, and possibly—although it is a largely and strangely silent possibility—other women. Amazons engage in troubling sexual practices, mating anonymously in the dark, killing men by exhausting them sexually, refraining from marriage until they have killed a man in war; one early modern author writes, "To none of the *Amazones* was graunted liberty to marry, excepte she had in warre valiauntly vanquished an enemy."[6] Amazons mystify sexual reproduction, undoing patrilineal connections, killing, maiming, or abandoning male children, raising their daughters in what becomes in effect a female parthenogenetic society. From this constellation of ideas about sexed bodies, sexual acts, and sex as an enforcement of desire, early modern texts invent and identify "Amazons."

Then they import them. In the early modern period, stories about Amazons become stories about mothers and children, husbands and wives, as texts ranging from *The First Blast* and *The English Gentlewoman* to *The Arcadia*, *The Faerie Queene*, and *A Midsummer Night's Dream* invoke amazonian exoticism in order to talk about the quotidian and the domestic. This is the double move of Amazon narratives, which project an image into an antisocial condition of sexual identity only to bring it back again. Back, that is, into articulations of male homosocial power and its perpetuation through domesticated heterosexuality, articulations that the intervention of "Amazon" can only disconcert. Jonathan Dollimore argues that the sodomite, as a figure for "deviant subject positions," threatens to provide a space for those positions within social norms: "The deviant was the point of entry into civilization for the unnatural, the aberrant, and the abhorrent, the wilderness of disorder which beleaguered all civilization; a disorder in part, but rarely only ever, sexual."[7] Amazons, like sodomites in Dollimore's account, are figures of errant subjectivity, embodiments of otherness in which the condition of distance has failed. But in amazonian narratives a response of desire, implicit in the fascination with sodomy, comes to the surface and becomes the matter of plot. If, as Dollimore argues, a figure incorporated in spite of efforts to exclude it opens a gap in social defenses, the effect escalates when inclusion is deliberate and even aggressive, when female masculinity becomes a way of understanding mothers and lovers and wives. Early modern stories about Amazons draw on a thoroughly modern set of causal clichés, reasoning from an incongruous relationship between gender and sex to the assumption of deviant sexuality. That that deviance implicates *hetero*sexuality only compounds the effect; if women who do strange things with each other impose their own distance, the same cannot be said of women who do strange things to men.

If "Amazon" becomes a sexual identity because of what Amazons do to men, it becomes a gendered identity because of what Amazons do *like* and *with* men, the image of female masculinity precipitating a crisis at the intersection of sociality and sex. It is in part a crisis of language: What words describe amazonian desires? Addressing the question of terms, Valerie Traub distinguishes between heterosexuality and homoeroticism through their connection to social categories of identity: "My use of the linguistic root 'sexuality' is meant to imply heterosexuality's institutional and political mandate, in which identity was situated in relation to one's sexual congress as a socially ascribed subject-position." She continues, "Homoeroticism was a position taken in *relation* to desire — a position, however, that was neither socially mandated nor capable of conferring identity or role."[8] Eve Kosofsky Sedgwick implicates both the social and the sexual in her term "homosocial desire": "In any male-dominated society, there is a special relationship between male homosocial (*including* homosexual) desire and the structures for maintaining and transmitting patriarchal power: a relationship founded on an inherent and potentially active structural congruence."[9] Sedgwick describes a continuum that connects the social to the sexual through desire; Traub distinguishes the erotic and the sexual based on their social legibility. In using the suffixes "erotic," "social," and "sexual" in the discussion that follows, I engage the relationship between distinction and continuum as it takes shape in Amazon encounters. The fantasy of amazonian eroticism confuses kinds of affiliation; at the same time, the project of amazonian domestication reflects a deep investment in categories of identity and desire. Interactions marked as social both slide into sexuality and are aggressively held apart from it; desire between men and women both looks like and cannot be allowed to be like desire among men.

My references to sociality and sexuality reflect both the attempt to make these conditions of relation separate and a profound skepticism, not only on my part but on the part of early modern texts, as to whether that attempt can succeed. The ordering principle that turns sexuality to the service of social convention is prone to failures of discretion, and Amazons catalyze erotic slippage. Amazonian eroticism mediates among terms, both between the hetero- and the homo- and between the social and the sexual. Homoeroticism, in Amazon encounters, might consolidate homosociality, but it also tends toward both homo- and heterosexuality; heteroeroticism does not simply produce marriage and children, but upsets the constitution of homosocial identity and the value judgments of heterosocial difference. When I use the terms "homoerotic" and "heteroerotic," I refer to this convergence of effects, this collision of ordering impulses and their discomfiture. The erotic is not only unruly, any more than it is only a consolidation of right relations; it does not map out categories, but reveals their interpenetration. Eroticism, like Amazons, implicates both bodies and fantasies, its presence both domesticating and estranging the intersection of social normativity and sex.

In this book I take up formulations of social normativity that are structured through, rather than against or in spite of, representations of a socially deviant sexual identity. Theories of patriarchy as a set of male relations mediated through women foreclose the possibility of unsocialized desire, drawing sharp distinctions between eroticism that works productively and eroticism that does not, between the social and the aberrant, between bodily acts that matter and those that signify only in their punishment and their exclusion. Recent work in early modern studies shows where and how those distinctions fail, allowing antisocial sexuality to occupy the space of the social itself. As Judith Butler has argued, the "domain of unthinkable, abject, unlivable bodies" against which normativity is constituted cannot, by definition, be excluded from the norm; she describes "an abjected outside, which is, after all, 'inside' the subject as its own founding repudiation." [10] Antisocial sexuality, as part of the early modern period's articulation of the abject, compels representation, appearing throughout the texts that — in their governing assumptions, their generic imperatives, their happy endings — should make it unthinkable. So Bray finds links between idealized friendship and unacceptable desire; Richard Rambuss traces signs of transgressive eroticism in devotional literature; Dorothy Stephens describes a pattern of "conditional relationships between errant women" in chivalric texts; Traub argues for a conflation of "chaste female friendship" with the dangerous grotesqueries of tribadism; Bruce Smith identifies "six separate myths of homosexual desire, each of which involves a different combination of characters and plot, a different set of ideas about sodomy, a different way of enacting homosexual desire in imagination"; Jeffrey Masten theorizes "a paradigm that insistently figured writing as mutual imitation, collaboration, and homoerotic exchange." [11] Such analyses demonstrate that intercourse is never entirely social, never completely safe; as Jonathan Goldberg writes in his introduction to *Queering the Renaissance*, "Sexuality is only phantasmatically cordoned off to some private sphere; in truth, sexuality structures and destructures the social." [12]

Any effort to restrict eroticism to social utility assumes discrete effects: homoeroticism is consummated in the production of social power between men, and heteroeroticism is consummated in the production of children by women. The studies I have cited here demonstrate that attempts to demarcate and patrol such a taxonomy reveal their own inadequacies, failing to suppress recognition that homoeroticism might always produce homosexuality, and that heterosexuality must often be an inadequate prophylactic; as Gregory Bredbeck writes, "Homoeroticism, then, can be perceived as something other than the margin of sexual meaning; it can also signal where the margins end and, in the process, indicate through implication the limited status of heteroerotic epistemology." [13] My work is deeply indebted to these studies and continues their pursuit of the unexpected, simultaneously fascinating and unsettling modes of eroticism that Traub theorizes through the interplay of anxiety and desire, and that Goldberg describes as "the sites of sexual possibilities, the syntax of desires not readily named." [14] But such possibilities, rather than being coded or concealed, are the plain matter of amazonian narratives, and my project in this way differs from those in which the presence of erotic errancy must be detected before its implications can be unpacked. Smith writes of homosexuality before the nineteenth century, "To see the pattern we have to know, first of all, what to look for. To decipher the message we have to know the code."[15] The pattern, the "secret," of Amazon encounters—that the response of desire has only a loose and shifting relationship to the perception of gender—is not their subtext or our metatext, but the plot. Operating on and as the surface, amazonian perversion (itself a curiously redundant term) does a different kind of work, and the nature of that work is my central question.

I am concerned, then, with what happens when the production of social normativity explicitly, rather than implicitly or clandestinely or inadvertently, presumes the presence of what Dollimore has termed "transgressive reinscription." Intimations of proximity and resemblance, Dollimore argues, may be more troubling than claims about absolute otherness, creating "instabilities within repressive norms."[16] The eroticism catalyzed by Amazons, in which continuity overwhelms discretion, disrupts the relationship between hetero- and homosocial conventions from within. In a story in which a man responds erotically to idealized masculinity only to find himself married to a woman, or in which a man responds erotically to idealized femininity only to find that his wife is much like a man, we do not need to look hard for the transgressive desire that underlies the repressive norm; indeed, we would be hard-pressed to look away. As texts locate the figure of the Amazon at the heart of social negotiations, the convergence of multiple similarities into imminence—Amazons are like men; Amazons are like mothers, wives, and queens; Amazons are *right there*—reveals the perversity of the inside. As a theory of the relationship between identity and misrecognition, amazonian sexuality anticipates our own, in this sense belated, theoretical discoveries, defining the processes that socialize desire as not only open to the enterprise of queering, but themselves already and self-consciously queer. Amazon encounters are strange dreams invested with the production of conventional meaning: a set of relations conceived as imaginary enters, if not into the real, then perhaps more transgressively into the symbolic.

In "The Agency of the Letter in the Unconscious," Lacan defines desire as metonymy, infinitely progressive and inevitably frustrated. He then equates metaphors with symptoms, describing symptoms as bodily articulations that stand in a complex and mediated relationship to an underlying story: "Between the enigmatic signifier of the sexual trauma and the term that is substituted for it in an actual signifying chain there passes the spark that fixes in a symptom the signification inaccessible to the conscious subject in which that symptom may be resolved—a symptom being a metaphor in which flesh or function is taken as a signifying element." [17] In this sense, Amazon myth is both a narrative and a figure, a desire that is also a symptom. Stories about Amazons metonymically push toward an end for which they are themselves a sign, referring to idealized relationships in which male homosociality produces and governs heterosociality and bonds between women do not matter. Idealized and simplified beyond possibility, the set of relations pursued by these stories is not social history or even social theory, but an articulation of desire. Domesticity in this context is a fantasy about appropriate relations between women and men rather than a question of economics or physical space; femininity is an idealized balance of titillation and acquiescence, not a matter of dangerous maternity, insurgent shrewishness, and menstrual blood. Amazonian narratives catalyze the fantasy of such symbolic relations by failing to produce them. These narratives do not begin with social order, but imagine its invention out of a set of recalcitrant and deforming terms, naturalizing not an ordered state but a state of resistance: categories and hierarchies are imposed, often inadequately and unpersuasively, rather than presumed. The Amazons of early modern narratives, as characters, exempla, or "real" women, constitute "a metaphor in which flesh or function is taken as a signifying element." Amazon encounters are symptoms in the sense that they look nothing like the thing to which they refer, even as they expose its presence; ideals of ordered relation appear in their alteration and their failure.

Here I want to be explicit about the use value of a narrative that insists on its own material plausibility without ever apparently being true. Describing her project of "history at the level of the signifier," Catherine Belsey writes, "Culture is lived, but we have no direct access to early modern 'life'. The materials of cultural history reside in the signifying practices of a society, and these include its fictions, where meanings and values are defined and contested for the delight and instruction of an audience which is expected to understand a proportion, at least, of what is at stake."[18] Amazons cannot, as far as we know, provide evidence for a historical argument about early modern conditions of social domesticity. That is to say, real men are not, in early modern culture, marrying real Amazons, although there is extensive interest in the possibility that real Amazons exist. As objects of an ontological debate in which fascination with the question overshadows the pursuit of answers, Amazons are both alien and immanent, available to representational appropriation and intractable in their evocative effects. This is the force of stories that represent Amazons within conventionally domestic space. Such stories are not, from an early modern perspective, historical or anecdotal, but they are also not entirely disqualified from that position, and their construction within the space of the subjunctive enables them to figure a set of concerns as closely related to everyday life as they are mythologically remote. In *Mythologies*, Roland Barthes writes, "Myth has the task of giving an historical intention a natural justification, and making contingency appear eternal."[19] For the early modern period, stories about Amazons often begin as attempts to naturalize the artifacts of gender and end by interrogating the stuff out of which those artifacts are made.

In my readings of such stories, I argue that they work as theoretical structures, revealing and analyzing tensions within systems of socioerotic connection. Like the stories proposed by psychoanalytic theory — the mirror stage, the primal scene, the Oedipal conflict — stories about Amazons *might* happen or, in the opinion of an individual author, perhaps even *did* happen, but their narrative power lies in their larger articulation of a structure of identity and desire. In the course of the twentieth century, we evolved a range of strategies and terms to reflect the signifying contradictions that inhabit intersections of sociality and sex: Freud's uncanny; Lacan's interplay of being, having, and seeming; Butler's gender trouble; Sedgwick's conjoining of "homosocial" and "desire"; Garber's "third"; the supplement; the phallus; the subversive; the abject. Throughout the discussion that follows, I place such paradigms alongside narratives of Amazon encounters, not to map our methodologies onto early modern texts, but to illuminate the ways in which those texts are themselves engaged in similar work.[20] Amazonian narratives of the early modern period are historically particular, in that they reflect specific conditions—events or ideas generated out of such issues as female sovereignty, geographical expansion, contested gender roles, emerging literary conventions—but they are consistently metacritical and hypothetical in their relationship to those conditions. In this book, I pursue the theoretical arguments that Amazon encounters present.

FAMILY ROMANCES

In 1558, in one of history's more striking convergences of misogyny and bad timing, John Knox expressed his views on female sovereignty. *The First Blast of the Trumpet Against the Monstrous Regiment of Women* describes the horrors of female power, and for Knox horror takes the form of Amazons. "I am assuredly persuaded that if any of those men, which illuminated only by the light of nature did see and pronounce causes sufficient why women ought not to bear rule nor authority, should this day live and see a woman sitting in judgment or riding from parliament in the midst of men, having the royal crown upon her head, the sword and scepter borne before her in sign that the administration of justice was in her power; I am assuredly persuaded, I say, that such a sight should so astonish them that they should judge the whole world to be transformed into Amazons." [21] The judges here invoked understand an unnatural state through a mythographic analogue: Amazons, who notoriously invert the structures of government, can be used to explain—although never to excuse—the presence of a queen on the throne.

I take this moment as my starting point, not only because it incorporates Amazon myth into political rhetoric, but because it synthesizes a range of domestic concerns. Knox expresses the conviction that female rule is a dangerous thing to a nation; however, this notion of domesticity as a category of patriotism or national identity is not separate from anxiety about more local domesticity, and specifically the nature of women's roles within the family. In *Fashioning Femininity*, Karen Newman observes, "The overdetermined relation between the family and society, between familial and political authority, with which power relations were represented in late Elizabethan and early Jacobean England made the family at once a site of contest and containment." [22] *The First Blast*, having begun with an attempt to contain particular queens, moves on to express a larger sense of domesticity as a contested space: "To the further declaration of the imperfections of women, of their natural weakness and inordinate appetites, I might adduce histories proving some women to have died for sudden joy, some for unpatience to have murdered themselves; some to have burned with such inordinate lust that, for the quenching of the same, they have betrayed to strangers their country and city; and some to have been so desirous of dominion that, for the obtaining of the same, they have murdered the children of their own sons. Yea, and some have killed with cruelty their own husbands and children" (44). Knox here imagines what will happen if not only the nation but its households are ruled by women. His argument progresses spatially, moving inexorably closer to home: women make bad enemies; women will betray their cities to their enemies; women will become the enemy within the family, killing their children and their men. This, Knox argues, is what happens under the aegis of female sovereignty; this is what happens in a nation of Amazons.

It is a strange threat. Amazons work more logically as signs for what is "out there," at the edge of the world or beyond that edge. Talking about Amazons, in early modern England as before and since, is a way of referring to the unknowable and the unreachable; Amazons are repeatedly associated with such other mythic figures as headless men, cannibals, Prester John, and the lost tribes of Israel. Although the debate over whether Amazons exist continues in this period—explorers and historiographers claim ocular proof, even as skeptics refer dismissively to "amazonian dreames"—interest inheres more in the space of not knowing. Turning to this "manly foeminine people," this "Amazonian, or Unimammian Nation," in his theological survey of the world, Samuel Purchas writes, "Religion it were to speake of their *Religion*, of whose being we have no better certainetie." [23] The quality of uncertainty persists. Amazons are variously imagined as Asian, African, American, and Northern European, as black and white, as divinely, monstrously, and parthenogenetically conceived. Accounts of their social practices range from rigid hierarchy to egalitarianism, from child killing to fostering, from random sex with male captives or neighboring tribes to intimations of lesbianism to various and usually violent forms of heterosexual marriage. Confronted by such contradictions, one early modern editor is driven to exasperation, writing of an explorer's account, "The Amazons are still further off: I doubt beyond the region of Truth; if the title be properly meant of such as are described." [24] And later historians often seem to have a similar response, looking back on the age of discovery as, at least in the matter of Amazons, an age of disconcerting unreason.

The authority of Amazon myth might lie less in its truth-value than in its status as a story with a moral. Abby Wettan Kleinbaum writes, "To win an Amazon, either through arms or through love or, even better, through both, is to be certified as a hero. Thus men told of battling Amazons to enhance their sense of their own worth and historical significance." [25] In classical Amazon encounters male heroism rests on the death of Amazons, producing a long tradition of high-minded conclusions. Diodorus writes, "Then the nations of barbary . . . so hardely asawted the Amasons incessantly with cotidian warre, that, as historiers repoort, they distroyed that name and all the hole nation." [26] An Athenian funeral oration by Lysias makes a similar claim: "They perished on the spot, and were punished for their folly, thus making our city's memory imperishable for its valor; while owing to the disaster in this region they rendered their own country nameless. And so those women, by their unjust greed for others' land, justly lost their own." [27] The myth of amazonian ascendancy produces the necessity of a fall. "But as it is the property of tyme to consume all thinges," William Painter concludes in his account, "even so the kingdome and power of the *Amazones* grew to utter decay, no one sutch nation at this day to be found." [28] Louis Montrose argues that such conclusions compensate for a threat to patriarchal government: "But if Amazonian myth figures the inversionary claims of matriarchy, sisterhood, and the autonomy of women, it also figures the *repudiation* of those claims in the act of Amazonomachy." [29]

But amazonian mythography is a series of intertextual returns, ending only to begin again somewhere else. Moving from Asia to Africa to America, from Herodotus to Diodorus to *The Palace of Pleasure*, stories about Amazons suggest that the satisfaction of conclusion is less compelling than the pleasure of the text, and in early modern texts that pleasure takes new forms. In classical accounts, as Page duBois argues, Amazons validate social contracts by providing a counterexample: "Even as such mythical creatures as the Amazons seemed to question the boundaries between male and female, the myth as a whole ended by denying the viability of single-sex female culture, and by affirming the traditional pattern of exchange of women by citizen men." [30] William Blake Tyrrell makes a similar point: "In the classical period matriarchy functioned as a tool for thinking, explaining, and validating patriarchal customs, institutions, and values by postulating the absurdities and horrors of its opposite."[31] Inversion proves the logic of the original proposition; normativity takes shape against the forms it excludes. But in the early modern period, the gesture outward is increasingly complicated by an impulse inward, a tendency to see Amazons not only at the edge of the world but at its center. Even accounts that reiterate the conceit of a great and final battle produce a domestic model from among the corpses, as in Thomas Gainsford's version of the story: "The better sort conspired against the women, and by degrees ware them out of the Countrey with many slaughters, teaching the obstinate the vicissitude of things, and admitting the submissive under the warmth of loving embraces, by which occasion the men at last prevailed; and in time this vast Countrey was proud to be the life infuser into many valiant sonnes."[32] Absolute conquest becomes a prelude to the Amazon at home, imagined as lover or wife, mother or queen; processes of consolidation and control, traditionally imposed through wholesale slaughter, depend instead on the ordering power of social expectations. And if martial triumph requires repetition from a distance, its domestic analogue looks still more precarious up close.

This is the energy behind Knox's condemnation, the significance of the analogy on which he insists: the Amazon at home is something that could happen in and to Britain itself. Despite the estranging efforts of polemicists, there is something disconcertingly *English* about the Amazons who appear in early modern English texts. During this period, classical amazonian histories appear in translation and are further popularized by such "novelizations" as *The Palace of Pleasure;* amazonian excess becomes a cautionary tale in contexts ranging from gender debates through conduct manuals to political tracts; and exploration narratives are collected and published by Richard Eden, Richard Hakluyt, and Samuel Purchas. Rather than defining otherness, Amazons in these contexts inspire analogy. For Painter as for Knox, the Amazon is an exemplary type that produces an anthology of derivative narratives: "The maners and qualities of which nation, bycause they were Women of no common spirite and boldnesse, bee thought good in the front of this second Volume to be described: bycause of dyvers Womens lives plentifull variety is offered in the sequele."[33] Painter builds a palace of pleasure on the grounds of Knox's call to arms, producing spectacle rather than horror show; but *The Palace of Pleasure*, like *The First Blast*, puts "Amazons" in contiguous relation to "women."

As rhetorical figures, Amazons serve a wide and often contradictory range of purposes, naturalizing men's superiority to women and historicizing women's violence against men, exemplifying chastity and summarizing sexual excess, celebrating and castigating queens.[34] Linda Woodbridge terms them "*exempla* most congenial to the formal defense," whereas Margaret King locates them on the other side of the exemplary debate: "Hostile representations of such disordered nature cautioned matrons and brides to respect their natural limits."[35] Amazons signify both ways, a doubleness made explicit in *The English Gentlewoman*. Having described a woman who embodies sexual transgression, Richard Brathwait concludes by asking, "Tell me, were not his spirit armour of proofe, who durst encounter with so couragious an *Amazon*?"[36] Having presented a parable in which a woman defends her chastity by force, Brathwait appends the marginal note, "An English Amazon" (126). As a sign of sexual excess, "Amazon" is proverbial; so, too, is "Amazon" as an index of militant virginity. It is less conventional to illustrate both conditions with the same figure, but *The English Gentlewoman* uses two versions of amazonian shorthand at once, glossing "Amazon" as sexual monster and as sexual ideal in the space of two pages. The references, in each case transparent, add up to something opaque.

Attempts to conventionalize amazonian sexual identity produce the familiar figures of virgin and whore, but they produce both at once, complicating the exemplary project. For Amazons to confirm the sexual categories that determine social value, validating a taxonomy of women, amazonian sexuality itself must be imaginatively discrete. Some Amazons promise that discretion: Penthesilea, who is militantly chaste; Hippolyta, who marries Theseus; Thalestris, who seduces Alexander the Great. The figures may raise questions—Should chastity involve weapons? Is it romantic to fight your wife?—but the virgin/wife/whore distinctions seem to hold. Maryanne Cline Horowitz reads the practice of "playing with Amazons" as a statement of mastery: "An apparently amusing 'male' game, presented for the enjoyment of conventional men and women . . . is refashioning autonomous female figures along traditional gender lines, that is, appropriating them to conserve the status quo."[37] But the conservative project is flawed. Painter's references to Hippolyta, Penthesilea, and Thalestris allow the boundaries dividing kinds of women to disappear:

> For what monstruous Sexe was this that durst not onely by many armies encountre with puissant nations, but also by single Combate, to fight with that terrible personage *Hercules*, whose unspeakable and incredible labours and victories, are by antiquity reported to be sutch, as none but he, durst ever adventure the like . . . What like besieged towne as that of *Troy* was? and yet *Penthesilea* one of their Queenes with hir mayny, indevoured to rayse the *Greekes*, that so many yeares had lien before the same. What Queene (nay what Stalant) durst sue for company of meanest man? and yet one of these presumed to begge the matche of the mightiest Monarch that ever ruled the world.[38]

Painter displaces the question of what the Amazons are with an account of what they do, submerging sexual distinctions in the commonality of violent acts. His account suggests a more general fragility in the taxonomic project: it is difficult enough to sustain categories without involving Amazons.[39] Newman writes, "Though there is no question that Renaissance discourses of femininity advanced social controls and the policing of female behavior, they also enabled opposing discourses, which though they often speak with the same vocabulary and from the same categories, were nevertheless tactically productive."[40] Amazonian narratives accumulate to such an "opposing discourse," revealing a tension between polemicism and overdetermination in which devices of meaning might always mean too much.

Texts nonetheless generate strategies for separating good Amazons from bad ones, an enterprise hard at work in Spenser's distinction between Britomart and Radigund.[41] Spenser celebrates Britomart's martiality through reference to Amazons: "Ioy on those warlike women, which so long/Can from all men so rich a kingdome hold."[42] At the same time, he justifies the slaughter of Radigund and her amazonian followers, his language closely recalling that of Knox:

> Such is the crueltie of womenkynd,
>   When they haue shaken off the shamefast band,

With which wise Nature did them strongly bynd,
T'obay the heasts of mans well ruling hand,
That then all rule and reason they withstand,
To purchase a licentious libertie. (5.5.25)

The stanza's conclusion—"Vnlesse the heauens them lift to lawfull soueraintie"—may be the most famous caveat in literary history. Finding himself engaged in a wholesale condemnation of female rule, Spenser wisely if belatedly leaves space for "lawful sovereignty," authority tautologically validated by the structures through which it governs.[43] The martial woman is manifestly unnatural—unless she is already your queen.

The narratives with which I am concerned ask what happens if Amazon encounters occur within conventional structures—occur, that is, in places that, politically, socially, and erotically, *matter*. For Elizabethan England, the image of female sovereignty could not matter more. Yet Elizabethan Amazons do not usually or explicitly refer to Queen Elizabeth I; in her exhaustive essay "The Amazons in Elizabethan Literature," Celeste Turner Wright states categorically, "I have not found any Elizabethan comparing the queen directly to an Amazon."[44] Direct comparison may not be the whole story, however; as Knox's disgrace and Spenser's anxious "unless" demonstrate, metonymic association is an unpredictable effect, and the tactful separation of queens and Amazons is less absolute than occasionally contrived. This is true in part because, whatever the policies of royal compliment, early modern historiography does not separate Amazons from queens at all. "All the great Monarchies were instituted by the councell of women," Anthony Gibson writes in *A Womans Woorth*, and the presence of Amazons in catalogues of such monarchies becomes an exemplary commonplace.[45]

For Heinrich Cornelius Agrippa, Amazons fit seamlessly into the history of nationalism: he lists "*Semiramis, Dido,* and the *Amazons,* for both *skil and success* in War; *Thomiris,* Queen of the *Massagetae,* who conquer'd *Cyrus,* that great Monarch of the *Persians;* as also *Camilla,* of the Nation of the *Volci;* and *Valisca,* of *Bohemia,* both potent Queens . . . with many other *Illustrious Viragoes,* who in the greatest *exigencies,* and most desperate *shocks* of Fortune, have preserv'd their *gasping* Countreys."[46] Gainsford's *Glory of England,* with its investment in a more specific nationalism, separates

Amazons from English queens, but even in this narrowly patriotic context the distinction is precarious. "In *Bohemia* even of late daies *Libussa* and *Velasca* obtained the Diadem," he writes, "and when they supposed themselves seated in firmenesse, they gathered a company of Ladies, and upon a light credulity, that the story of the *Amazons* was to be beleeved, would have erected such a foolish Common-wealth. Amongst our selves before the conquest we had a *Guendoline* Queene of *Brittaine,* a *Cordelia Vaodicea,* and some other; and since two Daughters of HENRY the 8." [47] Both skepticism and bad government intervene in the progress from Bohemia to England; but Gainsford's narrative, like Agrippa's, makes the move from ancient history to "late daies," from other countries to "amongst our selves," without leaving Amazons behind. Woodbridge writes, "Renaissance defenders of women often take this tack when faced with military-minded females; they praise martial women only when they act in defense of their country or their children." [48] This strategy, like Knox's, implicates female martiality in the most intimate negotiations of home.

The implication is generalized beyond particular queens. "Who can endure a virago for a wife?" Burton asks in *The Anatomy of Melancholy,* but it seems, at least in the imagination of early modern texts, that such endurance may routinely be required of men.[49] Theseus marries Hippolyta, Artegall marries Britomart, Achilles wants to marry Penthesilea, and wishes that he had not killed her first. Such unions, with their political, erotic, and generative implications, are not isolated as lapses in conjugal judgment but analogically generalized: in early modern discourses of courtship and marriage, Amazon encounters inspire larger claims about heterosocial relations. In Lady Mary Wroth's *Urania,* when the character Musalina disguises herself as an Amazon, the narrator says, "Like an Amason Musalina attires her selfe, though unfit habits for her, who was no hater of mankind"; the comment recalls the classical tradition of amazonian misandry summarized by Aeschylus, who refers in *The Suppliant Women* to "the unwed barbarous Amazons" and in *Prometheus Bound* to "the Amazons, the race of women who hate men." [50] But for most early modern texts, separatism is both less interesting and less threatening than integration. *A Womans Woorth* describes Hippolyta in aggressively domestic terms, adjuring Theseus to be grateful "to have faire *Hippolita,*/So worthy noting every way,/In thy house to waite on thee"; *The Honest Man* goes farther, claiming that "Amazon" is a term of conventionalized courtship. "If shee be too leane or too little, she will be so much the more active and nimble; if too fat, it will be gracefull: the excesse in height will passe for the stature of a Queen or Amazon; and in the end hee will cover every imperfection with the perfection that is nearest unto it." [51] And William Heale, in his argument against domestic violence, uses amazonian examples to warn that women might take their revenge: "If I shoulde chaunce to marrie with a stoute and valiant woman, such as either *Pentheselaea* was amongst the *Amazons,* or the Lady *Parthenia* of *Greece* . . . and after a while from *Cupids* warres fal unto Martial armes, I doubt my learning woulde not save mee from some unlearned blowes." [52]

In such examples, stories about Amazons theorize marriage rather than oppose it, illuminating the ways in which domesticity functions as a system of roles. Ian Maclean writes of exemplary texts, "The heroic exploits of exceptional women are noted, but moralists do not advise emulation of them, but rather their translation into domestic and private terms." [53] If such translation takes place in the case of Amazons, it is at best incomplete. Women are like Amazons — or Amazons are like women — when they play Hippolyta's submissive part in *A Womans Woorth* or the part of the object satirized in *The Honest Man,* but women and Amazons also meet in the images of Burton's virago and Heale's conjugal pugilist. According to such models, men may find themselves negotiating relationships to women across the gap between feminine and masculine conventions; or they may find that there is no gap at all, instead confronting a version of masculinity that mirrors their own. Through the conceit of the amazonian wife, exemplary symbolic function and a sense of disruptive plurality converge, synthesizing a range of performances in a single body and demonstrating that definitions shift. Amazonian domesticity encompasses both a servile Hippolyta and the radical inversion described in Charles Butler's allegorical account of bees: "I am enforced (unles I wil choose rather to offend in *rebus,* than in *vocibus*) by their leav and thine (learned Reader) to strain the ordinary signification of the woord *Rex;* and, in such places, to translate it *Qeene:* sit the males heere bere noe sway at all: this beeing an *Amazonian* or *feminine* kingdom." [54]

Butler's use of "Amazonian" and "feminine" as interchangeable modifiers of "kingdom" indicates the extent to which queens and wives converge. John Aylmer, responding to *The First Blast,* reasons from domestic to political government in his justification of female sovereignty: "If then [women] may governe men in the house by saynt Paules commission, and an houshold is a lytle common welth, as Socrates in Xenophon saith: Then I can not see howe you can debarre them of all rule, or conclude that to be heads of men is against nature." [55] Natalie Zemon Davis explains the utility of such microcosm/macrocosm analogies: "In the little world of the family, with its conspicuous tension between intimacy and power, the larger matters of political and social order could find ready symbolization." [56] As an example from William Bercher's *The Nobility of Women* suggests, extrapolation might make both family and state unsafe spaces for men. "As for strengthe we rede of the Amasones and manye other that wer wont to go to batteyll and have braught home manye tryumphes and victoris and yf this use were in o[u]r dais we shoulde see what the strengthe of wymen cowlde doe. and nature hathe allso preferred them in the order off generac[i]on ffor Gallen and Avicen sayethe, that the woman hathe the pryncypall office to conserve and conceyve the seede whearby the more parte of chyldren be lyke theyre mothers." [57] The "strengthe" Bercher describes works indistinguishably to produce war and reproduction, nationalism and maternal influence; the generation of both countries and children depends on women identified in amazonian terms. Amazons may lead explorers to the edge of the world, moralizers to exemplary extremes, and chroniclers to the beginning of historiographic record, but in early modern texts each of these pursuits tends to describe a circle.

Why, though, is this effect qualitatively different from that of those other recurring figures, Semiramis and Valasca and Zenobia and Thomiris? Why is "Amazon" not a trope of the same generality as Burton's "virago"? Why is it not just another metaphor, or another historical example? In part because Amazons are in one sense both, and in another sense neither. As Gainsford's comments suggest, they do not have the same historical status as Semiramis or Valasca, and yet they are invested with enough historical specificity to complicate tropic generalization. If one says "Amazon," one may, as *The Honest Man* argues, simply mean "tall," but one may also mean Penthesilea; the term is at once a metaphor and a series of events, which are in themselves only dubiously grounded in history and may instead be exemplary myths. More urgently for early modern texts, "Amazon" is doubly a figure: "figure" in the sense of body as well as in the sense of trope. In the sixteenth century, under the simultaneous pressures of exploration and myth, the Amazon encounter is a fantasy pursued by its own potential literalization; using Amazons metaphorically or referring to them historically coincides with looking for them in Africa or Asia or America or Northern Europe. Amazons may be far away in terms of time, space, or general unlikelihood—or, in the convergence of ideas about what "Amazon" means, they may not be far enough away at all.

If "Amazon" can refer to history or myth or the new world or your queen or your wife, Amazons might be at once undiscovered and already known. The drive to find a body out there somewhere sometimes gives way to recognition of a body that isn't "out there" at all. Juan Luis Vives argues that women may become amazonian by association: "Therfore whan I can not tell, whether it be mete for a Christen man to handle armour, howe shulde it be lefull for a woman to loke upon them, yea thoughe she handle them not, yet to be conversant amonge theym with harte and mynde, which is worse?" [58] Reading about martiality or watching it performed produces a dynamic of mirroring, admiration transformed to identity; looking for martial women is difficult to separate from looking at martial men. Painter's account of amazonian origins posits a still more disruptive causality: "The newes of [their husbands'] death knowen to their Wyves dwellinge in theyr countrey, caused them to conceive great heavinesse, and dolor extreme. And although they were women, yet did they put on manly courage . . . And that they might all be equall, and their sorrow common, they murdred certaine of their husbandes which remayned there." [59] The process that fills the place of husbands with the "manly courage" of wives—who, almost incidentally, kill any husbands who remain—suggests the shifts, displacements, and appropriations imaginable within the rigidity of domestic roles.

The speaker of *Muld Sacke,* a response to *Hic Mulier,* argues that the breakdown of difference resides not in extraordinary appearances, but in commonplace infringements of everyday rules. "A Woman was created to honour her Parents, and obey her Husband; Fathers, to use their lawfull authoritie over their Children; Husbands to overrule and command their Wives: as he therfore is an effeminate man, that transfers his birthright upon his Daughter or Wife, so is shee a Masculine Woman that bereaves Parents of authoritie, Husbands of supremacie, or debords from the modestie required in her sexe: shee then, that dare presume to overrule her Husband (or sometimes for his owne good beate him) although shee neither paint, cut her haire, or be deformed with new invented fashions, is notwithstanding *Hic Mulier.*" [60] Domesticity is a set of stories that generates its own counterplots, and amazonian narratives make this clear. In these narratives, the identities and oppositions that separate men from women and unite men with one another change their terms as the story moves on; patriarchy is less a conclusion than a pause among acts.

"Amazon" cannot signify in any singular or straightforward way. A narrowly defined "we" may know what it means, but the intersection of contexts, figures, and stories ensures that "we" will never be defined narrowly enough. This might be sufficient motivation for keeping Amazons at a distance. Bringing them close to home invites chaos: as separatists they are a threat, but as mothers and lovers and wives and queens they are a disaster, participating in and altering the structures that should work to keep them out. Yet even as texts from this period locate the alien within the familiar, they suggest the sense in which that process is already redundant: in representations of Amazons as in representations of women and men, challenges to conventional identities and hierarchies are at least as familiar as conventions themselves. The imaginative power of domestic Amazons lies not only in the inherent perversity of the term, but in its exposure of the incongruities that underlie social and sexual acts.

MIRROR GAMES

In the most famous of Amazon encounters, Achilles, having killed Penthesilea in battle at Troy, removes her helmet and falls in love. Thomas Heywood gives a highly conventional account:

> No sooner was the battaile done
> Her golden helme laid by,
> But whom by armes she could not take,
> She captiv'd with her eye.[61]

Achilles' intentions, according to *The Fall of Troy* and other chronicles, are strictly honorable: "Achilles' very heart was wrung/With love's remorse to have slain a thing so sweet,/Who might have borne her home, his queenly bride." [62] They are also necessarily subjunctive. If the hero is indeed "captiv'd" by the beauty of the Amazon, her conquest of him assigns a dubious version of agency to a body that is already a corpse. The story goes only so far, proposing that a hero can conquer an Amazon, can desire her and disarm her, but cannot take her home. As Tyrrell writes, "The Argives long for a wife like Penthesilea, and Achilles wants her as his wife, only *after she is dead.*" [63] The hero's softer side appears not as transformation, but as short-lived anachronism.

Herodotus describes a different Amazon encounter, less epic in its causes and considerably more social in its effects, which closely anticipates the stories told in early modern texts. He gives this account of the first encounter between the Amazons and the Scythians: "The Scythians could not make sense of the business. They had no knowledge of the speech or the clothes or the nation of the Amazons but were in great wonder as to where they came from. They thought that they were men of the same age and fought against them. After the battle, the Scythians took possession of some of the dead and so came to know that they were women." [64] Like Penthesilea, these Amazons are dead. But here even necrophilic eroticism can be appropriated to productive ends: "So they held a debate and decided that by no means should they kill any more of the Amazons but should send the youngest of their men to them . . . The Scythians determined to do this because they wanted to breed children from these women." Achilles' subjunctive response becomes practice; the discovery that Amazons are women requires their accommodation as wives. Conquest, in this narrative, is not a metaphor for desire, but a preliminary step in its consummation.

Where, though, is the eroticism that drives this love story? What is in it for the Scythians? In brief, Herodotus's Amazon encounter rewrites narcissism as a successfully generative economy. Men see men who are like themselves, and end up with women and children; if Amazon encounters synthesize identity and difference as catalysts of desire, that synthesis might endlessly reproduce idealized masculinity in its own image. This is very nearly a parthenogenetic fantasy come true: Amazons, at least in the anticipation of Herodotus's Scythians, reproduce men in the sense both of mirroring and of sexual generation. In her reading of Plato's *Timaeus*, Butler writes of the "figuration of masculine reason as disembodied body" that it is "a figure in crisis, for this body of reason is itself the phantasmatic dematerialization of masculinity, one which requires that women and slaves, children and animals be the body, perform the bodily functions, that it will not perform." [65] Homosociality, as a logic that identifies men with one another, produces this sense of crisis and of need; Narcissus may have everything he wants, but social pragmatism requires a second body and a third term, a more integral use of Echo. Amazons enable a narrative version of the theory that David Halperin derives from Plato's Diotima; Halperin writes that "her presence endows the paedagogic processes by which men reproduce themselves culturally—by which they communicate the secrets of their wisdom and social identity, the 'mysteries' of male authority, to one another across the generations—with the prestige of female procreativity." [66] As they allow men to confuse women with themselves, Amazon encounters might appropriate the necessity of sexual reproduction to the ideological project of consolidating male identity, and if there is a shaky assumption here—Amazons are like men; therefore Amazons will reproduce men in the service of men—no one needs to look too closely.

By implicating Amazon encounters in narcissistic fantasies, I assume that narcissism might be understood as something other than absolute self-involvement. Linking narcissism to melancholia, Lynn Enterline theorizes an experience of loss: "When the mirror becomes an instrument of reflection that produces an image like the viewer, it produces startling images for a kind of sorrow that impoverishes the self and for which there seems to be no compensation." [67] Early modern readings of the myth often describe this sense of frustration and lack; so George Sandys argues that Narcissus can only want what he is and can never have what he wants, concluding, "for the mind doth not truly affect the body, but its owne similitude in a bodily forme. Such *Narcissus*, who ignorantly affecting one thing, pursues another; nor can ever satisfie his longings." [68] In failing to distinguish between other and self, Narcissus might lose himself entirely. Such private processes have larger effects, making the narcissist a spectacle of devalued identities and fruitless contracts. Geffrey Whitney describes a highly visible preoccupation:

> Bicause selfe love doth wounde our hartes,
> And makes us thinke, our deedes alone to bee.

> Whiche secret sore, lies hidden from our eyes,
> And yet the same, an other plainlie sees.[69]

Abraham Fraunce also imagines a performance that is public in its causes and consequences: "*Narcissus* is a lover of himselfe, and so it falleth out, that vaunting and bragging loves self-love: He is turned to a flower, florishing to day, and fading to morrow, as such overweeners alwayes doe."[70] Illusion leads to self-love, self-love to self-loss, self-loss to social abnegation. Having fooled himself and been caught in the process, the narcissist has nowhere to go but in.

Yet narcissism can also be understood as a structure of connection, its privileging of identity reflecting value judgments that are social rather than mythological or solipsistic. As a perfectly self-enclosed economy, narcissism summarizes a logic of male bonding that orders relationships according to degrees of likeness, extrapolating self-recognition into consolidations of alliance. Based in the processes through which men recognize idealized masculinity in one another, this system of connection subordinates as it obscures women. Sandys writes that Narcissus's desire causes "the babling Nymph *Eccho*" to disappear: "Well therefore was vaine-glory fained to affect selfe-love; who rejected, converts into a sound; that is, into nothing."[71] As a social arrangement, narcissism makes its hierarchical assumptions clear. Male homosociality orders heterosocial relations through the exclusiveness of its priorities, the completeness of its distinctions between affinities that are valuable and those that are merely necessary. In his discussion of object choice, Freud argues that narcissism refers to the future and to the past: "What he projects before him as his ideal is the substitute for the lost narcissism of his childhood in which he was his own ideal."[72] But for Ovid's Narcissus, frozen in contemplation of his image, the equation of identity and desire occupies an endlessly expansive *now*. The myth presents a merger of subject and object characterized by an immediacy as irresistible as it is mistaken, enabling a fantasy in which men experience social intercourse as a system of infinite returns.

In their introduction to *Premodern Sexualities,* in a reading of the proem to William Caxton's *Policronicon,* Louise Fradenburg and Carla Freccero write, "The production of homosociality cannot take for granted sameness between men; this sameness must be created, and it is created out of men's very strangeness to each other." [73] As they intervene in male homosocial identifications, Amazon encounters create an explicit and temporary illusion of sameness that presumes its own exposure. Playing on misrecognition, such encounters suggest that there is something attractive about being so radically wrong; female masculinity both sets up a mirror in which women reflect men and translates that reflection into something else. Looking at an image of idealized masculinity, men who confront Amazons discover a body that can be incorporated into generative marriage. By making narcissism the cause of a heterosexual effect, Amazon encounters seemingly ensure that the eroticism implicit in the privileging of likeness will consolidate homosocial power without implying homosexual desire. [74] Male bonding may generate authority, but it poses a possible source of uneasiness as well; taking up Sedgwick's analysis of the relationship between the homosocial and the homosexual, Bruce Smith writes, "If fifth- and fourth-century Athens exemplifies 'ideological homosexuality,' if our own society exemplifies 'ideological homophobia,' the society of Shakespeare's England quite clearly exemplifies conflict." [75] Amazon encounters at once reveal and negotiate that conflict, using gestures of closure — normative heterosexuality, a happy ending — to disarm and socialize a story in which men want women who act and often look a great deal like men.

Traub writes of Shakespearean drama, "The relative ease or dis-ease with homoerotic desire seems to depend on the extent to which such desire is recuperable within a simultaneous homoeroticism and heterosexuality that will ensure generational reproduction. Specifically, in these plays the dramatized fantasy of eliding women in erotic exchanges seems to initiate anxiety." [76] In Amazon encounters, women are not elided but temporarily unperformed, enabling the doubleness that Traub describes: the encounters idealize and eroticize male homosocial bonds, but consummate those bonds in heterosexual generation. Social abstractions are perpetuated among men, but the literalism of sexuality is transported elsewhere, becoming a commodity rather than a threat. In his essay "Homosexuality and the Signs of Male Friendship," Bray describes slippage between acceptable eroticism and illicit sexuality. He argues that accusations of homosexuality did not need to be true: "They turned rather on a sharp-eyed recognition that the public signs of a male friendship—open to all the world to see—could be read in a different and sodomitical light to the one intended."[77] Amazon encounters guard against such recognition; the suffixes "social" and "sexual" are distinguished, not by their force or their cause or even by the players involved, but by the different utility of their effects.

But introducing female bodies into narcissistic strategies of representation has complicated results. "How is gender difference produced if the trajectory of desire is not determined by the gender of its object?"[78] Goldberg asks. It is a question that might well be put to the heroes of Amazon encounters. The intersection of homosocial and heterosexual attachments works against categorical discretion, precluding neat allocations of desire. One version of the Narcissus myth imagines the consequences of inserting a woman into narcissistic preoccupations: in *Mythologia*, Natalis Comes recounts a story told by Pausanias, in which Narcissus loves a sister who closely resembles him. After her death, this Narcissus looks at his own reflection to console himself, and finally dies of grief.[79] If the story absolves Narcissus of homoeroticism (itself a questionable assumption), it has its own pathologies, substituting incest and necrophilia for an Ovidian mistake. Enterline writes, "Like psychoanalysis, Pausanias's story places incestuous desire at the heart of family relations. And also like psychoanalysis, it places autoerotism at the heart of any loving relation whatsoever."[80] In this case, at least, it does not help to imagine that Narcissus might have been thinking about a woman while looking at himself; heterosexual intentionality makes things worse. Desire for an other who resembles the self results not in the union of social power and sexual generation, but in loss. In the Pausanias story, as in Amazon encounters, self-involvement resolves itself into a failure to tell the difference, and the narcissistic subject recognizes himself in an image that holds him in danger. Enterline's analysis of this effect in *The Duchess of Malfi* might describe all male subjects of Amazon encounters: "The relationship between sexual difference, doubling, and melancholia in the play has everything to do with visual trauma: male perception of itself in the female form becomes a traumatic event that decisively changes the very eyes doing the looking" (290).

As Enterline's language suggests, seeing is an act that returns upon its agent, not only to confirm but to transform. This effect shapes stories about Amazons; female masculinity, however efficient a synthesis, puts pressure on the processes through which a mirror image becomes recognizably a woman and explicitly an object of heterosexual desire. Reading the gender politics of Shakespeare's comic conclusions, Belsey writes, "Closure depends on closing off the glimpsed transgression and reinstating a clearly defined sexual difference. But the plays are more than their endings, and the heroines become wives only after they have been shown to be something altogether more singular—because more plural."[81] Making a transvestite hero a wife is not, or not completely, a solution, and in Amazon encounters the problems may be just beginning. For men who look at Amazons and suddenly see women, sexual difference underlies gendered identity, and the result is not closure but a jarring shift. Ovid's story of Narcissus describes the paralyzing effects of looking and mistaking:

> He feedes a hope without cause why. For like a foolishe noddie
> He thinkes the shadow that he sees, to be a lively boddie.
> Astraughted like an ymage made of Marble stone he lyes,
> There gazing on his shadow still with fixed staring eyes.[82]

That phrase, "like an ymage made of Marble stone," opens the way for an insidious intertextuality. Assuming the reference of image to body, Narcissus is caught looking, for while desiring oneself may be one thing, being turned to stone is surely the result of an other. With the shift from gender to sex, an ideal becomes a monster: Narcissus becomes Medusa.[83]

In connecting Amazons to Medusa I have taken the long way around, for Medusa sometimes appears as an amazonian queen. Sandys writes, "*Pausanias* reports this *Medusa* to be the daughter of *Phorbus;* who after the death of her father raigned over those people who border on the lake of *Triton:* whom she accustomed, with the neighboring *Africans,* to conduct to the warrs."[84] Diodorus Siculus, in his chronicle of Amazon nations, records that "oone maner nation of thise women was called Gorgones, agayne whome Perseus made mortall debate and warre."[85] André Thevet describes "iii sorts of *Amazones,* all a like, differing only in places and dwellings," and writes, "The most ancient sort were in *Affrica,* among the which were *Gorgonists,* that had *Meduse* for their Queene."[86] Ralegh, in the account of his Guiana voyage, follows Thevet: "The memories of the like women are very ancient as well in Africa as in Asia: In Africa those that had Medusa for queene."[87] In early modern iconographies such as

Vincenzo Cartari's *Imagini*, the warrior-queen Medusa mingles with the story of Perseus and the gorgon's head: "Diodorus writes that the gorgons were warlike women in Africa who were overcome by Perseus, who also killed their queen Medusa; this may be historical."[88]

"This may be historical." Cartari's implicit distinction—between history and fiction, history and convention, history and myth?—raises the question of why Medusa and Amazons appear as versions of the same thing. The interpenetration of the myths reflects several interrelated connections: both make the reciprocity of violence and sexuality explicit; both link eroticism to monstrosity; both obscure distinctions between agency and victimization; both, in the early modern period, inspire an exemplary didacticism. For Cartari, the figure of Medusa refers not to mythological bodies or historical acts but to processes of signification. "These things show the power of knowledge and prudence," he writes, "which through wonderful works and wise counsels can astonish men and render them like stone with amazement, so that it can obtain whatever it wishes, provided it can suitably expound it: it is language that is expressed by that terrible head" (129). Sandys offers analogous abstractions: "[Perseus] attempts [Medusa] alone; in that she of all the *Gorgons* was only mortall: to show that we should pursue what is fecible; and not such designes as are vast and endlesse."[89] The list of values Sandys extrapolates from the story includes reason, knowledge, wisdom, experience, perspicacity, policy, quickness of wit, deep apprehension, glorious action, and honest fame. Medusa does not embody this catalogue of virtues, but through her it becomes legible; for Sandys as for Cartari, this most famous of monstrous female bodies disappears into text.

Like the morality tales in which "Amazon" signifies virginity or domestic insurrection, such exegeses make Medusa a device, a generalization, a trope. The process of reading her tells men about themselves; so Freud, in his essay "Medusa's Head," follows Cartari in imagining an excess of knowledge, fantasizing a Perseus-like hero who requires an apotropaic intervention to survive the encounter. Having identified Medusa with the female genitals, Freud concludes, "The sight of Medusa's head makes the spectator stiff with terror, turns him to stone. Observe that we have here once again the same origin from the castration complex and the same transformation of affect! For becoming stiff means an erection. Thus in the original situation it offers consolation to the spectator: he is still in possession of a penis, and the stiffening reassures him of the fact."[90] Rather than being deadly, Medusa offers full-body reassurance, her petrifying effect producing that comparatively rare kind of synecdoche that takes the whole for the part. But such readings, as they rework the moment of crisis, generalize it outward and inscribe it in large terms. The myth of a hero and a monster becomes the experience of women and men; as a symbol Medusa, like the Amazon, might refer to something other than the story told in her myth, but the extrapolation of that "something other" makes heterosexual panic general and explicit. In Sandys's words, "*Medusa*, lust and the inchantments of bodily beauty, which stupifies our senses, make us altogether unusefull, and convert us as it were into marble, cannot be subdued."[91]

Medusa, or rather the image of Medusa, cannot be subdued because it turns the effects of heterosexual victimization back on men. In Ovid's account, Medusa is twice a victim: Neptune rapes her, and Athena holds her responsible for the act. "And least it should unpunisht be, she turnde hir seemely heare/To lothly Snakes."[92] If there seems to be a gap in the reasoning behind this response, a logical swerve, it is not inscrutable but disturbingly familiar: Medusa is beautiful, and so she is raped; she is raped, and so she is punished. In a strong ideological revision, Hélène Cixous rereads the figure of Medusa in her challenge to Freud: "Wouldn't the worst be, isn't the worst, in truth, that women aren't castrated, that they have only to stop listening to the Sirens (for the Sirens were men) for history to change its meaning? You only have to look at the Medusa straight on to see her. And she's not deadly. She's beautiful and she's laughing."[93] The two stories, Ovid's and Cixous's, play out a game of containment — Medusa as victim — and subversion — Medusa as agent — that seems absolute in its oppositions. But the nature of Medusa's victimization undermines the distinction between an object that is acted on and a subject that acts, for in being punished, Medusa executes punishment, her transformation possessing the power to transform.

In his analysis of fetishism, Robert Stoller writes, "A fetish is a story masquerading as an object."[94] Fetishism, like iconography, initiates a process of reasoning backwards: if specific fetishes appear peculiar, even inexplicable, they refer to a narrative that is common enough, invoking possession and display to compensate for the sense in which women's bodies threaten men. Medusa's head has a similar effect, inspiring readings that take up an apparently idiosyncratic example in order to articulate and defuse conventional anxieties about sex. If looking at a woman turns a man to stone, it is because (according to Cartari) he suddenly knows too much, or because (according to Sandys) he suddenly wants too much, or because (according to Freud) he suddenly has (is?) an extensive erection. To interpret Medusa in these terms is to recognize female bodies less as objects than as object lessons, generating images that tell men something about themselves. Iconographically preoccupied, such readings look away from the narrative development through which sexual violence returns to do damage to its agents. Yet Medusa's story takes shape through that development, differentiated from the stories of other Ovidian victims because her victimization results in indiscriminate violence against men.

Medusa's story reveals the dangers of separating responsibility from agency, of confusing the roles of transgressor and victim, of holding the object responsible for the consequences of desire. Men who have been turned to stone may be knowledgeable or reasonable, just, moderate, or sexually potent, but they have also been turned to stone. If Medusa becomes a monster because in some misogynist syllogism she asked for it, her monstrosity is a weapon; through this return of the oppressed, the myth suggests that heterosexuality, however carefully its hierarchies are defined, might always disrupt the narcissistic economy that keeps women in their place. Reading the Medusa image in Dante's *Inferno*, John Freccero links that image to "the sensual fascination celebrated in the literature of love," and writes, "Its threat is the threat of idolatry. In terms of mythological *exempla*, petrification by the Medusa is the real consequence of Pygmalion's folly."[95] Medusa's is not just a story about the ways in which sexuality is dangerous to women; and indeed, if it is an object lesson at all, it seems most aptly directed at the men who are turned into objects. Fraunce glances at yet another version of Medusa's myth, in which she is punished not for rape but for ambitious self-absorption: "*Medusaes* hayre (either for that *Neptune* in *Minervaes* temple used her irreligiously . . . or, for that she gloried so much in her golden locks, as that she durst compare with goddesses) were turned into snakes, and the beholders thereof into stones."[96] Parodying narcissism, the Medusa myth turns tautology into horror show. Medusa's alternative identity as a warrior queen in this sense does not change her at all: that transition, from self-satisfaction to paralyzed horror, is the effect of Amazons. " 'I am not afraid of you. I defy you. I have a penis,' " Freud's subject tells Medusa.[97] "Look," Medusa might reply, "I have a sword."

Let me return briefly to Herodotus's Scythians and to the consequences of their Amazon encounter. Having turned the terms from war to love, they find themselves flirting with homosocial disaster. " 'If you want to have us as your women and want to be thought to be honorable men,' " the Amazons tell them, " 'go to your parents, take the allotted share of your property, and then come and let us live together on our own.' The young men agreed and did this . . . And from then on the women of the Sauromatians follow their old way of life; they go on horseback, hunting with their men and without them, and they go to the war, too, and wear the same dress as the men do." [98] Herodotus's history exposes a flaw in narcissistic fantasies, recording that assimilation of the heterosexual by the homosocial produces not better men but women who are more like Amazons. The Scythians anticipate the social uses of desire—"they wanted to breed children from these women"— but if there is social parthenogenesis here, it reproduces an amazonian society. Amazon encounters might always go wrong in this way, and early modern fictions raise the stakes. Unlike the Scythians, these texts do not send men out but bring Amazons in, and Amazons come in only to turn the inside out. Dollimore writes, "The female transvestite of the earlier period appropriated, inverted, and substituted for, masculinity— in a word, perverted it. This was primarily a question of style rather than sexual orientation." [99] In the case of Amazons, style gives sexuality the effect of an ambush: social order comes to crisis not through sexual separatism, but through its failure. If female masculinity seems a representational bargain, producing figures who are both erotically charged and sexually useful, early modern narratives count the costs.

One of those costs is the exposure of a gap between abstract ideas of male homosociality and the representation of relations among men. In a discussion of Sedgwick's conception of male homosocial desire, Traub warns against simplistic application: "The uncritical use of this model thus risks reproducing a homophobic discourse in the interest of advancing a particular feminist agenda. That the model also tends to deny the availability of female agency is a related, though separate problem." [100] By theorizing the relationships between men and women in terms of the relationships among men, we risk both equating male homoeroticism with patriarchal hegemony and relegating women to the status of objects. In a sense, the interpretive practices Traub critiques reproduce the implicit agenda of amazonian narratives, which would make desire between men evidence of social power, not sexual consummation, and identify desire for women as a transitive rather than a reciprocal act. But amazonian narratives, as I have begun to suggest, take apart their own agendas, making explicit the extent to which the social organization of gender and power is an ideal emptied out in the pursuit of realization. Eroticized male bonding does not, or does not only, consolidate the homosocial, any more than eroticized male-female bonding civilizes the heterosocial. Instead, these narratives reveal the desire for such consolidating and civilizing effects, desire articulated most clearly in its frustration. Stories about Amazons sever social theory from practice in a way that complicates male interactions as much as it does those between women or between women and men. The modes of relation assembled under the idea of the male homosocial—patronage, narcissism, rivalry, desire—do not accumulate to a seamless theory of patriarchy in these stories. Instead, the interaction of men and masculine women challenges any abstract conception of homosociality, linking men not only to women but to one another in destabilizing ways.

Conventional homosocial relations have force in the texts with which I am concerned: Ralegh, Shakespeare's Suffolk, and Jonson claim to speak within the conventions of patronage; Artegall, Pyrocles, and Theseus claim to act within the definition of heroism; and everyone claims to pursue a version of desire governed by men and directed at women. As they attempt to articulate a theory that unites men in a condition of government, these texts make the usual distinctions between agents and patients, subjects and objects, selves and others, conquerors and victims. Their male characters add up to a kind of catalogue of patriarchal subject positions: colonialists, kings, an allegorical figure of justice, a legendary prince, a duke who is also a mythological hero. But these roles are complicated in their enactment and compromised in their ideological force. Unsuccessful explorers, ineffectual rulers, an allegorical figure repeatedly dislocated from the quality he represents, a prince whose heroism is in the past, a duke of deus ex machina—none of these sustains a condition of agency or focuses a set of bonds. In these texts that focus on Amazons, men and the relations among them destabilize the governing fiction of patriarchal authority, not by operating against or outside it—as sodomites or witches, cannibals or traitors—but by occupying it without authenticating its terms.

To take up and turn the second point of Traub's critique, male bonding looks rather different in the light of female agency. Amazonian narratives disrupt the idea of masculine hegemony by showing that women can intervene in its constitution and performance, and this disruption raises further questions about the relationship of men to the abstract ideal of patriarchal control. In *The Politics and Poetics of Transgression*, Peter Stallybrass and Allon White describe a relationship between "top" and "bottom" in which the first term not only depends on but includes and eroticizes the second. "The result," they write, "is a mobile, conflictual fusion of power, fear and desire in the construction of subjectivity: a psychological dependence upon precisely those Others which are being rigorously opposed and excluded at the social level. It is for this reason that what is *socially* peripheral is so frequently *symbolically* central." [101] Amazon encounters play out this "conflictual fusion" as a hand-to-hand fight, closing any gap between self and other, peripheral and central, social and symbolic, and leaving no high ground from which to articulate exclusive conditions of power. The men of amazonian narratives are often as remote as are the women from the univocally repressive high-mindedness that the term "patriarchy" assumes. In these narratives, relationships predicated on the assumption of mutual masculinity are erotic, idiosyncratic, inconsistent, violent, selfish, and sometimes, simply, mistakes; but they are rarely successful ideological propaganda. From Ralegh's split focus between his patrons and his queen, to Suffolk's seduction of the wife he has provided for his king; from Artegall and Scudamour's squabble over False Florimell, through Basilius's passion for a disguised prince, to Theseus's arbitrary betrayal of Egeus, male bonds do not advertise the fact of patriarchal consolidation but emphasize the distance of many men from it. Male homosocial power may be a fantasy in these texts, but it is a fantasy both troubled and obscured by the players who act it out.

Amazonian mirror games work in two ways in early modern texts. The first is an accumulation of effects: women in appropriately feminine roles — wife, mother, mistress, queen, object of aesthetic or erotic desire — engage in inappropriate performances, becoming recognizable as amazonian. The second is a disguise plot, in which the interchangeability of Amazons and men creates a crisis of difference. Both narratives put any exclusively male claim to agency or masculinity in question; both disrupt the male homosocial processes of connection and exchange. The first structure follows Painter's account of "the originall of the Amazons," in which women defined by apparently conventional relationships to men become amazonian when their domestic circumstances shift, but assume agency in the process, moving from being themselves victims of circumstance to making victims of men. The second structure approximates that described by Herodotus; here Amazons appear to be men until the processes of homoerotic violence give way to those of heteroerotic negotiation. These are variations on a single story, for the husbands who die to make their wives Amazons in Painter's story are the Scythians whom, in Herodotus's story, the Amazons will marry. The story can be imagined from two directions — wives might become Amazons, Amazons might become wives — but it always alters the look of heterosocial normativity.

In *Staging the Gaze*, Barbara Freedman describes "a Renaissance tradition of learned ignorance, trick perspectives, and optical experiments, all of which answer to our paradoxical desire to see how we cannot see ourselves seeing."[102] Amazon encounters catalyze and reflect that paradoxical desire. The process of recognizing female masculinity within domestic conventions is both a trick and a revelation, both a claim to and an effacement of knowledge. In the causality through which wives become amazonian, a transparent object becomes opaque: the conceit of female bodies as matter without signification, allowing a clear line of sight between men, fails as male subjects confront the spectacle of female agency. Connections that work across women must suddenly work through and indeed against them, as the adjective "amazonian" indicates the surfacing of a submerged third term. When Amazons become wives, that transition imposes another kind of spectacular shift: the idealized masculine mirror image in which men recognize themselves vanishes, leaving behind the far messier transactions of difference. The erotic continuity that links homo- to heterosocial bonds may be efficient, but that efficiency leads to dangerous condensations.

The first section of this book, "Abroad at Home: The Question of Queens," takes up narratives in which women defined within familiar structures become recognizably amazonian. In my first chapter, "Falling off the Edge of the World," I place Ralegh's account of his Guiana voyage in the context of other exploration narratives that imagine encountering Amazons. These narratives construct a triangulated relationship among explorer, patron or reader, and commodities of exchange, in which new world women and the feminized new world appear as often interchangeable objects of desire. Amazons, possessing not only exotic female bodies but land and gold, synthesize such objects, and my reading of Ralegh and other explorers considers Amazon quests both as figures of acquisition and as structures of infinite pursuit. Looking for Amazons maps an old set of narrative terms onto a new space; even as explorers claim to find "real" Amazons, their narratives and those of later commentators suggest that these Amazons are "really" something else, women who participate in social structures that can be contrasted—and, more insidiously, compared—to those already known. Ralegh's translation of the strange into the strangely familiar is particularly acute, referring all objects and desires to conditions at home.

The texts considered in my second and third chapters look more directly at the amazonian within England itself. Shakespeare's *Henry VI* plays record a progress inward: from Joan la Pucelle, who is named an Amazon as she defines the edge of English male heroism, to Margaret of Anjou, who becomes England's queen. In *1 Henry VI* Joan la Pucelle does a good deal of damage, but she does it from outside. But when Queen Margaret takes on the martial role that characterizes her appearance in *3 Henry VI*, she does so in domestic terms: as the queen of the country, the wife of the king, and the mother of his son, she is termed "Amazonian" by York and accused of "playing the Amazon" by his son, suggesting that the adjective might be more dangerous than the noun. Pursuing this notion of dangerous tropes, my discussion of early Jacobean queen's masques considers another invasion of the amazonian, taking up the exotic identities invented for female masquers by Samuel Daniel and Ben Jonson. From *The Vision of the Twelve Goddesses* to *The Masque of Queens*, a genre that exists to praise the king does so through an embodied history of martial women, making female masculinity an iconographic conceit. Court masques construct themselves in terms of commodified narcissism, inviting the king to look at an idealized version of himself; but their generic imperative takes an odd swerve when the masquers look like Amazons.

Each of these narratives makes England and Englishness its terms of reference; each implicates English queens; each describes a process of importing alien women to articulate the power of chauvinistic containment. Women—new world women, French women, exotic queens— take part in the homosocial and heterosocial operations of domesticity, proving that those operations work. But increasingly the familiar comes to appear strange, as representations of domestic structures are shaped by the images they contain. Stories about amazonian wives and queens become exercises in the uncanny, explications of the process through which, as Freud argues, *heimlich* and its opposite come to mean the same thing: "Thus *heimlich* is a word the meaning of which develops in the direction of ambivalence, until it finally coincides with its opposite, *unheimlich*. *Unheimlich* is in some way or other a sub-species of *heimlich*." [103] Defined as domesticated women, Amazons expose the ambivalence of that term, causing conventional categories to coincide with the image of their disruption.

If amazonian queens and wives are uncanny, the Amazons I discuss in this book's second section, "Splitting the Difference: Homoeroticism and Home Life," work like the supplement, that figure of which Jacques Derrida writes, "It adds only to replace. It intervenes or insinuates itself *in-the-place-of*; if it fills, it is as if one fills a void. If it represents and makes an image, it is by the anterior default of a presence." [104] Demonstrating that women and men might be performatively interchangeable, Amazons at once substantiate the signifiers of masculinity and threaten to replace the bodies to which they are attached. Female masculinity is an addition that presupposes the possibility of loss, a break in the referential statement linking masculinity to men. Judith Halberstam writes, "If what we call 'dominant masculinity' appears to be a naturalized relation between maleness and power, then it makes little sense to examine men for the contours of that masculinity's social construction. Masculinity . . . becomes legible as masculinity where and when it leaves the white male middle-class body." [105] In Spenser's *Faerie Queene*, Sidney's *Arcadia*, and Shakespeare's *A Midsummer Night's Dream*, masculinity appears detachable from heroic male bodies, becoming visibly a project, a synthetic invention of terms. Amazon encounters raise the possibility that "dominant masculinity" might simply be the version that wins. Tending toward an efficiently heterosocial conclusion, in which Amazons become wives because they are women, the narrative might always go astray: *someone* will be feminized by this encounter, but femininity is no more firmly attached to women than masculinity is to men. All bodies matter; none prescribe.

In my fourth chapter, I argue that Britomart's quest in *The Faerie Queene* summarizes these troubled eroticisms and shifting identities. As it invents a knight to consummate a marriage, that quest synthesizes heroic masculinity and female reproductive sexuality, complicating chivalric beginnings with domestic ends. And desires proliferate in between: in the multiplication of disguise plots and allegorical intentions men admire men, women desire women, and men and women confront one another in conditions of hostility, idealization, abjection, and marriage. As a woman who fights like a man in order to find one, Britomart at once conceals sex and insists on it, making her own masculinity the means to a happy ending. The perils implicit in this scheme become apparent when Britomart finds the man whose image she has assumed: at their first encounter she defeats him, at their second she unmans him, and at their third she finds him in women's clothing, set to spin. Imitation is appropriation; female masculinity crowds out men. This cannibalistic narcissism finds its mirror image in *The Arcadia*, the focus of chapter 5: when Prince Pyrocles disguises himself as an Amazon, his disguise plot, like Britomart's, multiplies desires. As an Amazon, Pyrocles inspires erotic response from a woman who wants a woman, from a man who wants a woman, from a woman who wants a man, and from a man who wants a transvestite. But this irresistibility is a calculated risk, and, again like Britomart, Pyrocles finds that amazonian disguise incorporates more than he had bargained for. Having catalyzed a constellation of desires, he cannot resolve them into a single body of unambiguous gender and uncontested sex; the invention of an Amazon overwhelms and almost eclipses the fact of a prince.

My final chapter takes up Shakespeare's Hippolyta. Hippolyta is the early modern Amazon that everyone remembers, yet she has little obvious chance to be an Amazon at all. Both the play and its critical tradition present her marriage to Theseus as a frame narrative for comedy; here is a narrative of socialized desire that, by its very unlikelihood, asserts the success of the genre. Yet *A Midsummer Night's Dream*, from Theseus's opening nostalgia for the past to Oberon's closing anticipation of the future, has a problem with time. Through inappropriate gestures forward and back, as well as through the repetitive sexual conflicts of the here and now, Hippolyta's amazonian role is multiplied rather than foreclosed, its effects bracketing and inflecting the play. Her entry in the dramatis personae—"Hippolyta, queen of the Amazons, betrothed to Theseus"— might summarize resolution out of conflict. But it might also identify a syntagmatic doubleness, asserting that "betrothed" intersects without displacing the effects of "Amazon." Hippolyta's story begins in violence and ends in tragedy, leaving little space for the production of domestic models. To tell that story as comedy requires a suspension not only of disbelief but of knowledge, and the various love matches of *A Midsummer Night's Dream* reflect the effort involved.

In these three narratives, Amazons not only precipitate recognition of the ways in which heterosexuality may be dangerous to men; they also focus a system of erotic response to which men are not relevant at all. The aggressive pursuit of heterosexual closure produces, oddly but repeatedly, self-contained economies of female desire. Britomart is distracted from her search for Artegall first by Malecasta and more effectively by Amoret; Cleophila inspires in Philoclea an extraordinary frankness of what we, having more vocabulary than she has for what women could possibly do with other women, would term lesbian desire; Hippolyta focuses female characters' nostalgia for erotic exclusivity. In the 1970s, Amazon myth became a pattern for lesbian feminist separatism, suggesting alternative structures of connection, government, and desire. In early modern texts such alternatives are already, however inarticulately, in place, expanding the supplementary effect: Amazons not only threaten to replace male bodies in the performance of masculinity, but demonstrate that homosocial privilege, as a claim about value based in power, may not belong only to men.

The narratives with which I am concerned in this book invoke heterosocial hierarchies both to reinforce male homosocial power and to make female homosociality invisible. Governed by such hierarchies, desire has little to do with women, and desire *between* women has little to do with anything. In her introduction to *Immodest Acts,* Judith C. Brown attempts to account for the curious silence about lesbianism in the early modern period: "Whether common or rare, sexual relations between women could have only one purpose, to enhance and glorify real sex, i.e. sex with a man. This is one of the reasons why some contemporaries may have felt they could safely ignore lesbian sexuality." [106] If, as Brown suggests, this is not the whole story, it is certainly the story of a wish fulfillment. Female sexuality disappears in such an account, obscured by the importance of transactions among men; it is this ideal of mastery that texts invoke by domesticating Amazons. Explorers seduce patrons with the eroticized commodities of the new world; heroes who fight over women enhance their own value in other men's eyes; historians record the consolidation of alliances through marriage, and dramatists celebrate that consolidation on stage; the author of the court masque and its royal referent construct a perfectly closed economy in which women's bodies are aestheticized metaphors for something else. But men who encounter Amazons pay too much attention to women, allowing female sexuality to intervene in masculine consolidation. In a discussion of Shakespeare's sonnets, Sedgwick writes, "For a man to undergo even a humiliating change in the course of a relationship with a man still feels like preserving or participating in a sum of male power, while for a man to undergo any change in the course of a relationship with a woman feels like a radical degeneration of substance." [107] Amazon encounters are structured by the indistinguishability of these effects, conflating the bonds through which men reassure one another and those that connect men and women at their mutual expense.

Female masculinity proves less that women's bodies can take the place of men's than that that place was always overcrowded. "As concernyng strength and valiaunt courage, whiche ye surmise to lacke in them," Sir Thomas Elyot writes in *The Defense,* "I could make to you no lesse replicacion, and by old stories and late experience prove, that in armes women have ben found of no littell reputacion, but I will omit that for this time, for as muche as to the more parte of wise menne it shal not sound muche to their commendacion." [108] Agrippa dismantles even the implicit essentialism of Elyot's moral reservations, concluding his catalogue of martial female performances with a comment on social inventions:

> From what hath been said, appears conspicuously, as if written with *Sunbeams* on a Wall of Chrystal, That this Sex are not *incapable* of, nor were in the primitive and more innocent Ages of the World, *debarr'd* from managing the most arduous or difficult affairs, till the *tyranny* of Men usurpt the dispose of all business, and *unjust Laws, foolish Customes,* and an *ill mode* of education, *retrencht* their liberties . . . By which unworthy, *partial* means, they are forc'd to give place to Men, and like wretched *Captives* overcome in War, submit to their *insulting Conquerors,* not out of any natural or divine reason, or necessity, but only by the prevalency of *Custome, Education, Chance,* or some *tyrannical* occasion.[109]

Gender, writes Agrippa in 1509, is a contingent compensatory back-formation dependent on time. Or, in Cartari's words, "This may be historical."

"If gender attributes and acts, the various ways in which a body shows or produces its cultural signification, are performative," Butler writes in *Gender Trouble,* "then there is no preexisting identity by which an act or attribute might be measured; there would be no true or false, real or distorted acts of gender, and the postulation of a true gender identity would be revealed as a regulatory fiction." [110] The fragility of absolutist taxonomies returns us to the conclusion implicit in Herodotus's story: when Amazons are incorporated into domestic structures, the conditional nature of those structures is exposed. Categories and hierarchies are vulnerable to the conditions of their production, and neither the exclusion of women from male negotiations nor their inclusion in support of those negotiations quite works. Both ways of dealing with sexual difference — making it invisible and making it useful — appear inadequate in the face of amazonian interventions. Abandoned by men, the domestic space of Amazons becomes a spectacle of female homoerotic separatism; invaded by men, it presents a state that looks less like naturalized patriarchy than like a deliberate heterosexual distribution of the identities of butch and femme. In "Toward a Butch-Femme Aesthetic," Sue-Ellen Case writes, "The female body, the male gaze, and the structures of realism are only sex toys for the butch-femme couple." [111] Encounters between men and Amazons effect this displacement of literalism through the intervention of performative play, but here, in the context of heterosocial and heterosexual hierarchies, the lack of a naturalized causality between bodies and roles is not enabling but profoundly disruptive. In the absence of a presumptive relationship between sexed bodies and gendered acts, or between gendered bodies and social value, regulatory fictions are simply fictions.

I have on occasion been asked what it means that the authors of these stories about amazonian women are, overwhelmingly, men. [112] The critique implicit in this question is problematic, relying as it does on an idea that male-authored texts cannot create enabling, surprising, disruptive, or otherwise unconventional possibilities through their representations of women. But it is interesting that stories about Amazons inspire such a question, especially in a critical climate both wary of intentionality and dismayed by essentialism. When we are surprised that men write so much about Amazons, what are we surprised at? The answer may have to do less with sex than with canon. The texts on which my chapters focus are written by authors who, both in their own historical moment and in ours, constitute the literary mainstream, populating unreconstructed *Norton Anthologies* and fueling defenses of high art. Shakespeare, Spenser, Sidney, Ralegh, and Jonson are among the figures whose writings inform our most traditional understandings of early modern culture: of the Elizabethan world picture, the great chain of being, and the Renaissance frame of mind. They are also the figures who produce the period's most elaborate stories about Amazons. That odd fact raises the question of what we are looking for when we look to these authors, of whether our own desires reside in recognition or estrangement. Discussing the relationship between historicist and transhistoricist perspectives, Fradenburg and Freccero write, "If the practice of queer theory has taught us that neither alterity nor similarity is an inevitable conceptual guarantor of oppositional political force, that the construction of desirous identifications can be potentially destabilizing as well as totalizing, then we must see that positing the power of the past to disrupt and remake the present is not necessarily to adopt a naïve continuism." [113] "The Renaissance" has imposed a number of mythic legacies as the location of the present has changed over time—sensibility, modernity, humanism, capitalism, the subject, the Bard—and the contested relations of amazonian narratives make up part of the vehicle through which those inheritances have been conveyed. If, as I argue, early modern Amazons are startling in relation to domesticity precisely because they appear so thoroughly at home there, the same might be said of their relationship to the literary canon.

In focusing on canonical texts written by male authors, I approach the intersection of familiarity and strangeness from a different direction: we know about these authors, as we know about Amazons, but like early modern Amazons these authors are not doing quite the work we expect. The question, "Why don't women write more about Amazons?" is a symptom of our historical frustration, a subset of the question, "Why don't women—enough women, different women, the right women—write at all?" The fact that men *do* write about Amazons is another kind of symptom, a hint that such concepts as hegemony and normativity are not only under attack from without, but deeply messy and contradictory on their own terms. Stories about Amazons are not voices from the margins, but part of the statement of the center; if our ideas about patriarchal ideology in the early modern period derive largely from canonical literary texts, our sensitivity to the elements that trouble that ideology comes, at least in part, from the same source. The mainstream texts of male authors cannot define women exclusively as objects of exchange, vessels of reproduction, or catalysts of narcissistic pleasure, not only because the work of female or less talented or racially different or socially unconsidered or queer readers and writers intervenes, but because the system of ideas contained in the concepts "mainstream" and "male" is not tight enough to sustain patriarchy as an exclusive fiction. Of course, we know this already; the interplay of subversion and containment would not have captivated us so thoroughly for so long if we did not. But amazonian narratives make the illusions both of patriarchy and of canon highly visible, revealing that to sustain an opposition between in and out requires a set of assumptions—*shaky* assumptions—about the nature of "in."

Analyzing the processes through which such assumptions are constructed and maintained, Newman writes, "In the early modern period, the female body is the site of discourses that manage women: by continually working out sexual difference on and through the body, the social is presented as natural and therefore unchangeable, substantiated, filled with presence."[114] In amazonian narratives, as I have argued, the line of reasoning that runs from the sexual to the social, from difference to hierarchy, falls apart. If men "win" in Amazon encounters, they reconstitute patriarchal structures through an aggressive artificiality; if they lose, they occupy the narrow space left by women who act at once as women and like men.[115] Incorporated into the structures of socialized desire, Amazons expose that desire as a system of roles that might always be detached from the bodies they exist to regulate. In early modern English texts, the agency of imagining Amazons lies almost entirely with men, suggesting that such possibilities, however counterintuitive, are built into social logic itself; again, this is not a fear of invasion or alienation, but an acknowledgment of causalities already in place. Is every amazonian dream a wish fulfillment? Perhaps, but desiring subjects do not know what they are looking *for* until they know what they are looking *at*, and there is something perilous in this interpretation of dreams.

Part One

ABROAD AT HOME:

THE QUESTION

OF QUEENS

Men are attracted to Amazons and
strong women. They are a challenge
for one thing. (Studies have shown that
bitchy women always get married.)
—Martha Mattson, *Amazons:*
The Forgotten Tribe

CHAPTER ONE

Falling off the Edge of the World: Ralegh among the Amazons

QUEENE ELIZABETH

The Amazons are still further off:
I doubt beyond the region of Truth; if the
title be properly meant of such as are described.
—Samuel Purchas, *Hakluytus Posthumus*

When you have eliminated the impossible, whatever
remains, however improbable, must be the truth.
—Sir Arthur Conan Doyle, *The Sign of the Four*

In a letter describing his first voyage, Christopher Columbus offers the following catalogue of persons.

> Thus I have neither found monsters nor had report of any, except in an island which is the second at the entrance to the Indies, which is inhabited by a people who are regarded in all the islands as very ferocious and who eat human flesh . . . they are no more malformed than the others, except that they have the custom of wearing their hair long like women . . . These are those who have intercourse with the women of *Matremonio*, which is the first island met on the way from Spain to the Indies, in which there is not one man. These women use no feminine exercises, but bows and arrows of cane, like the abovesaid [cannibals]; and they arm and cover themselves with plates of copper, of which they have plenty. In another island, which they assure me is larger than *Española*, the people have no hair. In this there is countless gold, and from it and from the other islands I bring with me Indios as evidence.[1]

The passage exemplifies a particular kind of new world voice, which mingles the claims of proximity and hearsay to demonstrate that it speaks the truth. A fabulous population, heard of but not seen, introduces a land identified by a mistake; the narrative conflates female violence, male effeminacy, cannibalism, and wealth, and hopelessly blurs the distinction between finding things and hearing reports. As a later account of the voyage makes clear, Columbus describes what evades him: "[Columbus] passed by many Ilandes: among the whiche was one called

Matinina, in whyche dwell only women, after the maner of them, called *Amazones."* [2]

The process of "passing by," paradigmatic for accounts of new world Amazons, suggests a larger point about exploration narratives. As they connect knowledge and even acquisition closely to failure, amazonian quests play out tensions between the impulse to explore and the claim to discover. These quests, like exploration more generally, are governed by an uneasy relationship among representational strategies, yoking figures of possession to figures of endless pursuit. As mythical objects, Amazons can never be found, identifying the edge of knowable space by remaining just beyond it. But for explorers they are also linked to all the objects that *can* be found, from gold to cannibals to women to land, and stories about them invoke not only frustration but the richness of presence. In *The Conquest of America,* Tzvetan Todorov writes, "Just as for modern man a thing, an action, or a being is beautiful only if it finds its justification in itself, for Columbus 'to discover' is an intransitive action." [3] Amazons preserve this quality of the intransitive, ensuring that ambition is never satisfied, possibilities are never exhausted, the end of the quest is never reached. Yet there is serious materialism behind the belief that Amazons have what explorers want.

Stories about Amazons in the new world reflect the doubled and to some extent contradictory workings of metonymy as a narrative trope. Metonymy is in one sense closely akin to synecdoche, using a part or attribute to signify a thing or things and assuming a natural and recognizable relationship between the representative and the represented. The examples listed by one dictionary of literary terms — " 'The Stage' for the theatrical profession; 'The Crown' for the monarchy; 'The Bench' for the judiciary" [4] — indicate that metonymy offers access to objects or concepts through aspects that can be felt, seen, and understood; metonymy in these instances symbolizes constellations of ideas through their associations with specificity and presence. But metonymy is associative in another sense as well, indicating the impossibility of full presence and signifying that which cannot be comprehended or reached. The term then describes an endless progression along a signifying chain, in which moving from one reference to the next proves only that the object remains elusive. This is the version of metonymy that Lacan describes in "The Agency of the Letter in the Unconscious," defining it as "being caught in the rails—eternally stretching forth towards the *desire for something else.*"[5]

Lacan's description seems more apt both to Amazon quests and to exploration narrative as a discursive form. The process of exploration depends on the frustration of desire, and Amazon myth is symptomatic in its perpetuation of quests and quest narratives: mountains, rivers, winds, storms, the threat of enemies and the orders of authorities intervene between the Amazon discoverer and his discovery. More than this, epistemology intervenes; knowledge of a new space is fundamentally incompatible with its occupation by Amazons. Describing the quest for El Dorado in terms of this kind of metonymic logic, Mary Fuller writes, "We must say not that we have arrived but that we have reached some point of exhaustion."[6] Amazons are past that point, representing the last—and inevitably missing—link in the signifying chain.

But to understand exploration narrative only in these terms is to ignore the fact that explorers and their patrons are deeply invested, in all senses of that word, in the end of the quest. Through their close association with other objects of desire, Amazons function metonymically in the representative as well as the elusive sense of that term, compelling interest in exploration by promising its translation into discovery. The pursuit of Amazons implicates and symbolizes more obviously material goals—gold, land, women who don't fight back—and the fact that Amazons themselves remain not only hard to find but epistemologically opaque proves irrelevant. If finding them would stimulate belief in a further constellation of desirable objects, almost finding them has much the same effect.

André Thevet writes of American Amazons, "Some may say, that they are not *Amazonists,* but as for me I judge them suche, seeing that they live even so, as we finde the *Amazonists* of *Asia* to have lived. And before passing further, ye shall note, that these *Amazones* of which we speake, are retired, inhabiting in certaine Ilands which are to them as strong holdes, having alwayes perpetuall warre with certaine people, without any other exercise, even as those of whom have spoken the Historiographers."[7] Thomas Gainsford registers a far more skeptical response to "*Amazons,* as supposed to flie hither, when the Kings of *Europe* repined to see women the equall sharers of honour amongst them"; he writes, "But for my owne part, I rather suppose it the error of ignorant Cosmographers, who when they cannot, or dare not certainly deliniate a countrey, then will they fill up a place with monsters and formidable creatures both men and women."[8] Mythological historiography and geographical inaccessibility prove two points at once, both authorizing amazonian presence and making it manifestly unlikely. Such interpretive disparities characterize the responses that early modern explorers, their readers, and their editors have to the question of Amazons, but even the most outraged disbelief only reinforces fascination with its object. Texts in which explorers claim experience, editors append doubt, and readers express incredulity do not cancel out Amazon encounters but redouble their production of narrative.

The quest for Amazons occurs at an intersection of conflicting desires. Amazonian stories are at once too familiar not to be true and too strange to be believed, reflecting a mixture of motives: Is discovery about revelation or recognition? Even as they claim the privileges of novelty, new world narratives reason by analogy, so that objects found or imagined are contextualized by and referred to objects already known. From the interpretation of native languages to statements about sovereignty, marriage, and exchange, exploration narratives construct a new world that signifies in old ways. Familiarity and strangeness intersect, conflating home and away and creating tension between moments of discovery and presumptions of knowledge. At stake is the process that translates exploration into conquest: as an anticipatory revision of the unknown, recognition becomes a statement of possession, translating objects from things that are strange to things that can be had. Amazon encounters, at once impossible and well-known, become shorthand for a larger uncanniness in which mapping familiar stories onto strange places articulates a strangeness already present in the familiar. The pursuit of Amazons produces a doubled discourse that claims what has not yet been found, but at the same time threatens to alienate what is already possessed. Metonymy, I have suggested, is the synecdoche of desire, the taking—in all senses of that word—of a representative object to consolidate objectification as a process; but metonymy is also the process of desire, Lacan's "being caught in the rails." As amazonian pursuits in the new world make clear, it is at once a possessive figure and the figure for loss.

Falling off the Edge of the World

Abby Wettan Kleinbaum describes 1542 as "The Year of the Amazon in America."[9] In that year, Francisco de Orellana took a party from Gonzalo Pizarro's expedition and sailed into a notorious confrontation, of which Gaspar de Carvajal gives this account: "It must be explained that [these Indians] are the subjects of, and tributaries to, the Amazons, and, our coming having been made known to them, they went to them to ask help, and there came as many as ten or twelve of them, for we ourselves saw these women, who were there fighting in front of all the Indian men as women captains, and these latter fought so courageously that the Indian men did not dare to turn their backs."[10] Carvajal struggles to recreate the immediacy of the encounter: We have seen the Amazons, and there were twelve of them. But the moment of recognition immediately inspires doubt, as one early skeptic's summary suggests, "Francisco de Orellana, in descending the river, had some skirmishes with the Indians inhabiting that shore, who were very fierce, and in some parts the women came out to fight, with their husbands. On this account, and to make his voyage the more wonderful, he said that it was a land of Amazons, and besought His Majesty for a commission to conquer them."[11]

The language of wonder evokes the power of Orellana's experience, but wonder itself appears as something constructed, a deliberate manipulation of response. Stephen Greenblatt writes of new world encounters, "The expression of wonder stands for all that cannot be understood, that can scarcely be believed. It calls attention to the problem of credibility and at the same time insists upon the undeniability, the exigency of the experience."[12] Orellana claims that undeniability; the river must be "Amazon" because the Amazons are there. But Greenblatt's "problem of credibility" is there as well, and even for Orellana himself the name becomes a source of rather than a response to the immediacy of the thing. He pursues not Amazons but Amazon myth, extracting it in all its classical detail from a prisoner he interrogates; Carvajal assures the reader, "He now understood him by means of a list of words that he had made" (219), but whatever the efficacy of that list, foreknowledge structures Orellana's questions and, it seems safe to imagine, the answers as well.[13] "The Captain asked him what women those were . . . The Captain asked him if these women were married . . . The Captain asked him about how they lived . . . The Captain asked if these women were numerous . . . The Captain asked if these women bore children . . . The Captain asked him how, not being married and there being no man residing among them, they became pregnant" (220). Todorov writes of Columbus, "He knows in advance what he will find; the concrete experience is there to illustrate a truth already possessed, not to be interrogated according to preestablished rules in order to seek the truth." [14] Orellana, like Columbus, knows what he wants to know. His information concerning Amazons depends less on a sporadically intelligible captive than on mythographic clichés; his questions do not elicit a narrative, but reveal one.

That narrative has always been subject to critique. Cristobal de Acuña writes of Orellana's discovery, "Time will discover the truth," and with time skepticism has only increased.[15] For recent historians, Orellana's Amazon encounter is an aberration in an otherwise credible history, a flight of fancy from a prosaic text. José Toribio Medina traces doubts about the entire account to the presence of this story: "As the existence of these women could be nothing but a fiction, a serious charge was raised against both Orellana and his chronicler for having sponsored a fable destitute of all verisimilitude." [16] Boies Penrose refers to the river's name as "the misnomer which has survived through the centuries." [17] Paul Herrmann blames not the narrator, but widespread cultural fallacies, concluding, "We have no reason for branding Gaspar de Carvajal, Archbishop of Lima, as a shameless liar." [18] But however thoroughly the episode has been discredited, it cannot be repressed; if the Amazon encounter is a fiction, a misnomer, and a lie, its effects are tangible. The river has had a number of names, including Marañón and Fresh Water Sea; Samuel Eliot Morison records that one explorer called it the Ganges, and it was even, briefly, called after Orellana himself.[19] Yet "Amazon," inspired by women whom few but Orellana ever believed were Amazons at all, is the name that persists.

If no one believes that Orellana has found the Amazons, this does not mean that no one believes in Amazons. Rejection of easy and accidental discoveries preserves them as at once evasive and useful; doubt drives exploration forward; skepticism informs the need to find and find out. Closely linking failure to the promise of future success, Amazon quests produce a pragmatic opportunism already acknowledged in the first critique I cited: having seen the Amazons, Orellana "besought his Majesty for a commission to conquer them." [20] Material optimism produces such artifacts as the Amazon Company, a trading company founded in the early seventeenth century. Accounts of its founding refer indistinguishably to "the Amazon" as a river and "the Amazons" as a population; Amazons may not be the goods to be traded, but they provide tacit assurance that those goods are there. In what seems suggestively like nominal determinism, the company fails, but "Amazon" continues to signify the presence of desirable objects.[21] Greenblatt describes a causal connection between awe and acquisition: "The marvelous is a central feature then in the whole complex system of representation, verbal and visual, philosophical and aesthetic, intellectual and emotional, through which people in the late Middle Ages and the Renaissance apprehended, and thence possessed or discarded, the unfamiliar, the alien, the terrible, the desirable, and the hateful." [22] Amazon quests follow the fault lines of these processes, conflating the impulse to possess and the need to sustain a state of mystification.

Such ambivalence returns to the metonymic doubleness with which I began. Association with Amazons lends objects value, but Amazons guarantee value most effectively when they escape the condition of possession. If this is paradox for the sake of paradox, it is not mine; claims about amazonian discovery repeatedly take back as much as they give away. Gonzalo Fernández de Oviedo promises "an account of the dominion of Queen Conori and the Amazons, if Amazons they ought to be called." [23] A chapter in an account of Prester John is headed, "Of the kingdom of Damute, and of the great quantity of gold there is in it, and how it is collected; and to the south of this are the Amazons, if they are there." [24] At once linked to geographical specificities and veiled by epistemological doubt, Amazons both appear and recede through fantastic associations. Not only do they live next to Prester John; according to Mandeville, they are also the keepers of the lost tribes of Israel.[25] A marginal note in Samuel Purchas's collection titled *Hakluytus Posthumus* describes "An Unicorn or Asinus Indicus not that which Painters present with horne in the fore-head. Amazons." [26] Mandeville writes "Of the Land of Job, and of his age; of the array of men of Chaldea; of the Land where women dwell without company of men; of the knowledge and virtues of the very diamond." [27] In the region of Amazons, anything is possible, and the result is a collection of fabulous objects that are not out of the question but just out of reach.

Practical and fantastic pursuits converge most closely in the association of Amazons with gold. Quoting Cortés's comment on the Island of Amazons — "They told me also, that it is very rich in pearls and gold" — Irving Leonard writes, "For the Conquistador the New World, Amazons, and wealth became inseparable." [28] Alvares, in *The Prester John of the Indies,* informs his readers, "They also say that there is an infinite amount of gold in this kingdom of the Amazons." [29] De Acuña, optimistic about the truth of Orellana's Amazon encounter, takes gold as its touchstone: "If these are the Amazons made famous by historians, there are treasures shut up in their territory, which would enrich the whole world." [30] But as the rhetoric of "if" and "they say" indicates, amazonian gold proves as elusive as lost tribes, unicorns, and true diamonds. The experience of the particularly hapless explorer Ulrich Schmidel, whom Purchas somewhat mysteriously renames "Hulderike Schnirdel," reminds readers that conquest and acquisition work only in the subjunctive. Schmidel writes, "The Amazones have neither Gold nor Silver in this Iland, but they are reported to have great Treasures in the firme land, which the men inhabit." [31] We are still in the space of reports, in which "firme land" is at best shaky ground. The quest begins with optimism — "Mention of the Amazones and of their riches, was very pleasing to us to heare"; progresses through frustration — "We could not goe to them by water but by land, and that in two whole moneths journey"; and arrives at the impossible: "But our Captaine asked the Petie-King of this Nation, how many dayes Journey we yet had to the Amazones? from whence he receiveth answere; That wee must yet travell one whole moneth, besides that all the Countrie was full of water" (17: 33–35). We seem to have been reduced, or perhaps conveyed, to the insecure premises of what the ever skeptical Purchas terms "Amazonian Dreames" (18:59).

Such explorers as Schmidel are tremendously specific about what they do not find. In their synthesis of materialism and frustration, these accounts suggest an endlessly expanding world that still never offers quite the right returns. Purchas writes of the effect, "The Amazons are still one nation further then the relaters or their authors have traveled. In two places of Asia, two of Africa, two of America; the Amazons have bin, till that men came there and found none."[32] One twentieth-century author argues that Amazons are most useful as markers of the points at which exploration has failed: "Fabulous creatures such as the kynocephali, the monoculi, or the pygmies, the tradition of which is closely linked with that of the Amazons, are still to be found on geographical maps of the sixteenth century, but, alas! they have been driven to the South Polar regions!"[33] The point, it seems, is that one can never get past the edge of the map; obstacles proliferate at the levels both of geography and of interpretation. So de Acuña watches Amazons recede through a chain of language in which the barriers to understanding multiply: "Thirty-seven leagues from this village, and lower down the river, on the north side, is the mouth of that of the Amazons, which is known among the natives by the name of Cunuris. This river takes the name of the first Indians who live on its banks, next to whom follow the *Apantos,* who speak the '*lingoa geral*' of Brazil. Next come the *Taguaus,* and the last, being those who communicate and traffic with the Amazons themselves, are the *Guacarás.*"[34] Amazons are connected to known space and common language only by recurring interventions, and pursuing them is not only difficult but potentially ill-advised. Anthony Knivet writes, "I would have perswaded the Tamoyes to have warred against the Amazons, but they durst not, for they said, we know that their Countrie is very populous, and we shall be all killed."[35]

Amazonian narratives locate the spectacular, the marvelous, the fabulous—Greenblatt's "wonder"—not in a moment of confrontation, but in the processes of anticipation and reinterpretation. They prove less about the new world than they do about desire and the interpenetration of texts. Explorers well or sketchily versed in myth bring back "news" of Amazon encounters; romance, at the peak of its popularity, takes their accounts as raw material; explorers who read popular romances go to the new world to discover Amazons yet again. John Cartwright describes the "Women Archers" he sees as "very skilful and active in shooting, and managing any sort of weapon, like the fierce Amazones in antick time," suggesting the reciprocal production of knowledge and discovery.[36] Do well-read explorers have a better chance of finding what they are looking for? Or of knowing what they are looking at? Todorov argues that exploration is always intertextual, describing Columbus's account of the new world in those terms: "One might say that Columbus has undertaken it all in order to be able to tell unheard-of stories, like Ulysses; but is not a travel narrative itself the point of departure, and not only the point of arrival, of a new voyage? Did not Columbus himself set sail because he had read Marco Polo's narrative?"[37] As a product of invested rereadings, the new world Amazon might be not a discovery, but a pretext.

In the other Amazon event of 1542, myth again works as an interpretive device rather than a declaration of experience. California, named for *Amadis*'s amazonian Queen Calafie, does not appear to explorers as a land of gold, griffins, and seductively pagan warrior women; it does not even display the more ordinary wonders that lead to Bernal Díaz's famous analogy in *The Conquest of New Spain*. "These great towns and *cues* and buildings rising from the water, all made of stone, seemed like an enchanted vision from the tale of Amadis."[38] "California" emerges both from and as a recognized fiction, commemorating the recognition of incongruity. Explorers apply the name to identify what they have not found; unlike Orellana's Amazons, who become fantastic in retrospect, the kingdom of Queen Calafie is an illusion invoked through its exposure. In her study "California: The Name," Ruth Putnam concludes, "The point to bear in mind is that, once suggested, the application was probably in derision pure and simple."[39] The western margin of a land in which the land of Amazons has for fifty years moved inexorably west takes a name that claims only fictional reference, marking an end, an edge, an exhaustion of progress.

Leonard writes of Montalvo, author of the Calafie episodes in *Amadis*, "While he was engaged in writing this tale it is possible that there reached his ears an echo of Columbus's report of Amazon-like women on some islands past which he had cruised and of their alleged proximity to the Earthly Paradise."[40] As Columbus sails in search of Marco Polo's Isle of Female only to return with what may become Montalvo's Queen Calafie, so later explorers model conquest on *Amadis* and incorporate Calafie in California. Medina gives a vivid instance of such mutual production, recording that Orellana's adventures almost immediately appeared in popular plays. In his chapter "Orellana in the Drama" he offers a few excerpts but declines to discuss them, saying only, "It would be foreign to my purpose, as well as displeasing to the reader, for me to go into an analysis of a work so preposterous."[41] Criticized for their claims about fabulous figures, explorers return to find themselves on stage with them, in fictions no more—or less—preposterous than the accounts that lend them authority. With Amazons as an index, it is not always easy to distinguish leaving for the new world from coming back again.

That circularity, in which not only fact and fiction but home and away become difficult to distinguish, produces the effect of seeing twice. Early accounts of discovery are filled with double visions, in which a second look dispels illusion and reveals fool's gold, fabled cities transformed into abandoned villages, cannibals who never offer to eat their discoverers. California's aggressively fictional name articulates a common conviction: If the treasure has been found, it isn't the right treasure. Appearing frequently in the catalogues of oddities and monstrosities that map desire onto the new world, Amazons are subject to such narrative double takes, but the fantasies surrounding them are more complicated than those involving, for example, men with their heads in their chests. As I argued in the introduction to this book, Amazons in early modern texts appear not only in the new world but in the social categories that structure the world at home. Second looks at Amazon encounters reflect this circumstance, producing not an emptying out of the term "Amazon" but a reevaluation of the new world bodies to which that term refers. Endlessly metonymic quests sometimes give way to moments in which Amazons are found, only to be reconsidered, rediscovered as something already known.

The practice of replacing the strange with the strangely familiar produces a series of strategic rereadings. Lopez Vaz, in another early critique of Orellana's Amazon encounter, argues for a reconsideration not of woman warriors, but of their relationship to men: "There were of these women upon divers partes of this river, who seeing the Spaniardes fighting with their husbandes came in to succour them, and shewed themselves more valiant then their husbandes; for which cause it was named, The river of Amazones." [42] Antonio de Herrera repeats this argument in the sixth decade of his *General History of the West Indies*: "Some of the Spaniards were of opinion that Captain Orellana should not have given the name of Amazons to these women who fought, because in the Indies it was no new thing for the women to fight, and to use bows and arrows." [43] In *Purchas his Pilgrimage*, Purchas writes, "These Amazons were but the wives which exercised armes, and followed warfare with their husbands." [44] *Hakluytus Posthumus* multiplies this interpretation: Purchas refers, in a note to the account of Francisco Alvares, to "Amazones, the warlike wives of those parts"; comments on Knivet's account, "Amazons, not a one-breasted Nation, but warlike women"; writes of Vaz's discovery, "Note the truth of that which hath mocked men touching Amazons in Asia, Africa and America. None other have yet by credible reports beene found but warlike wives, and not solitary unimamians"; and entirely dismisses the findings of Ulrich Schmidel. "The Amazons are still further off: I doubt beyond the region of Truth; if the title be properly meant of such as are here described. For warlike wives living in societie with men, are many." [45] Such narratives domesticate violence, engaging in an uncomfortable substitution that produces, not Amazons, but wives with weapons.

As they replace "solitary unimammians" with women defined through their connections to men, these accounts focus not on the anomaly of female separatism, but on the nature of heterosocial bonds. Amazon myth becomes a cover story; so Morison, in his description of Columbus's second voyage, recounts a strange masquerade. "Here, his first shore party was met by an army of Carib women armed with bows and arrows, from which everyone concluded that this was the Isle of Amazons; and such they understood it to be, from a woman they captured. She said, records Ferdinand Columbus, that 'the island was only inhabited by women, and that those who would have hindered the men landing were women, except four men who were there accidentally from another island; for at a certain time in the year they come to sport, and lie with them.' None of this was true, except that the women were good archers." [46] Amazon pretenders are exposed by the discovery that they live within conventional family structures, and the revelation makes them amenable to colonial conquest. The account concludes, "The lady casique and her daughter, so Columbus declared, volunteered to accompany him to Spain, and were accepted." When Amazons become warlike wives, it becomes possible to bring them home.

Peter Martyr d'Anghiera tells a still stranger story, which aggressively asserts editorial privilege. "There are also other Ilandes sytuate about this *Colluacana* or *Caluacam*, the whiche are inhabited onely with women lyving without the coompanye of men after the maner of the *Amazones.* But they that ponder the matter more wisely, thinke them rather to be certeyne women whiche have vowed chastitie and profesed a solytarie lyfe as the nunnes doo with us, or as the virgins cauled *Vestales* or *Bonae Deae*, were accustomed to do amonge the gentiles in oulde tyme. At certeyne tymes of the yeare, men of the other Ilandes resorte unto them. But not for the intent of generation, but moved with pitie to helpe them to dresse their gardens and tyll their grounde." [47] Hindsight intervenes between the explorer and his experience, explaining that the women discovered are not Amazons but nuns, who live apart not out of militancy but out of piety; men visit them regularly, but only to help with the garden. Again, this extraordinary substitution does not deny that Amazons exist: what the author terms "corrupte women," who mutilate one breast, give away their boy-children, and show an unseemly interest in "carnall copulation," occupy another island. Rather than vanishing or being discredited, the Amazons have simply, metonymically, moved next door, leaving something more familiar behind.

Such interventions repeatedly assert that Amazons are not in fact Amazons at all because they are chaste, because they have husbands, because they have two breasts. But the process of revision does not end the quest; false Amazons, manufactured through misreading or imposture, seem only to reinforce the conviction that real Amazons must be out there somewhere. More urgently, these belated reconsiderations suggest that neither the explorer nor the reader can tell the difference, that wives, impostors, and even nuns may look like Amazons and that Amazons may be indistinguishable from wives and impostors and nuns. Purchas's assertion, that "warlike wives living in societie with men, are many," opens up more problems than it forecloses, locating female excess within domestic conventions. If it is true — and exploration narratives seem to have an odd investment in *making* it true — it has a disruptive effect on categories of distinction. Amazons might be taken as counterexamples that validate the social logic of the feminine, but it is difficult to know what has happened to that logic when the structure of marriage accommodates a multitude of warlike wives.

Exploration narratives that make this move reject the unknown for a deliberate invention of the uncanny. Marriage is a system read onto the new world through the terms of the old; whether praised for conjugal restraint or denigrated for its lack, the people scrutinized by explorers inhabit a prefabricated structure of expectation. The reiterative insistence on "warlike wives" comes close to home, its focus not merely anthropological but self-aware. Hakluyt's note to Vaz's account effects the transition from separatist to domestic violence by positing a structure of alliance — "Amazones women which helpe their husbands in the warres" — but Alvares makes explicit the darker intimation of hegemony reversed. "The Husbands of these women are no Warriors, because they will not suffer them to manage Armes."[48] Women warriors, "more valiant than their husbandes," reflect uneasiness about women more generally; discovering Amazons means rediscovering old anxieties and well-worn debates. Wives with weapons metonymically refer to embattled domesticity, even as "real" Amazons metonymically recede. The revision of Amazon encounters inserts the uncanny in the place of discovery, making the strange familiar, marking the new world as a repetition and a return.

THE REGION OF TRUTH

In "Love, Guilt and Reparation," Melanie Klein offers the following theory of exploration. "In the explorer's unconscious mind, a new territory stands for a new mother, one that will replace the loss of the real mother . . . Here both the escape from her and the original attachment to her find full expression. The child's early aggression stimulated the drive to restore and to make good, to put back into his mother the good things he had robbed her of in phantasy, and these wishes to make good merge into the later drive to explore, for by finding new land the explorer gives something to the world at large and to a number of people in particular. In his pursuit the explorer actually gives expression to both aggression and the drive to reparation."[49] For Sir Walter Ralegh's *The discoverie of the large, rich, and beautifull Empire of Guiana*, this structure is a fantasy of textual effect. Klein describes a triangle, linking child to mother, explorer to "the world at large," through the "good things" of a new mother and a new world. Driven by "both aggression and the drive to reparation," this successfully mediated system of connection is the goal of *The discoverie:* whether we privilege the rhetoric of persons, in which a man solicits the favors of a woman, or the rhetoric of politics, in which a subject negotiates with his sovereign, Ralegh's narrative presents itself as the matter of bonds.

In his introductory letter to Howard and Cecil, Ralegh offers his body, his time, his money, and, if necessary, his life in an attempt to regain the favor of the queen. "I did therefore even in the winter of my life, undertake these travels, fitter for bodies lesse blasted with misfortunes, for men of greater abilitie, and for mindes of better incouragement, that thereby, if it were possible, I might recover but the moderation of excesse, and the least tast of the greatest plenty formerly possessed." [50] Ralegh presents self-denial as reparation for past excess, a strategy which, for Louis Montrose, yields a cartographic pun: "In short, Ralegh's discovery of a new continent discovers him to be newly continent." [51] Fuller offers a similar observation: "The *Discoverie of Guiana* reenacts and rewrites the scene of Ralegh's transgression, enacting fidelity and continence over and over." [52] And Jeffrey Knapp writes, "In fact, allegorizing the poor returns from his Guianan venture as a personal triumph, a demonstration of the self-restraint he had previously seemed to lack, Raleigh paradoxically celebrates virginity even more than had the earlier Virginian writers." [53] Throughout *The discoverie*, Ralegh emphasizes his restraint: "I have chosen rather to beare the burden of poverty, then reproach, and rather to endure a second travel and the chances therof, then to have defaced an enterprise of so great assurance, untill I knew whether it pleased God to put a disposition in her princely and royal heart either to folow or foreslow the same" (343). By mediating his desires through those of the queen, Ralegh might unwrite past transgressions; the right kind of return could be a lucky escape.

But if *The discoverie* attempts a process of self-refashioning, it takes a complicated route. "I have undergone many constructions," Ralegh writes in his prefatory letter to Howard and Cecil. "I have bene accompanyed with many sorrowes, with labour, hunger, heat, sickenes, and perill: It appeareth notwithstanding that I made no other bravado of going to the sea, then was ment, and that I was never hidden in Cornewall, or els where, as was supposed. They have grosly belied me, that forejudged, that I would rather become a servant to the Spanish king, then returne, and the rest were much mistaken, who would have perswaded, that I was too easefull and sensuall to undertake a journey of so great travell" (339). Having "undergone many constructions," Ralegh attempts to intervene in the process, inventing two sets of relations. In the first, *The discoverie* mediates his relationship to Elizabeth; in the second, he conflates Guiana as an objective and Elizabeth as an obstacle in courting the patronage of men.[54] And if the first of these strategies identifies *The discoverie* as an exercise in self-definition, the second offers it as proof of presences other than the speaker's own. The narrative takes failure as its referent on the one hand, and on the other asserts the ease of success. In its doubled triangulation, *The discoverie* relies on the sense in which metonymy works twice, both invoking the processes through which objects of desire recede and standing for the promise of their availability. Meaning accumulates for one audience along the surface of signification, and refers for another to an underlying materiality; Ralegh's rhetoric both claims to be and promises to provide a commodity that will reconstruct his relations to power.

Ralegh writes *The discoverie* in response to claims that he never went to Guiana at all, but was "hidden in Cornewall, or els where, as was supposed." To counter such accusations, he promises a description that is natural, mimetic, transparently experiential; the Ralegh of these opening remarks might be the ideal narrator fantasized by Montaigne. "We had neede of Topographers to make us particular narrations of the places they have beene in. For some of them, if they have the advantage of us, that they have seene *Palestine*, will challenge a priviledge, to tell us newes of all the world besides. I would have every man write what he knowes, and no more: not onely in that, but in all other subjects." [55] Guaranteeing a particular narration of the place he has been in—and insisting that it is *not* Cornwall—Ralegh opposes his narrative of experience to the misrepresentations imposed on him by others. But such a narrative cannot escape its own status *as* narrative, and in the end, writing *The discoverie* might prove nothing more tangible than that Ralegh has written a book. Considering the limitations of texts as material standins, Fuller writes, "Models that tend toward describing memory or discovery as modes of transportation applied to images or even objects, and that attempt to secure discovery and memory in a milieu of voiceless physical procedures, arrive immediately in the midst of figurative language, the poet's lie." [56] For Ralegh, despite the ambitious assurances of his introductory epistles, "the poet's lie" seems always to be the destination of choice.

Referring to Ralegh's poem "On the Life of Man," Barbara Herrnstein Smith discusses distinctions among kinds of discourse. "We are at some peril if we fail to distinguish the unreality of dreams from the unreality of waking experiences or unreal representations of tigers from unreal tigers—a peril that I shall not call 'real' but, as Sir Walter Raleigh put it, at least 'in earnest.' It may be argued that all natural utterances are themselves fictive. But the distinction between natural and fictive discourse does not thereby collapse: it simply, so to speak, moves over one ontological notch." [57] As a discourse that claims to reflect rather than invent experience, *The discoverie* relies on this distinction between the natural and the fictive. But the nature of Ralegh's ontological moves, of his statements about what is and is there, obscures the difference, causing objects described as real to work like and indeed as tropes. Discovery, as Fuller argues, always appears through such linguistic processes as metaphor and metonymy, bringing the new world to the old only through the mediating mechanisms of signification. But Ralegh's text, as if anticipating our own deconstructive impulses, foregrounds those mechanisms, using them to confound the familiar and the strange. Objects of discovery are privileged not in their novel materiality, but in the constellations of figures they invoke. Metonymy operates at the level of metaphor; conceits lead not to referents or the illusion of referents, but to conceits; and the processes of association tend indistinguishably toward the old world and toward the new.

Freud writes, "An uncanny effect is often and easily produced when the distinction between imagination and reality is effaced, as when something that we have hitherto regarded as imaginary appears before us in reality, or when a symbol takes over the full functions of the thing it symbolizes." [58] Exploration narratives should always, at least arguably, produce this first kind of uncanniness, generating moments at which "something that we have hitherto regarded as imaginary appears before us in reality." But as a record of experience, *The discoverie* is uncanny in Freud's second sense, its rhetorical processes a series of symbolic mirror games: the practices of cannibals look like the traffic in women; new world gold conjures up the image of the queen; conquest is a mode of patronage; novelty recalls myth. All objects here work like those Amazons who are reread as warlike wives, identifying the strange as a condition of the familiar. *The discoverie*'s own Amazon encounter summarizes this sense of a narrative never fully committed to the experience it exists to describe. "[I] was very desirous to understand the truth of those warlike women, because of some it is beleeved, of others not. And though I digresse from my purpose, yet I will set downe that which hath bene delivered me for trueth of those women" (366–67). Ralegh's Amazons are already twice-told, and his new world informant has both the same authority and the same information as old world texts. The truth that *The discoverie* delivers is a list of clichés, impressive in the thoroughness with which it reconstructs classical myth and in the insouciance with which it eschews experiential claims. History and geography, time and space, become indistinguishable in the distance they impose between Ralegh and his objects: "In many histories [Amazons] are verified to have bene, and in divers ages and provinces" (367). This is perhaps inevitably true of Amazon encounters, and certainly true of those I have described; in the absence of new experience explorers rely on old news. But for Ralegh the gesture of circularity, of explicit recycling, becomes paradigmatic, even as the status of Amazon myth ("of some it is beleeved, of others not") anticipates responses to his own text. Ralegh's Amazons do not stand out in their unlikelihood or in their frankly derivative nature. Instead, they fix the status of his narrative; if, as Medina argues, Orellana's amazonian dream is an aberration, Ralegh's is an index.

The prepositional conditions that structure Amazon encounters — hearing about, looking toward, sailing past, stopping before — shape all experiences in *The discoverie*. Knapp considers Ralegh in the context of English writers who, he argues, "have little choice but to confine their expansionism to an indirection variously conceived as unworldliness, superstition, error, incapacity, introversion, distraction, or disgrace — modes of contrary idealization that I subsume under the larger rubric, again, of trifling." Reading *The discoverie* in these terms, Knapp writes, "Raleigh exploits the tradition of English otherworldliness in order to disguise his material failure." [59] *The discoverie* constructs referentiality not by claiming to be transparent but by putting its opacity on display. When explorers look at the new world with *Amadis* in mind, they imagine a trip through the looking glass, in which the things encountered are at once alien and oddly everyday. For Ralegh there is no *through;* the looking glass is a flat, hard surface that reflects back what he has brought with him.

Exploration narrative, I have suggested, presents itself as a chain of signification laid above a chain of experience, sometimes promising the reader access to that experience, sometimes drawing endlessly away. But

Ralegh is not the source of one experience but a reader of many, and *The discoverie* presents anthology as mimesis. On top of one object the text stacks a number of names: "By that way followed Orellana (by the commandement of Gonzalo Pizarro, in the yere 1542) whose name the river also beareth this day, which is also by others called Marannon, although Andrew Thevet doeth affirme that betweene Marannon and Amazones there are 120 leagues: but sure it is that those rivers have one head and beginning, and the Marannon, which Thevet describeth, is but a branch of Amazones or Orellana, of which I will speake more in another place" (358). And underneath a few words—gold, cannibals, women, the queen—the text layers a multitude of possible objects, leaving the relationship among them indistinct. Referentiality, as a correspondence of word to thing or as a fantasy necessary to the genre of exploration narrative, is both multiplied and emptied out.

Terms shift without warning in *The discoverie*, so that a river can be "Amazones or Orellana" and both 120 leagues from and the source of Marannon; clarification is always deferred to "another place." And "Amazones" takes on its own multiplicity, seeming to mean Amazons and Amazon River interchangeably. Ralegh recounts one explorer's discovery that "no entrance could be found by the branches or body of Amazones," and writes of another, "By the Amazones hee was utterly overthrowen" (362, 363). As it indicates both geography and the bodies that inhabit it, the figure lends agency to impediments; bounded by "Amazones," Guiana resists discovery. And under the influence of such resistance, Ralegh's entire quest sounds like an amazonian pursuit. "For mine owne part," he writes, "(as we were not able to march it for the rivers, neither had any such strength as was requisite, and durst not abide the comming of the Winter, or to tarie any longer from our ships) I thought it were evill counsell to have attempted it at that time" (413). Ralegh cannot reach his objective because the weather is wrong, the rivers intervene, he has insufficient manpower. Like "Amazones," these obstacles appear at once natural and oddly personal.

Ralegh's reliance on the power of representation, not only to recount discovery but to constitute it, presumes that elaborations on failure prove the value of the goal. His obtrusive manipulation of textual processes—addresses, quotations, ellipses, references, conceits—attempts to invent a world that he has failed to experience, constructing it not as a persuasive simulacrum but as an image of desire. Greenblatt writes, "In the midst of pessimism and disgust, Ralegh kept alive within himself the opposing vision, the conviction that role and reality can come together, so that by the power of the imagination the world is recreated in the image of man's desires. And this vision did not spin itself out in ethereal dreams but found a clear and worldly focus: Guiana." [60] For *The discoverie*, that "clear and worldly focus" becomes the quest for Guiana's gold: "I wil hope that these provinces, and that Empire now by me discovered shal suffice to inable her Majestie and the whole kingdome, with no lesse quantities of treasure, then the king of Spaine hath in all the Indies East and West" (348). Through gold, Ralegh might fulfill *The discoverie*'s doubled purpose, delivering both the economic rewards that motivate patronage and a revitalized vision of sovereign power. Gold is a touchstone, its presence bringing together objects and desire without space for metonymic evasions or interpretive subjectivity; whatever might be said about the motives that drive exploration, finding gold is a transitive act.

Yet for *The discoverie* it is figurative and subjunctive, subject to the narrative's amazonian effect. Ralegh's references to the connection between gold and Amazons confuse the site of discovery, the agency of ownership, and the processes of exchange: "These Amazones have likewise great store of these plates of golde"; "Undoubtedly those that trade Amazones returne much golde" (367; 366). "Amazones" signifies both the presence of fabulous riches and the impossibility of attaining them; as Ralegh concludes, "Although, as I am perswaded, Guiana cannot be entred that way, yet no doubt the trade of gold from thence passeth by branches of rivers into the river of Amazones" (367). Evasion and frustration characterize the quest for gold throughout *The discoverie*: "But in those canoas which escaped there was a good quantity of ore and gold"; "to stay to digge out gold with our nailes, had been Opus laboris but not Ingenii"; "I could have returned a good quantity of gold ready cast, if I had not shot at another marke, then present profit" (389–90). The quest generates only a rhetoric of escape: the escape of the canoes with the most valuable cargo; the escape of the people with the most useful knowledge; his own escape into higher motives and enigmatic language ("another marke, then present profit"; "Opus laboris but not Ingenii"). In looking for gold Ralegh discovers what he lacks: "Whosoever hath seene with what strength of stone the best gold oare in invironed, hee will not thinke it easie to be had out in heapes, and especially by us, who had neither men, instruments, nor time (as it is said before) to performe the same" (345).

The "smal graines of gold" that Ralegh does bring back represent rather than constitute treasure. "I was not bound to satisfie any man of the quantitie, but such onely as adventured, if any store had bin returned thereof" (344; 345). Gold, discovered, becomes another figure that generates further text: "Because there have bin divers opinions conceived of the gold oare broght from Guiana, and for that an Alderman of London and an officer of her Majesties Mint, hath given out that the same is of no price, I have thought good by the addition of these lines to give answer aswel to the said malicious slander, as to other objections" (343). As the doubled production of evidence—grains of gold, "the addition of these lines"—suggests, proof is a question of reading. It is undermined by a case of *mis*reading; beguiled by the promise of the real thing, Ralegh's men fall for the simulacrum. "Such as had no judgement or experience kept al that glistered, and would not be perswaded but it was rich because of the lustre" (404). "Al that glistered" is not gold but fool's gold, and how surprising is it that Ralegh's men are taken in by a trope?

But the trope, according to Ralegh, matters. In the place of gold as a portable and fungible substance, *The discoverie* inserts a structure of reference in which fool's gold is a sign on the surface that rewards those who look beneath. "Al the rocks, mountains, al stones in the plaines, woods, and by the rivers side are in effect throughshining, and seem marvelous rich, which being tried to be no Marcasite, are the true signes of rich minerals, but are no other then El madre del oro (as the Spaniards terme them) which is the mother of gold, or as it is said by others the scum of gold" (344). False gold, in a semiosis mediated by translation, is the sign of real gold; bringing home shiny rocks of no intrinsic value does not demonstrate failure, but proves that "it was El Madre del oro, that is the mother of gold, and that the Mine was farther in the ground" (405). The argument works as a kind of reverse alchemy, turning gold into the things it is not in order to prove its worth. In an extraordinary literalization of the structure of metaphor, Ralegh brings back "the true signes of rich minerals," arguing that Guiana works as a system of tropes.

When he valorizes fool's gold by substituting referential for intrinsic

value, Ralegh appends a disclaimer: "But it shall be found a weake poli-
cie in me, either to betray my selfe, or my countrey with imaginations"
(405). But as his repeated recourse to the argument indicates, "imaginations," fantasies of interpretation, are what Ralegh has to offer; if his
exploration narrative is a mimetic response to experience, the experience is that of reading. Fool's gold substantiates a structure of belief that
works only within *The discoverie*'s terms as a text, and proves that those
terms mirror the textual logic of Guiana itself. It is a neat tautology,
in which bringing back gold from the new world proves that there is
gold in the new world, and yet we are far from the tightly constructed
sign that I earlier proposed. Ralegh's discovery of gold does not foreclose metonymic evasion, but relies on it; does not replace interpretive
subjectivity, but privileges it. Real gold is hard to get to, because false
gold is in the way; but to those who know how to read the signs, false
gold proves that real gold exists. Like the "Amazons" encountered by
explorers, who are not Amazons at all but who indicate their presence,
"the scum of gold" asserts discovery by radically shifting the conditions
of exchange. New lands, like the women who inhabit them, affirm value
but resist commodification.

Talking to men, Ralegh might signify Guiana's accessibility and desirability by exploiting the tropes of a feminized new world, but images of
female agency complicate the conceit. Conflicting images of women who
have things, women who are things, women who represent things, and
women who dictate the meaning and distribution of things overlap and
interpenetrate. Montrose writes of Ralegh's amazonian speculations,
"Implicit in the conceptual shift from *the land as woman* to *a land of women*
is the possibility of representing women as collective social agents." [61]
Where women govern the spaces of discovery, those spaces cannot easily
appear as feminine objects subject to masculine appropriation; images
of sovereign female power oppose the ideal of a receptive passivity. And
the multiple meanings of "Amazones" indicate a larger problem with
the syllogism that links women to land, land to value, value to conquest:
as it denotes both geography and the people who inhabit it, the word
suggests not only the resistance of women who have land but the recalci-
trance of the land itself. If agency attaches itself to female bodies, identifying new territories with those bodies fails to convey their openness
to acquisition. The uncomplicated exchange of women by men might

substantiate a set of statements about commodification and possession, but *The discoverie* makes such statements difficult. Can a woman be a trope if the audience is the queen? In the structures of exchange, who is the agent, who is the object, and who gets to say?

Ralegh claims that he does not want to traffic in women, striking a bargain with one local ruler that sharply distinguishes kinds of property: "He yeelded for a chiefe cause that in the warres with the Epuremei, they were spoyled of their women, and that their wives and daughters were taken from them, so as for their owne parts they desired nothing of the golde or treasure, for their labours, but onely to recover women" (412–13). Like Ralegh's insistence on sexual restraint, the king's proposal — "their women for us, and their gold for you" — assures readers that Englishmen know the difference between appropriate and inappropriate objects of desire (413). The encounter asserts a division, between gold and conquest as reasonable pursuits and women as an economy best left to the native inhabitants. Ralegh's tone is anthropological, a strong statement of difference: "And in truth they war more for women then either for gold or dominion." His king might be one of the cannibals, idealized but unmistakably other, of whom Montaigne writes, "All their morall discipline containeth but these two articles; first an undismayed resolution to warre, then an inviolable affection to their wives." [62]

Ralegh's own cannibals, however, relate to women not through an "ethical science" but through an economy. Cannibals are linked to other exotic populations in *The discoverie*, as they are in exploration narratives more generally: "To the West of Caroli are diverse nations of Canibals, and of those Ewaipanoma without heads"; "On the South side of the maine mouth of Orenoque, are the Arwacas; and beyond them the Canibals and to the South of them the Amazones" (423, 424). But in Ralegh's text they more often appear engaged in processes of heterosocial commodification and homosocial exchange. Describing "a great nation of Canibals," Ralegh writes that "their chiefe towne beareth the name of the river, and is called Acamacari: at this towne is a continuall market of women" (407). In cannibalistic transactions women are valuable objects, equated with and bartered for other treasures; Ralegh describes a local population's journey "to trade for golde, and to buy women of the Canibals" (387). Men trade gold to cannibals for women, and the traffic links European markets to those of the new world: "Among many other trades, those Spaniards used canoas to passe to the rivers . . . which are on the south side of the mouth of Orenoque, and there buy women and children from the Canibals" (376).

Why does Ralegh identify cannibals not as men who eat men but as men who trade women? And what does this have to do with the Spanish? The easy answer is otherness. Linking cannibals to Spaniards through women separates all of them from Ralegh himself; this is not, he points out, the right kind of male bonding. But Ralegh's idiosyncratic definition of cannibalism also distances him from any version of male homosocial power. The customs Ralegh finds alien are governed not by the violence of men against men, but by the ordered trade in women; using female bodies to form alliances and preserve property rights, cannibals reinvent patriarchy. Cannibalism, for *The discoverie*, means the social consumption of women, a practice less obviously grotesque than the literal devouring of human bodies, but more thorough in its hierarchical impositions: people might eat each other interchangeably, but women are constantly defined and disposed of by men. The system of values mirrors the familiar one that Ralegh, through his appeal to male patrons, attempts to reenter, in which agreement over a feminized object—Guiana or, more dangerously, Elizabeth herself—signifies a distribution of power that privileges men. But when Ralegh rediscovers that structure in the new world, he finds it irrecoverably strange. At one moment in *The discoverie*, he is himself implicated in cannibalistic practice: "This Arwacan Pilot with the rest, feared that wee would have eaten them, or otherwise have put them to some cruel death (for the Spaniards, to the end that none of the people in the passage towards Guiana or in Guiana it selfe might come to speach with us, perswaded all the nations, that we were men-eaters, and Canibals)" (390). Intriguingly, cannibals become men-eaters when they also become Englishmen; authentically strange new world practices appear most clearly when Ralegh discovers them attached to himself. He of course denies the false identity; his implication in conspicuous consumption is not a poet's lie, but a Spanish one.

Ralegh's participation in the exchanges of the new world impoverishes him. The only gold available to him is already marked by the queen, and he brings home less than he took away: "I gave among them manie more peeces of gold, then I received, of the new money of 20 shillings with her Majesties picture to weare" (415). This is more than a story about the expense of exploration. Ralegh reproduces the cult of Elizabeth in the new world, presenting the queen's image as an object of exchange; again defining figure as commodity, he draws on narrative and iconographic resources to produce material effects. "I shewed them her Majesties picture which they so admired and honoured, as it had bene easie to have brought them idolatrous thereof," he writes, and, of a later encounter, "Dilating at large (as I had done before to those of Trinidad) her Majesties greatnesse, her justice, her charitie to all oppressed nations, with as many of the rest of her beauties and vertues, as either I could expresse, or they conceive: all which being with great admiration attentively heard, and marveilously admired, I beganne to sound the olde man as touching Guiana" (354, 399). But the queen's image does not confer power on the men who exchange it; acknowledging political realities, Ralegh offers the inhabitants of the new world the same subjected condition that he enjoys in the old. "I made them understand that I was the servant of a Queene, who was the great Casique of the North, and a virgine, and had more Casiqui under her then there were trees in that yland: that shee was an enemie to the Castellani in respect of their tyrannie and oppression, and that she delivered all such nations about her, as were by them oppressed, and having freed all the coast of the Northren world from their servitude, had sent mee to free them also" (353–54). Female sovereignty governs male subjectivity, and freedom, in this rhetorical contract, is a willed change of servitude. Setting up a transaction among men in the new world, Ralegh refers its conditions to the queen who governs the old one.

Karen Newman writes of early modern England, "Patriarchalism was a dominant trope through which social relations were perceived, a strategy whereby power was embodied and institutionalized."[63] In *The discoverie* patriarchalism is a trope like any other, vulnerable to commodification and rereading; in the absence of any naturalized relationship between agents and objects, the bargains made by men might subject them to women, and the agency of women might objectify men.[64] Like the warlike wives and female captains of other exploration narratives, women in Ralegh's text have power within, rather than apart from, heterosocial relations. Contextualized by such populations as "the Canuri, which are governed by a woman (who is inheritrix of that Province)" (*The discoverie*,

423), the idiosyncracies of Amazons threaten to become general practice, saying something both unimaginable and long-suspected about women and making a particular point about queens. In the new world as constructed by Ralegh and other amazonian dreamers, the logic that reasons from Amazons to other, more familiar versions of female sovereignty seems inescapable. Ralegh's rhetoric continually intermingles Amazons, amazonian queens, and queens, and, as he attempts to draw his own queen into the politics of the new world, he risks implying that she is already there.

Describing Guiana's boundaries, Ralegh writes, "This river falleth into Amazones, by which Osua with his companies descended, and came out of that province which is called Mutylonez: and it seemeth to mee that this empire is reserved for her Majesty and the English nation, by reason of the hard successe which all these and other Spanyards found in attempting the same" (362). *The discoverie* makes iconography a topographical proposition: Guiana, being hard to enter, must belong to the virgin queen. Like the "branches or body of Amazones," Guiana offers no entrance, but is preserved from invasion as is the body of Elizabeth herself.[65] And Guiana, like Elizabeth, is unique in this; the Spaniards who could not enter there have been everywhere else. Comparing Spain's excess to England's lack, Ralegh writes, "I will thus conclude, that whatsoever kingdome shalbe inforced to defend it selfe may be compared to a body dangerously diseased, which for a season may be preserved with vulgar medicines, but in a short time, and by litle and litle, the same must needs fall to the ground, and be dissolved" (347). Conquest is a patriotic necessity; the equation that links Guiana's impenetrability to the queen's produces the imperative that Guiana be invaded in the queen's name. That paradox in turn produces the most notorious passage of *The discoverie:* "To conclude, Guiana is a countrey that hath yet her maydenhead, never sackt, turned, nor wrought, the face of the earth hath not bene torne, nor the vertue and salt of the soyle spent by manurance, the graves have not bene opened for golde, the mines not broken with sledges, nor their Images puld downe out of their temples. It hath never bene entered by any armie of strength, and never conquered or possessed by any christian Prince" (428).

Interpretations of this passage have credited Ralegh with everything from rapacious anticipation to proto-postcolonialist guilt. However we pathologize the narrator, his representation of Guiana seems to reassert conventional gender politics, linking male sexuality to masculine agency and identifying femininity, embodied in women or sketched out on maps, as the prize. Montrose reads this moment as a mutual naturalization of male and colonial power: "The ideology of gender hierarchy sanctions the Englishmen's collective longing to prove and aggrandize themselves upon the feminine body of the New World, and, at the same time, the emergent hierarchical discourse of colonial exploitation and domination reciprocally confirms that ideology's hegemonic force." [66] If Ralegh links Guiana's militantly intact boundaries to those of the virgin queen, his conclusion offers both gift and threat. As Klein writes, "We can see that through the interest in exploring (whether or not aggression is openly shown) various impulses and emotions—aggression, feelings of guilt, love and the drive to reparation—can be transferred to another sphere, far away from the original person." [67]

But if Klein theorizes exploration as a displaced, and thus estranged, processing of domestic relations, in *The discoverie* displacement fails. Writing to defend himself against accusations that he has never left home, Ralegh cannot keep the *heimlich* out of his story. Freud writes, "There is a joking saying that 'Love is home-sickness'; and whenever a man dreams of a place or a country and says to himself, while he is still dreaming: 'this place is familiar to me, I've been here before,' we may interpret the place as being his mother's genitals or her body. In this case too, then, the *unheimlich* is what was once *heimisch*, familiar; the prefix *'un'* ['un'-] is the token of repression." [68] Countries that appear strangely familiar become women, who inspire both the impulse to return and the need to escape. Imaginative power resides in the "mother's genitals or her body" as it does in the maidenhead of Guiana, but it is not the male subject's power; for Freud's dreamer as for Ralegh, the sense of familiarity generates uneasiness rather than aggression. Ralegh is not "Charles the 5. who had the maidenhead of Peru" (346); Spaniards both buy real women from cannibals and figuratively rape a feminized new world, but Ralegh, throughout *The discoverie*, asserts his distance from such transactions. In his text, the land figured in terms of virginity is familiar precisely because it is mystified, inaccessible, unknown. Impenetrability works as an analogy, but it is also a fact: the only material discovery of Ralegh's *Discoverie* is that no one gets in.

In *The discoverie*'s conclusion, Ralegh turns from maidenheads to Amazons, again conflating the land and its militant population of women in another tribute to female sovereignty. "Her Majestie hereby shall confirme and strengthen the opinions of all nations, as touching her great and princely actions. And where the South border of Guiana reacheth to the Dominion and Empire of the Amazones, those women shall hereby heare the name of a virgin, which is not onely able to defend her owne territories and her neighbours, but also to invade and conquer so great Empires and so farre removed" (431). In conquering Guiana, Elizabeth will prove something to Amazons, opposing virginity to whatever it is that Amazons do. But Ralegh's statement of opposition is a rhetorical turn that turns back on itself to become another mirror game, in which sexual difference is less significant than the identity of gendered performance. Reading this moment as part of Ralegh's strategic "withholding of male desire," Fuller writes, "In that space of absence, the power of the queen can be celebrated in a new and flattering way, as a power between women that relegates men to an instrumental status." [69] This may reduce the equation too far; associating Elizabeth with Amazons is at best a risky business, by no means sure to flatter, and Ralegh veils coincidence with a claim of distinction. But the figure does create a closed economy, in which the pursuits of empire belong only to queens. Rather than identifying Elizabeth as the referent of Amazons, we might understand Ralegh's rhetorical move as another triumph of conceits, which links the signifiers of sovereignty and agency to iconographic and mythological images of women instead of referring them to men.

In the doubling of female sovereignty, metonymic logic comes full circle: if amazonian objectives recede across strange landscapes even as amazonian signification implicates familiar structures, these processes converge in *The discoverie*'s last encounter. Elizabeth prevents the violation of Guiana; "Amazones" preclude the invasion of Guiana; the barriers are imported; the barriers are already there. In his last sentence Ralegh attempts to open up the self-contained system of abstractions into which he has written himself, reinventing discovery as a teleology imposed on feminized objects by male subjects: "I trust . . . that he which is King of all Kings and Lord of Lords, will put it into her heart which is Ladie of Ladies to possesse it, if not, I will judge those men worthy to be kings thereof, that by her grace and leave will undertake it of themselves" (431).

But the men who might be kings must first obtain permission from the queen—a condition that tends to rob the subjunctive imperialist coup of its momentum. And Amazons, as Ralegh writes, "are sayd to be very cruell and bloodthirsty, especially to such as offer to invade their territories," turning violence back on its intentions (367). The strategy that renders invasion as rape falls apart in the absence of any penetration at all, and Elizabeth's own Amazon encounter is not a colonial catalyst but a tautology of female power. Ralegh's rhetorical strategies resolve themselves into this final structure, in which women signify their own acts of conquest and the act of spectatorship is the only one available to men. If this structure bears little resemblance to the actual politics, sexual and otherwise, of colonialist expansion, we might perhaps say the same thing of *The discoverie.*

CHAPTER TWO

Fearful Simile:
Stealing the Breech in
Shakespeare's Chronicle Plays

QUEENE MARGARET

The quene perswaded and encouraged by
these meanes, toke upon her and her husbande, the
high power and aucthoritie over the people and subjectes.
And although she joyned her husbande with hir in name,
for a countenaunce, yet she did all, she saied all, and she
bare the whole swynge, as the strong oxe doth, when
he is yoked in the plough with a pore silly asse.
—Edward Hall, *The Union . . . of Lancastre and Yorke*

A domestick fury makes ill harmony in any family.
—Richard Brathwait, *The English Gentlewoman*

Critically speaking, Shakespeare's *Henry VI* plays tend to go to pieces. If the project of carving up these plays and giving the best parts to Shakespeare has passed out of fashion, it has been replaced by discussions of the plays as self-fragmenting artifacts mirroring the state they describe. The logic of this Henriad appears as repetition rather than linear progress: heroic flourishes, treacherous acts, the crowning, capturing, and killing of kings recur as patterns that all but eclipse the individuals concerned,[1] and the female characters might be less distinct than they are variations on the themes of repetition and excess.[2] But as the plays progress, images of female transgression come ever closer to home, and look rather different when they are inside than they did when they were out. As Jean Howard and Phyllis Rackin observe in *Engendering a Nation*, "The French women who threaten to subvert the English historical project in *Part I* are unmarried; in *Part II*, the dangers they embody quite literally come home to England in the form of ambitious wives, married to the men who govern the land."[3] In the first, second, and third parts of *Henry VI* female agency moves from margin to center, a movement that begins with the claim that the enemy is an Amazon and ends in the recognition of something distinctly amazonian about the woman who is queen, mother, and wife.

Conventions of female excess distinguish between the domestic and the imported, between misbehaviors that oppose socialized femininity and those that inhabit it. In *Still Harping on Daughters* Lisa Jardine draws such a distinction between viragoes and shrews: "The threat of the scold is local and *domestic;* that of the Amazon/virago is generalised 'rejection of her sex', a strangeness which travesties nature." [4] The amazonian references of Shakespeare's first tetralogy reflect fascination with the possibility that distinctions might fail, that the two categories of transgression might, through the image of the amazonian wife, become one and the same. The result is an excursion into the uncanny, what Freud defines as "that class of the frightening which leads back to what is known of old and long familiar." [5] Amazons in socially conventional roles locate the strange—and, indeed, the frightening—within the familiar, producing the anxieties of conflation, displacement, and loss that Freud describes as the uncanny's effect. In the case of Joan la Pucelle, rhetorically held at arm's length, the threat that the familiar might converge with the strange remains largely implicit; but Margaret, who follows Joan in the role of female masculinity, uncannily performs it from within the terms of domesticity itself.

It is a shift inward bracketed by the two kings' bodies: Henry V, who is mourned in his fallen presence and celebrated for his glorious past at the beginning of *1 Henry VI*, and Henry VI, whose corpse appears onstage in the far more muted procession that begins *Richard III.* These royal corpses summarize the threat to sovereign male authority, a threat embodied in the tetralogy's women. Readers have always recognized that the women of these plays have an enervating effect on the men: they are "domineering females," "typically defined as opponents and subverters of the historical and historiographic enterprise," "associated with bloody rites of violence and 'misrule,' " "known to be from hell because of the confusion of gender," representative of "illegitimate and therefore unnatural power," possessing "all the coded and recognizable ambiguities of the castrating woman." [6] Such vigorous consensus obscures the fact that its explanation is doubled, conflating feminizing and effeminating processes that do not add up to quite the same thing. Women, these readings suggest, destabilize male privilege through their appropriation of masculinity; at the same time, women sap male potency through feminine sexuality. We might get around this paradox by asserting that, in the early modern imagination, female masculinity is a sign of heterosexual excess, which is a conventionally feminine trait: "In life as on the stage,"

Rackin argues, "masculine women were regarded as whores."[7] But I want to take seriously the fact that explanations of Joan and, to a still greater extent, of Margaret call on notions of femininity and masculinity in the same breath. This simultaneity generates the disruptive effect of female agency; by invoking two sets of conventions at once, the *Henry VI* plays complicate the hierarchical relationship not only of men to women but also of homosocial systems of power to heterosocial interactions and roles. Joan and Margaret challenge rather than consolidate the naturalized referential assumptions of masculinity, and the tetralogy chronicles an increasingly acute failure to use women to negotiate bonds among men.

Judith Butler describes gender as "an identity tenuously constituted in time, instituted in an exterior space through a *stylized repetition of acts.*"[8] For the female characters of the first tetralogy, gender is not only highly and self-consciously stylized but double; femininity and masculinity appear not as oppositional or mutually displacing terms but as simultaneous performative effects. In the course of the *Henry VI* plays, the nature of that doubleness, summarized in references to Amazons, changes; although readers have tended to equate Joan and Margaret as figures of the French, the feminine, or the theatrical, these plays stage a significant shift. In *1 Henry VI*, Joan is called "Amazon" (1.2.104).[9] Constantly forced on the awareness of spectators both onstage and off, her position as a manly woman generates an essentializing rhetoric that traces her disruptive effect to the fact that she "is" a variety of contradictory things. Margaret, by contrast, is termed "amazonian" and subjunctively described as "play[ing] the Amazon" (1.4.114, 4.1.106). Multiple identities give way to multiple performances. Joan functions only problematically within an economy governed by men because her value, as a sexual commodity and as an iconographic figure, does not remain constant; the qualities assigned to her accumulate not to consensus but to an unsocializable collection of extremes. Margaret instead manipulates the terms of the social, occupying the middle ground of domestic convention; her performance of the roles of mother, wife, and queen brings masculinity and femininity into their most ruinous conflation.

The distinction between Joan and Margaret mirrors a larger difference within monitory texts. Joan is described in the language of exemplary catalogues, which define conventions through the reification of polarities; figures that embody extremes oppose one another to suggest a socialized space between, and Joan's existence outside that space makes her a threat. Margaret recalls the representational strategies of conduct manuals, in which conventions are acted out rather than framed; as she appropriates domestic roles to her own ends, she suggests the transgressive potential of the terms that define women's place. Both strategies assign value to sexual and gendered acts; but if the first essentializes that value as self-evident, the second implies, often against its declared ends, that essentialism may be obscured by feminine performance. In *The English Gentlewoman*, Richard Brathwait writes of the virtuous woman, "Her desire is to *be*, rather than *seeme*, lest *seeming* to *be* what she *is not*, shee gull the world, but her selfe most, by playing the counterfeit." [10] Beneath this benevolent warning against self-deception lies another, self-interested concern: If seeming—counterfeiting, playing—is a mode accessible to women, they threaten both to evade and to appropriate the defining structures of men.

Brathwait's terms anticipate another theory of the relationship between the embodied and the performed. In "The Signification of the Phallus," Lacan describes "the intervention of a 'to seem' that replaces the 'to have,' in order to protect it on the one side, and to mask its lack in the other." [11] Theorizing the conditions of being, having, and seeming, Lacan imposes a shift from the rhetoric of identity as difference to the rhetoric of seeming as masking or appropriating the place of difference. In linking this structure to the roles played by Joan and by Margaret, I do not mean to argue that the plays' women occupy the place of the phallus—although, considering the fantastic materiality and infinite metonymic retreat that I described in the previous chapter, the association has a certain imaginative power. I suggest instead that the tetralogy's representational strategy mirrors Lacan's in representing the conventional signs of discrete sexual identity first as embodied paradox and, more powerfully, as a performance that is also a veil.

The three parts of *Henry VI* complicate the connection of masculinity to men through changing relationships not only between "masculine" and "female" but between "amazonian" and "Amazon." Such complications of identity and referentiality are to some extent the inevitable result of theatricality itself, which, in Barbara Freedman's reading, is constituted through a strategy of misreading analogous to the events of the Lacanian mirror stage: "Both tragic and comic narratives stage misrecognition in the quest for recognition. Whereas Shakespeare's tragedies address the need and failure to find a place in another's eyes, the comedies are more concerned with dislocating perspective; they suggest that only a limited perspectival space defined by error constitutes identity." [12] The *Henry VI* plays conflate the effects that Freedman describes. If Margaret's appearance as Henry's bride at the end of *1 Henry VI* shifts the play's register from tragic to comic conclusions, and if the results of that marriage turn comedy back toward tragedy, the plays mix up conventions of recognition and misrecognition as well. "A woman's general. What should we fear?" Richard asks in *3 Henry VI*, the false causality between statement and question marking the intersection of understanding and its failure (1.2.68). Any attempt to relegate women to their place within masculinist hierarchies through the simple fact of recognizing them *as women* runs up against another of the plays' simple facts: women may be masculine as well.

TO BE

With relentless thoroughness, *Henry VI, Part 1* defines Joan as an outsider. Opposed to an English male aristocratic ideal, she is a woman, a peasant, a virgin, a whore, a saint, a witch, an Amazon, French. Her aggression, while it challenges English idealizations of heroic significance, might consolidate those ideals as well: if the English, at the end of *1 Henry VI*, return to a smaller England, they bring with them a clarified sense of what Englishness means. Coppélia Kahn writes, "As virgin prophetess, mannish amazon, and seductive courtesan, Joan is a composite portrait of the ways women are dangerous to men." [13] Such comprehensive otherness reflects the convention of subjectivity that produces identity through a negotiation of difference; recognition of Joan and violent disassociation from her construct the male heroic subject. In Rackin's terms, male historical abstractions oppose the presence of female bodies: "The whole issue of physical presence vs. historical record, dramatized in *1 Henry VI* as a conflict between English men and French women, is central, not only to this particular play, but to the history play genre itself." [14] Joan's femaleness, however theatrically contingent, is an ideologically absolute condition against which the play constructs its privileged terms.

In this sense, *Henry VI, Part 1* stages a process of deliberately oppositional self-construction, what Butler describes as "a repudiation which produces a domain of abjection, a repudiation without which the subject cannot emerge." [15] The play's representation of a figure of otherness is useful in that it clarifies categorical and hierarchical values by defining that figure against them. But as Butler argues, distance is an illusion, otherness always contingent, in a structure that makes abjection a function of subjectivity. In the particular case of Shakespeare's Joan, the process of repudiation constructs her as uniquely efficient, able to do what she does because of what she is; 1 Henry VI most successfully links act to name in a figure who is neither English nor male nor conventionally heroic. The threat posed by Joan is not simply her evident otherness—which might, after all, only tell the hero what he wants to know—but the fact that that otherness produces a persuasive referential relationship between identity and performance. 1 Henry VI undermines essential male subjectivity by displaying its mirror image in the space of the abject. If the play's resolution depends on the naturalized attachment of masculinity, kingship, and authority to English men, that resolution is parodied and proleptically disrupted in the characterization of Joan la Pucelle.

The play insists on the verb of equation that links Joan to descriptive nouns: Joan "is" a range of things, contradictory but always extreme. In her first encounter with the dauphin, Joan offers a warning: "My courage try by combat, if thou dar'st,/And thou shalt find that I exceed my sex" (1.2.89–90). The implications of the dauphin's response—"Stay, stay thy hands! Thou art an Amazon,/And fightest with the sword of Deborah" (1.2.104–5)—follow Joan throughout the play. His statement conflates what Joan is, what she has, and what she does, reasoning from identity through equipment to act and back again. Joan's body may not display the missing breast invoked by "Amazon," but it has been transformed by her purpose: "And, whereas I was black and swart before,/With those clear rays which she infused on me/That beauty am I blessed with which you may see" (1.2.84–86). Her sword, if not actually the sword of Deborah, has been chosen by supernatural intervention, placed in her hands by a force that is not her own. The literalism of what should be metaphors gives Joan a curious singularity, tying the figures that describe her closely to the identity she claims and the purpose she pursues. "Assigned am I to be the English scourge," she says, and throughout *1 Henry VI*, her identity will be defined by the rhetoric of "I am" and "you are" (1.2.129).

Kahn writes, "The patriarchal world of Shakespeare's history plays is emphatically masculine. Its few women are relatively insignificant, and a man's identity is determined by his relationship to his father, son, or brother."[16] Women in such a context should work as the matter from which male homosocial bonds are formed, a function as important in the consolidation of hostility as it is in the making of friendship. In *Sexual Dissidence*, Jonathan Dollimore writes of the relationship between antagonism and alliance, "What are in one sense dramatically opposed kinds of relationship are in another simply alternative celebrations of masculinity . . . In both kinds of relationship men recognize and reinforce each other's sexuality in the triangle man-man-woman."[17] Figured as individual chivalric conflicts or as wars among nations, battles between men display women as prize, as motive, and as cause. Such displays presume that men have the power to define women in terms of sexual and social value. That value may shift—how Helen of Troy looks to the Trojans may differ from how she looks to the Greeks—but women are always excluded from its determination. Fighting for women consolidates a male homosocial universe only as long as the place of women themselves remains constant.

In *1 Henry VI* such constancy is an impossible fiction. Rather than being fought for, Joan la Pucelle is fought against, entering into the play's privileged masculine terms through the condition of masculinity itself. The result is a kind of exemplary chaos, in which Joan is defined in terms that respond to evidence of her agency rather than demonstrating the determinative power of men. When the French argue among themselves or with the English over what her intervention means, the terms of disagreement suggest the confusion of her sexual and martial roles. Is she given to the dauphin as a gift, or does she come to him as an ally? Is she like the French in fighting for their cause, or are the French and the English united against her in being men? Are her grounds of battle those of nationalism, chivalric heroism, lust, or some odd, early version of what we might now term women's rights? Responses to the play have suggested that Joan's presence onstage unites the English against the French, the men against the women, the audience against the French, the audience and the English and arguably the French against Joan.[18] Multiple gestures toward some consolidation of alliances suggest that Joan la Pucelle has anything but a consolidating effect.

Gabriele Bernhard Jackson reads Joan's multiplicity as a reflection of heterogeneous iconographic values: "The disjunctive presentation of Joan that shows her first as numinous, then as practically and subversively powerful, and finally as feminized and demonized is determined by Shakespeare's progressive exploitation of the varied ideological potential inherent in the topically relevant figure of the virago . . . At no stage is the allocation of value clearcut." [19] "Virago," or, in the play's word, "Amazon," might accommodate Joan's extremes: a mythological system that locates Penthesilea, chaste hero of Troy, beside the sexually ravenous women of the new world can surely find space for a saint who is also a high-minded strumpet. Virgin and whore, saint and witch, Joan makes inevitable the punning paradox of Talbot's "Pucelle or pussel." Identified as an Amazon, she is by nature a challenge to the conventionally male prerogatives of definition and possession. Explanations of her disruptive effect range from the political to the mythological to the sexual to the economic to the theological, but behind each of these terms lies recognition that she interrupts the processes that consolidate homosocial masculinity.[20] In *1 Henry VI* the prescriptive assumptions that put women in their place are very much in play, but they look rather suspect when women take the place of men.

Joan's performance is not a transvestite disguise plot, for there is no moment of redeeming revelation; when Bedford asks, "A maid? And be so martial?" he recognizes that her female body is always visibly the referent of masculine acts.[21] "Where is my strength, my valor, and my force?" laments Talbot; "Our English troops retire; I cannot stay them./A woman clad in armor chaseth them" (1.5.1–3). If Talbot is the touchstone of English male chivalric valor, female masculinity threatens to unman him, in a process of unraveling certainties that culminates in his line, "I know not where I am nor what I do" (1.5.20). Joan does not kill him; they are simply two objects that cannot occupy the same space at the same time. Rackin writes, "Talbot, the English champion, and Joan, his French antagonist, speak alternative languages," and, when Joan speaks her deflating words over Talbot's corpse—"Him that thou magnifi'st with all these titles/Stinking and fly-blown lies here at our feet" (4.7.75–76)—she proves that he has come too far into her field of discourse.[22] Their opposition marks the edge of the English world, as Amazons always identify such edges; but here as in the accounts of early modern explorers, the distinction between outside and in threatens at times to disappear. Bedford articulates this possibility in one of the play's earliest speeches, while the body of Henry V still lies onstage:

> Posterity, await for wretched years,
> When at their mothers' moistened eyes babes shall suck,
> Our isle be made a nourish of salt tears,
> And none but women left to wail the dead. (1.1.48–51)

England becomes a place of women, a space defined by the loss of men.

In his introduction to *Saint Joan*, George Bernard Shaw writes, "She is the most notable Warrior Saint in the Christian calendar, and the queerest fish among the eccentric worthies of the Middle Ages." [23] *1 Henry VI* surrounds Joan with names that reflect her contested symbolic status: in Act I alone, she is "a holy maid," "an Amazon," "Pucelle or pussel," "a witch," a "high-minded strumpet," "Divinest creature," "Astraea's daughter," and "France's saint." [24] In the multiplicity of epithets and encomia, Shakespeare echoes his sources. Hall calls her "monster," "orgayne of the devill," and "this wytch or manly woman (called the maide of GOD)"; he ascribes her virginity (if it exists) simultaneously to her "foule face" and to her sexual resistance, and makes her at once a negligible peasant and an agent provocateur among rulers, "wise men," and "lerned clarkes." Of her celebrity he writes, "O Lorde, what dispraise is this to the nobilitie of Fraunce: What blotte is this to the Frenche nacion?" [25] France may, in Hall's account as in Shakespeare's, be opposed to England, but still Hall laments the fact that Joan la Pucelle devalues anything redeemable — noble, heroic, male — in the French. Catalyzing an effect of fragmentation that exceeds national boundaries, Joan's condition of difference not only separates her from men but divides men among themselves. This becomes explicit when she persuades Burgundy to change his allegiance: "Done like a Frenchman — [*aside*] turn and turn again!" (3.3.85), she says, and suddenly Burgundy is connected to national identity — *any* national identity — only by the relationship of treason.

Burgundy's disconnection, like the stutter in Hall's patriotic insularity, hints that Joan might blur the national distinctions that *1 Henry VI* so violently asserts. In *Female Pre-eminence*, Heinrich Cornelius Agrippa writes, "The *English Nation* were most ungratefull, should they ever forget their Obligations to this Sex," but follows this almost immediately with a brief history of Joan, describing the obligations that she has conferred on France through her attack on the English: "Taking *Arms* like an *Amazon*, [she] *arrested* their fortune, put a stop to the *torrent* of their victories, and by degrees restor'd the *withering de Luces* to their former lustre." [26] Anthony Gibson, in *A Womans Woorth*, subordinates both the English and the French to Joan's instrumentality; he writes of "the marvaylous constancy of *Joan* the Pucel, whose life the Englishmen had gladly saved, if she would simply have said, that shee was holpen by charmes, extraordinarie meanes, and supernaturall power in execution of her perillous enterprises: but she preferred her honor before life," and praises "her valour, which made Fraunce more famous then ever it had beene before, yea, more then at this daye it hath attainde unto." [27] Christopher Newstead's *Apology for Women* includes Joan in a list of warrior women that disregards nationalism entirely, placing her in the company of Semiramis, Boadicea, Elizabeth I, and the Amazons of classical mythology.[28] Thomas Heywood conflates her with his own national heroines; a chapter of his GYNAIKEION is titled "Of English Viragoes. And of *Joan de Pucil.*" Each of these accounts accepts the virginity that *1 Henry VI* puts in question; each recognizes militance as a mode of nationalism not incongruously embodied in women.[29] Most strikingly, all of these accounts imply that Joan's exemplary effect may be less a distinction between the English and the French than an authorization of women at the expense of men.

Tracing the implications of Joan's iconography, Leah Marcus finds resemblances between the English scourge and Shakespeare's own English sovereign. "In *1 Henry VI*, Joan La Pucelle functions in many ways as a distorted image of Queen Elizabeth I. She, like Elizabeth, is a woman who 'acts like a man.' She collects about her a markedly similar set of idealized symbolic identities. Yet she belongs to the enemy camp. The figure of Joan brings into the open a set of suppressed cultural anxieties about the Virgin Queen, her identity, and her capacity to provide continuing stability for the nation." [30] Here is the extreme event of such border crossing, its consummation in symbolic collapse. If Joan looks like Elizabeth, if Elizabeth looks like Joan, this does not domesticate the strange but estranges the domestic. The metonymies that lead from queen to biblical heroine to classical Goddess should never be pursued to the boundaries occupied by devils and witches and whores. Understood in the terms that define Joan La Pucelle, Elizabeth would present a version of sovereignty in which the ruler, rather than embodying the bond that draws men together, makes monstrous the hierarchical connection of monarch to male subject and disrupts the lateral connections that define male subjectivity itself. Such disruption, in *1 Henry VI*, is the danger posed by female martiality; in the associations traced by Marcus, that danger is unimaginably escalated by a martial female queen. The land of Amazons, such interpenetrations suggest, is closer than you think.

Or perhaps the *heimlich* is simply farther away. The moments that threaten the center suggest less an invasion than a dispersal; Joan la Pucelle never comes close, but the elements that converge to produce the conventions of the familiar might always move apart. Whether we imagine that Joan exists simultaneously through contradictory identities or moves through a range of registers or "is" one thing but is erroneously read as another, the extremes of her characterization preclude any socialized role. In heterosocial interactions as in the homosocial violence of the battlefield, Joan confounds conventional expectations.[31] She embodies no recognized social or sexual value on which men can agree; her notorious virginity coexists with her castigation as a whore. Vives writes, "We have red of women, that have ben taken and lette go againe of the moste unruly soudyours, only for the reverence of the name of virginite, bicause they sayde that they were virgins."[32] Such reverence does not govern the soldiers who capture Joan, for there is no common language in which her claims might make sense to them. The speeches that condemn her, recalling Talbot's pun on her name, reflect only her inscrutability: "Now heaven forfend! The holy maid with child?"; "And yet, forsooth, she is a virgin pure!/Strumpet, thy words condemn thy brat and thee" (5.4.65, 83–84). The compromise of excess and restraint that domesticates sexuality is precluded both by what others say about Joan and by what Joan says about herself; however broadly the term is understood, she is never imaginably at home.

This becomes explicit when she tries to define herself in socially legible terms. When her statement of virginity fails to save her, Joan performs a startling reversal, not only claiming to be pregnant but showing disconcerting flexibility about the identity of the father. In a belated and doomed attempt to act out conventional femininity, she claims social and sexual value as the embodiment of connections among men. Inevitably the scheme backfires, for Joan's multiple claims represent paternity as a statement that can be interpreted and revised. With an indifference that goes beyond English contempt for any child who is French, the men of the play do not care whether Joan's claims are true or false; the literal fact of pregnancy cannot, for her, be equated with the social fact of motherhood. Like the stories in which Amazons return male children to anonymous fathers, Joan's version of maternity does not translate into patriarchal terms. This last scene has sometimes been read as feminization, putting an unruly body back into a socially calculable place; yet Joan's plea for mercy, more clearly than any other element of her story, demonstrates that for her such a place does not exist.[33]

That displacement, the result of a powerful desire to keep Joan La Pucelle outside the terms of the familiar, informs readings not only of dramatic structure but of canon. If Joan is clearly not English and in some sense not French, she is also sometimes not Shakespeare's. Tillyard describes the argument: "Apart from the queer reluctance to allow Shakespeare to have written ill or like other dramatists when he was immature, the chief reason why people have been hostile to Shakespeare's authorship [of 1 Henry VI] is the way he treats Joan of Arc. That the gentle Shakespeare could have been so ungentlemanly as to make his Joan other than a saint was intolerable. This is precisely like arguing that Shakespeare could not have written King John because he does not mention Magna Carta."[34] Not, perhaps, precisely. Tillyard's "queer reluctance," like Shaw's queer fish, hints at something more than usually estranged. The gesture that defines Joan La Pucelle as "not Shakespeare's" is not simply a defense of gallantry or good historicism, but a symptomatic reproduction of the play's own logic. If idealized Englishness is constructed against France's Joan, then the idealized Shakespeare, in controversies over the authorship of this play, has been constructed against a Joan who belongs to someone else entirely. To allow Joan into the canon is, in such readings, to endanger the most important connection of all, the connection that links Shakespeare to "the Shakespearean." In metatextual negotiations, as in those that take place onstage, the appearance of Joan La Pucelle reveals the fragility of privileged bonds.

Possession may, as Lacan asserts, be an illusion; it is also a way of thinking about women in 2 *Henry VI*. As York speaks his last line to Joan— "Curse, miscreant, when thou com'st to the stake" (*1HVI*, 5.3.44)—the finality of the word *Exeunt* is immediately undermined by another stage direction: "*Enter Suffolk, with Margaret in his hand.*" For Joan, being a Frenchwoman in the hands of the English is an experience of violence that demonizes sex. For Margaret, the position is conventionally eroticized, her body defined as a valuable commodity: "She's beautiful, and therefore to be wooed;/She is a woman, therefore to be won," says Suffolk (5.3.78–79). As an object of desire, Margaret has a version of power that, like the power of all Petrarchan objects, returns to the man who describes it. "Fie, de la Pole, disable not thyself," Suffolk says,

> Hast not a tongue? Is she not here?
> Wilt thou be daunted at a woman's sight?
> Ay, beauty's princely majesty is such
> Confounds the tongue and makes the senses rough. (5.3.67–71)

The idea that Margaret might disable men—an idea to which the play will come back with a vengeance—here inspires Suffolk to an articulate and self-congratulatory speechlessness that recalls Sidney's Astrophil.[35]

Suffolk imagines a triumph of mediated desire, in which Petrarchan tropes subject Margaret to King Henry and King Henry to Suffolk himself.

> Solicit Henry with her wondrous praise;
> Bethink thee on her virtues that surmount,
> And natural graces that extinguish art;
> Repeat their semblance often on the seas,
> That, when thou com'st to kneel at Henry's feet,
> Thou mayest bereave him of his wits with wonder. (5.3.190–95)

With Henry's capitulation—"So am I driven by breath of her renown/ Either to suffer shipwreck or arrive/Where I may have fruition of her love"—the scheme seems well underway (5.5.7–9). But the equation of sovereign privilege and erotic compulsion will return to haunt the men who desire Margaret. If Suffolk reads Margaret as a mediating term, for Margaret herself Suffolk mediates effectively, and briefly, between a position of disadvantage and one of power. Margaret's body does not long remain passive text, and in Shakespeare's own text Petrarchan conventions anticipate a more material fragmentation. *Henry VI, Part 2* stages Margaret's transformation, from "Queen Margaret, England's happiness!" to "blood-bespotted Neapolitan,/Outcast of Naples, England's bloody scourge!" (1.1.37, 5.1.117–18). Represented as the matter of male bonds, Margaret becomes the cause of their disintegration, precipitating the representational violence not of sonnets but of civil war.

Echoes of familiar language attach themselves to Margaret long before York's castigation of the English scourge. "Such commendations as becomes a maid,/A virgin, and his servant, say to him," she instructs Suffolk at the end of *1 Henry VI* (5.3.177–78), recalling that other virgin who has just left the stage.[36] But if Margaret's pedigree—female, French, desirable, and of dubious descent—recalls that of Joan la Pucelle, her performance is markedly different. She moves inward as decisively as Joan remains out, her body focusing projections of the future as the body of Henry V had summoned nostalgia for the past: "Her valiant courage and undaunted spirit,/More than in women commonly is seen,/Will answer our hope in issue of a king" (*1HVI*, 5.5.70–72). Even here, in Suffolk's early words, Margaret is already both in and curiously out of place, her courage and spirit analogous to the conquests of Henry V, while Henry VI has only an indirect relationship to both.

> For Henry, son unto a conqueror,
> Is likely to beget more conquerors,
> If with a lady of so high resolve
> As is fair Margaret he be linked in love. (*1HVI*, 5.5.73–76)

Newly crowned, Margaret already threatens to displace the king. "She should have stayed in France, and starved in France," Gloucester says (*2HVI*, 1.1.133), but marginalization does not work against Margaret as it did against Joan, for Margaret's role—wife of this king, mother of the next—puts her at the heart of English national identity.

Margaret disrupts structures of male government in *2 Henry VI*, not by rebelling against convention, but by participating in it. The qualities that make her desirable to Suffolk and to Henry become her own means to power; imagined as a royal accessory, she is acquired at a cost, gaining control of the English succession as England loses control of France.

The marriage, which Henry reads as a triumph of desire and Suffolk as a strategic climax, is for Margaret only the beginning. "Margaret shall now be Queen and rule the King;/But I will rule both her, the King, and realm," Suffolk says at the end of *1 Henry VI* (5.5.107–8). It is a prophecy perhaps best answered by a stage direction from *2 Henry VI*: *"Enter the King with a supplication, and the Queen with Suffolk's head"* (4.4,s.d.).

We have come a long way in a short dramatic time, from "Suffolk, with Margaret in his hand" to "the Queen with Suffolk's head." And why, we might pause to wonder, is she carrying his head? Margaret does not directly cause Suffolk's death. But as she walks onstage with her monstrous burden, she has a transformative effect on the received wisdom, erotic and political, that presents fragmentation as synthesis: metaphors that figure the ruler as the head of the body politic, like Petrarchan tropes that dissect women for the pleasure of men, are replaced by an economy in which men's bodies come apart. Margaret's mourning takes darkly comic form—"Here may his head lie on my throbbing breast,/But where's the body that I should embrace?" (4.4.5–6)—as it literalizes Suffolk's earlier conceit.

> If I depart from thee, I cannot live,
> And in thy sight to die, what were it else
> But like a pleasant slumber in thy lap? (3.2.388–90)

"Leaving you would kill me," the Petrarchan lover tells his mistress, claiming her through her claim on him; but the dynamics of power look rather different if he is right. Appearing with the fragmented body of her object of desire, Margaret displays the consequences that result when conventions of objectification go wrong.[37] Henry, it would seem, has gotten rather more than Suffolk had bargained for.

"These are no women's matters," Gloucester tells the queen as dissent threatens England (1.3.117). But the fragmentation central to *2 Henry VI* is precipitated first by male attempts to acquire Margaret and finally by Margaret's own strategies of acquisition, as she transforms passion into action, an object to an agent, within explicitly feminine conditions of performance. Margaret effects disruption through adultery, envy, lust, shrewishness, extravagance, and conceit, her excesses conventionalized even as they are held responsible for the increasingly precarious state of

England. The Duchess of Gloucester recognizes Margaret's role playing as dangerous to male sovereignty, warning Henry, "She'll hamper thee and dandle thee like a baby" (1.3.145). The erotic and maternal clichés of feminine behavior, interrupting the processes of statecraft, infantilize a king. Margaret here is not the "Captain Margaret" of Part 3, who emasculates her husband by assuming his armor and his armies. She is dangerous in 2 *Henry VI* because she is conventional, because desire for her makes her husband an effeminate cuckold and because her own vanity makes her a formidable political conspirator. Henry's marriage guarantees not the continuity of father and son but the intervention of women in negotiations among men, and men are victimized by Margaret's performance of femininity as effectively as they will be by her sword.

Kahn argues that, in history plays, "liaisons with women are invariably disastrous because they subvert or destroy more valued alliances between men."[38] Naturalized through repetition in the *Henry VI* plays, this conclusion should be decidedly *un*natural; it suggests that heterosexuality, rather than playing a proper part in perpetuating male homosocial power, violates the hierarchical relationship on which that power is based. In the place of the logic that draws men together through processes of evaluation and exchange, these plays present a system in which female agency disrupts male control over the significance of conventional roles. Domesticity becomes the site of disjunction rather than consolidation. In 2 *Henry VI* the enemy is at home, and Henry's marriage, which Joyce Green MacDonald calls "a marriage contradicting in every particular the patriarchal mandate for the union of a prince," strips him of the conditions of agency that, in 3 *Henry VI*, Margaret will take on.[39] "In this place most master wear no breeches," the Duchess observes (1.3.146).

Echoing the chronicles, Gloucester holds Henry's marriage responsible for the fragmentation of England.

> O peers of England, shameful is this league!
> Fatal this marriage, canceling your fame,
> Blotting your names from books of memory,
> Razing the characters of your renown,
> Defacing monuments of conquered France,
> Undoing all, as all had never been! (1.1.96–101)

Fearful Simile

Margaret undoes the fame of England as Joan la Pucelle had erased dead Talbot's catalogue of titles. In the case of Margaret, however, what Rackin describes as women's "antihistorical" effect is produced and recognized from within. Both Joan and Margaret threaten to obscure the terms by which men recognize one another and identify themselves, but in 2 Henry VI history is unmade not by a battle but by a marriage. "My wife was wise and good had she bene rightly sought,/But our unlawful getting it, may make a good thing nought," Henry says in The Mirror for Magistrates.[40] In 2 Henry VI the "thing" to be "got" recoils upon the getter. Wanting to be queen, Margaret marries Henry; wanting to be first in importance, she ousts Gloucester; simply, apparently, wanting, she acquires Suffolk, in whole and then in part. As a desiring subject she works indirectly, appropriating masculine assumptions about agency and acquisition to her own ends. If Joan la Pucelle opposes an English male aristocratic ideal, Queen Margaret gets under its skin.

Proximity, in this context, fails to reassure. There is no space, literal or mythological, between Margaret and England as there is between England and Joan, and Margaret's implication in nationalist and familial tropes fragments the political state even as she appropriates the rhetoric of statecraft. Where Joan's identities exist in simultaneous contradiction, Margaret's work and change across time: chastity makes her a queen, sexuality makes her the mother of a prince, and, in 3 Henry VI, maternity will make her an effective king. Because her roles begin in femininity and persist into usurpation, Margaret is difficult to put in her place; even Heywood, who places her among his "English viragoes," prefers to say as little as possible, acknowledging that iconography cannot contain her. "Of queene Margaret the wife of Henrie the sixt, her courage, resolution, and magnanimitie, to speake at large, would aske a Volume rather than a compendious discourse, to which I am strictly tyed. And therefore whosoever is desirous to be further instructed in the successe of those many battailes fought against the house of Yorke, in which she was personally present, I referre them to our English Chronicles, that are not sparing in commending her more than womanish spirit, to everlasting memorie." [41] With uneasy reference to Margaret's "more than womanish spirit," Heywood directs readers away from his own exemplary project and toward the chronicles, suggesting that this figure must be read not according to what she is but according to what she does. The

privileging of action—or, in the context of Shakespeare's plays, of acting—is implicit in Margaret's manipulation of femininity in 2 *Henry VI*;
it will emerge fully in the aggressive performances of Part 3.

TO SEEM

As 3 *Henry VI* begins, the king has become "Base, fearful, and despairing
Henry," and Margaret claims his place (1.1.178). When Henry placates
York by disinheriting his own son, Margaret asserts the authority of her
maternal and sovereign roles, arguing that Henry's denial of his heir
invalidates his own relationship to kingship as well.

> Hadst thou but loved him half so well as I,
> Or felt that pain which I did for him once,
> Or nourished him as I did with my blood,
> Thou wouldst have left thy dearest heart-blood there,
> Rather than have made that savage duke thine heir
> And disinherited thine only son. (1.1.220–25)

A tautological relationship between maternity and good sovereignty excludes the king, who is dismissed by Margaret in both marital and martial terms: "I here divorce myself, / Both from thy table, Henry, and thy
bed"; "The northern lords that have forsworn thy colors, / Will follow
mine, if once they see them spread" (1.1.247–48, 251–52). If Margaret is
the means through which a father is connected to and reproduced in his
son, here the means becomes an end. Margaret's declaration of agency,
rather than her passively receptive body, validates the identity of Prince
Edward as that identity is threatened by the king's paternal failure. Her
martiality does not replace maternity, but emerges from it, making violence a function of the domestic; in Henry's words, "Poor Queen! How
love to me and to her son / Hath made her break out into terms of rage!"
(1.1.264–65). The conventional femininity of 2 *Henry VI* leads inexorably
to the "ruthless queen" of Part 3. "*Henry VI, Part III*, then, is spectacularly
marked by the dissolution of every kind of male bond," write Howard
and Rackin, and Margaret's role is not this dissolution's symptom but
its cause.[42] She seems always to be between men in these plays, but as
she shifts her investment from Suffolk to Henry, from Henry to his
son, the dynamics of power implicit in that position become distinctly
double-edged.

Fearful Simile

For the chronicles Henry is "a ruler not Ruling," and Margaret, in consequence, becomes "quene Margaret his wyfe, in whom the whole rule of the realme consisted"; "The Quene, which bare the rule"; "the Quene, whiche then ruled the rost and bare the whole rule"; "Quene Margarete, whose breath ruled." [43] In such accounts Margaret's agency results from the king's abdication; as Hall writes, "The Quene encouraged her frendes, and promised great rewardes to her helpers: for the kyng studied nothing but of peace, quyet, and solitarie life." [44] Because there is no working king, there must be Queen Margaret. Howard and Rackin argue that this logic obtains in Shakespeare's plays as well: "Margaret's prominence in the action immediately suggests a weakness in the patriarchal structures that should have rendered her less visible and less powerful." [45] But there is more to Shakespeare's Margaret than sovereignty by default. In its conflation of marital, maternal, and martial agency, her statement "I here divorce myself" has the force of a speech act, creating a role that exceeds the space left vacant by the king. Heywood's *Exemplary Lives and Memorable Acts* offers this poetic tribute to her effect:

> Who can this Queenes heroicke spirit expresse,
> A foe to Peace, in field, a Championesse,
> Usurping all that Majesty could claime,
> Leaving her Husband, nothing save his name,
> He weares the Crowne, she Sword and Scepter bore,
> What could the brave *Semiramis* doe more?

Or, in the marginal note that glosses the beginnings of English civil war, "The Queene the instigator of all combustions." [46]

Richard Barckley, in *The Felicitie of Man*, recounts a popular story about the origins of Amazons, in which women react to their husbands' deaths in war. "This newes was so grievous to their wives, that were left behind in their owne countrey, that they determined to arme them selves like men, and to revenge their husbands death. And that the fortune of them all might be equall, and the sorrow common, they slue the husbands of them that remained behind, when the others departed out of their countrey." [47] The loss of husbands produces amazonian wives who kill their husbands. In such a story, women who come to power through the absence of men alter the conditions of power itself, making it difficult if not impossible for men to return. "How ill-beseeming is it in thy sex/To triumph like an Amazonian trull/Upon their woes whom fortune captivates!" York says to Margaret, his amazonian simile identifying her not as a placeholder but as a willful opportunist (1.4.113–15). "I would Your Highness would depart the field./The Queen hath best success when you are absent," Clifford tells Henry, and Margaret adds, "Ay, good my lord, and leave us to our fortune" (2.2.73–75). This differs subtly but significantly from the account given by the chronicles, in which Margaret's success only contextualizes Henry's failure: "Happy was the quene in her two battayls, but unfortunate was the kyng in all his enterprises, for where his person was presente, ther victory fled ever from him to the other parte, and he commonly was subdued and vanqueshed." [48] In *3 Henry VI* Margaret's possessive — *our* fortune — exiles Henry from England; he does not lose the battle so much as vanish from its terms of representation, as when his son tells him, "When I return with victory from the field,/I'll see Your Grace. Till then I'll follow her" (1.1.261–62). The dyad of mother and son, like that of sovereign and subjects, excludes the king. Margaret has made maternal and national obligation the same thing, and to fight for her son is to fight for the integrity of England.

Margaret makes the contradictions of her identity — masculine and feminine; maternal and violent; French and English — work together as conditions of performance. Having appropriated the terms of Englishness, she disrupts them through a theatrical presence that confounds materiality and illusion. Butler writes, "The regulatory norms of 'sex' work in a performative fashion to constitute the materiality of bodies and, more specifically, to materialize the body's sex, to materialize sexual difference in the service of the consolidation of the heterosexual imperative . . . what constitutes the fixity of the body, its contours, its movements, will be fully material, but materiality will be rethought as the effect of power." [49] In early modern drama, the contingent, belated, and socially governed production of sexed bodies reflects dramatic necessity. But the privileging of performance in *3 Henry VI* goes beyond the exigencies of a transvestite stage, locating a perverse and contested relationship between body and act not in the person of the boy actor, but in the character of Queen Margaret. If, as Butler suggests, heterosocial norms construct and make use of certain kinds of bodies, Margaret in turn makes efficient and disruptive use of heterosocial norms. Within the fiction of the play, intersections of power, performance, and heterosexual imperatives produce a female sexual identity that revises the significance of men.

Margaret's acts cross the lines between national and familial preoccupations, between domestic violence and its more acceptable public forms. When she captures York, Margaret traces his political failure across the body of his youngest son: "Look, York, I stained this napkin with the blood/That valiant Clifford, with his rapier's point,/Made issue from the bosom of the boy" (1.4.79–81). For Margaret this death is a logical consequence of this kind of war; for York it is a monstrous surprise.

> O tiger's heart wrapped in a woman's hide!
> How couldst thou drain the lifeblood of the child,
> To bid the father wipe his eyes withal,
> And yet be seen to bear a woman's face?
> Women are soft, mild, pitiful, and flexible;
> Thou stern, obdurate, flinty, rough, remorseless. (1.4.137–42)

York chastises Margaret by describing her deviation from what women should be, opposing the natural to the unnatural in essentializing terms. But as Margaret demonstrates in 2 *Henry VI*, femininity is less a collection of truths than a set of tools, and even in York's own language static identity gives way to the operations of display. His verb of equation connects Margaret to adjectives rather than to nouns; where Joan la Pucelle is Amazon, witch, strumpet, scourge, Margaret is stern, obdurate, flinty, rough, remorseless. Margaret does not act or seem as she should, and York's image of a "tiger's heart wrapped in a woman's hide," figuring the female body itself as a disguise, implicates sexual essentialism in the rhetoric of performance.

Drawing on the language of costume and mask — "But that thy face is, vizardlike, unchanging,/Made impudent with use of evil deeds,/I would assay, proud queen, to make thee blush" — York echoes early modern conduct manuals in their critique of artifice (1.4.116–18). York's epic horror gives way, in texts such as *The English Gentlewoman*, to a kind of disillusioned resignation; the monstrous and the unnatural become monitory clichés. "What prodegy fuller of wonder, then to see a woman thus transform'd from nature?" Brathwait writes. "Her *face* is not her owne, note her *complexion;* her *eye* is not her owne, note her *straid motion;* her *habit* is not her owne, eye her *strange fashion.* Whilest *loose weares* imply *light workes;* and thin cobwebbe covers promise free admittance to all sensuall lovers."[50] Having denounced such women for feminine intemperance, Brathwait characterizes their sexual depravity as masculine; female excess, inherently theatrical, is at once a snare for men and an appropriation of apparent maleness. Transgressive in her enactment of both masculine and feminine conventions, Margaret presents a spectacle of strangeness that reflects the anxieties of everyday life. In a discussion of male uneasiness about femininity, Joan Riviere refers to "the conception of womanliness as a mask, behind which man suspects some hidden danger."[51] For men who encounter Margaret the danger is doubled: to interrogate one masquerade is to be confronted by another. "Tell him my mourning weeds are laid aside/And I am ready to put armor on," she says in answer to Edward's challenge (3.3.229–30); to which Edward responds, "Belike she minds to play the Amazon" (4.1.104–6).

The anxiety produced by such playing appears in the only simile of York's great speech: "How ill-beseeming is it in thy sex/To triumph, like an Amazonian trull" (1.4.113–14). Margaret is not an Amazon but amazonian, a player of Amazons; if she marks the space beyond the margins of Englishness, maleness, and a natural condition of power, she does so from so far inside the structures defining those terms that it is not clear where the English male aristocratic hero can safely go. In both her political and her familial roles, Margaret occupies heterosocial hierarchies, demonstrating their vulnerability to revision from within. Her presence reveals a space of transgression inside conventional social logic; her conditions of seeming — or, to take up York's term, ill-beseeming — are not unprecedented but exemplary. Her demystifying effect on gender politics is both public and personal, a function of being a woman and of being the queen. Performative appropriations, with their devastating effect on hierarchy, might always shift from the public sphere to the private and back again, as when Knox's *First Blast* indiscriminately condemns amazonian queens and amazonian wives;[52] the damage can neither be limited to a unique political position nor disarmed by confinement to the home. When Margaret offers York the blood of his son, she both parodies and breaks the patrilineal connections that pass through women on their way to sons and heirs. Bringing family ties and affairs of state simultaneously to crisis, she demonstrates that when women mediate between men, it might always be an act of violence.

The first victims of that violence, as Knox argues, are husbands and children, whose identity conventional femininity should protect and define. Early in *3 Henry VI*, Warwick says of Henry,

> The proud insulting Queen,
> With Clifford and the haught Northumberland,
> And of their feather many more proud birds,
> Have wrought the easy-melting King like wax. (2.1.168–71)

Subjecting her husband to desire, Margaret acts out the Petrarchan conceit of the desired object's power. *3 Henry VI* proposes that such conceits have real consequences, leading as naturally to "Captain Margaret" as they do to erotic consummations.[53] Warwick, describing Henry as "My sovereign, with the loving citizens,/Like to his island girt in with the ocean,/Or modest Dian circled with her nymphs," makes the king himself a Petrarchan object (4.8.19–21); feminized, aestheticized, and made chaste, a Diana more modest than martial, Henry is protected from the obligations of maleness and of kingship. As Diodorus writes of the Amazons, "Theire husbondes stonde in like condition as women and wives doo among us in oure contrey, ordeyned of purpose to kepe the house at home, to be buxom and obedient unto theire wives, clerely discharged from all maner of warre, beryng no rome nor office of worship in theire contrey."[54]

Richard wishes of Margaret "That you might still have worn the petticoat,/And ne'er have stol'n the breech from Lancaster" (5.5.23–24).[55] But Henry is always contingent, displaced by his wife, mediating between memories of his father and hopes for his son. It seems impossible to identify sovereign male authority with presence in this play, and Prince Edward himself appears only through nostalgia and anticipation: Oxford says of him, "O brave young prince! Thy famous grandfather/Doth live again in thee: long mayst thou live/To bear his image and renew his glories" (5.4.52–54). The connection is ultimately a false trail. Prince Edward calls to mind not a heroic past but the presence of his mother; York's son Edward calls Margaret "You, that are King, though [Henry] do wear the crown," and her intervention snaps the thread connecting king to king (2.2.90). Identifying kingship as something that can be constructed and revised, Margaret effectively disinherits her son through her efforts to restore him to his father's place. When women cease to be objects that prove a connection among men and become agents who attempt to impose one, the register of the connection shifts, making it not a fact but an invention.

Margaret constructs her amazonian performance in the service of a masculinist and chauvinist attempt to preserve patrilineality in its established form, but there is something deeply problematic about using female masculinity to prop up men. Prince Edward becomes vulnerable because his mother protects him, a playground logic that, in *3 Henry VI*, has serious effects. Margaret's performance at once detaches masculinity from maleness and makes visible the sense in which maleness is contingent on the actions of women; she simultaneously appropriates and undermines the privileges attached to the identities of father, hero, and king. The effect of her actions reflects the suspicion, traceable throughout early modern texts, that women might upset patriarchal structures simply by embodying their conventions and fulfilling their demands. For a period that blames the mother's thoughts during conception and pregnancy for everything from a child's sex to its race to its potential deformity, the perpetuation of male privilege through female bodies is hardly risk-free.[56] In response to the question "Why are children oftener like the father then the mother?" the collection of popular information titled *The Problems of Aristotle* gives the following answer: "That proceedeth of the imagination of the mother, which thinketh of the disposition of the father in the act of carnal copulation: and therefore by reason of the strong imagination in the time of conception, the children get the disposition of the father."[57] Paternity, this text assures us, is a figment of maternal imagination.

3 Henry VI plays out the fear that the destructive effect of mothers on their sons might be less a deliberate act than an effect of maternity itself.[58] Queen Margaret, after all, is a very good mother. She is not amazonian in the sense of maiming or killing or abandoning her son; it is her refusal to let any of these things happen to him that does the damage. Her agency becomes most dangerous when it is turned to patriarchy's own ends, and in a sense this is always the flaw in the system: it is difficult to give women significance without at least lending them power. If heterosexuality is the silent partner in the perpetuation of male homosocial privilege, Shakespeare's Queen Margaret plays out the consequences of breaking that silence. It is an open secret that male homosocial structures are vulnerable to the conditions of their production, and *3 Henry VI* exposes that vulnerability not through a woman who refuses to bear or raise or claim her husband's son, but through a woman who does those things too well. Maternal intervention, whether malignant or benign, brings about the fate of the amazonian son. The terms of Prince Edward's death — "Take that, thou likeness of this railer here" (5.5.38) — make it clear that, here as in *The Problems of Aristotle*, a mother's body signifies as a father's name does not.

Prince Edward recalls not his patrilineal heritage but the woman who has made him what he is; in Richard's words, "Whoever got thee, there thy mother stands" (2.2.133). In her efforts to make her son a man, a hero, and a king, Margaret recreates him in her own image. When he dies, her mourning is at once traditionally maternal and a sharp reminder of an earlier act of violence. Comparing his death to that of Caesar, she says, "He was a man; this (in respect) a child, / And men ne'er spend their fury on a child" (5.5.56–57). Men may not; Margaret already has. The death of Rutland reappears, not only as a linguistic ghost in a metatheatrical revenge plot, but as a reminder that what Margaret finds unimaginable she has also performed. *3 Henry VI* does not present a dynamic in which femininity gives way to agency only to collapse back into helplessness.[59] Grieving mother, like murderous queen, is a role, neither more nor less genuine than the condition of being beautiful or amazonian or tigerlike. The conditions of martiality are those of maternity, and mourning, like violence and conspiracy and seduction, is a piece of a larger performance.

That performance, I have argued, disjoins men from one another and from the natural condition of masculinity, identifying male heroism as a conscious act. Before the final battle, it is not Prince Edward's presence or the king's name but Margaret's example that makes men act like men, as the prince himself observes:

> Methinks a woman of this valiant spirit
> Should, if a coward heard her speak these words,
> Infuse his breast with magnanimity,
> And make him, naked, foil a man at arms. (5.4.39–42)

Battles take place only through a female catalyst, and from the beginning the play is explicit about Margaret's responsibility not only for local conflicts but for civil war. According to Edward, Duke of York, it is her role playing that brings England to irrecoverable fragmentation:

> For what hath broached this tumult but thy pride?
> Hadst thou been meek, our title still had slept;
> And we, in pity of the gentle King,
> Had slipped our claim until another age. (2.2.159–62)

At once political and theatrical, Margaret's intervention causes the battle and the play. "Hadst thou been meek, our title still had slept"—or, in Edward's next condemnation, "No, wrangling woman, we'll no longer stay./These words will cost ten thousand lives this day" (2.2.176–77). Conventionally feminized as a "wrangling woman" even as she plays her most violent part, Margaret inspires men to fight by conflating politics and mourning: "Lords, knights, and gentlemen, what I should say/My tears gainsay; for every word I speak,/Ye see, I drink the water of mine eye" (5.4.73–75). Her domestic chaos coincides with England's own, and, at the moment of his victory, Edward IV finds it difficult to banish this reminder of contingency and loss: "Away with her. Go, bear her hence perforce"; "Away, I say! I charge ye bear her hence"; "Away with her, and waft her hence to France" (5.5.68, 81; 5.7.41). The last question in this play full of questions—"What will Your Grace have done with Margaret?" (5.7.37)—suggests that disposing of an amazonian queen is a difficult speech act indeed.

The answer to this question is anticipated in another question. As he contemplates the captive Margaret, Richard asks, "Why should she live, to fill the world with words?" (5.5.44). The image has a particular historical—or perhaps, in Rackin's term, antihistorical—referent, for Margaret will live on ahistorically into the England of *Richard III*, continuing to comment on events long after she should have died in ignominious exile. Rather than disappearing in response to Edward's slightly hysterical orders, Margaret brings into the world of *Richard III* the economy of fragmentation and loss that had so distressed York, an economy in which kings are traded for kings, husbands for husbands, sons for sons.

Though not by war, by surfeit die your king,
As ours by murder, to make him a king!
Edward thy son, that now is Prince of Wales,
For Edward our son, that was Prince of Wales,
Die in his youth by like untimely violence!
Thyself a queen, for me that was a queen,
Outlive thy glory, like my wretched self! (1.3.197–203)

Through the anomalous presence of Queen Margaret, the language of reciprocal domestic violence, which defines men as the tokens and the victims of exchange while women survive to count the costs, persists into *Richard III*. Readers often argue about Margaret's agency in this play: Are her words curses, prophecies, or slightly heavy-handed indulgences in authorial foreshadowing?[60] But it is in a sense an empty debate; Margaret, unlike King Edward IV, does not need the power of speech acts, because the amazonian logic she had gradually imposed on *2 and 3 Henry VI* governs *Richard III* absolutely. Families in this play are not systems of alliance but sites of division and catalogues of loss; agency is disconnected from idealized masculinity; England is ruled by a sovereign utterly committed to the dissolution of bonds among men. What, in such a context, is left for Margaret to say? Stage productions and films can leave her out without drastically changing the play, not because she is irrelevant, but because she is implicit. Having survived the three parts of *Henry VI*, Margaret in this final appearance explicates the conflation of the national and the familial that she has so disruptively performed, theorizing the narrative of loss that equates civil war and family feud.

To return to Clarence's question, What is to be done with Margaret? In yet another metatextual revenge plot, her presence haunts not only *Richard III* but literary history itself. Robert Greene, in his notorious critique of Shakespeare, attacks him through the image in which York had figured Margaret: "Trust them not: for there is an upstart Crow, beautified with our feathers, that with his *Tygers hart wrapt in a Players hyde*, supposes he is as well able to bombast out a blanke verse as the best of you: and beeing an absolute *Johannes fac totum*, is in his owne conceit the onely Shake-scene in a countrey."[61] Greene's misquotation is a near-quotation that replaces "woman" with "player" in a gesture that is no substitution at all. In acting, in seeming, in the ruthless appropriation of plays, Shakespeare is equated with the Queen Margaret of his own reinvention.[62] If Joan la Pucelle has been taken to identify *1 Henry VI* as "not Shakespeare's," Margaret here becomes the sign that Shakespeare's text was never his to begin with — or perhaps such conventions of ownership, like Margaret's own paradoxical conventionality, produce only an infinite return, for what does it mean to attack Shakespeare for having no words of his own if the attack is formulated in Shakespeare's own words? Here again an attack from outside takes the form of that which is already in; again the terms of alienation reproduce even as they invade the *heimlich*; and again Margaret, brought up to articulate a relationship among men, becomes not the matter of connection but the sign of its failure.

CHAPTER THREE

Stranger in the Mirror:
Amazon Reflections in the
Jacobean Queen's Masque

PENTHISILAEA

Here come forth all the Anti-masques:
    7 Indians adoring their 1 Pagoda
    1 Hare
    2 Hounds
    4 Lyons
    3 Apes
    An Asse like a Pedante, teaching them Prick-song
    6 Barbarians
    5 Hogges.
  —Aurelian Townshend, *Tempe Restored*

Objects in mirror are closer than they appear.
    —Automobile warning label

SPECTACLES OF STRANGENESS

Between 1604 and 1609, four Jacobean court masques stage spectacles of women and identify Queen Anne as patron, actor, and even author: *The Vision of the Twelve Goddesses, The Masque of Blackness, The Masque of Beauty,* and *The Masque of Queens.* Anne appears in these productions as the star player, providing, according to Samuel Daniel and Ben Jonson, not only patronage but plots and tropes. The extent of her responsibility may be a politic conceit, but it has imaginative implications nonetheless: if, as a king's wife, Anne represents power once removed, Jacobean queen's masques remove her instead to a space in which female agency, as a dramatic fiction, might contest the fact of sovereign male control. Considering women's participation in the construction and enactment of masques, Marion Wynne-Davies writes, "The Queen's masque not only challenged the gendered preserves of authorship but questioned the legitimacy of absolute male power as symbolised by the Stuart King."[1] As they attach qualities of martial violence, sexual aggression, and racial difference to roles played by women, queen's masques define authority and identity, even on this closely governed stage, as changeable conditions of performance. In so doing, these masques tell stories that refer not to the king in the audience or even to the queen onstage but to the fantasy of female agency, a fantasy that takes shape through a recurring flirtation with Amazons. Staged in the form of unruly women, monarchical icons become amazonian symbols, their celebratory project double-edged. Queen's masques, displaying female bodies to the king, display as well an alternative theory of power.

According both to the texts of these masques and to the conclusions of later readers, the fantasies on display compliment as they refer to King James I: the king, occupying the best seat in the house, provides both the masque's occasion and its ideal reader, leaving the rest of the audience one step back from spectacular immediacy. Jonathan Goldberg, in *James I and the Politics of Literature,* traces a direct correspondence between the celebration and its subject: "In its form, the masque provides a mirror, too, for it elucidates the spectacle that the king presents sitting in state. The mysteries of the masque reflect the monarch's silent state: the masque represents the king. The king observes and is observed; as much as the masquers themselves, he is onstage." [2] As King James watches that which he already is, the masque becomes a progression of synecdoches, representing a kingly quality through each masquer's body and cumulatively staging a sovereign whole. The barrier between audience and stage, like the masque itself, is staged only to be discovered, revealed as artificial: as the king is mirrored in the masque, the separate space of dramatic narrative disappears in a blaze of royal tautology.

In Jacobean queen's masques, genre theory reflects social theory. Poets make artifacts out of women and offer them to the king; male bonding occurs across female bodies; reproduction as the work of women is at once displaced and transcended by the production of works of art by men. In *A Room of One's Own,* Virginia Woolf writes, "Women have served all these centuries as looking-glasses possessing the magic and delicious power of reflecting the figure of man at twice its natural size." [3] Women in masques are both windows and mirrors, transparently linking the king's gaze to the poet's, opaquely returning the king's gaze to himself. This is narcissism as an institution, playing out the social dimension of that term: the king, as male subject, looks both at an externalized version of himself and at that other male subject, the poet who constructs the equation of identity and desire. The court stage promises a space within which women, like and as dramatic fictions, are manifestly the third term, objects that signify but do not matter. According to their declared representational strategy, Jacobean queen's masques both impose rigidly hierarchical categories of identity and enact the ultimate mirror game.

But in some basic sense queen's masques don't play. David Lindley describes the masque genre as a whole in terms of conflict rather than certainty: "It is at the same time an art which aspires to translate its participants into an ideal contemplative vision and a kind intimately related to the flux of political reality. Its confident celebration and triumphant assertion are couched in a literary form that is full of inner tension." [4] In the early Jacobean celebrations written by Daniel and Jonson and performed by Anne and her courtiers, that tension takes a particular shape as images of female agency disrupt the reflective trope. Power in these fictions appears as something martial, exotic, and historically inimical to men. Martial women may be familiar objects of new world desire, frequent protagonists in chivalric romance, provocative figures for the popular stage, but they are not a logical idiom in which to celebrate a king. I have argued that Amazon encounters impose a kind of double vision in the early modern period: as subjects both of discovery and of history, they are a dream shadowed by its own potential realization. Female masquers, in their guises of power, recreate this sense of a myth which may at any moment produce a body, and which, onstage, *must* produce a body; and here, as in the new world or the Shakespearean world of King Henry VI, the effects of that body upset the expectations that motivate desire. Like Amazon myth, the genre of the queen's masque has been described as a wish fulfillment that tells men what they want to know about themselves. But queen's masques, again like stories about Amazons, exceed their conditions of invention.

Masquers and Amazons explicitly converge when Jonson stages Penthesilea in *The Masque of Queens*, but the fascination with martial women begins earlier, in Samuel Daniel's 1604 *The Vision of the Twelve Goddesses*. Considering the transition from Elizabethan to Jacobean celebrations, Barbara K. Lewalski writes, "While entertainments of various sorts had been a staple of Queen Elizabeth's progresses, the court masque became a major genre in the early years of James's reign, and Queen Anne was midwife to it." [5] If this generative conceit gives Anne agency, it does so in mediated terms, suggesting that the results of her intervention attach not to her but to someone else. For Daniel, the identity of that "someone else" seems clear; the masque's purpose, he writes, "was onely to present the figure of those blessings, with the wish of their encrease and countinuance, which this mightie Kingdome now enjoyes by the benefite of his most gracious Majestie." [6] Goddesses appear as aspects of sovereign virtue, idealized women transformed into fragments of the king, their individuality disappearing into synecdochic conceit. Daniel filters myth through an aggressively male aesthetic: "And well have mortall men apparelled all the *Graces*, all the *Blessings*, all *Vertues*, with that shape wherein themselves are much delighted" (ll. 61–63). The masque, itself a shape wherein men are to be much delighted, proposes twelve female bodies as a vision of the king.

The assembled compliment requires circumspection, a patrolling of mythological boundaries to ensure that goddesses do not overwhelm their celebratory role. Daniel describes his editorial principle: "And though these Images have oftentimes divers significations, yet it being not our purpose to represent them, with all those curious and superfluous observations, we tooke them onely to serve as Hierogliphicqs for our present intention, according to some one propertie that fitted our occasion, without observing other their mysticall interpretations" (188). "Divers significations" are, for this *Vision*, "mysticall," mystified, full of interpretive excess; Daniel's "Hierogliphicqs for our present intention" must be contained by their occasion. Proserpina should not remind us of rape or Ceres of revenge; the jealousy of Juno vanishes with the lust of Venus. And Daniel's martial woman loses her edge. The militant virginity of Diana gives way to a pastoral vision:

> Chaste *Diana*, in her Robes of greene,
>> With weapons of the Wood her selfe addrests
> To blesse the Forrests, where her power is seene,
>> In peace with all the world but Savage beasts. (ll. 110–13)

The violence of militant chastity is veiled by Daniel's narrative, and Diana finds a target only in the "Savage beasts" over which she exercises a sort of pest control.

Signifying as fragments and precluded from speech, the masquers recall Nancy Vickers's account of Petrarchan representation: "A modern Actaeon affirming himself as poet cannot permit Ovid's angry goddess to speak her displeasure and deny his voice; his speech requires her silence. Similarly, he cannot allow her to dismember his body; instead he repeatedly, although reverently, scatters hers throughout his scattered rhymes."[7] This might describe the closed system of king and poet, within which the only space for women is one of silence. Yet the single-mindedness of this vision cannot entirely suppress the plurality of myth, and, if the "divers significations" of goddesses threaten to disrupt the royal compliment, Diana introduces a more specific threat. As Vickers has shown, Diana and her victim Actaeon are never far apart in early modern representations, and their encounter is peculiarly suggestive for Jacobean queen's masques. "It is a confrontation with difference where similarity might have been desired or even expected," Vickers writes. "It is a glance into a mirror—witness the repeated pairing of this myth with that of Narcissus (*Metamorphoses* 3. 344–510)—that produces an unlike and deeply threatening image" (103).

The fantasy of purchasable narcissism, in which self-love accompanies rather than obscures self-recognition, is vulnerable to its own conceits, and Actaeon, rather than Narcissus, might figure the king's relationship to the queen's masque. Guilty of illicit spectatorship, of seeing too much, Actaeon becomes the victim of his own pleasures. George Sandys writes a sharply edged moral to his story: "I rather agree with those, who thinke it to bee meant by his maintaining of ravenous and riotous sycophants: who have often exhausted the Exchequors of opulent Princes, and reduced them to extreame necessity. Bountie therefore is to be limited according to the ability of the giver, and merit of the receaver: else it not onely ruinates it selfe, but looseth the name of a vertue, and converts into folly."[8] The king's opulent celebrations, his dramatizations of sycophancy in the form of masques, reproduce Actaeon's spectacular excess and hint at the violence that follows: the masque's multiple bodies might be ominous, turning synecdoche back toward fragmentation. If it takes twelve women to make a sovereign whole, then female masquers play to a watcher who, Actaeon-like, watches the progress of his own dismemberment.

Queen's masques, as they present a spectacle that is also a mirror and populate it with figures from myth, construct an observer who takes narrative risks; if the real king is not threatened, the fiction of power is less immune. Behind the fantasy of socialized narcissism, which idealizes men through their projection onto one another and the sovereign through his recognition of himself, is that other Narcissus for whom the illusion of otherness means self-loss. For this Narcissus, closely associated with Actaeon and the men who look at Medusa, an aggressively male gaze does not assert ownership but precipitates dispossession, the object's spectacular revenge. These myths of men who fall victim to their own appropriative gaze, I suggest, underlie Jacobean queen's masques, invoked both by specific references and by generic conceit. When the fact of sovereign male authority articulates itself as a spectacle and as a fiction, it opens itself to interpretation, so that the story that masques use myths to tell is not the only story. Images of female power hint at alternative structures even as they celebrate the king; the political truth that appears in the mirror might be upside down. Martial women are incorporated into royal spectacle without becoming congruent with it, drawn in but not disarmed. Arguing that transgressions that reflect dominant culture are not necessarily contained by that culture, Jonathan Dollimore writes, "Inversion becomes a kind of transgressive mimesis: the subculture, even as it imitates, reproducing itself in terms of its exclusion, also demystifies, producing a knowledge of the dominant which excludes it, this being a knowledge which the dominant has to suppress in order to rule." [9] The Jacobean queen's masque, as a tautology of male homosocial power built on myths that take such tautologies apart, is an inside story that tells too much.

As goddesses, Daniel's masquers recall mythological violence; as courtiers, they are disruptively individual, revealing familiarity through the veil of allegorical conceit. That familiarity concerns the king closely, for as Pallas Athene, Queen Anne appears with all the weapons of female martiality. "*Pallas* (which was the person her Majestie chose to represent) was attyred in a blew mantle, with a silver imbrodery of all weapons and engines of war, with a helmet-dressing on her head, and presents a Launce and Target" (190). Daniel's narrative claims to disarm this apparition: "war-like Pallas," with her "heroicall spirit," becomes the figure "in whom both Wit and Courage are exprest," springing forth full-formed from the collaboration of the poet's conception with the king's gaze. But the reading of women's bodies as aspects of men, like the reduction of Amazons to accessories of male heroism, wavers when confronted with the bodies themselves. Iris's demand for silence — "For who can looke upon such Powers and speake?" — invites literal-minded response, and

Dudley Carleton claims to have looked upon a surprising amount of Anne (ll. 74–75). "Only Pallas . . . had a trick by herself, for her clothes were not so much below the knee that we might see a woman had both feet and legs which I never knew before." [10] For Carleton, disguise becomes display, and the goddess of wisdom conveys transgressive knowledge. Suzanne Gossett writes of Carleton's comment, "He ignored the appropriateness of the costume to Pallas in observing its inappropriateness to Anne." [11] Questioning the fiction exposes its incongruity: masquers are only precariously disguised, and the body onstage might reveal not the wisdom of the king but the excess of a queen.

The martial form of that excess begs the question of *which* queen. Stephen Orgel, in *The Jonsonian Masque*, writes, "Even the first masque commissioned by the new king, Daniel's *Vision of the Twelve Goddesses* (1604), looks back to the traditional pageant." [12] Looking back at this moment, from this newly acquired throne, involves a potentially impolitic nostalgia: often identified with such chaste goddesses as Diana and Athena, Queen Elizabeth I might be a ghost on the Jacobean court stage. In the preface to his 1605 drama *Philotas*, Daniel describes "English Rime" as an enterprise cut short by Elizabeth's death, its full realization left in the past tense:

> For since that time, our Songs could never thrive
> But laine as if forlorne; though in the prime
> Of this new raising season, we did strive
> To bring the best we could unto the time. (ll. 77–86, v. 3)

Anne's militant appearance, like Daniel's poetry, solicits a gaze turned backward to Elizabeth's multiple and spectacular roles.[13] If the *Vision* is allusive, if its fictionality is not self-contained but refers outward from the stage, this "traditional pageant" seems to reach for a referent other than the one in the audience. Such Elizabethan nostalgia, as it looks away from the king, invites displacement, and within a year of Daniel's *Vision* Ben Jonson presents the next queen's masque, the *Masque of Blackness*.

Jonson, echoing Daniel, refers the figures of his masque to the king, "that majesty who gave them their authority and grace, and, no less than the most royal of predecessors, deserves eminent celebration for these solemnities." [14] But Jonson, again like Daniel, then turns to the queen, and describes a more specific intervention than that of her "heroicall spirit." "Hence, because it was her majesty's will to have them blacka-mores at first, the invention was derived by me, and presented thus" (ll. 18–19). Anne's will becomes the masque's conceit, filling the stage with Niger's "beauteous race":

> Who, though but black in face,
> Yet are they bright,
> And full of life and light,
> To prove that beauty best
> Which not the color but the feature
> Assures unto the creature. (ll. 81–87) [15]

Blackness is an abrupt departure that leaves traditional pageantry behind and threatens to strand its audience as well. Dudley Carleton writes, "Their Apparell was rich, but too light and Curtizan-like for such great ones. Instead of Vizzards, their Faces, and Arms up to the Elbows, were painted black, which was Disguise sufficient, for they were hard to be known; *but it became them nothing so well as their red and white, and you cannot imagine a more ugly Sight, then a Troop of lean-cheek'd Moors* . . . [The Spanish Ambassador] took out the Queen, and forgot not to kiss her Hand, though there was Danger it would have left a Mark on his Lips." [16] The masquers are inscrutable, "hard to be known." Their effect on men goes beyond a mark on an ambassador's lips; Carleton identifies *Blackness* as an indecorous object for the courtly gaze and a debased representation of sovereign identity. "Theyr black faces, and hands which were painted and bare up to the elbowes, was a very lothsome sight, and I am sory that strangers should see owr court so strangely disguised." This spectacle, he argues, should not be seen as a mirror; it produces neither an ade-quate nor an appropriate reflection of "owr court." Carleton's account concludes in a vividly evocative causality: "And one woeman amongst the rest lost her honesty, for which she was caried to the porters lodge being surprised at her busines on the top of the Taras" (10:449). The visible transgression of the queen's conceit leads to the sexual impropriety of a woman's "business"; versions of excess become indistinguishable, the loss of "honesty" implicating both sexuality and disguise. In this royal celebration the masquers are "too light and Curtizan-like," scandalous company for a king.

Like a glimpse of the queen's legs, the masquers' blackness dislocates metaphor, leaving watchers more concerned with figures as bodies than with figures as tropes: "At night was there a sumptuous shew represented by the Q. and some dozen Ladyes all paynted like Blackamores face and neck bare and for the rest strangely attired in Barbaresque mantells to the halfe legge, having buskins all to be sett with jewels, which a wave of the Sea as it weare very artificially made and brought to the stage by secrett ingines cast forth of a skallop shell to performe the residue of the devise of dansing etc. Which I saw not, nor harkened after further. But tell it you only for this that you discerne the humor of the tyme" (10:449). Implicit in the repeated critique is a sense that the masquers have abandoned or besmirched conventional femininity. In her discussion of *The Masque of Blackness*, Kim Hall writes, "It cannot be made too obvious that such discussions of blackness are almost inevitably yoked to problems of gender difference."[17] Queen Anne brings these discussions and problems, the marginalia of cultural anxiety, to court. The masquers of *Blackness* mirror the women of the new world, who appear simultaneously as masculine and feminine, black and white; so Nuño de Guzmán describes the Amazons for whom he searches as "whiter than other women," but a later historian refers to Guzmán's quest for "the elusive black Amazons."[18] The *Masque of Blackness*, like the new world narratives it echoes, conflates the confusion of race and the inappropriate performance of gender, displaying "the humor of the tyme" to spectators who remember only women's bodies engaged in indecorous display.

Jonson's masquers come to a land "Ruled by a sun that to this height doth grace it,/Whose beams shine day and night, and are of force/To blanch an Ethiop" (*Blackness*, ll. 223–25). Yet the masque ends, not with a recuperative display of sovereign male power, but with the masquers' promise to return, and for several years their transformation remains suspended. In 1608, after a delay that in itself seems irresistibly symptomatic, Jonson presents *The Masque of Beauty*. His preface to this sequel once again disclaims authority, crediting the queen with the sustained conceit: "It was her highness' pleasure again to glorify the court, and command that I should think on some fit presentment which should answer the former, still keeping them the same persons, the daughters of Niger" (ll. 2–5). The masquers again take the stage, "their beauties varied according to promise," and their cosmetic transformation is laid at the feet of the king (l. 5). "Which among these is Albion, Neptune's son?" asks Boreas, seeking the source of metamorphosis. The answer is a strangely evocative question: "Or can/A doubt arise, 'mong creatures, which is man?" (ll. 20–25). "Man" and "power" are not identical in this context, for the literal spectator-king and the allegorical Albion are equally removed from the action. Hall writes of *Beauty*, "This model explicitly reveals the ways in which imperial contact is shaped by an organization of racial values rooted in the control of gender mandated by patriarchy." [19] But as it fuses problems of race and gender in an attempt to govern both, the model leaves space for control to slip.

Allegorically, the separation of beauty and blackness appears as an exclusively female struggle, not opposing the obscurity of disguise to the vision of James, but setting Night against Aethiopia. Addressed in terms that identify his court as the site, himself as the agent of transformation—"Now expect to see, great Neptune's son, And love the miracle which thyself hast done"—the king is irrelevant to his own moment of glory (ll. 142–43). The consolidation of patriarchal ideologies has been left to women, and the masque cannot repress racial and sexual dissidence at the same time; as it invests in a racist aesthetic, banishing blackness, it leaves the stage full of women whose nature and value can change. The metamorphosis is another manipulation of femininity, confounding identity and artifice: Are these new bodies the real bodies? Or bodies that have been invented? Are we to privilege the masquers or their roles? *Beauty* recalls Shakespeare's Joan la Pucelle, refigured by her encounter with the Virgin Mary:

In complete glory she reveal'd herself;
And whereas I was black and swart before,
With those clear rays which she infus'd on me
That beauty am I blest with which you may see. (*1 Henry VI*, 1.2.83–86)

Transformed by a woman's intervention, bleached by the "clear rays" of a heretical iconography, Shakespeare's Joan anticipates the progress of Jonson's masques. It is a seditious intertextuality, for Joan's "assur'd success" is the defeat of England, and, where Jonson promises new decorum in his masquers' beauty, Joan's own beauty is a weapon. "My courage try by combat, if thou dar'st,/And thou shalt find that I exceed my sex," she promises the dauphin who desires her (1.2.89–92). This is the anxiety of *Blackness:* that the masquers, at once familiar and strange, may exceed their sex, becoming the inscrutable viragoes of Carleton's claim.

The concluding songs of *Beauty* reanimate the specter of sexual excess, turning again to unruly myths:

> If all these Cupids now were blind,
> As is their wanton brother,
> Or play should put it in their mind
> To shoot at one another,
> What pretty battle they would make
> If they their objects should mistake,
> And each one wound his mother! (ll. 280–86)

The "play" of Jonson's Cupids is a fantasy of incest, conflating eroticism and death; blind Cupids, as they find their objects in error, disrupt the hierarchies of paternal control and the boundaries of socialized desire. The song's second verse makes the audience's implication explicit: "For say the dames should, with their eyes,/Upon the hearts here mean surprise,/Were not the men like harmèd?" (ll. 292–94). The masque concludes that "women were the souls of men" (l. 310), ending in a vision of possession, of appropriation from within, strongly evocative for these masques that claim to contain the true spirit of the king.[20] As the masquers draw the watchers into the dance the masque overruns its boundaries, and "Beauty at large brake forth and conquered men" (l. 332). Through such images, Jacobean queen's masques erase a safe space of marginalization, bringing mythologically or geographically remote versions of female agency to center stage. In 1609, in Jonson's *Masque of Queens,* the practice climaxes in a parade of queens that begins with "Penthesilea the brave Amazon."

"It was my first and special regard to see that the nobility of the invention should be answerable to the dignity of their persons" (ll. 3–5). This is Jonson's introduction to *Queens,* his "first and special regard" recalling the theatrical indiscretions of *Blackness.* Having credited Anne with that alien conceit, Jonson describes her desire for a compensatory structure of distinction: "And because her majesty (best knowing that a principle part of life in these spectacles lay in their variety) had commanded me to think on some dance or show that might precede hers and have the place of a foil or false masque, I was careful to decline not only from others', but mine own steps in that kind, since the last year I had an antimasque of boys; and therefore now devised that twelve women in the habit of hags or witches, sustaining the persons of Ignorance, Suspicion, Credulity, etc. the opposites to good Fame, should fill that part, not as a masque but a spectacle of strangeness" (ll. 8–17). *Blackness* had been "a spectacle of strangeness" to its sequel of *Beauty*, but had estranged beauty as well; Jonson's comment reflects the need for a more discreet distinction.[21] The text of *Blackness* concludes, "So ended the first masque, which, beside the singular grace of music and dances, had that success in the nobility of performance as nothing needs to the illustration but the memory by whom it was personated" (ll. 337–39). Yet it is precisely the "memory by whom it was personated," the consciousness of particular identity, that lends transgression to disguise. In *Queens*, Jonson claims to isolate and subdue such excesses in the antimasque, making witches and queens perfectly separable fictions. His "twelve women in the habit of hags or witches" are played by male actors, distinguished from the female masquers by social hierarchy and the visible deformity of gender disguise. Gossett argues that the antimasque clarifies the masque's exemplary function: "The new method called for men or boy actors to play female roles in the antimasques, embodying the distorted vision of women, and for aristocratic women to play the masquers. The message conveyed to the audience is that 'real women' are, or should be, like the masquers."[22] Masque and antimasque engage in mutual elucidation, ensuring that "the nobility of the invention should be answerable to the dignity of their persons." In this masque no woman should find reason to lose her honesty.

The division of masque from antimasque polarizes female power at ideal and monstrous extremes, asserting that the difference can be seen, can be known. Yet no other masque fantasizes an Amazon invasion as explicitly as does *Queens*. Visually, verbally, and in the elaborations of its printed text, the masque plays out an amazonian synthesis of violence and desire, titillation and horror show. Jonson's narrator is Perseus, a man defined by his proximity to both goddesses and monsters. In "Jonson and the Amazons," Orgel identifies Perseus as an agent of male homosocial exchange: "Perseus is there because he confers—on the poet—the power of women, the power of the gorgon."[23] But as Orgel himself observes, Perseus's agency is contingent rather than heroically absolute. In myth he mediates between versions of female power, a role he reprises in *Queens:*

> I did not borrow Hermes' wings, nor ask
> His crooked sword, nor put on Pluto's casque,
> Nor on my arm advanced wise Pallas' shield
> (By which, my face aversed, in open field
> I slew the Gorgon) for an empty name. (ll. 346–50)

The masque describes Perseus as "expressing heroic and masculine virtue" (l. 342), but the qualities he expresses—rehearses, articulates, invokes—tend to be embodied somewhere else. Jonson emphasizes this by choosing Perseus over heroes who triumph unambiguously against unruly women. In his notes he writes, "The ancients expressed a brave and masculine virtue in three figures, of Hercules, Perseus and Bellerophon, of which I chose that of Perseus, armed" (542). Hercules captures the war belt of the Amazon queen, either killing her in the process or giving her to Theseus as a prize; Bellerophon is assigned the task of fighting Amazons and kills them all. But Jonson rejects these heroes in favor of Perseus, who, as he brings Medusa's head to Athena, conflates two dangerous women rather than neutralizing one.

As Perseus's mediating role in *Queens* suggests, masque follows myth in effecting such conflations: Athena wears Medusa's head upon her shield; the queens bind the witches' bodies before their chariots. Like the goddess who incorporates the power of the gorgon, Jonson's heroines are tied, figuratively as well as literally, to their antagonists. Wynne-Davies writes, "The defeat of the hags cannot finally suppress the linguistic and physical freedom of the women in the masque, as these qualities have already emerged in the characters of the queens."[24] The action of *Queens* attempts to avert the spectator's gaze from this synthesis; with the appearance of the goddesses, "not only the hags themselves but the hell into which they ran quite vanished, and the whole face of the scene altered, scarce suffering the memory of such a thing" (l. 335–37). But "the memory of such a thing," like *Blackness*'s "memory by whom it was personated," must be suffered. Shadowed forth in the chief hag, "her hair knotted and folded with vipers" (l. 88), Medusa is a cautionary tale for the watcher, another dangerous spectacle not entirely tamed by her appearance in this spectacular genre. As a victim, as a monster, as a chaste goddess's weapon, she demonstrates the extent to which stories about women resist reduction to single-minded and expedient ends. Sandys writes, "Thus provided, *Perseus* kills *Medusa*, reason corporall pleasure: yet lookes not on her, but only sees her deformity in the shield of *Pallas* (as we view without prejudice to our sight the eclyps of the sun in the water) since it is not safe to behold what our hearts are so prone to consent too."[25] The moralization concludes with a warning against desire, arguing that even a prophylactic gaze is not a safe one.

Perseus, in his campaign against female monstrosity, brings Athena the only weapon she lacks; as William Blake Tyrrell writes, "Restored within her and combined with her military attributes, the gorgon would make of Athena an Amazon."[26] Implicit in the conflation of Medusa and Athena, anticipated in the aggression of witches, the Amazon is Jonson's first queen. Penthesilea, that most palatable of Amazons, who guards her chastity and defends Troy, is nonetheless an awkward item on a patriarchal agenda: Virgil's *Aeneid* describes her as "A Queene of war, though maide she bee, with men she likes to trie," and Spenser calls her "bold *Penthesilee*, which made a lake / Of *Greekish* bloud so oft in *Troian* plaine."[27] Setting the tone for the cast that follows, Penthesilea identifies female sovereignty as an authorized assault on men. The masque's other queens are equally notorious for intemperance, often exemplifying it in political polemics and monitory texts, and Jonson recapitulates their histories in his elaborate notes. He cites Virgil on Camilla: "She had not accustomed her woman's hands to the distaff or the work baskets of Minerva; but, though a maiden, was inured to bear the hardships of war"; Xerxes on Artemisia: "Indeed men have shown themselves to me women, yet women have shown themselves men"; Xiphilinus on Bunduica: "[Her] mind was a man's rather than a woman's."[28] In *Impersonations*, Orgel takes up these images of appropriation, writing, "As with the image of Queen Elizabeth in armor, it is precisely the masculinity of the queens that constitutes their virtue."[29]

But "virtue," whether as chastity, as heroism, or as audience appeal, is a problematic term in the context of this masque, for the female masculinity that Jonson displays operates only and explicitly at the expense of men. The queens of *Queens* summarize a history of heterosexual violence that Jonson glosses in his notes: these queens wear armor, eat their enemies, kill their lovers, cut their hair. Lewalski writes, "While the masque spectators were not given the biographical accounts that Jonson provided in his elaborately annotated text for Prince Henry—accounts which emphasize their militancy, gender inversion, and conquests of men—the descriptive epithets in the text would evoke for many the familiar stories of these Queens and their claims to fame." [30] Jonson's eleventh queen makes it clear that these "familiar stories" pose a threat in both conjugal and political terms: "The eleventh was that brave Bohemian queen Valasca, who for her courage had the surname of Bold. That to redeem herself and her sex from the tyranny of men which they lived in under Primislaus, on a night and an hour appointed led on the women to the slaughter of their barbarous husbands and lords; and possessing themselves of their horses, arms, treasures and places of strength, not only ruled the rest, but lived many years after with the liberty and fortitude of Amazons" (546). The first step in the invention of Amazons is the death of the husband, the death of the king.

Valasca precedes Queen Anne, who "Possesse[s] all virtues, for which one by one/They were so famed" (ll. 393–94). As "a queen in whom all they do live" (l. 504), Anne appears without the mediation of an alien history; she is Bel-Anna, "Queen of the ocean," "the worthiest queen" (ll. 392, 398). Jonson explains her transparent disguise: "The name of Bel-Anna I devised to honor hers proper by, as adding to it, the attribute of *fair*, and is kept by me in all my poems wherein I mention her majesty with any shadow or figure" (547). In the daily life of the court, Anne's sovereignty might itself be a fictional representation, a transparent conceit; in the words of one early critic, "[James] had a very brave queen that never crossed his designes, nor intermeddled with state affaires, but ever complyed with him (even against the nature of any, but of a milde spirit) in the change of favourites; for he was ever best when furthest from his queene." [31] But in *Queens* Bel-Anna poses a powerful alternative to the mutual affirmation of masque and king. The queen onstage, rather than the king in the audience, concludes, solves, and explicates the masque's synecdochic riddle, her identity defined as the sum of its parts. Lewalski argues that Anne replaces the king entirely: "The attempted containment cannot succeed: these militant Queens whose force is directed against Kings and husbands need, and find, a female referent in Queen Anne, not in King James." [32] If the masque flirts with such a referential defection, it does so by transporting Queen Anne into the space of those other spectacular queens, a space inhabited by female sovereignty in its amazonian rather than its Jacobean form.

In *Queens*, as in Daniel's *Vision*, there are intimations of Elizabethan nostalgia; the line of queens extends back not only into myth but into the recent historical past. Thomas Heywood, in a later iconographic project, constructs a catalogue of queens very similar to Jonson's, concluding with an explicitly amazonian Elizabeth: "Let me not here forget the Campe at *Tilbery* in which her Majestie was in person, and that if the *Spaniard* had prevailed by Sea to have given him battaile by land, appearing in the head of her Troopes, and incouraging her Souldiers, habited like an *Amazonian* Queene, Buskind and plumed, having a golden Truncheon, Gantlet, and Gorget; Armes sufficient to expresse her high and magnanimous spirit."[33] Like Bel-Anna, Elizabeth is the queen toward whom celebration accumulates, and Penthesilea sets the stage for Heywood's Elizabeth as she does for Jonson's Anne. "All these Heroyicke Ladies are generally called *Viragoes*, which is derived of Masculine Spirits, and to attempt those brave and Martial Enterprises, which belong to the honour of men, in which number, this *Penthisilaea* hath prime place" (96). Heywood's valorization of Penthesilea recalls the implicit question of *Queens*, the question of who, exactly, has "prime place" on the Jacobean court stage. "Masculine Spirits" belong to "Heroyicke Ladies," and female masculinity seems to suggest more about women than it proves about men.

The iconographic project of queen's masques, taking women to signify men, presumes a privileged and integral male subjectivity. Male sovereignty, these masques propose, is a self-sufficient state, hierarchically distanced from other conditions of identity; the illusion of female masculinity thus pays tribute to the empowered masculinity of the king. In her reading of "The Signification of the Phallus," Judith Butler writes, "In order to 'be' the Phallus, the reflector and guarantor of an apparent masculine subject position, women must become, must 'be' (in the sense of 'posture as if they were') precisely what men are not and, in their very lack, establish the essential function of men."[34] In this mirror game, women tell men what they want to know about themselves. But might we not instead see the dynamics of the masque as an interplay of mirages, implicating not only women but what Butler terms "the foundational illusions of the masculine subject position"? Might not masculinity, as an essentialized condition of possession, become visibly fictional through being reflected in conceits?

The mirror game is a strategy of willed misperception, its subject positions ambiguous and contingent. Butler points out that the fantasy of reflection undermines, rather than enables, the constitution of gendered subjects as mutually affirming, distinct, and in any sense real: "In a strong sense, Lacan disputes the notion that *men* signify the meaning of *women* or that *women* signify the meaning of *men* . . . Part of the comedic dimension of this failed model of reciprocity, of course, is that both masculine and feminine positions are signified, the signifier belonging to the Symbolic that can never be assumed in more than token form by either position" (45). We can, I think, understand this function of the symbolic in iconographic as well as Lacanian terms: as a set of signs that accumulate to identity, the images presented in masques correspond to another set of images offstage, and in neither space are symbols fixed in their condition of reference. Masques occasion processes of signification, not conditions of being, and if men appropriate their meaning from the ways in which women signify, in so doing they expose that meaning as fragile and indiscrete. The relations between female masquers and the king, like those between Lacan's players, do not authorize an absolute male subject, but expose the willfulness of such a construction.

Jacobean queen's masques enact what Dollimore calls transgressive reinscription, "the return of the repressed and/or the suppressed and/or the displaced via the proximate."[35] A logic of association that resolves itself into Amazons preoccupies this most rigidly authoritarian of genres, playing out at least the fantasy of conquest from within. The "proximate" — the stage, the court, the court poet, the queen — becomes double-edged, producing uncanny spectacles of familiar artifacts with strange contents, familiar bodies in strange disguise. These spectacles, which claim a referential conceit that they cannot or willfully do not sustain, reflect the tensions between intimacy and danger, between structures of control and the return of that which they repress or exclude, from which the uncanny derives. In "Jonson and the Amazons," Orgel concludes, "None of the power of the Jacobean monarchy inhered in the queen, and Jonson's chivalric metaphor in effect deprived Anne and her ladies of the only real source of authority they possessed—their status as desirable consorts. Female chivalry, in this new formulation, leaves male power unaffected: unmoved, unthreatened, uncompromised."[36] This may, historically, be true; there seems to have been no danger that James's wife would depose him, although we might have some doubts about his son.[37] But in tracing amazonian effects we do not need to reason directly from court celebration to realized insurrection, at least, in 1609, not yet. Masques are fictional events, as well as leaving traces of historical ones, and in queen's masques the relationship between spectator and spectacle is an exchange of narratives, in which stories told onstage gloss the story of sovereign male authority. If the king's presence does not explain figures of female excess, those figures might explain themselves, appropriating, dismantling, and rewriting the presumption of referentiality that governs their appearance onstage.

That particular kind of story has brief tenure, although the authors of Jacobean masques continue to produce extravagant and often scandalous spectacles for the king. Decorum comes first, however: in 1610 *Tethys Festival*, commissioned by Anne and written by Daniel, celebrates Henry as Prince of Wales, and this queen's masque, the first to follow *The Masque of Queens*, rejects the antimasque and banishes the Amazon.[38] The action proceeds with aggressive propriety, and at its conclusion Mercury summons six noblemen to "bring backe the Queene and her Ladies in their owne forme."[39] The emphasis on their *own* form, on a return that is not an invasion, makes role-playing safe, and Daniel's final comment dispels even the illusion of disguise. "And in all these shewes, this is to be noted, that there were none of inferior sort, mixed amongst these great Personages of State and Honour (as usually there have beene) but all was performed by themselves with a due reservation of their dignity" (ll. 416–20). For Jonson's antimasque Daniel, in *Tethys*, substitutes "the Antemaske, or first shew," a dance of naiads that threatens neither sexual nor social confusion. In the context of such political and aesthetic circumscriptions, the vexed relationship of masque to antimasque appears as a transparent matter of perception (the ideal looks nothing like the monstrous) and of person (great personages of state and honor have nothing to do with inferior sorts). In "Of Masques and Triumphs," Francis Bacon puts the conceit of *Blackness* where, according to this logic, it belongs: "Let anti-masques not be long; they have been commonly of fools, satyrs, baboons, wild men, antics, beasts, sprites, witches, Ethiops, pigmies, turquets, nymphs, rustics, Cupids, statuas moving, and the like."[40]

Yet for five years Jacobean queen's masques tend toward Amazons, invoking paradoxes of female masculinity and horrific titillation that attach themselves to the bodies that live with the king. In their stage presence, through their staged powers, women in these masques pose a question to the discrete embodiment of royal authority. Privileged seeing doubles back on itself, invoking the fate of Actaeon, and synecdoche, representing women as the parts or the souls of men, hints at the fragmentation of the king. The frozen impotence of Medusa's victim is counterpoised against the generic promise of celebratory narcissism, offering a sharp reminder that the fate of Narcissus is itself a paralyzing mirror game in which self-recognition fails. Mistaking the referent, Narcissus might stand as a warning to the royal watcher who finds either confirmation or adoration in a pageant of Amazons. In one sense (the "real" sense?) the king always wins; in another he is endlessly caught up in a confrontation with the witches (Jonson's antic witches? James's own "real" witches?) who, in *Queens,* identify him as "you that to arm us have yourself disarmed" (1. 206).

CLAIMING THE ARTIFACT

This might all be far-fetched. King James I, after all, does not lose his throne to women, either on or offstage, and the polite fiction of Anne's authorial power may be exactly and only that. But the intersection of poet, masque, and royal spectator is an exchange described through its potential disruption; if masques are both gifts to and celebrations of the king, there is, as I have argued, something peculiar about this particular traffic in women. From goddesses to "lean-cheeked Moors" to queens, the women of queen's masques neither mirror male sovereignty nor substantiate the hierarchical assumptions of heterosociality. If the amazonian invasion here fantasized, at once temporary and artificial, is self-consciously a trope, it has disorienting effects, recalling George Puttenham's catalogue of "the figures which we call Sensable, because they alter and affect the minde by alteration of sence."[41] The circuitous processes that praise the king go out of their way to remain remote from their object; of such a figure, Puttenham writes, "But the sence is much altered and the hearers conceit strangly entangled by the figure *Metalepsis,* which I call the *farfet,* as when we had rather fetch a word a great way off then to use one nerer hand to expresse the matter aswel and plainer" (152). "The sence is much altered and the hearers conceit strangly entangled." In the context of Jacobean queen's masques, "sense" and "conceit" take both their meanings: sense as sensual experience and sense as signification; conceit as trope and conceit as the proper self-image of a king. Entangling sense and conceit through exotic figures, these masques proceed metaleptically, in what is, at least for Puttenham, a gendered effect. "And it seemeth the deviser of this figure, had a desire to please women rather then men: for we use to say by manner of Proverbe: things farrefet and deare bought are good for Ladies" (152). Queen's masques are far-fetched in that they are "farfet," imported into a context of privileged maleness within which they are both literally and figuratively "deare bought," "good for Ladies" but perhaps less so for men. And if any damage done by these masques remains speculative and subjunctive, at least one early modern fiction chooses to play it out: *Timon of Athens,* probably written between 1605 and 1608, stages a masque of Amazons as a social universe dissolves.

For the early modern period, Timon is a figure of misanthropy. Plutarch's life of Marcus Antonius takes Timon as quick shorthand: "*Antonius,* he forsooke the citie and companie of his frendes, and built him a house in the sea, by the Ile of PHAROS, upon certaine forced mountes which he caused to be cast into the sea, and dwelt there, as a man that banished him selfe from all mens companie: saying that he would lead *Timons* life, bicause he had the like wrong offered him, that was affore offered unto *Timon:* and that for the unthankefulnes of those he had done good unto, and whom he tooke to be his frendes, he was angry with all men, and would trust no man." [42] William Painter, in the introductory epistle of *The Palace of Pleasure,* makes Timon the figure for a narrative process in which storytelling is an antisocial rather than a communal act. "And for that my privat reading might not delyte and pleasure me alone, to avoid the nature of that cankred churle and foe of humain companye, *Timon of Athens,* that lived but for him selfe, I have (after my skill) culled some floures and fruites from that pleasaunt store of those my readinges to impart for universal gayne and benefyte." [43] Existing only in opposition, Timon is a sign rather than a subject in such references, representing the loss of identity as constituted through relations and bonds.

The play *Timon of Athens* reproduces this disconnection at all levels; it has been, from the beginning, the most problematic of problem plays. Formally it is probably unfinished, and certainly inconsistent: prose and verse interrupt one another, characters appear without stage directions and stage directions without characters, and Timon, dead, has two epitaphs. The play is titled a "life," labeled a tragedy, and most often performed as satire; it enjoyed its greatest popularity as a Restoration drama by Thomas Shadwell.[44] It is separated from Shakespeare by its lack of publication during his lifetime and by speculative attribution to Thomas Middleton;[45] it is distanced from early modern stage history by the fact that it was apparently never performed in that period. Rolf Soellner's book on the play names it "Shakespeare's pessimistic tragedy"; according to some critics it does not work as a tragedy at all.[46] Structural and thematic readings focus on its internal disjunctions, sharply dividing the first three acts from the last two.[47] It is a play of ruptures, which E. K. Chambers reads as evidence of Shakespeare's own breakdown: "Shakespeare's spirit must have been nearly submerged in *Lear*, and although the wave passed, and he rose to his height of poetic expression in *Antony and Cleopatra*, I think that he went under in the unfinished *Timon of Athens*. The chronology of the plays becomes difficult at this point, and it is therefore frankly a conjecture that an attempt at *Timon of Athens* early in 1608 was followed by a serious illness, which may have been a nervous breakdown, and on the other hand may have been merely the plague."[48] Not drama, but psychodrama; as the author of *Timon*, Shakespeare (if it was Shakespeare) is separated even from himself. "I do not suggest that *Timon* throws much light upon Shakespeare's normal methods of working," Chambers writes (1:483).

From its cast of characters to its stage history to its relationship to genre, authorship, and canon, *Timon of Athens* seems a symptom of its own subject, an essay on the processes of dislocation. As the central character of this unlikely play, Timon himself exists to expose a void; beginning with an excess of exchanges among men, *Timon of Athens* stages a fall into misanthropy that resolves homosociality into exile. The presumption of privileged male subjectivity reveals its darker side from the play's beginning: "Our poesy is as a gum which oozes/From whence 'tis nourishéd," the Poet says in the first scene, defining patronage as a loss of substance (1.1.23–24).[49] The Painter describes his portrait of Timon as "a pretty mocking of the life," to which the Poet replies, "Artificial strife/Lives in these touches, livelier than life" (1.1.38, 41). Mockery and strife inhabit the celebratory project even in its early, idyllic incarnations; "He that loves to be flattered is worthy o' the flatterer," Apemantus says. It is a debased tautology that reaches its climax in Timon's "Masque of Ladies [as] Amazons, with lutes in their hands, dancing and playing" (1.2.130.s.d.). The masque takes Timon both as author and as object — "You see, my lord, how ample you're beloved" (1.2.129) — and its concluding dance identifies him as the privileged spectator to whom its spectacle refers. "The Lords rise from table, with much adoring of Timon; and to show their loves, each singles out an Amazon, and all dance, men with women" (1.2.145. s.d.). In a play in which the only other female characters are prostitutes, this heterosocial intercourse appears as a pleasant fiction among men, but its effect is to reveal homosocial exchange as a corrupt economy on the verge of collapse. Susan Handelman writes, "The world which excludes woman splits itself apart; the man who denies the female divides his own self and like Timon becomes his opposite, Misanthropos, monster, and beast." [50]

Frank Kermode writes of the play, "At the first, all is sensual gratification, a theme reinforced by the masque of Amazons, which is in iconographical terms a Banquet of Sense." [51] As "a Banquet of Sense" the masque is a commentary, a gloss, a signifying feast. "What Timon presumably intends with the device of Cupid and the Amazons is to present the reconciliation of opposites; what he produces is ominously discordant," Soellner observes.[52] Coppélia Kahn describes that discord in gendered terms, linking the masque to Timon's "primitive identification with a powerful maternal woman": "In short, the masque responds to an image of Timon as one from whom, like Fortune, all bounties flow. But both masque and image are ostentatious and shallow, and the masque is a tissue of flatteries veiling a fantasy of female power, deceptiveness, and aggression." [53] Kahn calls Timon "Shakespeare's last narcissist," and narcissism here is not a mode of self-aggrandizement or a form of social attachment, but a failure of context. Timon, as epigrammatic shorthand or the subject of drama, is a figure for the breaking of bonds. The social world of *Timon of Athens*, composed entirely of men, embodies its potential for collapse in Timon and signifies the imminence of that collapse through a spectacle of Amazons. There is an odd literalism to the play's cultural commentary: the language of excessive appetite is table talk at a banquet, the rhetoric of spiritual impoverishment occurs at the moment of bankruptcy, and the moral failings of women are described to prostitutes. This constriction of reference, as it ties abstractions to their least noble conditions of production, finds a figure for the fact that women do not consolidate relationships among men: male bonding becomes self-consuming artifice as it takes place through Amazons.

For Apemantus, the Ladies (as) Amazons represent the conquest of Athens by its own indiscretions.

> Hoy day!
> What a sweep of vanity comes this way!
> They dance? They are madwomen.
> . . . .
> Who lives that's not depraved or depraves?
> Who dies that bears not one spurn to their graves
> Of their friends' gift?
> I should fear those that dance before me now
> Would one day stamp upon me. 'T has been done;
> Men shut their doors against a setting sun. (1.2.130–44)

Idealized both for its selective democracy and for its mythic heroes, Athens is the ultimate site of masculine exclusivity, the locus classicus of homosocial self-congratulation. In Apemantus's speech that closed world comes to pieces, disjoined from within. This is the fate of Timon's Athens: the dominant gesture of reciprocity among men is not exchange but mutual banishment. When Timon congratulates the Amazons and claims the masque — "You have added worth unto't and luster,/And entertained me with mine own device" (1.2.148–49)—he anticipates his own exile, confirming his implication in a system within which conditions of identity and alliance exist only to fail. Timon changes from privileged male patron to allegorical misanthrope; *Timon* changes from an extravaganza of homosocial intercourse to an orgy of isolation and antisocial revenge; and the causal progression of these transformations turns us back toward the paradox of Jacobean queen's masques. How does a stage full of martial women demonstrate male authority? How can goddesses, Amazons, witches, and queens validate heterosocial hegemony? The uneasiness occasioned by Timon's Masque of Amazons recurs throughout the first decade of Jacobean rule. Through images of profligacy and its costs, Shakespeare's play mirrors critiques of King James I;[54] and King James I, looking into the mirror of his own royal celebrations, finds images of Timon's Amazons. As a sign that it tends toward fragmentation, *Timon of Athens* stages the outlandish conceit of an amazonian masque. It is a conceit, in Puttenham's terms "farfet," which patrons in both Athens and England find "deare bought" as well.

Part Two

SPLITTING

THE DIFFERENCE:

HOMOEROTICISM

AND HOME LIFE

It was love at first fight.
—John Maddox Roberts,
Conan and the Amazon

CHAPTER FOUR

Dressed to Kill: Looking for
Love in *The Faerie Queene*

Where Hellen *is, there, will be* Warre:
For, Death *and* Lust, *Companions are.*

We are now obliged to recognize
that the little girl is a little man.
—Sigmund Freud, "Femininity"

Ladies can laugh at Ladies, Knights at Knights.
—Edmund Spenser, *The Faerie Queene*

I want to start with something familiar, and ask that it be read for the moment not as a theory, but as a story.

> The *mirror stage* is a drama whose internal thrust is precipitated from insufficiency to anticipation—and which manufactures for the subject, caught up in the lure of spatial identification, the succession of phantasies that extends from a fragmented body-image to a form of its totality that I shall call orthopaedic—and, lastly, to the assumption of the armour of an alienating identity, which will mark with its rigid structure the subject's entire mental development.[1]

As a paradigm, Lacan's description of the mirror stage is so familiar as to read like a trope, the projection backward of a myth of origin rather than a developmental narrative mimetically related to the process it describes. I would like to make it strange by making it plot. If the mirror stage is not necessarily the experience of every child, it is that of Spenser's Britomart, who falls in love with Artegall's magically generated reflection and disguises herself as a knight in order to pursue it. Like Lacan's subject, she looks in a mirror, sees an image of agency, is caught up in fantasy—and takes on "the armour of an alienating identity" in order to become what she desires.

I offer this less as a Lacanian reading of *The Faerie Queene* than as a suggestion about early modern mirror tricks, for Britomart's transformative look in the mirror reflects a larger fascination with the relationship between identity and misrecognition. In *Staging the Gaze*, Barbara Freedman writes, "Renaissance mirror games arrange for a flattering self-portrait to come into focus precisely in that moment when a distorted image could be relegated to a field of erring sight." [2] Britomart's quest takes place on that field. Through her disguise plot, *The Faerie Queene* plays out the processes of enabling misperception, with their constant if displaced reminders of the "distorted image" out of which they are produced. The mirror game that creates the Knight of Chastity stands in a supplementary relationship to allegorical and chivalric systems of identity, generating both the substantiation and the implicit threat that supplementarity implies. For Britomart, in her misunderstanding of Artegall's likeness and in her encounters with him while disguised, the play of knowledge and error, distortion and ideal, brings about a crisis of identity that implicates both the allegorical relationship between Chastity and Justice and the performative relationship of masculinity to men.

Like other narratives of knights and quests, *The Faerie Queene* presents chivalric encounters in which opponents, held in equation by the visible display of armor and the equally rigid apparatus of heroic codes, affirm identity through the mediating conceit of the mirror image. Because knights look and act alike, variations on victory and defeat consolidate a constant masculine chivalric ideal. Dependent on a logic within which difference affirms the larger fact of sameness, such consolidation is fragile, vulnerable to the conditions of its production. This becomes apparent when women play men, enacting masculinity without reference — or with disconcertingly effective reference — to the body beneath. In Britomart's quest as in other encounters between men and women who look like men, the identity constructed by apparent masculinity is at once true and false, illusion and effective performance. Through such encounters, early modern texts work out theories of subjectivity. As in the Lacanian mirror stage, chivalric narratives figure identity as a complicated compromise between likeness and difference, deception and revelation, violence and desire, in which self-articulation occurs through the intervention of an image that both is and is not logically connected to the body to which it refers. Identity depends on confrontation, emerging from an appropriative rather than a naturalized relationship between body and act. For both chivalric and Lacanian subjects, an idealized self-image emerges from aggressive misunderstanding, and "the armour of an alienating identity" is worth fighting for.

When that armor belongs to women, the process is complicated. Early modern fascination with this possibility suggests the sense in which self-construction is always in part contingent on mistake; the homosocial ideal that equates men to one another is undermined as women appear in unexpected places. Like Lacan's description of the *trotte-bébé*, the "support, human or artificial" that at once enables the subject's vision of self-sufficiency and provides a reminder of dependence, early modern narratives of encounters between men and armed women reflect a profound ambivalence toward the role women play in the formation of identity.[3] If chivalric encounters between men incorporate two bodies into the moment of mirroring, that doubleness resolves itself into a single heroic image. But when one of the men is not a man at all, the doubling of bodies exposes what Lacan terms the "fictional direction" taken by fantasies of mirroring. In her reading of Lacan, Jacqueline Rose writes, "The image in which we first recognise ourselves is a *misrecognition*," and for knights looking at women in armor the misrecognition does not remain in place.[4]

Assessing the relevance of Lacan's mirror stage to her discussion of embarrassment, Gail Kern Paster writes, "The mirror stage does locate shame socially, in the gaze of a desirable other, and thus brings it within the dynamic agencies of theater."[5] Transvestite chivalric encounters play out this convergence of desire and performance, of individual identification and public event. Female bodies performing masculine acts animate the anxiety of impersonation, of an effective assumption of the personal signifiers that chivalric convention predicates as innate. Martial female performances prove not only that gender is a construct, but that its shifting terms undermine the hierarchical relationship between homosocial structures of power and the heterosexuality through which they are reproduced. In *Between Men*, Eve Kosofsky Sedgwick glosses the phrase "male homosocial desire": "To draw the 'homosocial' back into the orbit of 'desire,' of the potentially erotic, then, is to hypothesize the potential unbrokenness of a continuum between homosocial and homosexual — a continuum whose visibility, for men, in our society, is radically disrupted."[6] In juxtaposing the terms "homosocial" and "heterosexual," I am pointing to a different and less obviously scandalous continuum, which links men's lateral interactions with one another to their hierarchical intercourse with women. But this link, like the one Sedgwick describes, becomes transgressive in becoming visible. When heroes confront Amazons, the assumption of identity between men gives way to assertions of difference between men and women, revealing that homo-social and heterosexual interactions are not hierarchically distinct but played out through the same bodies and in the same narrative space. If "social," as a suffix, implies an abstract notion of connection, and "sexual" invokes the literalism with which bodies collide, Britomart's disguise plot complicates that distinction through the processes of intersection and exchange. The sexual and the social do not become the same thing; indeed, *The Faerie Queene* chronicles the effort to keep them apart. But as the eroticism catalyzed by Britomart mediates between male homosociality and heterosexuality, and between heterosexuality and female homosociality, it disables presumptions concerning the agency or value conveyed by bonds.

This is the disruptive potential of Britomart's quest: she is connected to Artegall mimetically through allegory and armor and teleologically through her determination to marry him and have his child. Desire generates contradiction, working as a repetitive pattern, allegorical and homosocial, but also imposing a heterosexual and historical move into generation.[7] Maureen Quilligan writes, "To make a female an actor in an allegory is to complicate an already complicated set of gender distinctions in an already complicated genre of narrative."[8] In Britomart's story, kinds of narrative and categories of gender intersect: she is at once allegorically constant and sexually progressive, a mediating term between the iconographic and the domestic. There is a basically unreasonable relationship between her maternal destiny and the martial means she uses to get there, a gap in the syllogism between looking for and looking like a man.

GIRLS WILL BE GIRLS . . .

The eagerness with which Britomart pursues her quest has been characterized by some readers as unseemly, despite the narrator's assurance: "Not that she lusted after any one;/For she was pure from blame of sinfull blot."[9] Yet the fear of sexual excess is in some sense a displacement, for Britomart is less transgressive in desire than in recognition. Looking in the mirror, she at first sees only what is familiar: "Her selfe a while therein she vewd in vaine" (3.2.22.6). The image of Artegall follows, "A comely knight, all arm'd in complet wize," and Britomart's resolve to become a knight in order to pursue one causes the two moments of perception to merge. She speculates that she has become a new Narcissus:

> I fonder, then *Cephisus* foolish child,
> Who hauing vewed in a fountaine shere
> His face, was with the loue thereof beguild;
> I fonder loue a shade, the bodie farre exild. (3.2.44.6–9)

Glauce assures her that the identity is false, that Britomart is "nought like" Narcissus, who "was of himselfe the idle Paramoure;/Both loue and louer, without hope of ioy" (3.2.45.1–3). Britomart instead "lou'st the shadow of a warlike knight;/No shadow, but a bodie hath in powre," and the fear of becoming both subject and object of desire is countered by this certainty that there is a body out there somewhere, if Britomart can only find it (3.2.45.6–7).

Despite this reasoning, the image that intervenes between Britomart and narcissism is not Artegall but monstrous female sexuality. Glauce offers her a catalogue of negative exempla to define her desire against what it is not, beginning with incestuous Myrrha and ending with bestial Pasiphae. But Britomart, rather than recoiling from such monstrosities, recognizes them as instances in which desire possesses sufficient agency: "For they, how euer shamefull and vnkind,/Yet did possesse their horrible intent" (3.2.43.6–7). Forbidden union, as *successful* union, has its own appeal; these women get what they want. For all its containment within the subjunctive, this is one of the most transgressive moments in the poem. Britomart's desire produces not the deliberate masochism of Petrarchan conceits or the mistaken sterility of narcissism, but a specter of terrible acquisition. Saving Britomart from herself, various readers have argued that her desire is neither narcissistic nor monstrous, that her synthesis of masculine and female roles moves her away from these debasing or self-devouring models. Mihoko Suzuki writes, "Britomart, though androgynous, is not self-contained to the point of narcissism; unlike Virgil's Camilla, who suppressed her sexuality in order to wed herself to war, Britomart seeks Artegall to achieve that ideal union between the sexes which Spenser figures in the emblem of the Hermaphrodite." [10] Because Glauce is right, because Artegall exists, both Britomart's quest and her synthetic identity direct her desires outward.

But the models of desire that Britomart presents are paradigmatic.

Her readings of the mirror oppose narcissism to reproductive sexuality: incest and bestiality produce mothers and children, and in substituting the example of Pasiphae or Myrrha for that of Narcissus, Britomart imagines desire first as a pattern of homoerotic stasis and then as a story of generative heterosexual excess. There is tension here between ways of gendering the agency of desire, and between desire as triangulated homoeroticism and desire as heterosexually dyadic. Narcissus presents the static image of a man looking at a man and turning away from a woman—one way of understanding Britomart's glance in the mirror. But her moment of transformation is also a movement through time, for Britomart is a woman looking at and for the father of her child. These two structures characterize her quest: desire on that quest is synchronically triangulated through her apparent masculinity, but the quest itself progresses toward a reduction of triangles into pairs.

I will argue that the collapse of mutually affirming masculinity into heterosexuality is an anxiety expressed throughout the amazonian stories told and retold in early modern exemplary texts. For these texts as for *The Faerie Queene*, meeting the same partner in battle and in bed— never an easy transition—is a possibility that does a good deal of imaginative work. But I want to turn first to the image of the hermaphrodite which ends the original version of Book 3, and which is closely implicated in the tension between desire as structural, static, and iconographic and desire as progressively reproductive. Spenser's Hermaphrodite, formed by the union of Amoret and Scudamour, results from Britomart's heroic success, and she regards it with a sense of distance and of lack: "*Britomart* halfe enuying their blesse,/Was much empassiond in her gentle sprite,/And to herselfe oft wisht like happinesse" (3.12.46a.6–8). Restored to one another, Scudamour and Amoret have what Britomart does not; her masculine performance has completed a quest and enabled a union neither of which is hers. Yet at the same time the synthesis of woman and knight precisely mirrors her own condition, so that her distance from it suggests fragmentation, a pulling apart of function and form. Britomart herself is doubled, and, when the text describes her as "halfe enuying," we might pause to ask: Which half?

The hermaphrodite might represent not what Britomart wants but what she already is. Her quest can be seen as a series of iconographic moments in which her synthesis of qualities triumphs over more single-minded identities; Lauren Silberman writes, "In fashioning a female hero, one who dons armor in pursuit of love, Spenser moralizes and transforms Ovid's paradox that the triumph of Hermaphroditus' manhood is also its loss into the paradoxical giving and withholding of the self that defines chastity in Book III." [11] There is a certain risk to such readings, as Britomart's self-sufficient doubleness might displace Artegall, not by drawing her into narcissism or monstrosity, but by making the quest irrelevant: What, unwary readers could be tempted to ask, does she need *him* for? In the 1596 *Faerie Queene*, the hermaphroditic conclusion of Book 3 disappears, to be replaced by the enigmatic figure Scudamour encounters when he steals away Amoret:

> For, they say, she hath both kinds in one,
> Both male and female, both vnder one name:
> She syre and mother is her selfe alone,
> Begets and eke conceiues, ne needeth other none. (4.10.41.6–9)

Self-sufficiently double-sexed, this might be Britomart's emblematic twin.

But the possibility of Britomart's iconographic self-completion runs counter to her quest, and *The Faerie Queene*'s hermaphroditic images accommodate this tension, not only standing as symbols but gesturing toward a story. The hermaphroditic goddess of Scudamour's description, like the Roman statue to which Scudamour and Amoret are compared, is a static figure, a vision that stands still. The myth behind it, by contrast, in which the nymph Salmacis pursues the youth Hermaphroditus, is a narrative of transformation not irrelevant to Britomart's own. Hermaphroditus, like Narcissus, is fully self-absorbed, but the nymph Salmacis is no Echo; "willde he nillde he," "wound about him like a Snake," she imposes her body on his. [12] The result is synthesis: "They were not any lenger two: but (as it were) a toy/Of double shape: Ye could not say it was a perfect boy/Nor perfect wench: it seemed both and none of both to beene." Like Britomart's mirror-gaze, the spectacular desire of Salmacis—"She first the yongman did espie,/And in beholding him desirde to have his companie"—entangles the masculine in the female. And like Britomart, Salmacis become what she wants, but in so doing transforms her object. The Hermaphroditus myth is another return to the mirror stage, in which appetite reforms identity and detaches desire from any embodied condition of difference.[13]

If these are heterosexual consequences, Glauce's reassurance contradicts chivalric ideals: narcissism, rather than a cautionary tale, becomes a mechanism that preserves the exclusive masculinity into which Britomart deliberately and prosthetically enters. In the introduction to this book, I proposed a reading of narcissism as homosocial theory. Narcissus's preoccupation with identity, imagined not as a mistake but as a hierarchy of value, might be a template for patriarchal logic, organizing a system in which men look exclusively at and for their own images. As a condensation of male bonding that subordinates heterosexual to homosocial desire, narcissism is simply efficient. Disguised, Britomart participates in this economy, offering a mirror image to the knights she encounters that gains in value as she defeats them. For chivalric heroes as for Lacanian subjects, confrontation with a vision of agency precipitates desire for identity; men both want and want to be what Britomart is. Perhaps paradoxically, the revelation that she is a woman might further enable this system of masculine consolidation, rather than disrupting it. In chivalric heroic encounters, men bond with men across the bodies of women in a process of exchange negotiated through violence. Theorists from Gayle Rubin to René Girard to Eve Kosofsky Sedgwick to David Halperin have variously suggested the ways in which women perpetuate male relations of both rivalry and alliance; to quote Teresa de Lauretis's summary of Halperin, "It is the female, reproductive body that paradoxically guarantees true eros between men." [14] In this sense encounters between men and martial women are remarkably efficient, providing both the appearance of mutually idealized masculinity and the female body that lends male homoerotic violence a social fiction of cause.

Battles may be explained through women, but they are precipitated by envy, emulation, the seduction of the mirror. The fantasy that drives representations of Amazon encounters promises that that mirror will at once work and break, that the martial woman who looks like a man will play two parts in the triangulation that governs chivalry.[15] The hero of the Amazon encounter, confronting a body that looks like his own, responds with a simultaneity—and indeed causality—of identity and violence: the appearance of a mirror image creates the indistinguishable desires to admire it and to kill it.[16] The doubleness of martial women makes this doubled desire productive, enabling them to battle knights and at the same time provide the prize, the idealized feminized body that remains when the armor comes off. Such triangulation, at once narcissistic and heterosexually acquisitive, is a fantastic ideal, a synthesis of violence and sex composed of two bodies and an act. Girard has shown that desire works through violence and through triangles: "Nothing, perhaps, could be more banal than the role of violence in awakening desire," he argues, and adds, "Two desires converging on the same object are bound to clash. Thus, mimesis coupled with desire leads automatically to conflict."[17] Sedgwick has demonstrated that those violent rivalrous triangles are homoerotic as well; she writes of Girard's model, "The bonds of 'rivalry' and 'love,' differently as they are experienced, are equally powerful and in many senses equivalent."[18] It is perhaps surprising if one of the men between whom these bonds are formed turns out to be an Amazon, but it is also, if somewhat oddly, convenient.

Analyzing the relationship between identification and desire in Jacobean drama, Jonathan Dollimore writes, "The male is required to identify with other males but he is not allowed to desire them; indeed, *identification with* should actually preclude *desire for.* Conversely, those whom he is supposed to desire, and always in specified ways, namely women, he is discouraged from identifying with: that would equal effeminacy; so in relation to them *desire for* precludes *identification with*."[19] The convergence of "with" and "for" is transgressive, even dangerous. But in Amazon encounters such a conflation seemingly becomes safe: Artegall's encounter with Britomart consummates without compromising homosocial relations. Chivalric contests populate the narcissistic economy with two bodies, reinforcing the equation of identity and desire, and the revelation that one of those bodies is a woman's gives desire an acceptable place to go. The process through which eroticized contest becomes sexual conquest consolidates both homosocial and heterosexual bonds, reifying their mutual dependence and identifying their relationship as that between theory and practice: male homosociality both veils and makes use of heterosexuality. As Dollimore writes, "Within masculine sexuality the most significant other is the male—but it is a significance which presupposes, and is rehearsed in relation to, the female" (302).

But as the process of revelation denaturalizes masculinity, the shift from homosocial to heterosexual interaction gives a twist to the relationships and identities it is invoked to support. In *The Tears of Narcissus*, Lynn Enterline writes, "The entanglement of narcissism in melancholia, or of self-reflection in self-loss, disturbs the representation of a stable, or empirically knowable, sexual difference."[20] Encounters between men and masculine women, which both invoke and radically alter the narcissistic mirror, play out this failure of difference and its intimations of loss. Men who see martial women as women see themselves differently; if martial female roles are transformed by the moment of exposure, so, too, are the roles played by men. The transition from triangulation to conjugal pairs disrupts the symmetrical performance of masculinity on both sides, and, when Artegall strikes off Britomart's helmet with his sword, when sameness becomes difference and the martial body has a woman's face, he quite literally loses his grip.

> And as his hand he vp againe did reare,
>   Thinking to worke on her his vtmost wracke,
>   His powrelesse arme benumbd with secret feare
>   From his reuengefull purpose shronke abacke,
>   And cruell sword out of his fingers slacke
>   Fell downe to ground. (4.6.21.1–6)

Artegall, described by Scudamour as "now become to liue a Ladies thrall," is less like Narcissus here than like a victim of Medusa (4.6.28.8).

And if Medusa is both beautiful and deadly, Britomart possesses this doubleness as well, her body continuing to signify violence even as it is erotically transformed. As Artegall discovers, Britomart is an intimidating figure to defeat or to desire; her version of agency suggests not that bodies are veiled or displaced by acts but that both are insistently present, complicating the conditions of male response. The perception extends beyond Artegall, informing other reactions to Britomart as well:

> For she was full of amiable grace,
>   And manly terrour mixed therewithall,
>   That as the one stird vp affections bace,
>   So th'other did mens rash desires apall,
>   And hold them backe, that would in errour fall. (3.1.46.1–5)

While Britomart both looks and acts like a man, her martial encounters reinforce the structures of violence and exchange that make chivalric heroism work. Battling Scudamour over Amoret, or Artegall over False Florimell, she is dangerous only in a conventionally masculine sense. But at the moment of revelation, when it becomes clear that female sexual agency does not displace or disable masculinity but causes and constructs it, things change. Silberman reads the transition as a kind of chivalric Freudian slip: "The erotically charged rematch between Britomart and Artegall appears as an accidental slip from the homosocial into the heterosexual," she writes, and goes on to describe the resulting uneasiness. "Seen in the context of the homosocial camaraderie of Artegall and Scudamore, as well as their imagined homosocial rivalry with Britomart, the fight between Britomart and Artegall appears anomalous and disruptive." [21] The anomaly, revealing a conflict between conditions of desire, is less accidental than it is Britomart's role in the poem. As Natalie Zemon Davis writes, "The virtuous virago could be a threat to order after all." [22]

Britomart's identity as both masculine and female presents not a narrative of development or transformation but a problem of simultaneity. As the repeated image of her revealed face juxtaposed to her still-armored body suggests, she is not only both but aggressively both *at once*, making masculinity visible as a female performance. Her relationship to Artegall, first in disguise and then out of it, does not impose a distinction between the homosocial and the heterosexual; such a distinction might control the anxiety of doubleness by breaking the narrative in half, locating the homosocial chivalric encounter at the text's center and leaving heterosexual resolution in the conventional "happy ending" position offstage. Desire might be the cause of chivalric heroism, consummation its effect, as the narrator assures the reader at the beginning of Book 4: "All the workes of those wise sages, / And braue exploits which great Heroes wonne, / In loue were either ended or begunne" (Proem, 3.3–5). But chivalric heroism itself should occupy a space between, motivated but not interrupted by heterosexual preoccupations. Achieved, the union of Artegall and Britomart might resemble that of Scudamour and Amoret, or of Florimell and Marinell; postponed, it might echo that of Red Cross and Una. In these other cases, the relationship of sexual union to chivalric pursuit is one of reciprocal displacement, through which marriage truncates the quest or the quest defers marriage, each structure defining identity in distinct and discrete terms. Britomart's presence precludes such discretion. Her performance links homosociality to heterosexuality through the continuity of eroticism, suggesting that both systems of desire and the bodies within them may be vulnerable to mutual substitution. As John O'Connor observes of *Amadis de Gaule*, "Moreover, since Amazons in armor are indistinguishable from knights, two fighters frequently discover after many blows and perhaps a good deal of gore that they are lovers or even husband and wife." [23]

Transitions, whether from homosocial to heterosexual bonds or from chivalric to domestic narratives, are replaced by an economy of distributed—and implicitly redistributable—roles. Catalyzing constant erotic response even as she is herself radically inconstant in relation to gendered convention, Britomart embodies simultaneities that dislocate categories of difference, bringing wives onto the battlefield and knights into the home and, by giving these figures narrative continuity across the boundaries of coherent performative space, destabilizing assumptions about identity. The relationships between women and men are not subordinated to male homosocial bonds but intervene in their constitution. Rather than being identified in terms of difference that naturalize hierarchy—the other, the matter, the object, the abject—martial women figure the potential failure of difference itself. In his reading of the boy actor in women's clothes, Peter Stallybrass writes, "All attempts to fix gender are necessarily *prosthetic*: that is, they suggest the attempt to supply an imagined deficiency by the exchange of male clothes for female clothes or of female clothes for male clothes; by displacement from male to female space or from female to male space; by the replacement of male with female tasks or of female with male tasks. But all elaborations of the prosthesis which will supply the 'deficiency' can secure no essence. On the contrary, they suggest that gender itself is a fetish, the production of an identity through the fixation upon specific 'parts.' " [24] To impose domestic closure, *The Faerie Queene* must identify Britomart's disguise *as* a disguise, as a fiction cut short by a statement of fact. But that statement, as a displacement, a replacement, an elaboration, or an exchange, only exposes the need for an artificial and forceful assumption of what Stallybrass calls "parts."

Susanne Woods writes, "[Spenser] subverts his own message of masculine privilege, from the sympathetic features of the Radigund portrait to the ironic use of Britomart to restore masculine rule to the Amazons."[25] Such subversion is implicit from Britomart's first appropriation of armor; in Mary Villeponteaux's words, "Britomart's disguise unsettles identity, presenting a challenge to the patriarchal notion that authority is something biologically masculine, invested in the male at every social level."[26] The performance of female masculinity demonstrates not only that roles can be manufactured out of contradictions, but that this malleability of the apparently innate might be a source of power; not only that gender is a construct, but that constructed masculinity works most effectively when its relationship to the body is one of paradox. For men, chivalric heroism sets up a mutual dependence of sexual and martial agency, equating heroic victory and sexual potency, sexual failure and heroic defeat: male heroes claim the absolute condition of possession and become vulnerable to absolute loss. "Why is fixation on the penis (and by extension, the phallus) not called a fetish when it is attached to a man?" Marjorie Garber asks in *Vested Interests*. "The concept of 'normal' sexuality, that is to say, of heterosexuality, is founded on the naturalizing of the fetish. And this in turn is dependent upon an economics of display."[27] Swords are fetishes for heroes, providing protection not only through martial utility but through a naturalized connection to the male body; that naturalization has its risks and its costs. "*Hercules* served *Omphale*, put on an aprone, tooke a distaffe and spun," Robert Burton reminds his readers. "*Thraso* the souldier was so submisse to *Thais*, that he was resolved to do whatsoever she enjoyned . . . And as *Peter Abelhardus* lost his testicles for his *Helonissa*, he will I say not venture an incision, but life it self."[28] When the hero drops his sword, the fate of Abelard is not far behind.

Artegall seems particularly susceptible to this threat of detachment. He is a changeling; he wears another hero's armor; he is assisted by Talus, who attenuates Artegall's own link to allegorical function. When Artegall borrows Braggadochio's shield, Braggadochio easily takes credit for the resulting victory: "for Sir *Artegall*/Came *Braggadochio*, and did shew his shield" (5.3.14.7–8). To paraphrase O'Connor, knights in armor are indistinguishable from knights, and Artegall regains his position only by disarming to display his wounded body. As evidence, the gesture tends to work against itself. Heroic male identity cannot be proved by armor, which circulates; but it also cannot safely be proved by the body, exposure of which removes the objects through which identity has been defined. Shakespeare's Coriolanus knows what Artegall does not: a male body that is undeniably *his* and undeniably *there* discloses its vulnerability to damage. If Britomart's revelation asserts synthesis, Artegall's corresponding gesture reveals fragmentation. When Radigund disarms him, she reiterates a vulnerability already implicit in his own acts:

> Then tooke the Amazon this noble knight,
> Left to her will by his owne wilfull blame,
> And caused him to be disarmed quight,
> Of all the ornaments of knightly name,
> With which whylome he gotten had great fame. (5.5.20.1–5)

Judith Anderson writes, "[Artegall] has always a choice between being Justice, a virtue and an abstraction, and being a Knight, a virtuous man and a human being,"[29] but, deprived of the equipment that identifies him as a knight, an abstraction, and a man, he has no choice at all. In a revealing moment, he is described as "preseru'd from yron rust," as if nothing separates the man from his armor. When that separation is forcibly imposed, there may be nothing left.

A very different signifying structure identifies Britomart. Weapons for her are not fetishes or metaphors, but objects that get things done; if the sword lacks a genital referent, it is efficiently allied to the female body that uses it. Her performance produces effects without essentializing cause, undermining not masculinity but its exclusive connection to men. In *Female Masculinity*, Judith Halberstam writes, "Female masculinities are framed as the rejected scraps of dominant masculinity in order that male masculinity may appear to be the real thing. But what we understand as heroic masculinity has been produced by and across both male and female bodies."[30] Britomart's artifactual heroism creates a fissure in heroic referentiality. For Artegall, effective masculinity—the "real thing"—requires the visible causality that links body to act; feminization can never be only skin deep, for the revelation that a hero can be reinvented invalidates his property in his role. But the invented Britomart *is* the allegorical Britomart, the exposure of her body revealing not essence but contradiction and disabling not her but men. Gender becomes a performance less because women's bodies can replace

Dressed to Kill

151

men's than because masculinity was never male to begin with; if the game depends on artifice, then anyone can play. Spenser claims that women are precluded from heroic acts not by nature, but by a kind of historiographic petulance; "record of antique times," he argues, proves that female heroism was a commonplace, "Till enuious Men fearing their rules decay,/Gan coyne streight lawes to curb their liberty" (3.2.2.1, 5–6).[31] Femininity is an invention, and a fairly recent one at that.

"'Sex' is an ideal construct which is forcibly materialized through time. It is not a simple fact or static condition of a body, but a process whereby regulatory norms materialize 'sex' and achieve this materialization through a forcible reiteration of those norms," Judith Butler writes.[32] The "regulatory norms" through which sex, as reproductive sexuality and as the embodied referent of gender, is represented in *The Faerie Queene* complicate the notion of normativity. As Britomart, prosaically motivated by a desire for marriage and children, commits a series of transvestite acts, the conventions of domesticity become implicated in the shifting conditions of display. Domestic ideals, rather than reasserting the hierarchies disrupted by female masculinity, are produced out of that masculinity, and it is this understanding of the domestic — as performative, only paradoxically normative, and forcibly imposed not on women but on men — that connects Britomart to Radigund. If, as readers have always noted, the two women look almost exactly alike, this is less because Britomart is as bad as Radigund, or almost as bad, or potentially as bad, than it is because they want the same thing.[33] Britomart the hopeful wife, like Radigund the jilted mistress, constructs masculine violence out of heterosocial convention; both the Knight of Chastity and the Amazon Queen pursue a state in which men can be men and women can stop acting like them. Their desires anticipate the conclusion of the pamphlet *Haec-Vir,* in which the "masculine-feminine" speaker pleads, "Cast then from you our ornaments, and put on your owne armours: Be men in shape, men in shew, men in words, men in actions, men in counsell, men in example . . . Comelinesse shall be then our study; feare our Armour, and modestie our practice."[34] But the return to a normative distribution of gender roles exposes those roles *as* distributed, passed out in a process that reveals that sexual hierarchies, like sexual differences, are only as constant as they are constantly enforced.

The convergence of Britomart and Radigund might reflect a larger concern with extremes: stories about martial women accommodate both militant chastity and sexual excess, hinting at a connection between them. If Britomart is like chaste Penthesilea, and Radigund is like the sexually ravenous Amazons of the new world, they are somewhat like one another; both sexual excess and sexual resistance oppose the utilitarian middle ground of ordered sexuality. Yet it is the move onto that middle ground that most directly threatens Artegall. Once and nearly twice defeated by Britomart in battle, unmanned by the penetration of her armor, he postpones his happy ending only to reenact it. In his encounter with Radigund he loses another fight to female masculinity, and domestic bliss produces its own parodic mirror image: Artegall leaves a mistress behind only to be put in the place of one, dressed in women's clothing and set to spin.[35] The transition from homoerotic identity to heterosexual difference, however efficient as a chivalric economy, results in Artegall's downfall: from his horse, from his allegory, from the naturalized assumptions of masculine display.

This is the fault built into the fantasy. If Amazons promise a fabulous synthesis of chivalric and domestic ideals, the condensation of those ideals in a single body exposes the tension between them. That tension does damage to men: even as armed women fall victim to feminization, seduction, and other acts of violence, they produce a series of reciprocal victims who, like Artegall, choose the wrong moment to put down the sword. Desire for an Amazon, however thoroughly disarmed and objectified, precipitates a crisis of sexual discretion; if mirror games consolidate masculine identity through illusion, the illusion is as fragile as it is persuasive. Jane Gallop writes, "What appears to precede the mirror stage is simply a projection or a reflection. There is nothing on the other side of the mirror."[36] But the conflict between men and martial women materializes the relationship between image and object, placing two bodies uneasily in the same representational space and leaving them to fight it out. In such a narrative, what is on the other side of the mirror is not fiction, but women.

The Faerie Queene gives Artegall powerful models for the encounter: his armor is Achilles', his acts recall Hercules, and in myth both of these heroes, famously, win. Hercules's ninth labor requires the defeat of an Amazon queen; Ben Jonson writes that Penthesilea "was honored in her death to have it the act of Achilles."[37] Yet the aspect of these heroes most fully expressed in Artegall is less famous than notorious, exemplifying not invincibility but a condition of willed surrender. Achilles, whose mother fears his fate, dresses as a girl and hides among women; Hercules, in punishment for killing Iphitus, suffers transvestite enslavement at the hands of Omphale. This is Artegall's heroic precedent:

> Who had him seene, imagine mote thereby,
>   That whylome hath of *Hercules* bene told,
>   How for *Iolas* sake he did apply
>   His mightie hands, the distaffe vile to hold. (5.5.24.1–4)

Artegall is most like heroes when heroes are least like themselves. And Artegall's domestication, like that of Hercules, imposes a shift not only of clothing but of genre: from epic to comedy, from allegory to farce. In his "Defense of Poesy," Sidney takes the transvestite Hercules to illustrate his theory of comic effect: "Hercules, painted with his great beard and furious countenance, in a woman's attire, spinning at Omphale's commandment, it breeds both delight and laughter. For the representing of so strange a power in love procures delight, and the scornfulness of the action stirreth laughter." [38] Invoking spectacular triumphs in which heroes kill Amazons, *The Faerie Queene* turns these stories to reflect the everyday processes through which women laugh at men.

Men who encounter Amazons might always find themselves at the wrong point of the triangle. In homosocially governed processes of exchange, the third term is an idealized woman who, whether veiled by amazonian armor or displaced like the Echo of Narcissus, is always effectively absent, an abstraction masquerading as an object. But the third term of the Amazon encounter is a monstrous domestic product, a demonized woman or a broken man. For if heterosexual domesticity can be produced by chivalric violence, it cannot easily be separated from that violence; convergences of martial and marital roles, contingent on the belatedness of discovery, do not displace armed conflict with marriage but suggest an equation between the two, displacing instead the moment at which domesticity socializes desire. Britomart's anticipation of a meeting that might be a battle—"Tell me some markes, by which he may appeare,/If chaunce I him encounter parauaunt;/For perdie one shall other slay, or daunt" (3.2.16.3–5)—demonstrates that there is no gap between violent and erotic response. Marriage, rather than disarming female agency, brings it closer to home.

In his account of Guiana, Ralegh writes, "It was farther tolde me, that if in these warres [the Amazons] tooke any prisoners that they used to accompany with those also at what time soever, but in the end for certeine they put them to death." [39] A chronicler of the discovery of the Amazon river records, "An Indian farther up had told us that anyone who should take it into his head to go down to the country of these women was destined to go a boy and come back an old man." [40] As they replace triangulated homoeroticism with a direct confrontation between women and men, stories about amazonian sexuality confirm the fear of heterosexual emasculation. Narratives that progress from battlefield to bedroom often expose not objectified female bodies but the disabled bodies of men. Painter writes of the Amazons, "If by chaunce they kept any [male children] backe, they murdred them, or else brake their armes, and legs in sutch wise as they had no power to beare Weapons." [41] The threat synecdochically figured in the missing amazonian breast becomes explicit in these accounts of horrific maternal practice: fear of a devouring woman, left behind in the formation of masculine identity, reappears in the violence of Amazons. The result, for men, is in effect a projection back through the mirror stage, a return to disarticulated bodies without power to act. In "Of the Lame or Cripple," Montaigne reads this process erotically: "It is a common Proverbe in *Italie*, that *He knowes not the perfect pleasure of* Venus, *that hath not layne with a limping Woman.* Either fortune, or some particular accident, have long since brought this by-saying in the peoples mouth: and it is as well spoken of men as of women: For the Queene of the Amazons answered the Scithian, that wooed hir to loves-embracements. *The crooked man doeth it best.* In that feminine commonwealth of theirs, to avoyde the domination of men, they were wont in their infancie to maime them, both in their armes and legges and other limmes, that might any way advantage their strength over them, and made onely that use of them, that we in our World make of Women." [42] Montaigne's "in our World" suggests the deictic fragility of relations of gender and power, and Artegall in Radegone has clearly crossed a border.

Montaigne's narrative is less arcane than it is a causality written backward; as early modern texts pursue the link between female sexuality and male disintegration, they suggest that men are always potentially disabled by women's desire.[43] "What greater captivity or slavery can there be (as *Tully* expostulates) then to bee in love?" Burton writes. *"Is he a free man over whom a woman domineers, to whom she prescribes Lawes, commands, forbids what she will her self? That dares deny nothing she demands; she asks, he gives; she calls, he comes; she threatens, he fears;* Nequissimum hunc servum puto, *I account this man a very drudge."* [44] Artegall's experience in Radegone plays out the anxieties attendant on the transition from triangulation to duality, from martial to domestic spheres. Analyzing the Britomart/Radigund encounter in relation to Queen Elizabeth I, Quilligan writes, "Female authority here is not funny, because it is real."[45] It is "real" in a broader sense as well: as they become not enemies in arms but recognizable agents of female sexual desire, martial women might simply be women, Artegall's heroic fall reduced to the quotidian condition of Burton's "drudge." Spenser's narrator himself effects such a reduction, telling the reader who condemns Artegall, "Neuer yet was wight so well aware,/But he at first or last was trapt in womens snare" (5.6.1.8–9). The loss of heroism, of effective masculinity, is here neither cataclysmic nor even shocking, but simply inevitable.

Resolved into bad domesticity, Amazon encounters might be clichés that validate patriarchy by proving its point. Montrose describes Amazon myth as a reflection of cultural anxieties, a tacit recognition of hegemony's props: "Amazonian mythology seems symbolically to embody and to control a collective anxiety about the power of the female not only to dominate or reject the male but to create and destroy him. It is an ironic acknowledgment by an androcentric culture of the degree to which men are in fact dependent upon women."[46] The myth here is a compensatory structure, which acknowledges female power by estranging its effects or incorporating them into a dominant narrative. Describing "that various and conflicted set of ideologies we call Renaissance patriarchy," Stephen Orgel writes, "It is an ideology that contains its contradictions by allowing them to be contradictions; the contradictions—what it sees as threatening it—are essential to it, what make it work."[47] But the image of a self-serving heterogeneity is complicated by amazonian entanglements of the familiar and the strange. Is Amazon myth an acknowledgment or a displacement? a repetition or a difference? Do amazonian social and sexual practices reverse or reflect conventional ideas about women and men? Amazons, in the early modern imagination, might inhabit patriarchy as exemplary ideals or as clarifying counterexamples, or they might occupy an antithetical space, and their effect lies less in any of these situations than in their mutual plausibility. Like Derrida's supplement, stories about Amazons both support and undermine the agendas that produce them, offering a mirror image that might turn into an entirely different picture. If Amazon myth is a fiction, so is patriarchy; both are abstractions with pretensions to embodiment, and, where neither is demonstrable, either might be true. In *The Faerie Queene*, as in early modern texts more generally, Amazon myth does not oppose the normative to the monstrous — Britomart to Radigund, male to female power, marriage to ungoverned sexuality, heroism to emasculation — but makes it impossible to tell the difference.

Amazonian desires are dangerous, even — especially — when they mirror heterosocial ideals. The proem to Book 4, Canto 6 makes this clear: "*Both Scudamour and Arthegall/Doe fight with Britomart,/He sees her face; doth fall in loue,/and soone from her depart.*" Identified as the end of Britomart's quest, Artegall risks losing his own. Katherine Eggert argues that Book 5's shift into aggressive topicality enables his escape: "In the view of the male characters who are the necessary partners in this enterprise, marriage seems largely to replicate the dangers to heroism embodied in Acrasia's bower: marriage does not sharpen knightly instruments, it suspends them."[48] With Artegall's rescue and restoration, *The Faerie Queene* ends that suspension as it moves out of domestic space; the later events of Book 5 reinvent a world in which a man can be a knight. Yet this transition is itself enabled by a structure of homosocial triangulation that puts Artegall in the wrong place: in the battle between Britomart and Radigund, the vision of two knights fighting for a lady reappears, but the "lady" is Artegall.

According to Merlin, Artegall's marriage is destined to be deadly.

> Long time ye both in armes shall beare great sway,
> Till thy wombes burden thee from them do call,
> And his last fate him from thee take away,
> Too rathe cut off by practise criminall
> Of secret foes, that him shall make in mischiefe fall. (3.3.28.5–9)

As a mystified afterthought in a prophecy that has reached its more important conclusion, Artegall's death suggests the extent to which heroic male identity, confronted by amazonian synthesis, falls apart. The simultaneity of female body and masculine act leaves little space for men, and the chivalric triangle collapses first into an anxiety-ridden dyad and then into efficient singularity. This progression reappears in *The Feminine Monarchie*, Charles Butler's anthropomorphic essay on bees: "After which time [of breeding], these *Amazonian* Dames, having conceived for the next yeere, begin to wax weari of their mates, and to like their roome better than their company . . . You may soomtime see a handful or two before a Hive, which they had killed within: but the greatest part flyeth away, and dyeth abroad."[49] As a disposable husband, Artegall embodies a similarly stark definition of male utility: heterosexuality is necessary, but its tenure is brief.

I am not suggesting that Britomart kills Artegall, but rather that heterosexual desire removes him from allegory without giving him anywhere to go. Enacted by Radigund, this effect is connected to Britomart only implicitly by prophecy and analogy. Instead, our final vision of Britomart and Artegall shows us one last set of mirror games. After Artegall has been imprisoned, Britomart sustains his role, and Dolon, who shelters and betrays her, recognizes her in these terms: "For sure he weend, that this his present guest/Was *Artegall*, by many tokens plaine" (5.6.34.1–2). Britomart again becomes the image of the object of desire, her identity defined through and as an empowered illusion. When she reaches Artegall himself, she cannot look at him. Like Artegall earlier in the poem, she confronts an unexpected spectacle of femininity; unlike Artegall, she averts her gaze, her response to this final break in the mirror echoing that of Perseus, who avoids monstrous transformation by knowing when, and how, to look away.

> At last when as to her owne Loue she came,
> Whom like disguize no lesse deformed had,
> At sight thereof abasht with secrete shame,
> She turnd her head aside, as nothing glad,
> To haue beheld a spectacle so bad. (5.7.38.1–5)

For Radigund's tyranny to be redressed the Knight of Justice must be redressed, and Britomart, acting like and as Artegall, reconstructs him in her own armored image, "In which when as she him anew had clad,/She was reuiu'd, and ioyd much in his semblance glad" (5.7.41.8–9). Object and image reverse positions through the prosthetic distribution of armor, and Artegall, confronted by a rescuer who doubles as a wife, goes away again. His recession into allegorical distance restores the pattern: lives are threatened, armor is taken by violence and restored by grace, objects of desire are found and lost, and the chivalric repetition compulsion goes on.[50]

But putting distance between himself and Britomart cannot close the gap between Artegall's experience of chivalry and the idealized narcissistic system I have described. Having left his wife behind, Artegall meets his nominal soulmate in a confrontation that might restore the relations of identity and power:

> [They] ventailes reare, each other to behold.
> Tho when as *Artegall* did *Arthure* vew,
> So faire a creature, and so wondrous bold,
> He much admired both his heart and hew,
> And touched with intire affection, nigh him drew. (5.8.12.5–9)

This meeting, which begins in violence and ends in mutual admiration, should be the climactic fulfillment of chivalric ideals, concentrating mastery in the convergence of equals. Instead, Arthur, like Radigund, reprises Britomart in an Amazon encounter that looks exactly the same when played out between two male heroes.[51] As he leaves heteroeroticism behind, Artegall does not escape that first encounter but further implicates men in it. If Britomart and Arthur leave Artegall looking the same, looking in the same way, this continuity identifies the disruption of homosocial exclusivity as a general rather than a local effect. In its refusal to separate debilitating entanglements from enabling alliances, to distinguish by gender or isolate sex, *The Faerie Queene* invokes categorical abstractions only to show their failure. Homo- and heteroeroticism are distinct neither in their objects nor in their effects; desire is not contained by an idea of its target; boundaries between teleologies of response, between relations that are powerful and those that are merely useful, become obscure. Framed by Amazon encounters, the chivalric narcissistic fantasy is emptied out not only by the intervention of women, but by the interactions among men.

Dressed to Kill

So Britomart has been for Artegall a rather dangerous supplement, displacing him as an allegorical signifier and as a heroic performance in the very acts through which she restores him to himself. Pursuing a masculinist agenda—reestablishing Justice, restoring Artegall, returning Radegone to male rule—she recalls Orgel's description of contradictions that work; but female masculinity is at best a problematic guarantor of patriarchal effects. I have suggested that chivalric mirror games work like and indeed as theories of subjectivity: as an attempt to articulate links and tensions among gender, violence, eroticism, and social order, Britomart's quest anticipates our own preoccupation with signifying paradox. In *The Faerie Queene* as in texts of this period more generally, Amazon encounters reveal the precarious foundations on which conventions of identity rest, displaying oppositions and hierarchies in their natural if only potential state of collapse. Tacitly recognizing that effect, Artegall asks another amazonian victim, "Haplesse man, what make you here?/Or haue you lost your selfe, and your discretion?" (5.4.26.1–2). For *The Faerie Queene*, discretion, as categorical difference or as the ability not to tell the wrong story, is more easily lost than found.

. . . IN BED

The "wrong story" might be Britomart's chivalric imposture. What, to return to the beginning, does it mean for a woman to put on armor and go on a quest? At the level of plot, it is a deliberate revision of lived experience, a way of staying safe as a woman on the road; Glauce says, "That therefore nought our passage may empeach,/Let vs in feigned armes our selues disguize" (3.3.53.1–2). In historical terms, disguise situates Britomart in a national tradition of heroic women; the text names Bunduca, Guendolen, Martia, and Emmilen. Allegorically, Britomart's armor is not a disguise at all, but a realization of symbolically impenetrable virtue. Understood psychoanalytically, her disguise also engages the symbolic; as a king's daughter who appropriates his martial trophies, she takes an aggressive approach to the law of the father. As a negotiation of agency, Britomart's assumed role is a textbook case of the kind of up-by-your-own-bootstraps, be-all-that-you-can-be processes that characterize the more optimistic versions of self-fashioning. And seen through the lens of performativity, that role catalyzes the inconstancy of gender that implicates not only Britomart but everyone drawn into the progress of her quest.

Each of these readings focuses attention on the part that is played, the identity assembled and assumed. Red Cross describes Britomart's masculinity and femininity as equally the effects of disguise: "Faire Lady she him seemd, like Lady drest,/But fairest knight aliue, when armed was her brest" (3.2.4.8–9). Simply put, seeing is believing. This in turn produces an effect that is anything but simple: in her relationships with women, Britomart presents the text's most persuasive images of hetero-erotic conquest. Sheila Cavanagh writes, "While Britomart's story does not contain unequivocally lesbian undercurrents, she often manifests be-havior and responses to women which imply that her martial disguise muddles everyone's understanding of her gender and her heterosexu-ality, including her own." [52] Cavanagh concludes that what she describes as Britomart's "sexual naiveté" is prophylactic, ensuring that she neither desires women nor acts too much like them. But to read Britomart in terms of what she might think or want is to ignore what she looks like: dressed as a man, fighting other men to win possession of women, Brito-mart illustrates the heteroerotic as well as the homoerotic effects of chi-valric masculinity. *The Faerie Queene* is a world of arm candy, in which women prove things about men through the public fact of display. This economy produces the disguise plot's double twist: if heterosexual desire on Britomart's quest looks like male homoerotic violence, female homo-eroticism looks like consummated heterosexual desire.

The Faerie Queene is almost embarrassingly frank about the traffic in women, as the rules of Satyrane's tournament attest:

> And of them all she that is fayrest found,
>   Shall haue that golden girdle for reward,
>   And of those Knights who is most stout on ground,
>   Shall to that fairest Ladie be prefard. (4.2.27.1–4)

Even outside the structure of formal competition, Braggadochio, Blan-damour, and Ferraugh endlessly exchange False Florimell, who exists only to convey the privileges of ownership; and if the success of these bad knights is filtered through that modifier "false," their heroic counter-parts, who share the same desires, are still more conspicuous in their failures. Arthur does not catch Florimell, Scudamour does not save Amoret, Artegall does not win False Florimell, Marinell does not understand a prophecy and fights with a woman when he should be fighting for one. As such failures leave women in danger, they protect the condition of heroism. Sexual success is almost invariably a fall out of chivalric identity, whether into happy ending or into disgrace: Paridell, in his seduction of Hellenore, is more paramour than Paris; Scudamour, in the 1590 ending, dissolves into a hermaphroditic union that hints at loss; Argante and Olliphante charge through the text's landscape as instances of monstrous gratification. The homosocial transactions of chivalry, like those of sonnets, require an impossible object to keep their boundaries intact, and as long as all the knights chase Florimell together, there is little danger that any one of them will catch her. But the threat of sexuality is always at hand; the satyrs who possess Hellenore in common might only be knights who have chased a prize that did not run. The relationship between heroes and monsters is not opposition but continuum, the metamorphosis from one into the other only a capitulation away.[53]

This explains the unproductive nature of chivalric contests, in which knights come from miles around only to see Braggadochio win the prize. The narrator defines heteroerotic chivalry as a meeting of complementary values:

> For he me seemes most fit the faire to serue,
> That can her best defend from villenie;
> And she most fit his seruice doth deserue,
> That fairest is and from her faith will neuer swerue. (4.5.1.6–9)

Beautiful and virtuous women deserve the service of strong and brave knights, whose strength and bravery are validated in the service of beautiful and virtuous women; as the narrator comments, "either doth on other much relie" (4.5.1.5). In rewarding an unheroic figure, Satyrane's tournament seemingly violates this symbiotic tautology. But the system works best in the abstract and in the subjunctive, and Braggadochio's winning of False Florimell preserves it from the debasement of realization. The tournament efficiently quarantines immoderate desire, restricting it to two characters already chivalrically and allegorically devalued; having lost his credibility as a knight, Braggadochio is the only participant who can afford to win. The departure of the ill-conceived lovers not only banishes the specter of heterosexual excess, but unites the knights left behind.

Narcissistic contests between men enable the idealization of women, and desire for women motivates heroic acts by men. Under these rules, eroticism should never degenerate into sexuality; neither sodomy nor uxoriousness has a place in the chivalric world. But as examples ranging from the Squire of Dames to Artegall himself suggest, knights repeatedly fall out of that world, breaking the contract through which homoeroticism and heteroeroticism enable one another and exercise reciprocal restraint. For male heroes, eroticism is less often a self-contained mode of connection than it is a metonymic progress that falls abruptly into sex. Amazon encounters, as they represent the transition from homoerotic violence to heterosexual marriage, summarize concerns about the end of the quest: both desire for women and the mutual admiration of men, if taken too far, might unman heroes. Britomart is at once symptom and counterexample of this effect, embodying the female sexuality that precipitates falls from grace and enacting the idealized chivalry that avoids them. As she catalyzes Artegall's experience of emasculation, her own masculinity incorporates her into a different set of transactions, which illuminate the workings of heteroeroticism through the female homoeroticism precipitated by her disguise.

Reading Britomart's encounter with Malecasta, Silberman writes, "As Spenser adapts the Fiordespina episode from the *Orlando furioso* (25.4–70), he suppresses the undercurrent of lesbianism and, in its place, explores the permutations of heterosexuality."[54] Such a reading privileges the teleology of the quest, referring the eroticism through which it progresses to its sexual end. But Britomart's encounters with women do not simply tend toward heterosexual consummation; they look like it, taking up the "permutations of heterosexuality" in this sense as well. However effectively the quest's beginning predicates its conclusion, *The Faerie Queene* displays a powerful interest in what comes between, imposing a deictic double vision that is split between then and now. Eroticism implicates not only a body hypothesized from a look in a mirror, but bodies that exist in the present moment, and in that moment Britomart embodies heroic masculinity and catalyzes women's desires. Female homoeroticism may disappear at the point of heterosexual consummation—or, then again, it may not—but meanwhile it enables a flexibility of heteroerotic play inaccessible to women and men. With this in mind I would like to rethink that teleological imperative, opening up and complicating the relationship between means and ends even as *The Faerie Queene* does itself.

Rather than displacing possible sex between women by anticipating real sex between a woman and a man, the eroticism that shapes Britomart's quest causes desires to converge. Readers and characters respond to two different fictions—Britomart is a lady; Britomart is a knight—and the coincidence of assumptions revises as it reprises the triangulated structure of chivalric pursuits. In encounters with Malecasta, Amoret, and False Florimell, Britomart's female masculinity shapes an interaction made up not of two apparent men and a woman but of two women and the appearance of a man; and that appearance, whether Britomart banishes it by defeating a rival or simply dispels it by removing her own disguise, disappears. As it eliminates men, the story of Britomart and the women she wins offers the text's most sustained and most complicated treatment of the intersection of heteroerotic and homoerotic response. Refigured as a production in which desiring women play all the parts, heteroeroticism, like female masculinity, not only works but works *better*, both in its credibility as a performance and in its approximation of an ideal. But we are never allowed to forget that these exchanges involve only the illusion of men.

"Lesbian undercurrents," appearing by negation in both Cavanagh's and Silberman's accounts, suggest the possibility that Britomart's quest might go astray among women. In an effort to rescue her from such dangerous waters, readers point to her refusal to join Guyon and Arthur in pursuit of Florimell. The chase reveals the mixed motives of chivalry:

> But all spurd after fast, as they mote fly,
> To reskew her from shamefull villany.
> The Prince and *Guyon* equally byliue
> Her selfe pursewd, in hope to win thereby
> Most goodly meede, the fairest Dame aliue. (3.1.18.4–8)

Britomart's response distances her from these dubiously overlapping reasons for pursuit: "The whiles faire *Britomart,* whose constant mind,/ Would not so lightly follow beauties chace,/Ne reckt of Ladies Loue, did stay behind" (3.1.19.1–3). This is not a statement of sexual orientation; it is far from clear whether Britomart refuses to chase Florimell because it would be uninteresting to her as a woman or unbecoming to her as a knight. But as the excess of explanations leaves object choice opaque, it makes a different argument, critiquing the assumptions that cause Florimell to flee male knights. Britomart rejects the causal link between chivalric heroism and sexual reward; as the chase equates the obligation to protect women with the expectation of possessing them sexually, it leaves Britomart behind.

The vexed relationship between chivalry and sex structures Britomart's encounters with women throughout *The Faerie Queene.* Approaching Castle Joyous, she finds Red Cross under attack for his fidelity to his mistress, and defends his position: "For knight to leaue his Ladie were great shame,/That faithfull is, and better were to die" (3.1.25.3–4). Britomart articulates a chivalric tenet, but in which role does she speak: as the lady who deserves constancy, or as the knight who enacts it? Her role multiplies possible objects, as do the terms of the contest itself; the victorious knight "should aduaunced be to high regard,/(Said they) and haue our Ladies loue for his reward" (3.1.27.8–9). If this reward structure undermines the position of "him, that loues but one" that the challengers claim to uphold, Britomart's response complicates it further. "Loue haue I sure, (quoth she) but Lady none;/Yet will I not fro mine owne loue remoue,/Ne to your Lady will I seruice done" (3.1.28.2–4). Why, then, does Britomart fight? Her intervention has three results: it valorizes Artegall as an object; it defends Red Cross's virtue; it wins her a lady. Each has troubling implications, the first two putting male heroism in a dependent position, the third vitiating Britomart's earlier disclaimer. Invited "to enter in, and reape the dew reward" (3.1.30.8), Britomart does so, accepting that constancy's prize is another woman.

Like all supplementary processes, this wavers between addition and displacement. If Britomart, who previously had a love but not a lady, now has both, does this derail her quest? complicate it? advance it? Britomart herself deliberately prolongs her predicament, refusing to reveal herself even when Red Cross disarms (3.1.42). Malecasta wooes her, "all ignoraunt of her contrary sex" (3.1.47.2), and Britomart, in an odd turn of phrase that simultaneously declares and undercuts her innocence in the transaction, "dissembled it with ignoraunce" (3.1.50.8). Even when Malecasta declares her intentions clearly, Britomart sustains the charade:

For thy she would not in discourteise wise,
    Scorne the faire offer of good will profest;
    For great rebuke it is, loue to despise,
    Or rudely sdeigne a gentle harts request. (3.1.55.1–4)

Rather than a misunderstanding, this is a deliberate syllogism based in
the transitive property of desire: Britomart wants a man, and therefore
allows Malecasta to want her as a man. Eroticism is a condition of disguise, and the body inside the armor makes no difference; a flirtation
between women becomes a heterosocial contract. When Britomart finds
Malecasta in her bed, she is predictably dismayed. Forcibly shifted from
the formulaic interplay of gender to the embodied demands of sex, she
responds like those male knights confounded by her own revelations:

The noble *Britomartis* her arayd,
    And her bright armes about her body dight:
    For nothing would she lenger there be stayd,
    Where so loose life, and so vngentle trade
    Was vsd of Knights and Ladies seeming gent. (3.1.67.2–6)

Malecasta's court compromises chivalry with "ungentle trade," engaging devalued identities—"seeming gent"—in inappropriate exchange.
Britomart puts her armor back on.

  This is less homophobia than the horror of a fall, *any* fall, out of
chivalric identity. Britomart consolidates that identity through her relationship to another woman, in a heterosocial contract that remains at
the level of display. Her response to Amoret's imprisonment by Busirane
is prototypically chivalric: "For nothing so much pitty doth implore, / As
gentle Ladies helplesse misery" (3.11.18.5–6). Scudamour asks her, "What
couldst thou more, / If she were thine, and thou as now am I?"; like Red
Cross, he discovers that Britomart's help heroically effaces him (3.11.19.3–
4). In the 1590 ending Britomart returns Amoret to Scudamour, but
in the 1596 rewriting Scudamour has disappeared from the scene, and
Amoret recognizes that she has changed hands.

For well she wist, as true it was indeed,
    That her liues Lord and patrone of her health
    Right well deserued as his duefull meed,
    Her loue, her seruice, and her vtmost wealth. (4.1.6.1–4)

Amoret's notion of that contract, like Britomart's, privileges performance, putting the signifiers of possession in play. Love, service, and wealth belong to the knight who has saved her, but she hopes for a breach in the reasoning that, for Malecasta and for male knights, leads from ritual to sexual exchange: "Nathlesse her honor dearer then her life,/She sought to saue, as thing reseru'd from stealth" (4.1.6.6–7).

In a troubling passage, Britomart plays on Amoret's fear. "For other whiles to her she purpos made/Of loue, and otherwhiles of lustfulnesse,/That much she feard his mind would grow to some excesse" (4.1.7.7–9). What is happening here? The narrator's explanation that this "fine abusion" results from Britomart's wish "to hide her fained sex the better,/And maske her wounded mind" (4.1.7.2–4) seems deliberately feeble, but rejecting it implies either that Britomart is wildly unperceptive or that she is another Busirane. Unless, of course, we take seriously the games with pronouns—from her to she to she to his—which make gender an effect of rhetorical play. Dorothy Stephens reads the passage as a deliberate manipulation of conventions: "Britomart dallies more with Amoret than she ever does with Artegall, and it is tempting to say that at this stage of the game, she feigns only in order to flirt. By keeping her helmet on, Britomart can afford to raise the dialogue to a higher erotic pitch."[55] Replacing Scudamour with Britomart, the narrative moves from the hermaphroditic union of the first ending to performative doubleness, embracing the inconstant truth of appearances. Britomart acts out the implications of her disguise, even as the narrative reminds us that it *is* a disguise; sexuality, as threat or promise, is the symptom of an act. In the stanza following the description of Britomart's lustful behavior, the narrator asserts that despite Amoret's fears, "*Britomart* attended duly on her,/As well became a knight, and did to her all honor" (4.1.8.8–9). If this contradicts what immediately precedes it, the contradiction reminds us that both masculine aggression and masculine restraint are effective impersonations.

Rapid shifts among attitudes, pronouns, and conditions of knowledge demonstrate the elasticity of performance, and the effect again redoubles as Britomart and Amoret approach a castle that only knights who possess ladies may enter. Making short work of a challenger, Britomart tells him that "her loue to lose she was full loth,/But either he should neither of them haue, or both" (4.1.10.8–9). To have both is to have

Britomart, who has it both ways. When she disarms, she does not make the transition from knight to lady, but claims two privileged positions at once.

> She requir'd, that first fayre *Amoret*
> Might be to her allow'd, as to a Knight,
> . . . .
> Then since that strange Knights loue from him was quitted,
> She claim'd that to her selfe, as Ladies det,
> He as a Knight might iustly be admitted. (4.1.12.2–8)

The theoretical pronouncement that gender is performative can only, belatedly, echo Britomart's own. Like Ariosto's Bradamante, whose example this incident follows, Britomart disallows the moment of recognition, the reader's "Aha." After imposing three parts on two bodies, she invents four out of three, confounding homo- and heteroeroticism and making any gendered subject a plausible object of her desire. We have come rather far from that circumspect admission "Loue haue I sure, (quoth she) but Lady none."

Considering tensions among the expectations imposed by gender, Quilligan writes, "What seems to be at issue is the conflict within the terms of chivalric love—those pronounced by Arthur about ladies' undeniable rights, and those rights granted by conquest." [56] Britomart's inclusive identity subsumes that conflict, appropriating the various privileges of gender and putting contradiction to work. Having claimed two prizes and all of the subject positions, she takes Amoret to bed:

> And eke fayre *Amoret* now freed from feare,
> More franke affection did to her afford,
> And to her bed, which she was wont forbeare,
> Now freely drew, and found right safe assurance theare. (4.1.15.6–9)

Stephens writes, "It is wonderfully puzzling that the one happy bed scene in the whole poem appears here . . . While the text declares literally that each of the women longs to complete herself in her absent mate, the subtext at least momentarily believes in the self-sufficiency of their interaction with each other." [57] Heterosexism suggests that Britomart and Amoret can go to bed because nothing can happen there, but the text ironizes that assumption:

All that night they of their loues did treat,
And hard aduentures twixt themselues alone,
That each the other gan with passion great,
And griefull pittie priuately bemone. (4.1.16.1–4)

If loves, moans, and passions indicate a longing for men, they also evoke desire specific to these bodies and this moment. Again we are in two places at once, and, as Britomart has so recently demonstrated, erotic single-mindedness has no place at all.

Britomart's performance enables two women to go to bed and talk about their lovers, and, if this conjures up a sleepover, it also describes a triangle. In the place of men connected across women's bodies, the scene presents women who bond through stories about men, a recasting that not only shifts the agency of desire but emphasizes the fact that the men are not there. Only Britomart can take women to bed and remain a hero. The passion, sexual or confidential, which she exchanges with Amoret stands in illuminating contrast to Arthur sighing over his evasive fairy queen, or Scudamour lamenting his captive Amoret, or Artegall sulking over his unwon False Florimell. Britomart shares a bed with Glauce, who "her twixt her armes twaine/She straightly straynd, and colled tenderly,/And euery trembling ioynt, and euery vaine/She softly felt, and rubbed busily" (3.2.34.1–4); with Malecasta, who "by her side her selfe she softly layd/Of euery finest fingers touch affrayd;/Ne any noise she made, ne word she spake,/But inly sigh'd" (3.1.61.4–7); and with Amoret. Ate tells Scudamour,

I saw [Britomart] haue your *Amoret* at will,
I saw him kisse, I saw him her embrace,
I saw him sleepe with her all night his fill,
All manie nights. (4.1.49.1–4)

Whatever we may think we know, it is difficult to quarrel with Ate's facts or with her pronouns; even when Scudamour himself has been told that Britomart is a woman, he continues to call her Sir (4.6.34.5).

Winfried Schleiner analyzes relationships between female characters in *Amadis*, concluding, "Since this revaluation set female bonds above heterosexual relationships without challenging the necessity or need of the latter, the revaluation had no immediate practical or dynastic consequence."[58] In this sense, a chivalric contract formed with a woman should not threaten Britomart's sexual or allegorical status. But the display of female homoerotic desire might change the terms of chastity, the foundation of Britomart's identity and of patriarchally governed homosocial exchange. Valerie Traub writes, "Previously the rubric under which proper 'feminine' bodies and connections were situated, chastity itself becomes suspect, as the simple absence of male penetration is no longer deemed adequate to the task of maintaining the impenetrable security of the female body."[59] Traub describes this as a seventeenth-century development, but in *The Faerie Queene* its effects can already be felt. Desire between women does not leave the allegorical progress of chastity untouched, and Britomart's liaisons are in this sense dangerous, generating images of alternative consummations that might change the direction of her quest. There is, as Glauce assures Scudamour, no risk that Britomart will act as a man with Amoret. But her performance identifies both chivalric mastery and erotic conquest as representational effects; acting as a woman and like a knight, Britomart destabilizes the logic that, looking for heteroerotic agency, has recourse to men.

Where women who desire men and men who desire women risk expulsion from the exemplary space of *The Faerie Queene*, Britomart presents an idealized heteroeroticism that resolves itself into two women in bed. The collapse of male homoerotic triangles into heterosexual pairs poses a threat both to narratives and to men; the collapse of heteroerotic triangles into female homoerotic pairs restores order and protects a chivalric ideal. As recent scholarship has shown, sexual acts between women were both imaginable and imagined in the early modern period, and *The Faerie Queene* leaves its readers a choice: to look that way or not. But wherever we choose to turn our gaze, we confront the ways in which Britomart's female masculinity sustains the text's formal investment in desire as something potential rather than realized, a mode of eroticism rather than a claim about sex. The transition from representation to embodiment is as dangerous as it is easy, but only Britomart makes the transition back, and even she fails to do so when her excursions into heteroeroticism result in marriage to a man. As an accomplished fact, sexuality in *The Faerie Queene* works against its own hierarchical essentialism: the idealization of male homosocial bonds is undermined by the suggestion that they are a means to a heterosexual end, even as consummated heterosexuality is exposed as a fiction sustained among women. Female masculinity, as the site at which eroticisms converge, locates representational power in paradox and sexual teleology in the subjunctive.

When Britomart encounters more literal-minded heroes, she knocks them down and takes their women. She defeats Guyon, Paridell, Blandamour, Cambell, Triamond, Artegall, and Scudamour; only the titular heroes of the first and last books are safe, and of these Red Cross endures a rescue that has the effect of an assault. At Satyrane's tournament, Britomart appears at the moment of Artegall's victory, strikes him from his horse, and is awarded the lady he claims as his prize. She enters Amoret in the contest of virtue that follows — "At last the most redoubted *Britonesse,*/Her louely *Amoret* did open shew" (4.5.13.1–2) — but when it devolves into a beauty pageant and she is offered False Florimell instead, she declines, not because she is a woman but because she already has one.

> But *Britomart* would not thereto assent,
> Ne her owne *Amoret* forgoe so light
> For that strange Dame, whose beauties wonderment
> She lesse esteem'd, then th'others vertuous gouernment. (4.5.20.6–9)

Acting among men, Britomart passes in both senses of the word, neither faltering in the performance of masculinity nor failing the False Florimell test. *The Faerie Queene* puts us in a world in which heroes must be both men's men and ladies' men, proves that manhood is most effective when it is most incongruously embodied, and leaves us wondering where we are.

The answer, perhaps, is at a crux of chastity.[60] To assure readers of Britomart's positive exemplarity, *The Faerie Queene* makes two points: she is a woman, and she is an allegorical figure of sexual restraint. Here as elsewhere in the text, an excess of explanations fails to resolve itself into an answer. Neither a woman nor a knight should seduce virgins or kill heroes, and it should not be necessary to insist that Britomart does not (quite) do these things because she is both a woman and the Knight of Chastity, bound simultaneously by allegorical limitations, a chivalric code, and the fact that she doesn't have a penis. When Arthur rerescues Amoret, she fears him as she had feared Britomart, but the narrator has little patience for this:

Dressed to Kill

171

But cause of fear sure had she none at all
   Of him, who goodly learned had of yore
   The course of loose affection to forstall,
   And lawlesse lust to rule with reasons lore. (4.9.19.1–4)

This is a very different argument from that presented by Glauce, who attempts to defuse jealousy of Britomart. She tells Scudamour and Artegall,

   Ne thenceforth feare the thing that hethertoo
   Hath troubled both your mindes with idle thought,
   Fearing least she your loues away should woo,
Feared in vaine, sith meanes ye see there wants theretoo. (4.6.30.6–9)

Having constructed Britomart's masculinity, if not out of whole cloth at least out of borrowed armor, Glauce insists that there is nothing in it. But what is in it, of course, is Britomart's body, demonstrably unpredictable in its effects. For Arthur, "should not" produces "will not"; for Britomart, the top-heavy structure of good behavior rests on "can't." Where Arthur lacks the will, Britomart lacks the means, inspiring not a calmly authorized statement of chivalric and allegorical integrity, but a presumption of bodily insufficiency that threatens, under any sort of imaginative pressure, to empty itself out.

Britomart retains the agency of intention where Arthur does not, on the rather shaky premise that female sexual agency is perfectly safe. It is worth thinking here about Juan Luis Vives, who, in his discussion of embattled chastity, finds the intersection of women and chivalry particularly disastrous. He writes, "It can not lyghtly be a chaste mayd, that is occupied with thinkyng on armour, and turney, and mannes valiaunce. What places amonge these be for chastite unarmed and weake? A woman that useth those feates, drinketh poyson in her hart."[61] This may prove nothing in particular about Britomart's sex life, but it does remind us that she is always the subject of desire.[62] Appearing as a man among men or as a man with a woman or as a woman with a man or as a woman with whom other women go to bed, she governs both triangulation and its collapse; when three becomes two, Britomart gets what she wants. If anything, she has too many prizes: she must lose Amoret before she can find Artegall, and upon Artegall's departure she looks again for

Amoret. "Her second care, though in another kind;/For vertues onely sake, which doth beget/True loue and faithfull friendship, she by her did set" (4.6.46.7–9). It's a different kind of love, the narrator assures us; but in this endless game of acquisition and display, the precise point of difference may be more difficult to find than Amoret herself.

In the attempt to clarify relationships among kinds of desire, conditions of identity, means and ends, critical readings often turn to Britomart's defeat of Radigund. Here, according to various accounts, Britomart gets her man, justifies her allegorical existence, and destroys whatever is bad (conflicted, interesting) within herself.[63] Such quests for the moral of the story invoke templates ranging from allegory through psychomachia to feminist jeremiad, but even at the moment of triumph Britomart remains elusive, reflecting but not quite fulfilling critical desires. For, after all, we know that we are reasoning backward, that a moment of comic or even tragic conclusion does not uncomplicate the processes through which it has been achieved. There is nothing straightforward about either Britomart's story or our response. Is her frankly sexual motivation a good thing or a bad thing? Is her disguise an expedience or a transformation? Does she defeat male knights who have more experience and better training because she is pure of heart, has an enchanted spear, is a beautiful woman, or, as Glauce claims, is big and tall? Does she love Amoret more than she loves Artegall? Does she love Malecasta at all? Are we to understand her? Empathize with her? Emulate her? *Like* her?

These are unreasonable questions to pose to an allegorical or even a fictional character, but critical history proves that Britomart makes us ask. Susanne Wofford writes, "For Britomart, the illusion of innerness may partly be explained by the fact that the conceit of 'knight' is more clearly oxymoronic when applied to women."[64] Britomart's interest inheres in contradiction, and her quest concludes more persuasively in impossible triangles and implausible desires than in happy endings. She is not, or at least not obviously, a test case for polymorphous perversity, for her desires come with decorous explanations attached; but those desires are various, and the explanations make sense but do not cohere. She is a textbook example, but there are too many textbooks; she wants to be a good wife, but, when she achieves that position at the expense of men, what does it prove? *The Faerie Queene* makes a tautology of two contradictions: Female masculinity is governed and moralized by married chastity, and married chastity is enabled by female masculinity. But when chastity coincides with eroticism in the form of Britomart, a socially naturalized sexual hierarchy becomes difficult to imagine and impossible to prove. Whether she disrupts expectations or fulfills them, fits into conventions or transforms them, Britomart plays her role as an intersection of inventions that exposes their working parts.

CHAPTER FIVE

The Probable Impossible:
Inventing Lesbians in Arcadia

A fickle Woman *wanton growne,*
Preferres a Crowd, *before a* Crowne.

You have demolish'd the noble schooles of
Hors-manship (of which many were in this Citie),
hung up your Armes to rust, glued up those swords in
their scabberds that would shake all Christendome
with the brandish, and entertained into your mindes such
softnes, dulnesse and effeminate nicenesse, that it would
even make *Heraclitus* himselfe laugh against his nature
to see how pulingly you languish in this weake
entertained sinne of womanish softnesse.
— *Haec-Vir: Or The Womanish-Man*

Beware of all enterprises that require new clothes.
—Henry David Thoreau, *Walden*

STANDARD DEVIATIONS

In recent years, the terms "Amazon" and "lesbian" have been closely
linked. Publications from the 1970s include *Amazon Quarterly: A Lesbian-
Feminist Arts Journal; Amazon Expedition: A Lesbian Feminist Anthology; Amazon
Poetry: An Anthology of Lesbian Poetry;* and *The Lesbian Reader: An Amazon Quarterly Anthology,* published in 1975 by Amazon Press.[1] Despite counterexamples that include the overheterosexed film *Gold of the Amazon Women*
(1979), the connection remains firm in our cultural consciousness, as
Amazon All Stars: Thirteen Lesbian Plays, published in 1996, suggests.[2] Dispens-
ing with the need for subtitles, the word "Amazon" sometimes appears
as a statement of sexuality in itself; so both *The Amazon Trail* (Library
of Congress subject headings: "Lesbians—United States—Biography")
and the "Amazon" buttons worn at gay pride parades assume a self-
evident subject.[3] From the 1970s to the present, such references imply
an intuitive homology, between lesbian identity and the popular idea of
Amazons as large muscular women who live without men.

In previous chapters, I have argued that Amazon encounters in the
early modern period instead reflect a profoundly heterosexual preoccupation. The fascination with amazonian practices of childbearing and

childrearing, the narratives of random mating and tame husbands, the equation between the danger women pose on the battlefield and the danger they pose in bed, all define Amazons in relation to men. Men who talk about Amazons in early modern texts show more interest in consolidating their own erotic and reproductive practices than in speculating about what women do when they are alone. But there is also, in this period, a powerful and explicit amazonian discourse of desire between women. The catch is that one of the women is a man; in a recurring story, a hero disguises himself as an Amazon to get close to the lady he loves. Improbable as the approach might seem, it has evident appeal: transvestite amazonian disguise is central to Sir Philip Sidney's *Old* and *New Arcadias* and John Marston's *Antonio and Mellida*, appears in *Swetnam the Woman-Hater*, and defines the speaking subject of a poem by Thomas Carew. And for *Amadis de Gaule*, it seems to be a kind of repetition compulsion. In the index to his study of that romance, under the heading "Amazons," John J. O'Connor presents the subheading, "Knights in disguise as." [4]

If amazonian disguise helps the hero to attain his objective — and it does — it also veils heterosexuality with the appearance of an exclusively female bond, and that appearance, once constructed, is difficult to dispel. The Induction of Marston's *Antonio and Mellida* attests to the tenacity of assumed parts. Asked about his role, the protagonist replies, "Faith, I know not what: an Hermaphrodite; two parts in one: my true person being *Antonio*, son to the Duke of *Genoa*; though for the love of *Mellida*, *Piero's* daughter, I take this fained presence of an *Amazon*, calling myself *Florizell*, and I know not what. I a voice to play a lady! I shall nere doe it." [5] In response, a fellow character argues that the double role makes Antonio not a hermaphrodite, but an actor: "Not play two parts in one? away, away: 'tis common fashion. Nay if you cannot bear two subtle fronts under one hood, Ideot goe by, goe by; off this world's stage!" But as both Antonio's recourse to his "true person" and that recurring phrase "I know not what" suggest, this is a fear not of doubleness but of altered singularity.

> ANTONIO: I, but when use hath taught me action, to hit the right point of a Ladies part, I shall growe ignorant when I must turne young Prince againe, how but to trusse my hose.

FELICHE: Tush, never put them off: for women weare the breeches still. (7)

Antonio anticipates an irreversible transformation; Feliche assures him that the failure of sexual difference is a fact of life. As he shifts from "Amazon" to "woman" — "women wear the breeches still" — Feliche generalizes Antonio's predicament, reasoning from an idiosyncratic assumption of disguise to a statement about heterosociality. Playing Amazons, men make manliness a matter of playing as well; distinctions are fragile, even in love plots.

O'Connor writes, "Knights who disguise themselves as women invite embarrassment, and in *Amadis* they never escape it."[6] A transvestite hero might easily find himself scorned in battle, shunned by old allies, or courted by his prospective father-in-law. But perhaps the greatest embarrassment lies in the elimination of men from the field of desire; in amazonian disguise plots, female homoeroticism obscures heterosexual intent. Thomas Carew's poem, "A Lover, in the Disguise of an Amazon, is Dearly Beloved of his Mistress," summarizes a courtship that both rewards the male lover and leaves him out in the cold:

> Cease in cold jealous fears to pine,
> Sad wretch, whom Rivals undermine:
> For though I hold lock'd in mine arms
> My life's sole joy, a traitor's charms
> Prevail: whilst I may only blame
> My self, that mine own Rival am.[7]

The predicament of a man whose disguise has become his competition, of a lover who has what he was after but still cannot get what he wants, is deliberately contrived, and might tempt us only to admire the conceit. But I want to take seriously the rivalry that Carew's poem describes, pursuing the implications of a disguise plot that causally links female homoeroticism to heterosexuality even as it assumes conflict between them. If desire between women enables women to meet men, the relationship of means to end is more complicated than it might appear.

Carew's poem sets up three subject positions — a lover, a mistress, and an Amazon — in a relationship of triangulated rivalry. But this is not the familiar fantasy in which competition between two men results in one man's possession of a woman. In tranvestite amazonian disguise plots as in Britomart's flirtations with women, a surplus male does not vanish, leaving a man and a woman together; instead, the only male vanishes, leaving two women alone. As the logic of disguise locates gender and eroticism between women, acquisition of an object of desire takes place not as a purchase or a swap or an intersection of self-congratulatory narcissisms, but as a seduction that privileges female sexual agency. Even if we remain aware of the maleness of one of the women involved—itself a surprisingly difficult project—erotic exchange in this story is never a transaction between men. The story gestures instead toward a different fantasy, in which female homoeroticism prepares women for heterosexual consummation, and the disguise plot efficiently ensures that a man is already in place.[8] This reading, as it reclaims agency for male desire, draws attention to the ending and relies on its status as the last word. But amazonian transvestism is a complicated and potentially unruly instrument, and texts such as *Antonio and Mellida* and Carew's poem invite us to look at its erotic complexities, focusing attention not on heterosexual conclusions but on the subject of disguise.

The Countess of Pembroke's Arcadia presents a particularly elaborate version of this effect, and a correspondingly stubborn fascination with female homoerotic desire. Having fallen in love with a picture of the Princess Philoclea, Prince Pyrocles reinvents himself in her image, arguing that love "doth transform the very essence of the lover into the thing loved."[9] Desire, for Pyrocles, not only transforms its subject but closes the gap between subjectivity and objectification; as Clare Kinney writes, "Pyrocles perpetually reinvokes the prototype for both himself as desiring subject *and* Philoclea as object of desire, aggravating his Narcissistic confusion of the categories of desiring subject and desired object."[10] Musidorus finds something troubling in this equation between looking *at* and looking *like*, warning Pyrocles, "Sweet cousin, since you are framed of such a loving mettle, I pray you, take heed of looking yourself in a glass lest Narcissus's fortune fall unto you" (25). Defined indistinguishably as a lover and a narcissist, Pyrocles takes more than ordinary risks, submerging himself in a subordinate mimesis: "As for my name, it shall be Cleophila, turning Philoclea to myself, as my mind is wholly turned and transformed into her" (17). Desire is a claustrophobic tautology, in which Philoclea's image produces Cleophila's copy and Pyrocles disappears.

I have chosen to focus on the first version of *The Arcadia* rather than on the second to pursue the questions of where and how an amazonian disguise plot might end. In his unfinished revision, Sidney thickens the plot: Pyrocles names himself not Cleophila but Zelmane, taking the name of a woman who has disguised herself as a man named Daiphantus in order to pursue him and who, dying for love of him, causes him to take the name of Daiphantus as another disguise. The relationship among Zelmane the original (who was briefly Daiphantus), Zelmane the Amazon (who is Pyrocles and also Daiphantus), and Philoclea takes another turn when a portrait of the first Zelmane is described: "[She] at the first sight seemed to have some resembling of Philoclea; but with more marking (comparing it to the present Philoclea, who indeed had no paragon but her sister) they might see it was but such a likeness as an unperfect glass doth give, answerable enough in some features and colours, but erring in others." [11] Zelmane is a poor mirror of Philoclea, for whose sake Pyrocles becomes Zelmane, who seduces Philoclea by constructing herself as a mirror image. As it complicates the pattern of reflection, the revised *Arcadia* emphasizes sexual difference in various ways: through the invention of an "original" Zelmane; through greater attention to Musidorus and Pamela; through a proliferation of heroic male characters; through an increased emphasis on Pyrocles' own heroic past. These devices reflect without relieving uneasiness about narcissistic eroticism, multiplying distractions only to leave us, still, with a man who loses himself in a mirror. Some readers have argued that the revised *Arcadia* presents a more substantial—heroic, masculine, effective—Prince Pyrocles, but such a figure, if he exists at all, can appear only in the subjunctive and in the past tense; in the text's present moment, heroic masculinity is an effect of amazonian disguise. [12]

Concluding in midsentence, in midbattle, and on the note of a contested pronoun, the revised *Arcadia* suggests that the plot has become intractable, its teleology hard to imagine, as Margaret Sullivan writes, "Sidney seems to have revised himself into a corner." [13] The first *Arcadia*, by contrast, works its way to an ending that identifies it as a comedy, in which a series of misunderstandings and artificial obstacles resolve themselves neatly into heterosexual pairs. Amazonian disguise catalyzes intersections of male and female homoerotic desire and of accurately and mistakenly conceived heteroerotic pursuit: Musidorus would want Cleophila if he believed she was a woman; Philoclea wants Cleophila despite believing she is a woman; the duke Basilius wants Cleophila because he believes she is a woman; the duke's wife Gynecia wants Cleophila because she hopes she isn't a woman at all. As foreplay for comic conclusions, such confusion assumes a return, a moment at which the rhetorical gesture toward the real regains its determinate force. In giving us that moment, the first *Arcadia* demonstrates its inadequacy; the return of Pyrocles as Pyrocles is less an exposure of what is true than an exposé of the need to know. The great revelation of *The Arcadia* is that the male body we have at the story's end is the same one we have had from the beginning, mystified, contested, subject to revision. In turning to that body for narrative resolution, we find ourselves looking in the wrong place.

The Arcadia emphasizes this through the example of Gynecia, Philoclea's mother, who desires Cleophila because she presumes "Cleophila" to be a false front. "For so the truth is that, at the first sight she had of Cleophila, her heart gave her she was a man thus for some strange cause disguised" (43). This direct approach to consummation—Cleophila is a man, Gynecia is a woman who knows that—produces nothing at all; Gynecia's recognition of Pyrocles proves only the limited relevance of empirical facts. The language of revelation is repeatedly displaced by that of theatrical performance: "The part she played did work in both a full and lively persuasion," the narrator says of Cleophila (183), and Gynecia's inside information dispels neither the effect of disguise nor the pronouns that make it impenetrable. "I will not be the only actor of this tragedy," she tells Cleophila (162); when the masquerade continues, she assures herself, "this was but a prologue to the play she had promised her" (189). In pursuing the figure of the stage, *The Arcadia* does not distinguish between knowledge and ignorance, or among teleological and misconceived desires. "Fortune had framed a very stage-play of love among these few folk, making the old age of Basilius, the virtue of Gynecia, and the simplicity of Philoclea, all affected to one; but by a three-headed kind of passion" (49). Taking up the erotic implications of the boy actor's body in disguise, Peter Stallybrass argues that even moments of revelation may illuminate not what we are looking at, but what we are looking for: "The interplay between clothing and undressing on the Renaissance stage organized gender around a process of fetishizing, which is conceived *both* as a process of fixation *and* as indeterminable," he writes. "If the Renaissance stage demands that we '*see*' particular body parts (the breast, the penis, the naked body), it also reveals that such fixations are inevitably unstable. The actor is both boy and woman, and he/she embodies the fact that sexual fixations are not the product of any categorical fixity of gender." [14] Like the actor onstage, Pyrocles-as-Cleophila both lacks and exceeds the parts he and/or she might be imagined to possess, displaying and inhabiting a body that at once focuses desire and proves nothing about the conditions of its fulfillment. The male body that Gynecia wants may exist—indeed, it is crucial to *The Arcadia*'s erotic profusions that it does exist—but recognition of its presence neither explains nor disperses the compulsions engendered by disguise.

Heterosexuality as a fact about bodies does not generate persuasive heteroeroticism. Instead, it clarifies the extent to which desire is generated and sustained between women; whatever the sexual relations of bodies, eroticism is a contract among roles. Nor does disclaiming the disguise plot invalidate the identity that it has put into play, for, as Pyrocles discovers, it is easier to invent an Amazon than to make one disappear. Through consideration of the first *Arcadia*, and particularly of its attempts to arrive at a conclusion, I want to stress that we do not have to abandon desire between women as a temporary fiction simply because the ending tells us to. Indeed, it is far from clear that the ending *does* tell us to. The fact that Cleophila is "really" Pyrocles seems not to work as an answer, or perhaps to answer the wrong question; it may be true, but it does not impose resolution. If an amazonian invention enables a happy ending, it also constitutes an identity that, in its explicit and efficient artifice, alters the privileged originality of the body beneath the disguise.

DRESSING THE PART

In *Vested Interests*, Marjorie Garber describes the transvestite as a figure of "category crisis," writing, "The cultural effect of transvestism is to destabilize all such boundaries: not only 'male' and 'female,' but also 'gay' and 'straight,' and 'sex' and 'gender.' This is the sense—the radical sense — in which transvestism is a 'third.' " [15] In making heterosexuality the consequence of desire between women, *The Arcadia* constructs an erotic continuity that fails to draw lines between kinds; the hetero-eroticism of Pyrocles' initial desire intersects Philoclea's homoerotic response to produce a sexual contract. Under such pressures, the logic of sex as identity is emptied out; bodies matter, but they do not signify in the sorting out of categories. Female masculinity and male femininity demonstrate the pleasures and dangers of performative play, but even this sense of paradoxical reference loses force in *The Arcadia* as the naturalized conditions of "female" and "male" recede from the processes of definition. Detached from assumptions, even radically wrong assumptions, about bodies, subjectivity emerges as a collision of performative conventions, which do not prescribe identity but accumulate to it. *The Arcadia* makes Pyrocles an Amazon so that he can act like a man, and uses his male body to substantiate his claim to be a woman; in the production of a transvestite femme virago, femininity and masculinity are at once mutually productive and utterly confused. That confusion produces both identity and agency: as a sustained illusion of feminine masculinity, Cleophila is the text's best articulated subject.

Early modern heroes disguise themselves as Amazons, rather than simply as women, to sustain a claim, however odd and tenuous, to a state of masculinity. But when Pyrocles tells Musidorus, "I am resolved, because all direct ways are barred me of opening my suit to the duke, to take upon me the estate of an Amazon lady," Musidorus, like Marston's Antonio, reasons not from "manliness" to "man" but from "Amazon" to "woman" (16). He responds with textbook misogyny. "And this effeminate love of a woman doth so womanize a man that, if you yield to it, it will not only make you a famous Amazon, but a launder, a distaff-spinner, or whatsoever other vile occupation their idle heads can imagine and their weak hands perform" (18). As loving a woman and looking like one become indistinguishable, Pyrocles is excluded from the rhetorical positions inhabited by men. The familiar argument about the emasculating effects of heterosexual desire takes on new force as Musidorus imagines a permanent transformation: "You must resolve, if you will play your part to any purpose, whatsoever peevish imperfections are in that sex, to soften your heart to receive them" (18).[16] Pyrocles opens himself to a transformation that works from the inside out.

[His hair] was drawn into a coronet of gold, richly set with pearls, and so joined all over with gold wires, and covered with feathers of divers colours, that it was not unlike to a helmet, such a glittering show it bare, and so bravely it was held up from the head. Upon his body he ware a kind of doublet of sky-colour satin so plated over with plates of massy gold that he seemed armed in it; his sleeves of the same, instead of plates, was covered with purled lace. And such was the nether part of his garment; but that made so full of stuff, and cut after such a fashion that, though the length fell under his ankles, yet in his going one might well perceive the small of the leg which, with the foot, was covered with a little short pair of crimson velvet buskins, in some places open (as the ancient manner was) to show the fairness of the skin . . . Upon his thigh he ware a sword (such as we now call scimitars), the pommel whereof was so richly set with precious stones as they were sufficient testimony it could be no mean personage that bare it. Such was this Amazon's attire; and thus did Pyrocles become Cleophila. (25)

From golden hair to little crimson buskins, this is an extraordinary fashion statement. Reading the disguise plot in theatrical terms, Lisa Jardine writes of this first entrance, "The passage compounds the 'stage transvestism' polemic theme yet further, because the 'woman' Pyrocles disguises himself as is herself in *male* dress (the dress of the female warrior) . . . Cleophila wears 'wanton' warrior's dress, whilst Pyrocles impudently shows the 'smalle of his Legg', and the 'fayrenes of his skynn' through his short boots, as provocative boy/girl." [17] Pyrocles reveals as much as he disguises, and, if this is his idea of what an Amazon looks like, we might better understand his cousin's concern.

As he turns his male body to the performance of femininity, Pyrocles flirts with more than Philoclea. Thomas Laqueur has explored the ways in which the Galenic idea of a sexual continuum, which posits difference as a matter of degree rather than of opposition, implies that distinctions between men and women can fail.[18] But sexual hierarchy insists that they fail in only one direction: women may become men, but the reverse violates common sense. Ambroise Paré, in *On Monsters and Marvels*, summarizes this point of view: "We therefore never find in any true story that any man ever became a woman, because Nature tends always toward what is most perfect and not, on the contrary, to perform in such a way that what is perfect should become imperfect." [19] *The Arcadia*, aggressively not a true story, threatens just such an unnatural performance, for there is something disconcertingly final in that sentence "and thus did Pyrocles become Cleophila." Assuring Musidorus that his disguise will work, Pyrocles asserts that his own body makes it persuasive. "I have already provided all furniture necessary for it; and my face, you see, will not easily discover me" (16). Stephen Orgel writes of "the conviction that men can turn into—or be turned into—women; or perhaps more exactly, can be turned *back* into women, losing the strength that enabled the male potential to be realized in the first place." [20] If clothes deliberately unmake the man in *The Arcadia*, that effect reiterates a larger cultural conviction that such slippage can always and easily occur. The femininity of transvestite disguise is at once a costume and a preexisting condition, and, as long hair, fair skin, a beardless face, and a shapely leg conspire to construct the ideal woman, it becomes clear that Pyrocles is transformed not only by the part he plays but by the parts he already has.

Disguise not only creates the appearance of lesbian desire, but asserts that that appearance is at least skin deep. This transformative thoroughness changes language as well; having named Pyrocles "Cleophila," the narrator says, "[This] name for a time hereafter I will use, for I myself feel such compassion of his passion that I find even part of his fear lest his name should be uttered before fit time were for it" (25). Cleophila appears always as "she," an effect ascribed to Pyrocles' own intent: "You remember I use the she-title to Pyrocles, since so he would have it" (34). In her analysis of the bodily and rhetorical effects of transsexual surgery, Garber asks, "Is it the change of pronoun, finally, as much as surgical intervention, that makes so profound a difference?" [21] For Pyrocles, who has his pronouns altered on page 25, the narrator's "she" is a speech act; when all we have is narrative, a shift in gendered reference not only describes a sex change but is one. At the final trial scene, Pyrocles' accuser says that he "from a man grew a woman, from a woman a ravisher of women" (334), leaving it unclear whether that shift, from "a woman" to "a ravisher of women," confers a return to naturalized maleness or merely describes the multiplication of sexual monstrosities into which maleness has disappeared.

The Probable Impossible

Pyrocles, as Cleophila, conflates the conditions of being, having, and seeming like her object of desire. In her multiplied relations to possession and lack, subjectivity and objectification, she becomes irresistible: "[Philoclea] found a burning affection towards Cleophila; an unquiet desire to be with her; and yet she found that the very presence kindled the desire. And examining in herself the same desire, yet could she not know to what the desire inclined. Sometimes she would compare the love she bare to Cleophila with the natural goodwill she bare to her sister; but she perceived it had another kind of working. Sometimes she would wish Cleophila had been a man, and her brother; and yet, in truth, it was no brotherly love she desired of her" (85–86). Like Britomart confronted by Artegall's mirror image, Philoclea has practical concerns. Her desire perplexes her, but the fact that its object is a woman is a problem only in the sense that she cannot imagine what two women might do. Her wish that Cleophila could be made into a man seems to anticipate the plot, reassuring the reader even if Philoclea herself cannot yet be reassured; but she articulates that wish in problematic terms, imagining it as transformation rather than revelation and essentializing Cleophila's female homoerotic intent. " 'For,' said she, 'if she were a man I might either obtain my desire, or have cause to hate for refusal' —besides the many duties Cleophila did to her assured her Cleophila might well want power, but not will, to please her" (98). Sex is a wish fulfillment, and, basing her fantasy on a structure of desire already in place, Philoclea does not want Pyrocles; she wants Cleophila with added parts, which is not the same thing at all.

Richard A. Levin argues that we should take female homoeroticism seriously as an imaginative possibility: "Until that time—until Pyrocles discloses his male identity and the couple reforms as a heterosexual one—we are prompted to think of the relationship as involving two women." [22] The Arcadia sustains an extended flirtation with what we would term lesbian desire, presuming that that desire has both credibility and force; Pyrocles imagines his disguise not merely as a way to get close to Philoclea, but as a mode of seduction in itself. "If my beauty be anything, then will it help me to some part of my desires; otherwise I am no more to set by it than the orator by his eloquence that persuades nobody" (25). For Philoclea and Cleophila, the relation of likeness makes desire a natural consequence of mutual recognition. Orgel writes, "The nature of love is to strive to be like the beloved; women are therefore best wooed by imitation. It is, indeed, precisely Pyrocles' ability to perform as a woman that persuades Philocleia to love him." [23] The courtship narrative is not simply an exercise in empathy, or a statement that Pyrocles is in touch with his feminine side. When "Cleophila straitly embracing [Philoclea], and (warranted by a womanly habit) often kissing her, desired her to stay her sweet speech," it is on that "womanly habit" that seduction depends (104).

Pyrocles sustains his disguise for only a hundred pages. But when he claims to be a man, Philoclea sees not resolution but doubleness: "Alas, how painful a thing it is to a divided mind to make a well joined answer; how hard it is to bring inward shame to outward confession; and how foolish, trow you, must that answer be which is made one knows not to whom! Shall I say, 'O Cleophila'? Alas, your words be against it! Shall I say, 'prince Pyrocles'? Wretch that I am, your show is manifest against it. But this, this, I well may say: if I had continued as I ought Philoclea, you had either never been or ever been Cleophila" (106). Emphasizing the gap between what she hears and what she sees, between words and things, Philoclea both understands her own desire as the cause of this disjoining and defines it as an enduring effect. "O Cleophila (for so I love to call thee, since in that name my love first began, and in the shade of that name my love shall best lie hidden), that even while so thou wert (what eye bewitched me I know not) my passions were far fitter to desire than to be desired" (107). The appearance of a man, which is not in fact appearance but a statement that contradicts appearance, enables Philoclea to confess her love for a woman: Pyrocles may be the story's material conclusion, but Cleophila is its condition of desire.

Nor has the story ended yet. Philoclea's response to the revelation scene is described in an ambiguous figure: "The joy which wrought into Pygmalion's mind while he found his beloved image wax little and little both softer and warmer in his folded arms, till at length it accomplished his gladness with a perfect woman's shape, still beautiful with the former perfections, was even such as, by each degree of Cleophila's words, stealingly entered into Philoclea's soul" (106). When Pyrocles declares himself a man, Philoclea takes on the role of a man constructing a woman. Invoking the precedent of the Pygmalion/Galatea myth, *The Arcadia* hints that at some level the end of the disguise plot changes nothing;

"a perfect woman's shape, still beautiful with the former perfections" is the most appropriate point of reference for the now-revealed Pyrocles.[24] In this analogy, Pyrocles-as-Galatea takes shape through a desire that is not his own, and the transformation that brings him to life makes him a woman. The narrative carries out this proposition, maintaining in the present tense the nostalgia that Philoclea expresses for the past; for a hundred pages after the revelation scene, Pyrocles continues to appear always as "Cleophila" and as "she." The prince's declaration does not undo the narrator's speech act, and if Philoclea is at least half willing to reread Cleophila as Pyrocles, *The Arcadia* is not. Why, then, is it so easy to make Pyrocles into Cleophila, and so difficult to reverse the procedure?

The answer might be that Cleophila provides a logical connection between performance and identity, a causality that works. Paul Salzman argues that Pyrocles' amazonian role transforms not only the prince but the genre: "The princes in the *Old Arcadia* are reduced through their disguises to actors (role-players) rather than heroes."[25] The disguise plot identifies theatricality as the condition of heroism, and feminine masculinity captures its audience while men are banished to the eclogues. Linking theatrically produced bodies to the idealized body of the Lacanian mirror stage, Gail Kern Paster writes, "The actor's body offers to the spectator the contrast between fictional outer and insufficient inner which a mirrored image offers the baby, a body of behavioral completeness, significance, and desirability."[26] Behaviorally complete and infinitely desirable, Cleophila signifies as Pyrocles does not, the assumed identity at once enacting and obscuring the things that the "real" body cannot do. Described by Philoclea as "invincible Amazon," Cleophila fulfills the promise of that name, killing lions, protecting ladies, fighting battles, and ending a civil war. And her audience naturalizes these actions within the context of other female heroic performances: "The duke told with what a gallant grace she ran after Philoclea with the lion's head in her hand, like another Pallas with the spoils of the Gorgon" (48).

Determined to read masculinity as male, Gynecia counters with a different reference: "She saw the very face of young Hercules killing the Nemean lion" (48). But for early modern texts, Hercules represents not absolute maleness but sexual confusion; so in the pamphlet *Haec-Vir* the Womanish-Man calls the Man-Woman "most couragious counterfet of *Hercules* and his Distaffe," gesturing toward the layered opacity of identity and disguise.[27] For Gynecia, the presumption of maleness can be articulated only through the possibility of feminization; for other characters, virility makes Cleophila persuasive as an Amazon.[28] Amazonian expectations interrupt the processes that reason from masculinity to men, and only a few pages after the revelation scene, in an encounter with unruly peasants, Pyrocles has disappeared again, leaving Cleophila free to act. "Cleophila, whose virtuous courage was ever awake in her, drawing out her sword, kept a while the villains at a bay while the ladies gat themselves into the lodge . . . No blow she strake that did not suffice for a full reward of him that received it" (109). In this disguise plot, a sword signifies both ways.

For early modern texts, Amazons often mark the failure of legible difference; as one author writes, "If they had no more evident distinction of sexe, then they have of shape, they would be all man, or rather all woman: for the *Amazons* beare away the Bell: as one wittily, *Hic mulier* will shortly bee good latine, if this transmigration hold: For whether on horsebacke, or on foote, there is no great difference: but not discernable out of a Coach." [29] Where categories are invisible, "not discernable," we are back in Knox's "whole world . . . transformed into Amazons." [30] Men disappear in that world, not because they are absent but because their presence fails to signify; Pyrocles has taken on an identity that subsumes his own. In response to Musidorus's misogynist reproach, he does not insist on his manhood but idealizes his disguise: "And, for example, even this estate of Amazons, which I now for my greatest honour do seek to counterfeit, doth well witness that, if generally the sweetness of their disposition did not make them see the vainness of these things which we account glorious, they neither want valour of mind, nor yet doth their fairness take away their force" (19). In this argument, men sustain their exclusive claim to masculinity only because women do not interfere; male self-satisfaction is a function of female self-restraint, and at the edges of that restraint there are Amazons.

Pyrocles follows a tradition of gynophilic defenses, arguing that conventions of gender rely on forbearance by women and misrepresentation by men. In a reading of the revised *Arcadia*, Sullivan traces the processes through which masculinity is invented and jealously guarded: "To judge by the activities Pyrocles-Zelmane performs for the princesses . . . a male-dominated society systematically denies martial training to women to create a physical weakness that lends credence to the metaphysics of gender difference."[31] Early modern texts go farther, holding narrative manipulation, more than nature or even nurture, responsible for the restricted arena of women's acts. Ariosto offers a concise comment on the representation of women:

> And though of late they seem not to come nigh,
> The praise their sexe in former times have gain'd,
> No doubt the fault is either in backbiters,
> Or want of skill and judgement in the writers.[32]

Femininity is a false product of bad storytelling, and, submerging his identity in an amazonian name, Pyrocles claims to recover the truth about women. When Gynecia accuses him of deception, he says, "I am not acquainted with these words of disguising; neither is it the profession of an Amazon" (84). The argument—he is not disguised as an Amazon because Amazons do not assume disguise—hopelessly complicates the relationship between original and imitation, characterizing both men and women as narrative effects.

In response to such mystifications, Musidorus describes a loss of access to the real. "And is it possible that this is Pyrocles, the only young prince in the world, formed by nature and framed by education to the true exercise of virtue? Or is it, indeed, some Amazon Cleophila that hath counterfeited the face of my friend in this sort to vex me?" (17). Maleness is increasingly a fictional concept, a fantasy that recedes. Cleophila-as-counterfeit, like *Haec-Vir*'s "most couragious counterfet of *Hercules* and his distaff," has become opaque, merging feminine appearance and masculine performance into an identity impenetrable by a gaze that looks for Pyrocles. Explaining himself to Philoclea, Pyrocles presents a catalogue of loss: "Behold here before your eyes Pyrocles, prince of Macedon, whom you only have brought to this fall of fortune and unused metamorphosis; whom you only have made neglect his country, forget his father, and lastly forsake himself!" (105). Pyrocles' reclaimed identity is closely circumscribed, for he has left everything that identifies him as a man and as a specific man in the past, and his past exists only in the subjunctive and in the eclogues. At *The Arcadia*'s beginning the narrator says of the princes, "What befell unto them, what valiant acts they did, passing in one year's space through the lesser Asia, Syria, and Egypt, how many ladies they defended from wrongs, and disinherited persons restored to their rights, it is a work for a higher style than mine" (10). The heroism of Pyrocles as Pyrocles is at best a fragmented and allusive presence in *The Arcadia*, and Plangus, who looks for Pyrocles and Musidorus, finds only the traces of stories: "Yet he took upon him the quest of those two heroical princes who, in this mean time, had done such famous acts that all Asia was full of their histories. But he, having travelled a whole year after them, and still hearing their doings notably recounted, yet could never (being stayed by many misadventures) fully overtake them" (63).

The heroic history of Pyrocles cannot be attached to Pyrocles himself, and, when Gynecia forces him to a statement of maleness, it is another statement of loss. To her he offers the bald declaration for which the plot has been waiting: "The truth is I am a man" (179). But the explanation that follows detaches that statement from any claim to be masculine or heroic or Pyrocles. "The cause of this my changed attire was a journey two years ago I made among the Amazons, where having sought to try my unfortunate valour, I met not one in all the country but was too hard for me; till, in the end, in the presence of their queen Senicia, I (hoping to prevail against her) challenged an old woman of fourscore years to fight on horseback to the uttermost with me: who, having overthrown me, for saving of my life made me swear I should go like an unarmed Amazon till the coming of my beard did with the discharge of my oath deliver me of that bondage" (179). Pyrocles not only (presumably) invents his Amazon encounter, but claims to have lost his sword. As he disavows Cleophila, giving up her equipment and her acts, he plays another amazonian role, that of the male victim who is disarmed and disgraced. Maleness does not substantiate heroism, but displaces it; the loss of amazonian identity is a loss of masculinity as well.

END GAMES

Every time Pyrocles claims to be a man he loses something. The pattern reaches its climax in his seduction of Philoclea, which, rather than reconnecting gender to sex, precipitates the loss of masculine signifiers and the further mystification of the male body. "Neither doubt you, because I wear a woman's apparel, I will be the more womanish; since, I assure you, for all my apparel, there is nothing I desire more than fully to prove

The Probable Impossible

myself a man in this enterprise," he tells Musidorus when he assumes his disguise (21). That proof seems endlessly deferred; for a hundred pages after he declares himself to Philoclea, *The Arcadia* deploys female pronouns, importunate parents, unruly peasants, and a great deal of occasional poetry to hold the conditions of speaking as and acting like man apart. Kinney writes, "In the narrative present of Arcadia, immediate — and in particular *erotic*—action is repeatedly deferred as Sidney's lords and ladies demand (and supply) additional narrative performances."[33] When Pyrocles' seduction of Philoclea finally takes place, we do not see it; instead, the text presents an intensely conventional love poem that Pyrocles once heard from a friend. Rather than reading about the triumph of manhood, we contemplate a blazon that not only displaces sexual consummation with erotic potential, but closely recalls the terms in which Cleophila first appeared. If this device decorously screens Philoclea's body, it does the same to that of Pyrocles, leaving us where we began: with an idealized feminine body that obscures the fact that we are looking at a man.

Displacing the apparent source of masculinity — that Cleophila is an Amazon — with the actual source — that Pyrocles is a man — imposes its own anxiety, for if shifting from Cleophila to Pyrocles enables a climb up the sexual ladder, it risks leaving something behind. Discovering Pyrocles in Philoclea's bed, the servant Dametas has an extraordinarily symptomatic response: "Not thinking it good to awake the sleeping lion, he went down again, taking with him Pyrocles' sword (wherewith upon his shirt Pyrocles came only apparelled thither), being sure to leave no weapon in the chamber" (237). The causal progression from body to act, from disguise to identity, from desire to fulfillment, collapses into another narrative of loss; consummated heterosexuality leaves Pyrocles utterly disarmed. "The first ill handsel [Pyrocles] had of the ill case wherein he was was the seeing himself deprived of his sword, from which he had never separated himself in any occasion, and even that night, first by the duke's bed, and then there, had laid it as he thought safe, putting great part of the trust of his well doing in his own courage, so armed. For, indeed, the confidence in oneself is the chief nurse of true magnanimity; which confidence notwithstanding doth not leave the care of necessary furnitures for it" (251). Only when exposed as a man does Pyrocles fulfill Musidorus's fear that he may lose the signs of masculinity. Where a visibly feminine body had sufficiently explained masculine acts, a demonstrably male one is vulnerable to dispossession. If, as I argued in the previous chapter, swords are fetishes for male heroes, enabling a referential and therefore protective relationship between heroism and sexuality, weapons and male genitals, Pyrocles' losses in the first category radically undermine him in the second. The dislocation of a metaphoric relation among objects deprives the body of its power to signify, and Dametas leaves no weapon in the chamber.

Pyrocles seduces Philoclea through the medium of Cleophila, and the disappearance of that third term appears as loss. As a lover and a hero, Pyrocles loses place to his own amazonian performance; his sexual conquest only fulfills expectations that precede his reincorporation as a man. The introduction of his male body does not disallow the narrative of female homoerotic desire, but completes it, answering the question of what women do in bed. This may not sound new; it may indeed sound reactionary, like contemporary pornography that depicts lesbianism as two women waiting for real sex. But in transvestite amazonian disguise plots, desire does not tend toward heterosexuality in any direct or uncomplicated way, and there is no moment that consolidates identity and performance to a single-minded end. Instead, *The Arcadia* repeatedly separates embodied maleness from apparent masculinity as it turns each to the ends of sexual consummation. Through that consummation Philoclea gets what she wants, but exposure leaves Pyrocles in an inconclusive state. When Philoclea is ready for Cleophila to be Pyrocles, the narrative is not, refusing him his pronouns; and when the narrator informs us, in a transformation that takes place within parentheses, that Pyrocles "had at that present no more to play the part of Cleophila," Philoclea calls him "Cleophila or Pyrocles" and, still more suggestively, "false mankind" (200, 204, 205).

Cleophila works as a supplement. The disguise plot at once enables Pyrocles and, both linguistically and somatically, threatens to replace him; the conceit of amazonian transvestism is a seductive success, but generates a rhetoric of female homoeroticism that obscures the presence of men. Jacques Derrida writes, "The supplement adds itself, it is a surplus, a plenitude enriching another plenitude, the *fullest measure* of presence. It cumulates and accumulates presence . . . But the supplement supplements. It adds only to replace. It intervenes or insinuates itself *in-*

the-place-of; if it fills, it is as if one fills a void. If it represents and makes an image, it is by the anterior default of a presence." [34] The intervention of the supplement exposes as it compensates for lack, and this is the effect on heroes of amazonian disguise; when Musidorus, in the revised *Arcadia,* searches for Pyrocles without knowing that he has become Zelmane, his experience has a poststructuralist edge. "There indeed he found his fame flourishing, his monuments engraved in marble, and yet more durably in men's memories; but the universal lamenting his absented presence assured him of his present absence" (129). That chiasmus of absent presence and present absence structures the progress of heterosexual desire; in the courtship of Philoclea, Cleophila both enables and undercuts the fact of Pyrocles. Here as in Shakespearean comedy, the vicissitudes of disguise tempt us to be invested in the surface at the expense of the body beneath. But where Shakespearean transvestite plots are in a sense conventional in their triangulations, generating women out of the encounters between men, *The Arcadia*'s narrative represents consummated heterosexuality as an effect of female homoerotic desire.

Philoclea cannot imagine that such desire might have consequences. "But sweet Philoclea grew shortly after of all other into worst terms; for taking [Cleophila] to be such as she professed, desire she did, but she knew not what; and she longed to obtain that whereof she could not imagine the mean, but full of unquiet imaginations rested only unhappy because she knew not her good hap" (49). Reference to Philoclea's "good hap" reassures us that the dilemma is artificial and that we know how it ends, but resolution is not exempt from the condition of artifice. Insisting that the ending will provide the means opens up the question of whether sexual consummation, as material proof, proves anything at all. Desire is by nature perverse in *The Arcadia,* and if the statement "I am Pyrocles" has the effect, however delayed, of an answer, it is not the only one available; consummation does not automatically return the story to normative sex. Levin argues that Philoclea's naïveté is framed by a more knowing narrative voice: "Implied is that there is a 'how' and that the narrator knows to keep secret about it. A forbidden form of lovemaking would fulfill Philoclea's passion." [35] And Philoclea herself says more than she knows, demanding of Pyrocles, "What aileth this new conversion? Have you yet another sleight to play; or do you think to deceive me in Pyrocles' form, as you have done in Cleophila's? Or rather, now you have betrayed me in both those, is there some third sex left you into which you can transform yourself?" (205–6).

The possibility of a third sex preoccupies *The Arcadia* as it does early modern texts more generally. Valerie Traub has argued that tribades, as women whose bodies approximate possession of a penis, realize the supplementary effect that Derrida describes: "Early modern women's prosthetic supplementation of their bodies is, I would argue, both additive and substitutive: as a material addition to the woman's body and as a replacement of the man's body *by* the woman's, it not only displaces male prerogatives, but exposes 'man' as a simulacrum, and gender as a construction built on the faulty ground of exclusive, binary difference."[36] The anxiety surrounding this kind of exposure, in which something constructed rather than absolute emerges as the condition of sexual identity, runs throughout *The Arcadia*, articulated through a figure of ostensibly normative maleness. Pyrocles gains access to masculinity by becoming an Amazon, and this indirection defines his sexuality as well; seeing him in bed with Philoclea, Dametas "did not only perceive it was Cleophila (and therefore much different from the lady he sought), but that this same Cleophila did more differ from the Cleophila he and others had ever taken her for" (237). Naked and entangled in a sexual embrace, Pyrocles is still not Pyrocles; his exposure proves not that Pyrocles differs from Cleophila, but that Cleophila differs from herself. The ability to perform a sexual act seems curiously illegible as proof of sex itself; there is a gap in the reasoning that leads from "Cleophila has a penis" to "Cleophila is a man." And if that gap can be hurdled—if Pyrocles abandons Cleophila and stands trial as himself—its presence tells us something about the text's imaginative space. Philoclea may not be able to picture sexual acts between women, but *The Arcadia*, at the moment of Dametas's discovery, can describe nothing else. In a world that routinely explains unnatural desire in terms of bodily monstrosities, bodily supplements, and erotic intentionalities that transform the body, why, when Pyrocles reveals himself, don't we simply admire the tribade?

The statement that Cleophila is Pyrocles locates female homoeroticism and heterosexuality in a causal continuity that precludes distinction. And if this structure does not actually replace Pyrocles-the-boy with Cleophila-the-tribade, it does produce a version of maleness that cannot mean all that it is presumed to mean. In "The Rediscovery of the

Clitoris," Katharine Park writes, "Sex between women, removed from a heteronormalizing context, became significant as a social as well as a sexual threat; it imperiled not only marriage and reproduction, but also the 'natural' position of men as heads of household." [37] In Park's reading as in Traub's, the possibility that women might have sex that can be recognized *as* sex challenges the positions and assumptions of male privilege. Pyrocles' disguise plot incorporates such a challenge even as it claims to be a remedy: his story offers us two facts, that Cleophila seduces Philoclea and that Cleophila is a man, and the second accounts only incompletely for the first. Pyrocles tells Philoclea, "All, both men and women, owe this homage to the perfection of your beauty," and neither we nor they ever entirely escape that "both" (34–35). In formulating a sexuality that must be heterosexuality for the purposes of plot but is still rhetorically legible as the consequence of desire between women, *The Arcadia* opens up a condition of doubleness that it fails — or, more accurately, refuses — to close down. Female homoeroticism might be a plot device that enables heterosexual conclusions; just as plausibly, heterosexuality might be a sex toy for women.

Confronted with "a right Pyrocles countenance in a Cleophila face," Dametas addresses this vision as "thou woman or boy, or both, or whatsoever thou be" (29). The narrator refers to the reunion of Musidorus with "his dear he-she friend Cleophila" and, at the trial scene, describes "Pyrocles of a pure complexion, and of such a cheerful favour as might seem either a woman's face on a boy or an excellent boy's face in a woman" (326). During the trial itself, Philanax, Pyrocles' accuser, returns again and again to these images of simultaneity, blaming the disruption of Arcadia not on the emergence of Pyrocles but on his failure to banish the specter of Cleophila.[38] Philanax claims that "by an effeminate man we should suffer a greater overthrow than our mightiest enemies have been ever able to lay upon us" and calls Pyrocles "shameful and shameless creature, fit indeed to be the dishonour of both sexes," "mankind courtesan," "whorish beauty," "a player in disguising, a tiger in cruelty, a dragon in ungratefulness" (336, 337, 338). He says of the impersonation, "Any shape or title he can take upon him that hath no restraint of shame," and asks, "What can all the earth answer for his coming hither? Why alone, if he be a prince? How so richly jewelled, if he be not a prince? Why then a woman, if now a man? Why now Timopyrus, if then

Tough Love
196

Cleophila? Was all this play for nothing?" (334, 336). The answer is not nothing, but treason; Philanax holds Pyrocles-as-Cleophila responsible for the duke's death. This is category crisis with a vengeance, not only challenging or displacing sovereign male authority but killing it off altogether.[39] Unimpressed by the essential manliness of a specific sexual act, Philanax puts the multiplicity of performances on trial, reasoning from indeterminacy to the dissolution of patriarchal effect. Pyrocles resumes his former identity only to find that its meaning has changed, leaving him in the position not of Prince Charming but of saboteur; the trial sets out to distinguish debauchers from lovers, traitors from heroes, women from men, and ends in an accumulation of terms. In a proceeding designed to redress the seduction of Philoclea, the insistence on sexual definition does not reduce two to one, but reflects the image of a third.

Analyzing the idea of thirdness as "that which questions binary thinking and introduces crisis," Garber writes, "What is crucial here—and I can hardly underscore this strongly enough—is that the 'third term' is *not* a *term*. Much less is it a *sex*, certainly not an instantiated 'blurred' sex as signified by a term like 'androgyne' or 'hermaphrodite,' although these words have culturally specific significance at certain historical moments. The 'third' is a mode of articulation, a way of describing a space of possibility. Three puts in question the idea of one: of identity, self-sufficiency, self-knowledge."[40] In this sense Philoclea's suspicion of a "third sex" does not anticipate bodily transformation, but responds to a representational swerve. *The Arcadia* follows the intersections of desire, attaching identities to modes that work rather than to statements that are true. Sexual indeterminacy, which begins by complicating the relationship of bodies to acts and exploiting the pleasures of incongruity, ends by privileging the surface: getting what you want gives way to wanting what you see. Like the pamphlet *Hic Mulier*, the subtitle of which shifts its focus from "the man-woman" to "the masculine-feminine," the travels of Pyrocles begin with a sex plot and conclude in a state in which bodily acts illuminate the paradox through which they occur. Sex and gender, like Pyrocles and Cleophila, start out as self-evident distinctions and end up in a supplementary relationship through which the second invalidates the arguments of the first. Bodies work as instruments, but they neither return us to the real nor refer us to the symbolic.

To identify himself as a man, Pyrocles offers Philoclea not weapons or genitals or a chronicle of past heroisms, but letters from his father. "For a conclusion of proof [he] showed her letters from his father, king Euarchus, unto him; which hand she happily knew, as having kept divers which passed betwixt her father and him" (107). Pyrocles, as distinct from Cleophila, exists as a condition of his father's writing. Describing the "paternal function" that authorizes subjectivity, Lacan writes, "It is in the *name of the father* that we must recognize the support of the symbolic function which, from the dawn of history, has identified his person with the figure of the law." [41] Pyrocles' flirtation with the symbolic attempts to claim such a connection to agency and to knowledge, but he cannot be precipitated into discrete and articulate identity by the distinction between other and self implicit in alliance with the father's name. For him, as for Lacanian subjects, patriarchal authority is a mirror-game of illusions, but in *The Arcadia* the counterfantasy of paternal violence comes true. The law Pyrocles invokes excludes and turns against him: at the moment when he publicly stands trial as a man, his father, speaking for the state, orders him killed.

This is the double move of *The Arcadia*. Imagining a man disguised as a manly woman who looks like a woman and acts like a man, the text situates the male body in a parodic rather than a natural relationship to masculinity. Judith Butler discusses the parodic effects of drag: "Although the gender meanings taken up in these parodic styles are clearly part of hegemonic, misogynist culture, they are nevertheless denaturalized and mobilized through their parodic recontextualization. As imitations which effectively displace the meaning of the original, they imitate the myth of originality itself." [42] For *The Arcadia* the myth of originality is not Amazon myth, but Prince Pyrocles. If such figures as tribades and hermaphrodites incorporate parody, constructing an alternative causality between sexed bodies and sexual acts, transvestite amazonian disguise plots go farther. At the end of these plots the revelation of a male body lacks transformative power, its singularity an incongruous epilogue to the multiplicity of performative effects. Pyrocles' impersonation provokes misogynist response and is governed by feminine clichés; at the same time, it presents masculinity as a natural female state. Claims about the origins of this polymorphous identity lose force as its effects proliferate, and there is more to be lost here than the true sex of a prince. In

The Arcadia as in *Gender Trouble*, parodic performance undermines normative heterosexuality: if the comic conclusion brings together real women and real men, it does so through an awkward calling out of dramatis personae and an aggressive claiming of parts.

Levin reads the relationship between Philoclea and her apparent Amazon as a prototype of femme/butch role playing.[43] I have suggested instead that Cleophila appears in both conventionally masculine and conventionally feminine terms, her impersonation collapsing heterosocial oppositions. But *The Arcadia* does present a game of butch and femme, aggressively contrived and explicitly artificial in its conventions. It begins with the final appearance of Pyrocles:

> Pyrocles came out, led by Sympathus, clothed after the Greek manner in a long coat of white velvet reaching to the small of his leg, with great buttons of diamonds all along upon it. His neck, without any collar, not so much as hidden with a ruff, did pass the whiteness of his garments . . . On his feet he had nothing but slippers which, after the ancient manner, were tied up by certain laces which were fastened under his knee, having wrapped about (with many pretty knots) his naked leg. His fair auburn hair (which he ware in great length, and gave at that time a delightful show with being stirred up and down with the breath of a gentle wind) had nothing upon it but a white ribbon, in those days used for a diadem, which rolled once or twice about the uppermost part of his forehead, fell down upon his back, closed up at each end with the richest pearl were to be seen in the world. (325–26)

Whatever allowances we make for the Greek manner or the Elizabethan world picture, Pyrocles in this scene looks decidedly femme. He also looks just like Cleophila, and if the speech act that makes him "she" succeeds in part by referring to a visibly feminine body, that which makes him "Pyrocles" might fail by the same test. As it reproduces Pyrocles to prove that gendered performances refer to appropriately sexed bodies, *The Arcadia* either asks a great deal of the reader's investment in essentialism or undertakes a prodigious feat of construction. Pyrocles must be returned at least to the fiction of exclusive masculinity, made a man manqué in order to validate heterosocial exchange. His story, like the dialogue of *Haec-Vir*, ends with a renaturalization that works too visibly and too hard: "We will heere change our attires, as wee have chang'd our mindes, and with our attires, our names . . . Henceforth we will live nobly like our selves, ever sober, ever discreet, ever worthy; true men, and true women. We will bee henceforth like well-coupled Doves, full of industry, full of love." [44] Sexual difference is the artificial product of the pursuit of happy endings; heterosociality requires a rigid and artifactual insistence on roles. In "Toward a Butch-Femme Aesthetic," Sue-Ellen Case describes "a strategy of appearances [that] replaces a claim to truth," and writes, "These roles are played in signs themselves and not in ontologies." [45] In *The Arcadia*, the final union of Pyrocles and Philoclea is a similarly self-conscious semiosis, but its terms rely on implausibly categorical statements rather than exploiting the pleasures of play.

At the story's end, the narrator concludes of Basilius, "Many garboils passed through his fancy before he could be persuaded Cleophila was other than a woman" (360). However easy it may be to identify Basilius as a bad reader, it is hard to prove him entirely wrong. *The Arcadia* sustains its investment in desire between women even when the amazonian hairstyles and little crimson buskins come off, and does so at the risk of redistributing and even reinterpreting the cultural value of maleness. In "The Perversion of 'Lesbian' Desire," Traub argues that, by the end of the seventeenth century, female homoeroticism began to be perceived as dangerous even when enacted between conventionally feminine subjects: "Increasingly constructed as immoral, irrational, and narcissistic, the femme began to accrue the transgressive qualities associated before with the tribade." [46] *The Arcadia* anticipates this effect: the conviction that desire between women is an erotic irrelevance and the fear that it is a sexual fall converge in the masculine femininity of disguise. In a thoroughly amazonian paradox, Pyrocles' impersonation more explicitly engages the implications of female homoeroticism than do stories in which all the women are women. Locating a male body at the intersection of masculine and feminine conventions, *The Arcadia* constructs a progress of desire that insists on happy endings even as it inspires the catalogue of condemnations — "immoral, irrational, and narcissistic" — that Traub describes.

The persistence of desire between women revises the meaning of men: male sexuality is the addition that both consummates eroticism and makes it potentially monstrous, the part that at once completes and explodes the logic of the whole. In the letter that prefaces *The Arcadia*, Sidney describes the process of creation as an unnatural birth: "In sum, a young head not so well stayed as I would it were (and shall be when God will) having many many fancies begotten in it, if it had not been in some way delivered, would have grown a monster, and more sorry might I be that they came in than that they gat out" (3). For Philoclea, at the climax of seduction, the monster is the un-cross-dressed Pyrocles; and if Philoclea quickly gets over it, the narrative does not. The erotic and political crises that fill the last book, from Basilius's apparent death and Gynecia's self-accusation to Pamela's claim to her father's throne, follow in one way or another from the lack of Cleophila's mediating effect. An amazonian transvestite disguise plot has focused the text's systems of desire, and its disappearance works less as triumphantly comic resolution than as a kind of emptying out.

The Arcadia ends as a melancholic response to loss. In the place of last words, the narrator writes of forthcoming marriages and children that they must "awake some other spirit to exercise his pen in that wherewith mine is already dulled" (361). Like the princes' heroic history, the happy ending is not work for this pen; narrative truncations reprise the violence of transformation and loss. The fact that this was always after all a story about heterosexuality precipitates both a failure of desire and a sense of transgression: with the final appearance of Pyrocles, the narrative has reached some uneasy compromise between coming full circle and drawing a straight line, and the first *Arcadia* is in this sense no more finished than its successor. We know a version of the story it tells—boy meets girl; boy loses girl; boy wins girl—but where along the way does boy become girl? There seem to be more comic gestures available for making that move than for taking it back; and it is somewhat funny, but perhaps only in the serious sense of that word, that the discovery that a princess is sleeping with a prince instead of with an Amazon makes everyone want to kill the prince.

CHAPTER SIX

Tragical Mirth: Framing
Shakespeare's Hippolyta

When Mars, *and* Pallas, *doe agree,*
Great workes, by them, effected bee.

Tell me, were not his spirit armour of proofe,
who durst encounter with so couragious an *Amazon?*
or enter nuptiall lists with such a feminine *Myrmidon?*
—Richard Brathwait, *The English Gentlewoman*

Man for the field, and woman for the hearth:
Man for the sword and for the needle she:
Man with the head and woman with the heart:
Man to command and woman to obey;
All else confusion.
—Alfred, Lord Tennyson, *The Princess*

In 1994, The Ridiculous Theatricals produced *A Midsummer Night's Dream*
at the Charles Ludlam Theater in New York. Known for contemporary gay comedy and subversive productions of the classics, the company
took on Shakespeare as an essay in dragon-slaying: The Bard, their pub-
licity suggested, had met his match. As indeed he had, but in a more
literal sense than the statement implies. *A Midsummer Night's Dream* on
the Ridiculous Theatricals' stage looked very much like itself: aggressively performative, sexually twisted, and hard to cast. The production
made a virtue of that last necessity, turning "Pyramus" into "Paramus"
(a suggestion that Ovidian heroes and towns in New Jersey are similarly ill-fated) and staging the four lovers as follows: Hermia, an exaggeratedly feminine woman; Lysander, an exaggeratedly masculine man;
Demetrius, an exaggeratedly effeminate man; and Helena, a very large
man in very bad drag. The opportunities for camp received full play, and
the very funny interpretation that resulted was perhaps more faithful
than it had intended to be. Was this, after all, any more iconoclastic than
Mickey Rooney as Puck? than Calista Flockhart as Helena? than all those
"straight" productions in all those summer parks? than the BBC? There is
something innately parodic about *A Midsummer Night's Dream*, something
that tempts alternative readings. The poster-play for the argument that
Jack shall have Jill lends itself readily to other couplings and to second,

skeptical looks at heterosexual happy endings, and we do not need The Ridiculous Theatricals to tell us so. We have Hippolyta.

GREAT CONSTANCY

Sometime in the middle of the twentieth century, Hippolyta, whose lines make up less than 2 percent of *A Midsummer Night's Dream*, began to speak for the play. Her response to the playlet had been appropriated by earlier readers; Anne Barton, recalling Pepys's comment on "the most insipid ridiculous play that ever I saw in my life," writes, "He reacted much as Hippolyta does to 'the most lamentable comedy . . . of Pyramus and Thisby as performed by Bottom and his friends." [1] But as twentieth-century readers began a concerted effort to find something consequential in Shakespeare's comedy, Hippolyta provided a critical voice in a different sense. In 1957, Paul Olson made a claim about the play that would come to characterize this self-consciously serious understanding: "The dream becomes more than a fanciful illusion and grows, in Hippolita's phrase, 'to something of great constancy.' " [2] Extrapolating a validation of the play from Hippolyta's comment on the lovers' stories became conventional; set against Theseus's lines on lovers, lunatics, and poets, Hippolyta speaks directly to and for a specific critical desire. So James L. Calderwood writes, "Criticism of *A Midsummer Night's Dream* has on the whole followed the contrasting leads of Theseus and Hippolyta," and makes his own choice: "I suggest that something of constancy begins to take shape if we consider *A Midsummer Night's Dream* as one phase of Shakespeare's continuing exploration of the nature, function, and value of art." [3] In *Something of Great Constancy: The Art of* A Midsummer Night's Dream, David Young describes his intent "to establish the importance of *A Midsummer Night's Dream* in the development of Shakespeare's art, to redefine its place in the canon, and to emphasize its significance as a source of our knowledge of Shakespeare's own attitude toward drama, poetry, and the imagination," taking what he terms "Hippolyta's astute comment" as his point of departure. [4] In looking for knowledge, for poetry, for that mysterious commodity called "art," critics look to Hippolyta. [5] René Girard credits her with still larger answers; describing *A Midsummer Night's Dream* as "a serious genetic theory of myth," he writes, "The exchange between the bridegroom and his acutely perceptive but eternally overshadowed bride amounts to the first critical discussion of the

Tragical Mirth

play," and concludes with a rhetorical question. "How could we doubt that Hippolyta's words are the decisive ones, that they represent Shakespeare's own view of how the play really hangs together?" [6] Strange—admirable?—that the liminal voice of an Amazon speaks for this critical *Dream.*

"Theseus and Hippolyta are, as it were, a splendid frame for the picture," writes one nineteenth-century critic, and Hippolyta is in this sense a structural conceit as well as a critical voice.[7] She appears only at the play's beginning and end, and her first speech, beginning, "Four days will quickly steep themselves in night,/Four nights will quickly dream away the time," provides the sole solid temporal ground in this play shaped by fantasies and enchantments.[8] But if we accept the conceit of the frame narrative, what narrative is conveyed by her presence on stage? And who or what is being framed? Let me start by framing these questions themselves with a graphic detail. In 1877, Harper and Brothers published an edition of *A Midsummer Night's Dream* that William J. Rolfe, the editor, introduces through a collection of ruminations on Shakespeare and marriage. "There is the heroic magnificence of the princely loves of Theseus and his Amazon bride," writes one of the authorities he cites, "dazzling with the strangely gorgeous mixture of classical allusion and fable with the taste, feelings, and manners of chivalry; and all embodied in a calm and lofty poetry, fitted alike to express the grand simplicity of primeval heroism, and 'the high thoughts in a heart of courtesy,' which belong to the best parts of the chivalrous character." [9] Following a series of such remarks, Rolfe presents the text of *A Midsummer Night's Dream* "with illustrations." Opposite the title page, after the introduction, appears "HIPPOLYTA": classically amazonian, she leans on a pedestal, muscular right arm raised. And after the text, appearing without explanation opposite the page labeled "NOTES," is Rolfe's final illustration: "THE VENUS OF MILO." Her appearance mirrors that of Hippolyta, but if Hippolyta's body suggests martial power, the truncated body of the Venus of Milo evokes its loss. Bracketing the text, themselves bracketed by introduction and notes, Hippolyta and the Venus of Milo confront one another across *A Midsummer Night's Dream:* the armed woman, the woman disarmed.

"The first movement, the movement toward an orderly subordination of the female and her passions to the more reasonable male, is epitomized at the beginning of the first scene with the announcement of the prospective marriage of Theseus and Hippolita," Olson writes.[10] If there is something "constant" in this play, transfiguring, as Hippolyta argues, its stories all together, that constancy can apparently be found in her own marriage. The progression described in the dramatis personae — "Hippolyta, queen of the Amazons, betrothed to Theseus" — enables a larger understanding of the processes of domestication: as a defeated Amazon, Hippolyta validates the ordering principle that locates sexual authority in men. Framed by the symbolic implications of her body on-stage, the stories of unruly women that proliferate in *A Midsummer Night's Dream* have implicitly already ended, their rebellions foreclosed before they have begun. It is not, then, surprising that Hippolyta speaks for *A Midsummer Night's Dream* in readings that look for a coherent argument in its plots; taken as a model of an accomplished fact, she encapsulates the right relations of gender and the government of desire.

Barbara Freedman historicizes critical preoccupation with the play's coherence: "In the 1960s and 1970s we followed such critics as D. A. Traversi, Philip Edwards, and David Young through various takes of the 'structure and theme' variety, so that among British and American Shakespeareans the commentary on the play had indeed grown to 'something of great constancy' (5.1.26). And we liked to think of that line as *our* line, as the natural and well-earned product of our superior organizational skills." [11] Focusing instead on representations of distortion and conflict, her own reading again turns to the frame narrative for its terms, finding, in this instance, patriarchy and the opposition it has repressed. "When *A Midsummer Night's Dream* opens, then, the three characters on stage emblematically set out the relationship between the right vision of law and the erring vision of imagination" (182). James Kavanagh, too, reads the play in terms of a contested but ultimately triumphant patriarchal hierarchy, describing "a comic resolution that magically reconciles rebellious 'feminine' and individualist desire to a rigid social hierarchy of aristocratic and patriarchal privilege." [12] When the play begins, the inevitability of that reconciliation is already legible in "Hippolyta, Theseus's intended (who learns properly to submit to the man who literally won her in conquest)" (153).

In " 'Shaping Fantasies,' " Louis Montrose writes, "The festive conclusion of *A Midsummer Night's Dream* depends upon the success of a process by which the female pride and power manifested in misanthropic warriors, possessive mothers, unruly wives, and willful daughters are brought under the control of lords and husbands."[13] He, too, sees the ending written as the play begins: "The sexual act in which the man draws blood from the woman is already implicit, at the beginning of the play, in Theseus's vaunt" (52). Madelon Gohlke also takes up that "vaunt" and its implications:

> These lines, in which the sword may be the metaphoric equivalent of the phallus, in which love may be either generated or secured by hostility, and in which the two partners take up sadistic and masochistic postures in relation to each other, are not irrelevant to the concerns of the play. They may be seen to reverberate in the exaggerated submission of Helena to Demetrius, in the humiliation of Titania by Oberon, in the penetration by violence of the language of love. They even bear an oblique relation to the "lamentable comedy" of *Pyramus and Thisbe,* the failed marriage plot contained within the larger structure of successful heterosexual union celebrated at the end of the play.[14]

The conquest of Hippolyta by Theseus imposes a teleology on the reiterative violence, however subjunctive, displaced, metaphorized, or parodic, of Egeus against Hermia, Theseus against Hermia, Demetrius against Helena, Lysander against Hermia, Oberon against Titania, and fate and/or poor time management against Thisbe. The play's beginning both predicts and contains its end.

If my account of this pattern seems repetitive, I want the weight of that repetition to be felt. These readings have a constancy of their own, a framing certainty that answers the question of what *A Midsummer Night's Dream* is "about." The moral of the story has changed: *A Midsummer Night's Dream* was about the social and sexual subordination of women to men — which, for the play as for "us," was celebratory and natural; *A Midsummer Night's Dream* is about the social and sexual subordination of women to men — which, for the play as for "us," is a source of uneasiness and conflict. And the emphases continue to shift: Is the play primarily invested in or symptomatic of, for example, issues of aestheticism, formalism, psychology, sexuality, sovereignty, subjectivity, performativity, or class? But as they diverge widely in ideological preoccupations, readings of *A*

Midsummer Night's Dream share an interpretive impulse, finding emblematic condensation of the play's concerns in the story that Hippolyta — as queen of the Amazons, as bride to Theseus — tells.

What, then, is that story? Who, for Shakespeare, for his sources, for his audience, is Hippolyta? The biography that the early modern period inherits is anything but coherent. Plutarch summarizes its inconsistencies in his *Life of Theseus:* "*Philochorus,* and some other holde opinion, that [Theseus] went thither with *Hercules* against the AMAZONES: and that to honour his valiantnes, *Hercules* gave him ANTIOPA the AMAZONE. But the more parte of the other Historiographers, namely *Hellanicus, Pherecides,* and *Herodotus,* doe write, that *Theseus* went thither alone, after *Hercules* voyage, and that he tooke this AMAZONE prisoner, which is likeliest to be true. For we doe not finde that any other who went this jorney with him, had taken any AMAZONE prisoner besides him selfe. *Bion* also the Historiographer, this notwithstanding sayeth, that he brought her away by deceit and stealth." [15] Depending on the source, Hippolyta might be conquered, kidnapped, traded, or seduced. With these simultaneous and conflicting statements about agency in mind, let me present her story, extracted from its various early modern versions and told in short. The Queen of the Amazons has a belt that gives her prowess in war. Hercules, as the ninth of his labors, goes to get that belt. The queen: fights Hercules but loses/surrenders out of fear/surrenders out of admiration. Hercules: kills her in battle/kidnaps her and gives her to his friend Theseus/tells his friend Theseus about her, thus inspiring him to kidnap her. The Amazon acquired by Theseus is: Hippolyta, Queen of the Amazons/Hippolyta, sister of the queen of the Amazons/Antiopa, sister of Hippolyta, Queen of the Amazons/Menalippe. The Amazons respond to Theseus's kidnapping/rape/seduction of Hippolyta/Antiopa/Menalippe by: successfully invading Athens/unsuccessfully attempting to invade Athens. In the ensuing battle Hippolyta: fights with the Amazons/fights against the Amazons/is killed in battle/is killed while negotiating peace/is already dead.

What is "constant" about Shakespeare's Hippolyta? And what constancy does she impose on *A Midsummer Night's Dream?* As I will show, the sexual hierarchy that readers have often found inscribed in her presence is only inconsistently apparent in her story. In his critique of readings that present the play as an idealization of marriage, David Marshall writes, "We may discover in the play a scene of struggle — either a reflection of, or an engagement in, struggle — and not necessarily a display of power: a representation of power relations which confirms or reinforces a particular world-view." [16] The frame narrative makes the condition of struggle explicit. Theseus's Amazon encounter establishes gender relations as work, the product of processes that, in the fact of their repetition, betray flaws in the normative model they produce; and overdetermination, which characterizes the stories both of Hippolyta and of *A Midsummer Night's Dream*, hints at gaps in the narrative, an absence of solid ground beneath the proliferation of claims. Hippolyta demonstrates that patriarchally governed heterosociality rests on fragile and fluid distinctions: between men and women, between male and female homoeroticism, between homoeroticism and heteroeroticism, between means and ends. Her presence does not display suppression or repression or oppression already accomplished, but signals that these processes, at once necessary and dangerous to comic conclusions, are always ongoing and never complete. This, I suspect, is why readers return so persistently to Hippolyta: not because she embodies a foregone conclusion, but because she catalyzes a sense of narrative excess. Comedy makes sexual politics into literary conventions, taking socialized desire as plot and claiming an ordered hierarchical discretion as its narrative end. It seems an odd place to tell stories about Amazons.

BONDS OF FELLOWSHIP

In previous chapters, I have considered the ways in which stories about Amazons disrupt discrete categories of gender and hierarchical organizations of sex. That disruption is an effect of something extraordinary — a woman in armor, a man in amazonian disguise — which is turned to reflect on the everyday interactions of women and men. *A Midsummer Night's Dream* takes the next step, eliminating any sense of the extraordinary in its representation of amazonian effects. Presented as the frame narrative for comedy, the interaction of heroes and Amazons becomes a statement of normativity, shorthand for the workings of gender and power. The Amazon encounter is not tamed or revised by comic convention; instead, its tensions, reversals, and mistakes mirror the processes that produce happy endings. Hippolyta's story demonstrates that tragic and comic conclusions work in much the same way: each breaks up undesirable alliances, eliminates rebellious presences, and narrows the focus of power. And as Hippolyta's example makes clear, comedy, like tragedy, presents resolution as an act of violence. If, as so many readers have done, we take Hippolyta as the play's dramatic theorist, she only tells us what we already know about comedy: that socialized desire is an ordering impulse forcibly acted out. Yet that explicitness does a kind of generic damage, revealing that comic conclusions may not have the power to govern or dispel the excesses of comic plots.

Analyzing the relationship in comedy between male bonding and marriage, Bruce Smith writes, "Through scripts focused on wooing, courtship, and marriage, Shakespeare plays out the sexual conflict that the Myth of Combatants and Comrades poses for that other Renaissance ideal of human relations, the Myth of Companionate Marriage." [17] Both the bonds contracted among men and those formed between men and women preoccupy A Midsummer Night's Dream: the alliance of Theseus and Egeus, the doubling of Theseus and Oberon, and the rivalry of Demetrius and Lysander reflect an investment in male homosociality, while the play's four marriages (five, if one counts the ill-fated Pyramus and Thisbe) indicate that the heterosocial impulse is alive and well in Shakespeare's Athens. But these patterns of bonds, and their mutual enforcement, are troubled in the play by a tendency to overlap, to become not discrete categories of connection but a single system of roles. Smith concludes, "All of Shakespeare's comedies and tragicomedies end with male friendship yielding place to heterosexual love" (72). "Heterosexual love" clearly happens in A Midsummer Night's Dream, but by the play's end it is less clear that we know what it means. As men fight with women to establish the proper order of things—a process introduced but hardly concluded by Theseus's battle with Hippolyta—the distinction between male homosociality and heterosociality depends on increasingly precarious assumptions about identity as a condition of performance.

Montrose writes, "At the end of A Midsummer Night's Dream, as at the end of As You Like It, the marital couplings dissolve the bonds of sisterhood at the same time that they forge the bonds of brotherhood." [18] I will take up the question of sisterhood presently; what I would like to point out here is that the "bonds of brotherhood," if they are "forged" at all, represent forgery only in its counterfeit sense. When Theseus overrules Egeus at the play's end, reversing his own statement of law, he exposes a gap between patriarchal theory and the men who act it out, which in turn interrupts the connection of men to one another. The interactions of Demetrius and Lysander illustrate the pervasive nature of that interruption, exposing an inability to formulate homosocial contracts: doubled in their erotic connection to a single woman, nearly indistinguishable in their language of love and violence, they do not consolidate masculine agency through competition. "I would I had your bond, for I perceive / A weak bond holds you," says Demetrius, and that image of a weak bond haunts the play (3.2.267–68). Puck's intervention in the quarrel disjoins rivalry from identity and makes men into illusions: "Now follow, if thou dar'st, to try whose right, / Of thine or mine, is most in Helena," says Lysander to Demetrius, but the challenge does not establish property in women (3.2.336–37). Instead, Puck speaks in two counterfeit voices, presenting himself to Lysander as "drawn and ready" and assuring Demetrius, "We'll try no manhood here," a phrase that summarizes a larger condition of failure (3.2.402, 412). Rather than the battle of two men over a woman, *A Midsummer Night's Dream* displays two men pursuing a mirage that deliberately and effectively disrupts homosocial identification. Like battles between heroes and Amazons, the dispute between Demetrius and Lysander creates the appearance of masculine conflict, but that appearance is detached from men even as it detaches them from one another.

The only effective male bonding takes place through Hippolyta, in a set of rhetorical turns that brings her amazonian role into the play's present tense. Theseus refers to his wedding day as "The sealing-day betwixt my love and me / For everlasting bond of fellowship" (1.1.84–85), and, while "fellowship" might arguably describe companionate marriage, it has a masculine edge that Hippolyta's hunting scene brings into sharp focus.

> I was with Hercules and Cadmus once,
> When in a wood of Crete they bay'd the bear
> With hounds of Sparta; never did I hear
> Such gallant chiding; for, besides the groves,
> The skies, the fountains, every region near
> Seem'd all one mutual cry; I never heard
> So musical a discord, such sweet thunder. (4.1.111–17)

This is Hippolyta's longest speech, her only autobiographical moment, and one of the most impenetrable statements in the play. To begin with, it cannot be true. Cadmus, founder of Thebes, precedes Hippolyta and Hercules by several mythological generations, and Hippolyta and Hercules do not include hunting among their encounters. Editors' notes avoid Hippolyta's presence, glossing the story through Theseus, through Hercules, even through the etiquette of hunting. The Riverside edition defines terms—"hounds of Sparta," "bay'd"; the Arden explains Cadmus—"founder of Thebes; in legend, unheeded by Shakespeare, he belonged to an earlier epoch than Theseus and Hercules"; the Pelican notes "no corresponding episode in legend about Hippolyta, but in some accounts Theseus was a companion of Hercules in his Amazonian exploits, and hunted the Calydonian boar with other heroes." [19]

In an appended note the Arden takes a clearer path, resolving Hippolyta's claim back into the places where male bonding occurs between men. The note cites two passages from Plutarch, the first of which reads, "[The] fame and glory of *Hercules* noble deedes, had . . . secretly set [*Theseus*] heart on fire, so that hee . . . lovingly hearkened unto those . . . which had seene him, and beene in his companie, when he had sayde or done any thing worthy of memorie . . . [He] determined with himselfe one day to doe the like, and the rather, because they were neere kinsemen, being cosins removed by the mother side." The second passage describes the transaction in which Hercules gives Antiopa to Theseus.[20] The citations accumulate to a familiar story: Theseus desires to be like Hercules; Hercules gives Theseus a wife; male homoeroticism produces both bonds between men and generative marriage. This is not, however, the story Hippolyta tells in *A Midsummer Night's Dream.* In her version, she is the agent of male bonding rather than its sign; heroic masculinity is constructed between an Amazon and two men, neither of whom is Theseus; and even the Calydonian boar, object of Theseus's most famous hunt, becomes Hippolyta's bear.[21]

Here, as in the play's mythological references more generally, knowledge and ignorance leave the audience in the same place. If "we" do not know the details of Hippolyta's biography or the respective dates of Hercules and Cadmus, we take the story at face value—and contemplate Hippolyta, rearmed and reengaged in violent pursuits, nostalgically recalling her masculine past. Theseus becomes another hero in a series of heroes, his status as her conqueror overshadowed by the company she has already kept. But if, on the other hand, "we" know enough to reject this vision of heroic promiscuity, we are left with a blatant appropriation of the power of narrative, a retrospective revision that mirrors and rivals the nostalgic self-aggrandizement of Theseus himself. If the story is not true, then what does it mean? Hippolyta in this speech has the power to figure and refigure, to make things happen by making things up. Freedman writes of *A Midsummer Night's Dream* that "it presents knowledge as an effect of right censorship and figures metaphor as a dangerous instrument requiring close state control"; she goes on to argue that that control constitutes figurative narcissism. "Metaphor both appropriates and invalidates otherness by proving that everything strange can, in a moment of high narcissism, be made to reflect a part of oneself. When we imagine that everyone is like us, or can be compared to us, we are exploiting otherness as a commodity."[22] Hippolyta's stories—her own story, and the story she tells—open up that closed economy, realizing the danger that Freedman describes. Amazon encounters reveal that the desired self-image might not be an image of the self at all; narcissism becomes a trick of the imagination, and even when the narcissists win, their victory responds defensively to a convergence of other and self.

Like Hippolyta's nostalgia, Theseus's boast—"Hippolyta, I woo'd thee with my sword,/And won thy love doing thee injuries" (1.1.16–17)—recalls a martial amazonian past. In making that history explicit the play makes a deliberate choice, for there are other available versions of this marriage plot. The first account Plutarch considers, in which Hippolyta is Hercules' gift to Theseus, confirms that women are commodities exchanged by men, and that even Amazons have no agency in the process; as Gayle Rubin writes, "If women are the gifts, then it is men who are the exchange partners. And it is the partners, not the presents, upon whom reciprocal exchange confers its quasi-mystical power of social linkage."[23] But *A Midsummer Night's Dream* does not tell this story, nor is it the story preferred by early modern texts. Most of those texts follow the account that Plutarch describes as "likeliest to be true," in which Theseus does not seduce or acquire Hippolyta, but fights her. If the Amazon appears as a commodity, a patriarchal token, as *A Midsummer Night's Dream* begins, Theseus's lines remind us that this condition is recently imposed. As a former opponent and a future wife, Hippolyta reveals a lack of fixedness in the conditions of role playing; queen of the Amazons, betrothed to Theseus, she plays a part that implicates her both in heterosocial domesticity and in the bonds between men.

William Painter, in *The Palace of Pleasure*, does not distinguish war stories from love stories; in his account the second follow, as if naturally, from the first. "Certayne Historians do say that [the Amazons] were subdued in a pitched field, and appoynted battle. And that afterwards the two sisters were vanquished in singuler Combat . . . *Theseus* for no offer that [the queen] coulde make, woulde deliver *Hipolita*, with whom he was so farre in love, that he caried her home with him, and afterward toke her to wyfe, of whom hee had a sonne called *Hipolitus*." [24] In *Albions England*, William Warner suggests that such violent foreplay may be dangerous, putting both Theseus and the larger systems of gender politics at risk. Anticipating Spenser's Radigund, Warner's Amazons tell the Greeks, "And if your Champions vanquish ours, then we will tribute pay:/But if that ours doe vanquish yours, then you shall us obay." [25] Mastery is contested, not assumed, and, although Hercules wins easily, Theseus almost loses, until he deliberately invokes the relationship between male bodies and masculine acts.

But *Theseus* with his Combattesse in doubtfull battell fights,
Till, blushing at the Maidens blowes, he checks his mending sprights:
And laid so hardlie to her charge, not able to sustaine
his fresh-got force, that he also the second Prize did gaine. (26)

Describing Theseus's victory, the poem represents it as incomplete, claiming that he wins on one ground only to face defeat on another: "For he through Lance, his Foe through love went Victoresse away" (26).

As a conceit, Hippolyta's victory seems highly conventional: desire often appears as chivalric conflict, even as chivalric conflict often looks like desire. But in Amazon encounters neither set of relations metaphorizes the other, and the connection between violence and eroticism is not that of figure to referent, but of cause to effect. Heroic conflict and marriage take place through the same bodies and at the same narrative level, defining Hippolyta's identity less as a move toward truth—she's "really" a woman—than as a change in the conventions of desire. In

The Purple Island, Phineas Fletcher takes this farther. His account leaves martial combat unresolved, not granting heroic victory to Theseus but displacing it altogether:

> Th' *Amazon* Queen, *Hippolyta,*
> With *Theseus* entred lists in single fight,
> With equall arms her mighty foe opposing;
> Till now her bared head her face dislosing,
> Conquer'd the conqueror, and wan the fight by losing.[26]

Warner gives a different victory to each combatant, but here that balance is upset. Hippolyta does not lose on the field in order to win somewhere else, but short-circuits the terms of conquest by changing erotic contracts in midfight. Any distinction between her roles vanishes as hetero-eroticism intervenes in chivalric conflict, recalling the moment in *The Faerie Queene* at which Artegall's confrontation with an armed female body makes him drop his sword.

Theseus risks the same loss in his battle against Hippolyta that Hotspur suffers at the hands of Prince Hal, a loss not only of life but of heroic identity. Responding to Hippolyta on these terms, Theseus acknowledges her role within the closed system of heroism: narcissistically conceived, conflict within this system directs eroticized violence against an image of identity in a consolidation of masculine ideals. As Catherine Belsey writes of the courtship recalled in *A Midsummer Night's Dream*, "The text here proposes a parallel where we might expect an antithesis." [27] But Hippolyta is also dangerous to Theseus because she is different. Christine de Pizan, recounting the initial victory of the Amazons over Theseus and Hercules, writes, "These ii knyghtes were ashamed to be thus beten of these ii maydens," and adds, "This thynge sholde not be credyble to be trewe but yt so many antentyke doctours bereth wytnesse of it." [28] The story is incredible not only because undefeated heroes fall, but because their fall to women opens a rift in the heroic economy, unraveling narcissistic exchange. It matters a great deal in these accounts that Hippolyta is never mistaken for a man. Even Fletcher's version of the encounter, in which the sudden removal of the helmet is clearly indebted to the trope of misrecognition, is not itself based on mistake; the revelation of the Amazon's face may stun Theseus, but it does not convey new information. In the battle between Hippolyta and Theseus, a recognizably female body intervenes in the performance of masculinity, precipitating a conflict that both occurs through conventional chivalric codes and incorporates their violation. Unlike Amazon encounters that begin in misrecognition, this battle does not fantasize a transition from homoerotic to heteroerotic response, but asserts their simultaneity.[29]

Hippolyta is always marked—as her designation in the dramatis personae marks her—both as Theseus's prize and as his mirror image. *A Midsummer Night's Dream* might, in a teleological reading, prove that Hippolyta's masculinity is specious, her loss to Theseus demonstrating her essential femininity and her suitability as his wife. "Shakespeare's Hippolyta in *A Midsummer Night's Dream* illustrates that, properly tamed, Amazons could even be graceful, queenly heroines," Susanne Woods writes in her consideration of male fantasies of taming.[30] But the play insists on recalling Hippolyta's history; female masculinity is not detached, as prologue or as aberration, from heterosocial desire. Both chivalric masculinity and domestic femininity eroticize Hippolyta's relationship to Theseus, and the story of domestication itself has a catch, for the more aggressively the play feminizes Hippolyta, the more disruptive her intervention in masculinity becomes. If Hippolyta does not look as if she could ever have acted like a man, the conflict through which Theseus constructs heroic identity becomes opaque, either proving that masculinity is temporary and detachable or proving nothing at all. Victory, as so often for men among Amazons, looks uncommonly like defeat.

In some versions of the story this is literally true. According to Christine de Pizan, Menalippe fights with Hercules, Hippolyta with Theseus, and although the Amazons are eventually defeated, they first humiliate the heroes. In Anthony Gibson's account the Amazon wins: "*Hippolita* dissipated the troupes of great *Theseus*, dismounting himselfe in the fight," he writes, "yet afterward (on meere grace) made him her husband."[31] Gibson's account places Theseus, rather than Hippolyta, in the role of prize and concubine, reminding us that the husbands of Amazons are rarely heroes. That emasculating possibility surfaces in *A Midsummer Night's Dream* in the mechanicals' only corrected malapropism: when Quince says of Bottom, "He is a very paramour for a sweet voice," Flute replies, "You must say paragon. A paramour is, God bless us, a thing of naught" (4.2.11–14). Or, as Diodorus writes, "[It is] confirmed by statute decreed amonge [the Amazons] for evermore to be observed, that no man so hardy, uppon jeopardye of deth, afforce any enterprise of warre or to enure any maner fete of martiall adventure." [32] As it opens up such possibilities, Gibson's story demonstrates the malleability of gendered convention. If Hippolyta marries Theseus whether she wins, almost wins, or never has a chance, there is nothing essential about this causality; as the result of Theseus's victory, Hippolyta's condescension, or the generosity of Hercules, heterosexual marriage appears not as the triumph of real over mistaken identity but as a redistribution of roles. The play's frame narrative does not restore natural order, but highlights a state of contested performance. Men and women have access to the same set of acts, and Helena's protest—"Fie, Demetrius!/Your wrongs do set a scandal on my sex./We cannot fight for love, as men may do"— is an empty disclaimer (2.1.239–41).

A Midsummer Night's Dream exceeds its own boundaries, and both in looking forward and in looking back proves the intimacy of violence and desire. The amazonian tendency of war stories to merge into love stories also works in reverse, as Painter's account illustrates; having sentimentalized Theseus's conquest of Hippolyta, he writes, "Oritia certified of these news, beinge then out of her countrey, conceyved no lesse shame than sorrow . . . [and] perswaded Antiopa to be revenged upon the Grekes. For which purpose they made great preparation of warre." [33] That war of the Amazons against the Greeks is the next event in Hippolyta's history, the consequence of her seduction. Mythographers repeatedly describe it as an erasure of sexual difference: "For this is the same as saying that the men of those times were women and that the women were men," writes Strabo.[34] Plutarch tells the story only reluctantly, conceding that amazonian graves in Athens prove that it is true but maintaining that it is unnatural: "Now heare what was the occasion of the warres of the Amazones, which me thinckes was not a matter of small moment, nor an enterprise of a woman." [35] And Diodorus, in The Bibliotheca Historica, describes the amazonian invaders as "by emported resemblaunce of manly coraige, like unto men." [36]

If Shakespeare's play takes place between Painter's sentences, it shows the strain of that compression: inserting comedy between anomaly (women exist independently of men) and outrage (women challenge male government), A Midsummer Night's Dream averts our eyes from these phenomena by multiplying its stories of unruly women. It is a narrative double bind, or perhaps an inevitable return, replacing an amazonian invasion with rebellions from within. In *Bodies That Matter*, Judith Butler writes, "My purpose here is to understand how what has been foreclosed or banished from the proper domain of 'sex'—where that domain is secured through a heterosexualizing imperative—might at once be produced as a troubling return, not only as an *imaginary* contestation that effects a failure in the workings of the inevitable law, but as an enabling disruption, the occasion for a radical rearticulation of the symbolic horizon in which bodies come to matter at all." [37] That tension, between a "domain . . . secured through a heterosexualizing imperative" and "a troubling return," is played out in *A Midsummer Night's Dream*, in which the conclusion of male conquest and female submission proves less than final, becoming instead the beginning of an invasion, a revenge plot, a play. *A Midsummer Night's Dream* takes up time between courtship and marriage, but it also takes place between rape and revenge, a space within which acquiescent femininity is only erratically performed.

When Egeus says of his daughter, "I beg the ancient privilege of Athens:/As she is mine, I may dispose of her," he invokes an unassailable social premise; disposal is a paternal privilege, and Hermia's choice, "Either to die the death, or to abjure/For ever the society of men," is in this sense no choice at all, or at least no choice of hers (1.1.41–42, 65–66). But in another sense it is the choice made by Amazons. Female separatism, with its evasions and revisions of patriarchal control, is a powerful erotic presence in the play, from Hermia's reference to "the wood, where often you and I/Upon faint primrose beds were wont to lie" to Helena's famous speech about double cherries (1.1.214–15, 3.2.203–14). Valerie Traub writes, "*A Midsummer Night's Dream*, a play thoroughly concerned with the tension between unity and duality, merger and separation, oneness and twoness, presents Lysander's seductive come-on, 'One heart, one bed, two bosoms, and one troth' (2.2.42) as no different—qualitatively, emotionally, physically—from Helena's pained admonition." [38] She argues that the transgressive potential of this homology is vitiated by the play's heterosexual teleology: "Female homoeroticism is thus figurable not only in terms of the always already lost, but the always about to be *betrayed*. And the incipient heterosexuality of the woman who is recipient rather than enunciator of homoerotic desire comes to stand as the telos of the play" (72). *A Midsummer Night's Dream* moves away from homoerotic self-sufficiency, toward the "new friends, and stranger companies" of Hermia's early speech (1.1.219).

But we are again in the world of the supplement, in which something added has the power to displace. Luce Irigaray, in "This Sex Which Is Not One," writes, "Woman's desire has doubtless been submerged by the logic that has dominated the West since the time of the Greeks." In the time of Shakespeare's Greeks, that logic seems firmly in place, and yet women offer alternative articulations of desire. Irigaray goes on to ask, "Must this multiplicity of female desire and female language be understood as shards, scattered remnants of a violated sexuality? A sexuality denied? The question has no simple answer."[39] This must be said of *A Midsummer Night's Dream* as well. The multiplication of statements of desire opens those statements to interpretation: if the rhetoric of female homoeroticism sounds just like that of heteroeroticism, language, like masculinity, becomes portable, flexible in the ways that it defines and refers. A transition into heteroeroticism implies a possible transition out, and, in constructing a female homoerotic past tense, *A Midsummer Night's Dream* defines its present state in relative and contingent terms. Why give a homoerotic rhetorical space, however foreclosed, to characters who have already moved into heteroerotic articulation? If experience remains in the past, language does not, bringing bonds between women into a dramatic moment at which they intersect, rather than precede, the progress toward heterosexual consummation. Nostalgia for past pleasures, as it doubles and even displaces anticipation of the future, makes the erotic present a rather crowded place.

If this is a play of transition, the clean break is marred by rhetorical overlap. With a passion and a logic that do not belong in the present moment, Helena tells Hermia that heterosociality violates the expectations both of female bonding and of femininity:

> And will you rent our ancient love asunder
> To join with men in scorning your poor friend?
> It is not friendly, 'tis not maidenly;
> Our sex, as well as I, may chide you for it. (3.2.215–18)

As she claims that leaving the society of women for that of men is abandonment, betrayal, an act of violence, Helena implicitly retells Hippolyta's story. In "Male Bonding in Shakespeare's Comedies," Janet Adelman argues that connections between women in *A Midsummer Night's Dream* create a safe space of play: "At the same time as the male bond is essentially eradicated from this play, concern with same sex bonding is made comically safe and distant by its transfer to the women." [40] I suggest instead that traces of female exclusivity highlight the sense of something lacking in relationships among men, and that preoccupation with homosocial and homoerotic bonds makes heterosexuality an awkwardly subjunctive third term. Represented onstage only in the conflict between Titania and Oberon, consummated relations between men and women recede into the future as aggressively as eroticized relations among women return from the past. As a genre, comedy has a problem with time, striving to accomplish a consummation that cannot by its nature be accomplished *yet*. For a play hemmed in by amazonian history, the problem is rather more acute.

If *A Midsummer Night's Dream*'s frame narrative shows a troublesome tendency to intrude on the play, literary history has sometimes attempted to recontain it by invoking *The Knight's Tale*. Chaucer, this genealogical impulse suggests, provides authoritative precedent for wifely Amazons. But *The Knight's Tale*, like *A Midsummer Night's Dream*, invokes the story of Theseus and Hippolyta only to refer the audience elsewhere, leaving its own references both evocative and evasive.

> And certes, if it nere to long to heere,
> I wolde han told yow fully the manere
> How wonnen was the regne of Femenye
> By Theseus and by his chivalrye;
> And of the great bataille for the nones
> Bitwixen Atthenes and Amazones;
> And how asseged was Ypolita,
> The faire, hardy queene of Scithia,
> And of the feste that was at hir weddynge,
> And of the tempest at hir hoom-comynge;
> But al that thyng I moot as now forbere. [41]

Here, too, the amazonian history that brackets events is itself bracketed, enclosing a spectacle through which it cannot appear. Like *A Midsummer*

Night's Dream, The Knight's Tale presents amazonian domesticity as a frame narrative whose contents remain opaque, refusing either to tell the story or to leave it alone.

Evaluating the implications of the frame, we are again left with the question of knowledge, of what is available and how it matters. Could the characters in the play (the version of this question that privileges fiction) or the members of Shakespeare's audience (the version that privileges history) "know" enough about Theseus and Hippolyta for their presence in *A Midsummer Night's Dream* to have the effects I describe? The answer comes in two perhaps predictable parts: probably, and it doesn't matter. Amazons have a certain name recognition in early modern England, and the exploits of Theseus appear in contemporary English translations including Golding's of the *Metamorphoses*, Studley's of *Hippolytus*, North's of Plutarch's *Lives*, and Painter's of a variety of more or less bowdlerized authorities in *The Palace of Pleasure*. But, whether or not Hermia "knows" that Amazons do odd things to marriage, whether or not the groundlings "knew" that Amazons disrupt assumptions about masculinity, the play stages erotic complications both within and among homo- and heterosocial relations. And whether or not Shakespeare was thinking about the stories told by Plutarch and Ovid and Seneca—although for Shakespeare we seem less often to assume accident than design—*A Midsummer Night's Dream* constructs its own story around the tensions for which Hippolyta is a reference in brief.

JACK SHALL HAVE JILL

In his discussion of the "to seem" that intervenes between fantasies of being and having, Lacan writes that this intervention "has the effect of projecting in their entirety the ideal or typical manifestations of the behaviour of each sex, including the act of copulation itself, into the comedy." [42] For Lacan as for *A Midsummer Night's Dream*, comedy is a space in which sex, as gendered convention or as "the act of copulation itself," rests on a condition of seeming. This condition obscures qualitative or hierarchical difference, constructing a system of eroticized connection based in the constant possibility of revision and mistake; the dynamics of power implicit in Theseus's conquest are dynamic in the shiftiest sense of that term. I have argued that Amazon encounters make socialized desire recognizable as an invention, so that even when men win, their ascendancy does not approximate a naturalized state. Considering such essential failures, Butler, like Lacan, invokes comedy; she writes, "The persistent failure to identify fully and without incoherence with these positions reveals heterosexuality itself not only as a compulsory law, but as an inevitable comedy," and describes "heterosexuality as both a compulsory system and an intrinsic comedy, a constant parody of itself." [43] That convergence of law and parody ensures that social normativity is most visible as artifice when it most clearly states its case.

At the beginning of *A Midsummer Night's Dream*, Theseus summarizes patriarchy in six relentlessly conventional lines.

> Be advis'd, fair maid.
> To you your father should be as a god:
> One that compos'd your beauties; yea, and one
> To whom you are but as a form in wax
> By him imprinted, and within his power
> To leave the figure, or disfigure it. (1.1.46–51)

Asserting a set of relations that become true through his power to impose them, Theseus's speech claims the effect of a speech act. His language recalls the calm certainties of conduct manuals and other monitory texts: "Nothing sooner makes an impression in tender Years, than Precedents in Infancy, like Wax, taking and retaining the figure of that Seal which first impress'd it, unless it be rudely defac'd by another, or purposely destroyed." [44] But there is something risky about bringing an infrastructure out into the open; explicit description of hegemony defines it as an intention that generates acts. Theseus's declaration, secure in its status as a truth-claim, both identifies heterosociality as an imposition and links it to violence.

That link recurs throughout the play. As the couplings of Titania and Oberon, Titania and Bottom, Lysander and Hermia, Lysander and Helena, Demetrius and Helena, and Demetrius and Hermia reflect the shifting processes of identification through desire, they demonstrate that the socialization of sex requires constant enforcement. Freedman writes, "Patriarchal law rather than reason actually controls perspective in this play, and its vision is depicted as necessarily distorted and distorting. Since all power is necessarily a distortion, the problem the play poses is not how to correct distorted perspective but how to legitimize the distorted vision of the patriarchy."[45] Her reading evokes Oberon, who, by imposing distorted sight, makes it impossible to see in any way but his. But Oberon's interference among the lovers escalates misrecognitions and misalliances, and his victory over Titania rests on cuckoldry, bestiality, and the translation of a male body into a monstrous infantilized object of insatiable female desire. For Oberon as for Theseus, the forceful imposition of hierarchy emphasizes the disruptive possibilities it works to suppress. The argument that puts men in power is not prophylactic but defensive, as defensive as Theseus's heroic conquest. Women must be instructed and installed in their positions by men who must constantly assert control, and in the invention of gender violence and desire collide. That collision begins with Hippolyta and Theseus, who make the same story of abduction, seduction, rape, and war, but it does not end there.

A Midsummer Night's Dream presents erotic and violent acts not as working parts of a system of maintenance, in which violence is the barely hidden threat that keeps hierarchy in place; not as a system of differentiation between "good" and "bad" objects; but as interchangeable choices. Lysander, enchanted, says of Hermia, "What, should I hurt her, strike her, kill her dead?" (3.2.269). Demetrius threatens Helena in similar terms: "Tempt not too much the hatred of my spirit;/For I am sick when I do look on thee" (2.1.211–12). His threat of rape, like Oberon's revenge, defines sexuality as a weapon: "You do impeach your modesty too much/To leave the city and commit yourself/Into the hands of one that loves you not" (2.1.214–16). Even Pyramus and Thisbe reproduce the pattern in which heteroeroticism leads not to marriage but to rape and death: "Lion vile hath here deflower'd my dear," mourns Pyramus when he believes that Thisbe is dead (5.1.281). Made farcical by the rude mechanicals, spoken subjunctively by Demetrius and Lysander, authorized by Egeus's plea to Theseus, the mistaking of sex for death and of death for sex runs throughout the play.

This is the pattern of comedy, in which, at the last possible dramatic minute, erotic contracts replace death threats; it is also a pattern of cliché, in which an equation between love and death resolves one of those terms into metaphor. The lovers seem obsessed with such conceits. Hermia swears faith "by that fire which burn'd the Carthage queen"; Demetrius says of Lysander and Hermia, "The one I'll slay, the other slayeth me"; Hermia tells Lysander, "Thy love ne'er alter till thy sweet life end," to which Lysander replies, "And then end life when I end loyalty"; Lysander promises Helena, "And run through fire I will for thy sweet sake," and tells her, "Helen, I love thee; by my life, I do;/I swear by that which I will lose for thee." [46] Describing a critical tendency to dismiss conventions simply by recognizing them as such, Richard Rambuss writes, "Too often interpretation desists at the point of such a determination, as if the status of being conventional would make a discursive construct or a sentiment any less thick with significance." [47] In *A Midsummer Night's Dream* the love/death conflation becomes thick with significance through being thick on the ground; it has a darkening cumulative effect, and it is not consistently abstract. Hermia accuses Demetrius of real murder, although he replies with a metaphor: "So should a murderer look, so dead, so grim," she says, and he answers, "So should the murder'd look, and so should I,/Pierc'd through the heart with your stern cruelty" (3.2.57–59). His conceit clarifies by contrast, reminding us that Demetrius is not dead, while in Hermia's mind Lysander is. She imagines her own death as well— "Either death or you I'll find immediately" —and again this is not the wordplay that invokes fire and ice and Carthage queens (2.2.155). When Helena says, "Stay, though thou kill me, sweet Demetrius," or tells Hermia, "For love I follow'd him;/But he hath chid me hence, and threaten'd me/To strike me, spurn me, nay, to kill me too," she identifies death not as a metaphor for consummated sexuality but as an alternative plot (2.2.83, 3.2.311–13).

Laura Levine argues that *A Midsummer Night's Dream* never escapes the implications of its own immediate past, writing, "If the play begins then with Theseus turning to the revels to try to transform some original violence against women, what it depicts is a world in which this violence is not transformed but repeatedly deepened and amplified, a world in which the parameters of this original violence are always growing." [48] In *A Midsummer Night's Dream* as in Amazon encounters, violence begins in the confounded or belated recognition of gendered identity and its sexual implications. The lovers repeatedly define one another in terms of confusion. "Thou driv'st me past the bounds/Of maiden's patience," says Hermia, and orders Demetrius, "Henceforth be never number'd among men." "Have you no modesty, no maiden shame?" asks Helena, the play's most vocal arbiter of norms; "It is not friendly, 'tis not maidenly"; and again, "If you were men, as men you are in show,/You would not use a gentle lady so."[49] If that phrase "in show," like "not maidenly," has a certain resonance for this play that begins with Amazons, the lovers' language reflects a larger sense that identity rests on a failure of discretion. In *Shake Hands with Shakespeare*, a set of plays adapted for children, Albert Cullum writes, "If you like, you may have Hermia and Helena played by boys, and in this case the absurd chase through the forest can become a rough and tumble one."[50] In an apparently unconscious reinvention of early modern stage practice, Cullum reiterates the play's own proposition that identity is a matter of rough and tumble, and casting an arbitrary choice. Such instability is not merely a matter of play, and for the lovers mistaking might always be a prelude to dying. This is the possibility that allows readers to think of *A Midsummer Night's Dream* and *Romeo and Juliet* as the same story with different endings, and to understand the "Pyramus and Thisbe" playlet as a recuperative but still anxious acknowledgment of tragic potential. It is also a peculiarly amazonian understanding of the ways in which eroticism works. Transitions—from violence to desire, from mistaking to recognition—might come too late, as when Achilles kills Penthesilea and then looks for the first time at her face. Like heroes and Amazons, the lovers of *A Midsummer Night's Dream* repeatedly fail to recognize one another as subjects and objects of an acceptable response.

Such failures may create comedy and even farce, but they also reveal that love plots tend toward something terrible. "I'll follow thee, and make a heaven of hell,/To die upon the hand I love so well," Helena tells Demetrius (2.1.243–44). This is the lovers' danger, summarized in the amazonian marriage with which the play begins and ends: death may be a natural condition of erotic pursuits. It is a possibility that informs the play's preoccupation with inappropriate stories: Why does Titania invoke Philomel? or Helena Daphne? Why do the mechanicals play Pyramus and Thisbe? Why does Philostrate offer "the battle of the Centaurs," the story of a disrupted wedding involving a bride named— uncannily—Hippodamia? And why is this episode from Theseus's past sung by an Athenian eunuch?[51] These figures are conventions taken from a set of mythological signs, but like Hippolyta herself, such signs imply narrative. In a reading of Boccaccio's *Teseida*, Carla Freccero writes, "Although the poem works to contain the tensions produced by the abrupt transformation of Ipolita, and so Diana, into *dames courtoises*, right down to the finest numerological detail, there lingers a 'remainder,' the metaphorical consequence of the anxieties attendant upon such a process of courtly domestication." [52] I have argued that gestures of nostalgia and anticipation undermine the categorical statement of Hippolyta's presence in *A Midsummer Night's Dream*, that stories of before and after alter her exemplary significance. The play's system of references and conceits reflects and reiterates this effect—Freccero's "remainder," Hippolyta's excess—complicating the status of women as objects of acquisition by figuring them as either dead or deadly.

The fantasy of keeping women in their place is undermined by the fact that it will already repeatedly not have happened: if, at the play's beginning, Hippolyta, Hermia, and Titania articulate sexual rebellion in the past, future, and present tense, then the statement of mastery loses force in a tendency to repeat itself. Describing sex as an effect of repetition, Butler points out that multiplying an assumption exposes its flaws: "As a sedimented effect of a reiterative or ritual practice, sex acquires its naturalized effect, and, yet, it is also by virtue of this reiteration that gaps and fissures are opened up as the constitutive instabilities in such constructions, as that which escapes or exceeds the norm, as that which cannot be wholly defined or fixed by the repetitive labor of that norm." [53] As the "repetitive labor" of *A Midsummer Night's Dream* produces appropriate relations between women and men, it leaves the mechanics of production visible. If it is necessary to repeat a statement of mastery so often, might the statement in some way be not entirely finished, or not entirely true? Irigaray writes of women that "they are already elsewhere in that discursive machinery where you expected to surprise them," and Hélène Cixous expands on this fragmentation of singularity: "As subject for history, woman always occurs simultaneously in several places. Woman unthinks the unifying, regulating history that homogenizes and channels forces, herding contradictions into a single battlefield." [54] Hippolyta's story mirrors both Cixous's account of heterogeneic simultaneity and Irigaray's description of a discursive object that is always slightly elsewhere, and, as a response to such contradictory histories and multiple battlefields, a conqueror's narrative is never quite enough. There are too many stories in *A Midsummer Night's Dream*, pursuing too many objects across too much ground. Conquering an Amazon may prove that compulsory heterosexuality works, but restaging the act endlessly among young Greeks and fairies implies a certain lack of faith.

The eroticization of the conqueror's sword becomes a locker-room joke gone wrong, a sharp reminder that socialized desire is produced out of violence, deception, role playing, and unnatural acts. Hippolyta's domesticated state is neither itself naturalized nor does it naturalize heterosocial hierarchy; instead, it illuminates the effort involved in the invention of gender. Like the centaurs who invade the wedding of Pirithous, Hippolyta at her own wedding disrupts happy endings with the revelation that the outside has come in.[55] The play neither requires nor even invites us to believe that marriage forecloses sexual conflict; in their struggle over the changeling, Titania and Oberon identify marriage and generation as further battlefields. Paternal certainty rests on the assumption of married chastity, proposing that two opacities combine to make a fact, and the changeling, as an heir manqué with a mysterious past, exposes the fragility of this article of faith. Titania describes his birth in the absence of men, the result of a conception that literalizes metaphor:

> We have laugh'd to see the sails conceive
> And grow big-bellied with the wanton wind;
> Which she, with pretty and with swimming gait
> Following (her womb then rich with my young squire),
> Would imitate. (2.1.128–32)

The story recalls speculations about amazonian parthenogenesis, as in an account of Magellan's voyage: "Our oldest pilot told us that there is an island called Acoloro which lies below Java Major where there are not persons but women, and that the latter become mothers by the wind." [56]

But amazonian reproduction relies less on parthenogenesis than on casual sex. Strabo gives this account:

> They have two special months in the spring in which they go up into the neighboring mountain which separates them and the Gargarians. The Gargarians also, in accordance with an ancient custom, go up thither to offer sacrifice with the Amazons and also to have intercourse with them for the sake of begetting children,

doing this in secrecy and darkness, any Gargarian at random with any Amazon; and after making them pregnant they send them away; and the females that are born are retained by the Amazons themselves, but the males are taken to the Gargarians to be brought up; and each Gargarian to whom a child is brought adopts the child as his own, regarding the child as his son because of his uncertainty.[57]

This story of random lovers and guessing fathers is more ruinous than narratives in which amazonian sons are killed: partriarchy accommodates tragedy, but requires the means to know. In response to Titania's claims about female exclusivity and generative mystification, Oberon asserts that he *does* know. He quarrels with Titania, Puck explains, "because that she as her attendant hath/A lovely boy, stol'n from an Indian king" (2.1.21–22). The changeling boy becomes another man's heir, not mysterious but simply misplaced. The Arden edition of the play glosses this inconsistency: "*stol'n . . . king*"] as not incompatible with the story of his mother, below, ll. 123 ff.; Shakespeare may or may not already have conceived that."[58] Conception does, indeed, seem to be the question. And even after the issue of possession has been resolved, after Oberon's triumphant "Now I have the boy," other questions remain: What are the terms of changing, of exchange? What has been substituted for what, and who for whom?

A Midsummer Night's Dream is haunted by the possibility that generative heterosexuality may not generate as and what it should. This, after all, is the effect specific to Hippolyta: if her resistance to marriage is variously described and debated, there is nothing ambiguous about the results of her participation in it. In her battle with Theseus she may lose or win or perform some combination thereof; in the Amazon attack on Athens she may fight for Athens, fight for the Amazons, negotiate peace, or be dead; but she is always the mother of Hippolytus. His story is as relentlessly teleological as *A Midsummer Night's Dream* itself: wooed and betrayed by his stepmother Phaedra, he is banished by Theseus and torn to pieces as he flees from Athens. D'Orsay W. Pearson argues that Shakespeare names his Amazon Hippolyta, rather than Antiopa, to remind his audience of her ill-fated son: "He could have chosen his Amazon's name deliberately, working to stress Hippolyta as the feminine form of

Hippolytus, thus deliberately recalling the story of the son of the marriage the play celebrates."[59] The comic world of Shakespeare's play requires the suspension less of disbelief than of knowledge, and the play itself cannot leave knowledge alone. Hinted at in Oberon's heavily ironized blessing of "the best bride-bed" of Hippolyta and Theseus—"And the issue there create/Ever shall be fortunate"—Hippolytus stands in the future of *A Midsummer Night's Dream* (5.1.391–92).

In this sense the disputed Indian boy is a changeling stolen from another play. Excessively desired by his adoptive mother, jealously guarded by a father-figure obsessed with patrilineal and masculine continuity—"Jealous Oberon would have the child/Knight of his train"— the changeling might be Hippolytus (2.1.24–25). If the "Pyramus and Thisbe" playlet is a farcical version of the Pyramus and Thisbe myth or of *Romeo and Juliet,* the battle between Titania and Oberon is a comic mirror of *Hippolytus,* and not entirely or persuasively comic at that. Critical and stage history routinely double the ruling couples of *A Midsummer Night's Dream,* but Titania goes beyond identity with Hippolyta to forecast the role played by Phaedra.[60] A strange slip of reference makes this explicit. When Oberon charges Titania with adultery, he includes her in Theseus's catalogue of conquests:

> Didst not thou lead him through the glimmering night
> From Perigouna, whom he ravished;
> And make him with fair Aegles break his faith,
> With Ariadne and Antiopa? (2.1.77–80)

Oberon's list concludes with Antiopa, another name for Hippolyta in some of Shakespeare's sources.[61] But in *A Midsummer Night's Dream* Hippolyta is only Hippolyta, and the appearance of "Antiopa" begs a deictic question: How has "Antiopa" preceded "Hippolyta"? If Titania succeeds Antiopa, then she, like Phaedra, takes the place of Theseus's Amazon bride. Yet Hippolyta's marriage is still in the future, and Oberon locates the betrayal of Antiopa in the past. We are left not with the middle ground of domesticity, but with the two ends of a myth: the tragedy of Hippolytus makes its presence felt, but Hippolyta is still, unreasonably, onstage.

Is it going too far to see the story of Hippolytus in that of the changeling, to hear echoes of tragedy in a fairy dispute? Is this overinterpretation, as students say when analysis exceeds the comfort zone? Yes, of course, but only if we use "overinterpret" in the way that Freud does, to describe a process of multiple reading the results of which, however contradictory, nonetheless coexist. In his discussion of dream-work, Freud writes, "This ambiguity of the symbols links up with the characteristic of dreams for admitting of 'over-interpretation'—for representing in a single piece of content thoughts and wishes which are often widely divergent in their nature." [62] If *A Midsummer Night's Dream* is a wish fulfillment, it responds to contradictory desires. The play can be a comedy and still gesture toward an ending beyond its own, just as the play-within-a-play can be a farce and still flirt with catastrophe. Plutarch writes of the Hippolytus story, "And for that the Historiographers doe not in any thing speake against the tragicall Poets, in that which concerneth the ill happe that chaunced to [Theseus], in the persones of this his wife and of his sonne: we must needes take it to be so, as we finde it written in the tragedies." [63] Hippolytus belongs to tragedy, but like his mother he is incorporated into early modern domestic clichés. "Orpheus and hyppolytus had myserable endes for offendinge wymen," cautions William Bercher, advocating courtly behavior. [64] Richard Brathwait offers more detailed advice: "*Phaedra* fancied *Theseus* lesse than shee should, but young *Hippolytus* more than hee would. Which effects are usually produced, when either disparity of yeares breed dislike; or obscurity of descent begets contempt; or inequality of fortunes, discontent. Deliberate then before you marry." [65] The unimaginable becomes quotidian as epic myths inspire cautionary tales; Brathwait's language echoes the commonplaces that Lysander and Hermia exchange about the course of true love. Is it perverse to appropriate Hippolytus as a pedagogical tool for adjusting the workings of socialized desire? No more so, perhaps, than to present Hippolyta as a model for the marriages of *A Midsummer Night's Dream.*

The play underscores that perversity as it concludes with an incongruous spectacle. Occupying the place of a nuptial masque, the mechanicals' playlet generates a flurry of generic contradictions: tragical mirth, lamentable comedy, Hippolyta's own "He says they can do nothing in this kind" (5.1.88). "Nothing in this kind," like Philostrate's description of the playlet as "against your nuptial," suggests the problem of kind, of literary form, presented by "Pyramus and Thisbe" as masque or as farce.

In response to Theseus's declaration, "The best in this kind are but shadows; and the worst are no worse, if imagination amend them," Hippolyta replies, "It must be your imagination then, and not theirs" (5.1.208–10). She might here speak directly to the audience of her own unlikely comedy, reminding us that there is an end to this story that, like the violent ends of Pyramus and Thisbe, can be veiled in light words but not erased. In the last lines of his introductory speech, Peter Quince as Prologue says, "That you should here repent you,/The actors are at hand" (5.1.115–16). It is a moral to the story as apt as it is accidental, in which the Prologue, ruthlessly dismantling the suspension of disbelief, denies the audience the privilege of what Philostrate describes as "unbreathed memories" and ensures that the end is known from the beginning. But Theseus speaks the most suggestive lines, rejecting, significantly, the epilogue: "No epilogue, I pray you; for your play needs no excuse. Never excuse; for when the players are all dead, there need none to be blamed" (5.1.341–43).

In that other story in which the players are all dead, Theseus himself is blamed, not only for the tragedy of Phaedra and Hippolytus but for Hippolyta's death. In Ovid's *Heroides*, Phaedra tells Hippolytus of his mother's fate:

> The chiefe of all the *Amazons*
>   for prowesse and for fame
> Thy Mother was, who well deservde
>   great favor for the same.
> But if thou chaunce of hir what is
>   become, demaunde to make:
> Thou shalt descrie that she hir death
>   by *Theseus* sworde did take.[66]

In Seneca's *Hippolytus*, Theseus himself claims credit: "Now, now, to thee supernal Jove most hearty thankes I yeeld,/That with my first Antiope to dreary death I quelde."[67] The end of Hippolyta's story, already written in the play's refusal to separate violence from desire, literal death from figurative dying, shadows the end of *A Midsummer Night's Dream*. "I will get Peter Quince to write a ballad of this dream," promises Bottom. "It shall be called 'Bottom's Dream', because it hath no bottom; and I will sing it in the latter end of a play, before the Duke. Peradventure, to make it the more gracious, I shall sing it at her death" (4.1.212–17). It is a mark of Bottom's own symptomatic role in this play that his "her" has no referent, that "her death" is a signifier that, rather ominously, floats.

A Midsummer Night's Dream is bracketed by awareness of tragedy and excess; as Montrose writes, "The seductive and destructive powers of women figure centrally in Theseus' career; and his habitual victimization of women, the chronicle of his rapes and disastrous marriages, is a discourse of anxious misogyny which persists as an echo within Shakespeare's text, no matter how much it has been muted or transformed." [68] The play is always in context; in the Arden edition alone, the twenty-three-line hunting scene between Theseus and Hippolyta generates six notes to Seneca's *Hippolytus.* Theseus's job in the play is to defuse this awareness, embodying the authority of comic conclusions. Rolfe quotes one reader's vision of Theseus in this role: "The central figure of the play is that of Theseus. There is no figure in the early drama of Shakspere so magnificent. His are the large hands that have helped to shape the world. His utterance is the rich-toned speech of one who is master of events—who has never known a shrill or eager feeling. His nuptial day is at hand; and while the other lovers are agitated, bewildered, incensed, Theseus, who does not think of himself as a lover but rather as a beneficent conqueror, remains in calm possession of his joy." [69] There is a flaw in the argument, a gap in the progression from sexual desire to benign dictatorship, for by the time we see Theseus for the last time, we have already seen too much. With its aggressive statements of artifice and its defensive pose, a hands-on approach to patriarchy leaves us less with a vision of "calm possession" than with the uneasy awareness of what Theseus's "large hands" have failed to do and done.

A Midsummer Night's Dream offers the repetition of a beginning, with the assumption that that constitutes the end. If Hippolyta comes onstage as a consequence of conquest, that conquest implicitly reorders the play's other disrupted relations. But repetition threatens to transport comic processes into the space of parody. To return briefly to Butler's theory of parodic performances: "As imitations which effectively displace the meaning of the original, they imitate the myth of originality itself." [70] The "myth of originality," the original myth, of *A Midsummer Night's Dream* is Theseus's conquest of Hippolyta, but this act looks rather different in the presence of its imitations. How can we be finished when we have just started? And how successful is the extrapolated naturalization of "masculine" and "feminine," "husband" and "wife," or "sovereign" and "subject" from "hero" and "Amazon"? In *The Eighteenth Brumaire of Louis Bonaparte*, Karl Marx writes, "Hegel remarks somewhere that all facts and personages of great importance in world history occur, as it were, twice. He forgot to add: the first time as tragedy, the second as farce."[71] Like Hippolyta, Marx offers a statement of doubleness, reflecting the intervention of one set of performative terms into space that should be governed by another. Heroic conquest, repeated, might be bowdlerized; comic conclusions, overdetermined, might become unbearable. If, to return to Marx's comment via the mechanicals' dramatic efforts, the parody of tragedy is farce, the parody of comedy might be tragedy. As those phrases "lamentable comedy" and "tragical mirth" begin to hint, there is something troubling not only about the subject of the playlet but about the project of the play. To make an Amazon a blushing bride, to bless a bed that produces Hippolytus, is to ask a great deal of suspended disbelief; at the same time, any understanding of this play as tragic—or, to return to the critical project with which I began, as "serious"—requires a certain faith in overinterpretation. For *A Midsummer Night's Dream* generic categories, like those imposed by socialized desire, are not natural truths or even structural certainties, but the products of imagination.

"It must be your imagination then." This line should perhaps take the place of the lines concerning "great constancy" that have made Hippolyta *A Midsummer Night's Dream*'s dramatic theorist. Here, in this skeptical comment on the power of imagination—and perhaps on the imagination of power—is her own theory of drama, and it illuminates the sense in which any exemplary reading of her role must be attributed not to myth, or to generic convention, or even to Shakespeare, but to us. Hippolyta does not, after all, tell us what she thinks. Marshall writes, "Hippolyta speaks only once in the first scene—and she doesn't speak again until the fourth act—yet critics have usually acted as if they knew what was going on in her mind."[72] His examples, like Harold Brooks's claim that "[Theseus] is an ardent lover, and in her reply Hippolyta reciprocates his love,"[73] demonstrate the force of the critical desire that gives Hippolyta agency only in her own erotic conquest. That desire is hardly new; even Gibson, who claims that Hippolyta defeats Theseus in battle, later takes her as one of his examples of wifely humility. "*Hippolita* the Amazone was so humble and lowly to *Theseus*, that he having received a hurt with the Bulles horne of Praxila on his right shoulder: she used often times to lick the wound with her tongue: whereas even *Chiron* the Centaure grewe offended." [74] Here, as in the readings that Marshall critiques, Hippolyta is complacent, acquiescent, and above all silent, that silence turned to the advantage of heroes and readers who conclude that she has only gotten what she implicitly desired. Such conclusions require as much writing as they do reading, for in *A Midsummer Night's Dream* Hippolyta herself never speaks of desire. But if we are looking for dramatic theory, she says enough about plays to inspire a profound mistrust of her own role in this one.

Epilogue: Via *The Two Noble Kinsmen*

Shakespeare and Fletcher's *The Two Noble Kinsmen* looks like a conqueror's wish fulfillment, *A Midsummer Night's Dream* come true. Hippolyta in this play says the things that readers of Shakespeare's earlier Hippolyta have had to say for her, expressing a desire for marriage, kneeling to her husband not once but twice, and referring unambiguously to her place in the nuptial bed. Her simultaneously martial and sexual surrender encapsulates the fantasy of the Amazon encounter; according to one of the supplicant queens, Hippolyta "wast near to make the male/To thy sex captive," but Theseus proved an irresistible force.

> This thy lord,
> Born to uphold creation in that honour
> First nature styled it in, shrunk thee into
> The bound thou was o'erflowing, at once subduing
> Thy force and thy affection.[1]

Recalling Kleinbaum's formulation — "To win an Amazon, either through arms or through love or, even better, through both, is to be certified as a hero" — the Hippolyta here described guarantees both Theseus's chivalric worth and the patriarchal order he represents.[2] As a frame narrative, her marriage seems to guarantee the play's plot as well: through the figures of Palamon, Arcite, and Emilia, *The Two Noble Kinsmen* co-opts amazonian desires to the traffic in women, its relationships progressing from homoerotic identity through homosocial rivalry to heterosexual marriage.

That progress is not predicted by early appearances, in which the characters of the central love plot seem entirely preoccupied with erotic isolation. Emilia turns desire toward the past, describing her love for the now dead Flavina in a speech concluding, "The true love 'tween maid and maid may be/More than in sex dividual" (1.3.81–82).[3] Hippolyta interprets her speech as a declaration against marriage — "And this high-speeded pace is but to say/That you shall never, like the maid Flavina,/Love any that's called man" — to which Emilia replies, "I am sure I shall not" (1.3.83–85). And if Emilia lives up to expectations of amazonian separatism, Palamon and Arcite are still more literally cut off from heterosocial desire, imprisoned in a tower where they resolve to be content with one another:

> And here being thus together,
> We are an endless mine to one another;
> We are one another's wife, ever begetting
> New births of love; we are father, friends, acquaintance,
> We are, in one another, families;
> I am your heir and you are mine. (2.2.78–83)

An Amazon mourns her lost love, while two princes work out a fantasy of companionate marriage. As comic material, none of this looks very promising.

But we are in the world of romance, where things change quickly. The princes' idyllic raptures are interrupted by a glimpse of Emilia, and mutual admiration becomes rivalry within a hundred lines: "Friendship, blood,/And all the ties between us, I disclaim,/If thou once think upon her," says Palamon (2.2.174–76). Reciprocal murderousness defines their relationship for the rest of the play—"Arcite, thou art so brave an enemy/That no man but thy cousin's fit to kill thee"; "I am in labour/To push your name, your ancient love, our kindred/Out of my memory" (3.6.43–44, 5.1.25–27)—and the logic through which shared desire precipitates mutual violence appears as seamless, inevitable, unquestioned. Emilia is equally quick to shift her passions, and equally passionate in her conversion. Told that she must choose between the princes, she is confounded not by "whether" but by "which": "Out of two, I should/Choose one and pray for his success, but I/Am guiltless of election" (5.1.152–54). The play is firmly if suddenly committed not to homosocial exclusivity but to homosocial exchange, in which women cannot choose men but must be awarded to them; the princes' likeness is not an alliance but a contest, and Emilia is not an agent but the prize. "You are the victor's meed, the prize and garland/To crown the question's title," Theseus tells her; and again, "Know, of this war/You are the treasure and must needs be by/To give the service pay" (5.3.16–17, 30–32).

This is neither ambiguous nor subtle. Rivalry is not a tension or a metaphor but a fight to the death; the commodification of women is a royal speech act. Two men fight for an Amazon; one marries her; the other dies. Avoiding the complications of other Amazon encounters, in which one of the men is an Amazon, or in which there is only one man and he looks like an Amazon, or in which a man gradually realizes that his wife is an Amazon or that an Amazon is his wife, *The Two Noble Kinsmen* efficiently sets up its triangle and knocks it down.

But if we are in the world of romance, we are also still within the logic that identifies amazonian conquest as a pyrrhic victory. Jeffrey Masten argues that *The Two Noble Kinsmen* troubles its own conclusions: "Though the play seems to privilege a competitive mode eventuating in differentiation over a collaborative friendship in which Palamon and Arcite are inseparable, the play undercuts such a position, exposing Theseus's solution to insistent criticism."[4] Theseus may be the play's patriarchal guarantor, but his word, as law, precipitates a crisis of the symbolic. The undermining effect to which Masten refers is both vocal—Emilia's "Is this winning?" (5.3.138)—and structural. Having established a logic of rivalry and reward, the play collapses into caprice: Arcite, who wins the contest, dies in a bizarre accident when he is crushed by his horse; Palamon, by default, gains a bride instead of losing his head. "The conquered triumphs/The victor has the loss," says Theseus (5.4.113–14). Although it follows *The Knight's Tale* in its plot, *The Two Noble Kinsmen*'s conclusion is abrupt and starkly arbitrary, offering funerals and weddings as indistinguishable heroic vehicles and escaping the stage with a brief gesture toward incomprehensible gods. Bruce Smith writes of this play, and of its curiously unsatisfactory happy ending, "On the issue of male bonding versus marriage Shakespeare finished his career, not with one of the reconciliations that are the common theme of his other late plays, but with a fresh recognition of the impasse between the two."[5]

I suggested at the beginning of this book that, in early modern Amazon encounters, victory and defeat are interchangeable effects, both visiting confusion on the social articulations within which they occur. *The Two Noble Kinsmen* makes this its argument. In a play in which everything seems finally to be in place—men and women, homosociality and heterosexuality, frame narratives and the narratives they frame—the perversity of amazonian endings becomes fully clear. Heterosexual desire breaks up a homosocial utopia; heroic masculinity is self-destructive in its triumph; the winner dies, and the loser gets the Amazon. What are we to think?

Notes

PREFACE

1 Wilford, "Ancient Graves of Armed Women Hint at Amazons," B7.
2 Freud, "The 'Uncanny,' " 17: 245.

INTRODUCTION

1 Foucault, *The History of Sexuality, Volume I*, 43.
2 Bray, *Homosexuality in Renaissance England*, 16. See also Bredbeck, *Sodomy and Interpretation*, xi; Bruce Smith, *Homosexual Desire*, 10–11; Goldberg, *Sodometries*, 22; Traub, *Desire and Anxiety*, 111–13; Orgel, *Impersonations*, 37–42; Masten, *Textual Intercourse*, 5–7.
3 For an account of the legal status of sodomy in early modern England and an analysis of the relative infrequency of successful prosecution, see Bruce Smith, *Homosexual Desire*, esp. 41–53.
4 Scott, *Gender and the Politics of History*, 2.
5 Paster, *The Body Embarrassed*, 234. For her discussion of amazonian monomasty as a figure for the early modern infant's experience of inadequate or dangerous nurture, see 234–38. See also Schwarz, "Missing the Breast."
6 Oso'rio, *Five Bookes*, 25v.
7 Dollimore, *Sexual Dissidence*, 239. See also Bredbeck, who observes, "The entrance of sodomy into idealized languages of social order somehow also invokes the broader arenas of dissent trying to be controlled" (*Sodomy and Interpretation*, 21).
8 Traub, *Desire and Anxiety*, 112–13. See also Scott's useful discussion of the evolution of "gender" as an analytic term, in *Gender and the Politics of History*, esp. 31–33.
9 Sedgwick, *Between Men*, 25.
10 Judith Butler, *Bodies That Matter*, xi, 3.
11 Bray, "Homosexuality and the Signs of Male Friendship"; Rambuss, *Closet Devotions*; Stephens, *The Limits of Eroticism*, 19; Traub, "The Perversion of 'Lesbian' Desire"; Bruce Smith, *Homosexual Desire*, 20; Masten, *Textual Intercourse*, 9.
12 Goldberg, *Queering the Renaissance*, 6.
13 Bredbeck, *Sodomy and Interpretation*, 108.
14 Traub, *Desire and Anxiety*; Goldberg, *Sodometries*, 22.
15 Bruce Smith, *Homosexual Desire*, 13.
16 Dollimore, *Sexual Dissidence*, 33. Dollimore defines transgressive reinscription as "a mode of transgression which seeks not an escape from existing structures but rather a subversive reinscription within them, and in the process their dislocation or displacement" (285).
17 Lacan, "The Agency of the Letter in the Unconscious or Reason since Freud," 166.
18 Belsey, *Shakespeare and the Loss of Eden*, 8.
19 Barthes, *Mythologies*, 142.
20 A number of scholars have argued for close connections between contemporary literary theory and early modern texts. See, for example, Belsey, *Shakespeare and the Loss of Eden*, esp. 25; Bredbeck, *Sodomy and Interpretation*, esp. 94; Parker, *Literary Fat Ladies*, 1–7, esp. 5, and her introduction to *Shakespeare and the Question of Theory*, vii–xiii; and Quint's introduction to *Literary Theory/Renaissance Texts*, 1–19, esp. 6–7.

21 Knox, *The First Blast*, 43.

22 Newman, *Fashioning Femininity*, 16.

23 Purchas, *Purchas His Pilgrimage*, 268; 334; 269.

24 Purchas, *Hakluytus Posthumus*, 17: 35.

25 Kleinbaum, *The War against the Amazons*, 1.

26 Diodorus, *Bibliotheca Historica*, 202–3.

27 Lysias, *Lyrias*, 33.

28 Painter, *The Second Tome of The Palace of Pleasure*, 4.

29 Montrose, " 'Shaping Fantasies,' " 38.

30 duBois, *Centaurs and Amazons*, 111.

31 Tyrrell, *Amazons*, 28.

32 Gainsford, *The Glory of England*, 4.

33 Painter, *The Second Tome of The Palace of Pleasure*, 4.

34 For an extensive account of Amazon appearances in pamphlet wars and other polemi-
    cal texts, see Wright, "The Amazons in Elizabethan Literature." For a consideration
    of female exempla in the popular press, see Woodbridge, *Women and the English Renais-
    sance*.

35 Woodbridge, *Women and the English Renaissance*, 128; King, *Women of the Renaissance*, 189.

36 Brathwait, *The English Gentlewoman*, 124.

37 Horowitz, "Introduction," ix. See also Taufer's discussion of the pattern of amazo-
    nian conversion in the *Amadis* texts ("The Only Good Amazon Is a Converted Ama-
    zon," esp. 48), and Woods's discussion of the fantasy of Amazon "taming" ("Ama-
    zonian Tyranny," esp. 53).

38 Painter, *The Second Tome of The Palace of Pleasure*, 4.

39 For a discussion of the rigid formulation of women's roles, see Maclean, *The Re-
    naissance Notion of Woman*, 6–27, and Eaton, "Presentations of Women in the English
    Popular Press," esp. 176.

40 Newman, *Fashioning Femininity*, 30.

41 Shepherd argues for a successful distinction between demonized Amazons and
    idealized warrior women in the early modern period, introducing these categories
    through the Radigund/Britomart opposition. See *Amazons and Warrior Women*, esp.
    chaps. 1 and 2.

42 Spenser, *The Faerie Queene*, 4.11.22.1–2.

43 A number of readers have questioned whether Spenser's qualification, at once hasty
    and belated, succeeds in praising Elizabeth while condemning female rule more
    generally. See for example Stallybrass, who interrogates her status as an exception
    ("Patriarchal Territories," esp.132); and Parker, who describes her implication in "the
    monstrosity of the subjection of male to female power" (*Literary Fat Ladies*, esp. 60).

44 Wright, "The Amazons in Elizabethan Literature," 445n. See also Montrose,
    " 'Shaping Fantasies,' " 46–48; and Kleinbaum, *The War against the Amazons*, 98. Ville-
    ponteaux argues that Spenser does associate Elizabeth with Amazons in an implicit
    critique of her lack of an heir (" 'Not as Women Wonted Be,' " esp. 218). For analysis
    of other early modern references that link Elizabeth with Amazons, see Schleiner,
    "Divina Virago," 163–80. For a reading of texts that link Elizabeth to images of trans-
    gressive sexuality, see Carole Levin, "Power, Politics, and Sexuality."

45 Gibson, *A Womans Woorth*, 4. Agrippa, having defended women's skills in "schools,

court, and camp," writes, "No Strategem did warriour e're devise,/Which first he learnt not from their catching eyes" (*Female Pre-eminence*, 64).

46   Agrippa, *Female Pre-eminence*, 65.

47   G[ainsford], *The Glory of England*, 238.

48   Woodbridge, *Women and the English Renaissance*, 21.

49   Burton, *The Anatomy of Melancholy*, 569. The Latin text reads "Dominam quis possit ferre tonantem?"

50   Wroth, *The Urania*, 422; Aeschylus, *The Suppliant Maidens*, lines 287–88; *Prometheus Bound*, lines 723–24.

51   Gibson, *A Woman's Woorth*, 37r; Faret, *The Honest Man*, 266–267. Burton makes a claim similar to Faret's: "If she be flat-nosed, she is lovely; if hook-nosed, kingly; if dwarfish and little, pretty; if tall, proper and man-like, our brave Brittish *Bunduica*" (*The Anatomy of Melancholy*, 521–22).

52   H[eale], *An Apologie for Women*, 15. Observing that "it was the love stories of Hippolyta and Penthesilea, rather than their battles, which were commonly recounted," Belsey suggests that the evolving ideology of companionate marriage inspired authors to use masculine friendship as a model ("Disrupting Sexual Difference," 178).

53   Maclean, *The Renaissance Notion of Woman*, 58. Barnabe Rich offers a highly typical catalogue of representative virtues, in which his amazonian example — "for activitie in war *Penthesilea*" — contrasts sharply with the other virtues of providence, wisdom, poetry, policy, rhetoric, etc. (*The excellency of good women*, 3).

54   Charles Butler, "The Preface to the Reader," *The Feminine Monarchie*, sig. ₵4. I have modernized the appearance of "th," "ch," and "wh" throughout. Nicholas Culpeper takes up Butler's point in his *Directory for Midwives:* "Reade but *Butler his Book of Bees*, written altogether from experience, and you shall see what an admirable Martial Common-wealth they keep . . . The truth is, no Monarchy of men throughout the whole Universe was ever comparable to them" (43).

55   Aylmer, *An Harborowe for Faithfull and Trewe Subjectes*, sig. D1.

56   Davis, "Women on Top," 127.

57   Bercher, *The Nobility of Women*, 136.

58   Vives, *Instruction of a Christen woman*, 10.

59   Painter, *The Second Tome of The Palace of Pleasure*, iv.

60   *Muld Sacke*, sig. B1v–B2.

61   Heywood, *Exemplary Lives and Memorable Acts*, 104, lines 5–8.

62   Quintus Smyrnaeus, *The Fall of Troy*, lines 917–919.

63   Tyrrell, *Amazons*, 81, emphasis in original.

64   Herodotus, *The History*, 4.111.

65   Judith Butler, *Bodies That Matter*, 49.

66   Halperin, "Why Is Diotima a Woman?," 144.

67   Enterline, *The Tears of Narcissus*, 8.

68   Sandys, *Ovid's Metamorphosis Englished*, 160.

69   Whitney, *A Choice of Emblemes*, 149.

70   Fraunce, *The Third part of the Countesse of Pembroke's Yuychurch*, 15.

71   Sandys, *Ovid's Metamorphosis Englished*, 156.

72   Freud, "On Narcissism," 14: 94.

73   Fradenburg and Freccero, introduction, xv.

Notes to Introduction

74 Freud links such desire to narcissism. "[The ego-ideal] binds not only a person's narcissistic libido, but also a considerable amount of his homosexual libido, which is in this way turned back into the ego. The want of satisfaction which arises from the non-fulfilment of this ideal liberates homosexual libido, and this is transformed into a sense of guilt (social anxiety). Originally this sense of guilt was a fear of punishment by the parents, or, more correctly, the fear of losing their love; later the parents are replaced by an indefinite number of fellow-men" ("On Narcissism," 14: 101–2).

75 Bruce Smith, *Homosexual Desire*, 73.

76 Traub, *Desire and Anxiety*, 139.

77 Bray, "Homosexuality and the Signs of Male Friendship in Elizabethan England," 53. See also Bruce Smith's discussion of the tension between eroticized male bonding and the emphasis on marriage (*Homosexual Desire*, 72–73).

78 Goldberg, *Sodometries*, 37.

79 Comes, *Mythologia*, vol. 9, chap. 16, 523. For extensive discussion of this version of the myth, see Enterline, *The Tears of Narcissus*, 283–88.

80 Enterline, *The Tears of Narcissus*, 285.

81 Belsey, "Disrupting Sexual Difference," 187–88.

82 *Shakespeare's Ovid*, 3.521–24.

83 For a reading that links narcissism to Medusa in an attempt to define "the essential logic of superstition," see Siebers, *The Mirror of Medusa*. The quotation is from xiv. Stephens considers the implications if Medusa were to exchange gazes with a woman rather than a man; see *The Limits of Eroticism*, esp. 73–101.

84 Sandys, *Ovid's Metamorphosis Englished*, 221.

85 Diodorus, *Bibliotheca Historica*, 1: 287.

86 Thevet, *The New found worlde*, 101v.

87 Ralegh, *The discoverie*, 10:367.

88 Cartari, *Imagini*, qtd. in Orgel, "Jonson and the Amazons," 128–29.

89 Sandys, *Ovid's Metamorphosis Englished*, 221.

90 Freud, "Medusa's Head," 18: 273.

91 Sandys, *Ovid's Metamorphosis Englished*, 221. Other early modern readings of Medusa also incorporate multiple and even contradictory conclusions about the myth's meaning, including sexuality, aesthetics, knowledge, and martial law; see, for example, Fraunce, *The Third part of the Countesse of Pembroke's Yuychurch*, 29; and Bateman, *The Golden Booke of the Leaden Gods*, sig. Bv; sig. F.

92 *Shakespeare's Ovid*, 4.977–78. For a reading of the interplay of male and female sexuality in the Medusa story, and of the process by which male rhetoric appropriates the agency of Medusa's threat, see Vickers, "The Blazon of Sweet Beauty's Best," 109–12.

93 Cixous, "The Laugh of the Medusa," 289.

94 Stoller, *Observing the Erotic Imagination*, 155.

95 John Freccero, "Medusa," 8; 13.

96 Fraunce, *The Third part of the Countesse of Pembroke's Yuychurch*, 29.

97 Freud, "Medusa's Head," 18: 274.

98 Herodotus, *The History*, 4.114–16.

99 Dollimore, *Sexual Dissidence*, 34.

100 Traub, *Desire and Anxiety*, 105.

101 Stallybrass and White, *The Politics and Poetics of Transgression*, 5.

102 Freedman, *Staging the Gaze*, 4.

103 Freud, "The 'Uncanny,' " 17: 226.

104 Derrida, ". . . That Dangerous Supplement . . . ," 145.

105 Halberstam, *Female Masculinity*, 2.

106 Brown, *Immodest Acts*, 11.

107 Sedgwick, *Between Men*, 45.

108 Elyot, *The Defence of Good Women*, sig. C7v.

109 Agrippa, *Female Pre-eminence*, 76–77. Woodbridge, having discussed the elements of rhetorical paradox in Agrippa's text, writes of this moment, "Agrippa, as if his ingenuity had reached its outer limit with the eagles, phoenix, and basilisks, turns sober and begins arguing straightforwardly what was always the real issue—the case for equality" (*Women and the English Renaissance*, 42). See also Bercher, who writes, "Yff the wymen of our tyme do not exercyse armys yt is bycawse the Custom is other wyse, and not ffor lack of their boldenes" (*The Nobility of Women*, 131).

110 Judith Butler, *Gender Trouble*, 141.

111 Case, "Toward a Butch-Femme Aesthetic," 305. As is the case with the role playing produced by early modern patriarchy and by Amazon encounters, such readings of butch-femme relationship structures emphasize the intersection of social and sexual categories; the construction of those categories, however, is imagined as participatory, whereas both the patriarchal and amazonian heterosexual categories that I have considered are represented as coercively imposed.

112 For a reading of one early modern woman who explicitly compares herself to an Amazon queen, see Goldberg's account of female calligrapher Esther Inglis. Goldberg writes of the self-portraits that accompany Inglis's texts, "These are pictures of a humble Amazon, transcending the limits of her sex even as she retranscribes them and enters into the excessive sphere that copying opens up" (Goldberg, *Writing Matter*, 146–53; the quotation is from 150–52).

113 Fradenburg and Freccero, introduction, xix.

114 Newman, *Fashioning Femininity*, 4–5.

115 For comments on the asymmetry of redistributions of gender roles, see Woodbridge, *Women and the English Renaissance*, 146, and Rackin, "Historical Difference/Sexual Difference," 41.

1 FALLING OFF THE EDGE OF THE WORLD: RALEGH AMONG THE AMAZONS

1 Qtd. in Morison, *Christopher Columbus*, 211. For further discussion of the letter, see Morison's "Appendix: Columbus's Letter on His First Voyage," in ibid., 203–13.

2 "A treatyse of the newe *India* . . . after the description of Sebastian Munster in his boke of universall Cosmographie," in Eden, *The first Three English books on America*, 30.

3 Todorov, *The Conquest of America*, 13.

4 Cuddon, *A Dictionary of Literary Terms*, 394.

5 Lacan, "The Agency of the Letter in the Unconscious," 167; emphasis in original.

6 Fuller, "Ralegh's Fugitive Gold," 60. Fuller argues that metonymy, as a figure for objects that recede through association, displaces the "part-for-whole" logic of synecdoche in exploration narratives; see esp. 45.

7 Thevet, *The New Founde Worlde*, 101.

8 G[ainsford], *The Glory of England*, 75.

Notes to Chapter One

9   Kleinbaum, *The War against the Amazons*, 118.

10   Carvajal, *Discovery of the Orellana River*, 214.

11   Garcilasso Inca de la Vega, *The Expedition of Gonzalo Pizaro To the Land of Cinnamon*, 13.

12   Greenblatt, *Marvelous Possessions*, 20.

13   For further discussion of the role of translation and hearsay in amazonian narratives, see Leonard, *Books of the Brave*, 51–53, and Putnam, "California," 319.

14   Todorov, *The Conquest of America*, 17.

15   de Acuña, *A New Discovery of the Great River of the Amazons*, 123.

16   Medina, *The Discovery of the Amazon*, 25–26.

17   Penrose, *Travel and Discovery in the Renaissance*, 115.

18   Herrmann, *The Great Age of Discovery*, 213.

19   Morison, *The European Discovery of America*, 213–14. For discussion of these names, see Medina's chapter on the name of the river, in *The Discovery of the Amazon*, 153–63.

20   For discussion of contracts that specify the discovery of Amazons, see Leonard, *Books of the Brave*, 46–53.

21   For a history of the company, see Griffiths, *A Licence to Trade*, 208. J. H. Parry also mentions it in *The Establishment of the European Hegemony, 1415–1715*, 99.

22   Greenblatt, *Marvelous Possessions*, 22–23.

23   Qtd. in Medina, *The Discovery of the Amazon*, 399.

24   Alvares, *The Prester John of the Indies*, 455.

25   Mandeville, *Mandeville's Travels*, 1: 184–86. See also Penrose, *Travel and Discovery in the Renaissance*, 12.

26   Purchas, *Hakluytus Posthumus*, 7: 363. Purchas's comment on the amazonian discoveries of Don John Bermudez reflects a characteristic interplay of skepticism and belief: "Much of this Chapter seemeth to mee Apocrypha, but I leave libertie of Faith to the most licentious Credulitie, which shall thinke fitter to beleeve then to goe and see. And yet may Africa have a Prerogative in Rarities, and some seeming Incredibilities be true" (Purchas, *Hakluytus Posthumus*, 7: 364).

27   Mandeville, *Mandeville's Travels*, 1: 108.

28   Leonard, *Books of the Brave*, 48, 40; see also Kleinbaum, *The War against the Amazons*, 114.

29   Alvares, *The Prester John of the Indies*, 457.

30   de Acuña, *A New Discovery of the Great River of the Amazons*, 123. Nuño de Guzmán writes, "I shall goe to finde the Amazons, which some say dwell in the Sea, some in an arme of the Sea, and that they are rich" ("The Relation of Nunno di Gusman written to Charles the fift Emperour," in Purchas, *Hakluytus Posthumus*, 18: 59).

31   "The travels of Hulderike Schnirdel in twentie yeeres space from 1534. to 1554. abbreviated," in Purchas, *Hakluytus Posthumus*, 17: 33–34.

32   Purchas, *Purchas his Pilgrimage*, 334.

33   Rosenthal, "The Isle of the Amazons," 259.

34   de Acuña, *A New Discovery of the Great River of the Amazons*, 122.

35   "The admirable adventures and strange fortunes of Master Antonie Knivet," in Purchas, *Hakluytus Posthumus*, 16: 225.

36   "Observations of Master John Cartwright in his Voyage from Aleppo to Hispaan," in Purchas, *Hakluytus Posthumus*, 8: 489.

37   Todorov, *The Conquest of America*, 13. For accounts that connect this interdependence of voyage and text specifically to Amazons, see, for example, Rosenthal, "The Isle of the Amazons," 257, and Herrmann, *The Great Age of Discovery*, 213.

38 Díaz, *The Conquest of New Spain,* 214.
39 Putnam, "California," 353. See also Leonard, 52–53.
40 Leonard, *Books of the Brave,* 39. For further discussion of Columbus's influence on Montalvo, see Putnam, "California," 316.
41 Medina, *The Discovery of the Amazon,* 33.
42 "A discourse of the West Indies and South sea written by Lopez Vaz a Portugal," in Hakluyt, *Principal Navigations,* 11: 247.
43 de Herrera, *The Voyage of Francisco de Orellana Down The River of the Amazons,* 34.
44 Purchas, *Purchas his Pilgrimage,* 334.
45 Purchas, *Hakluytus Posthumus,* 7: 205; 16: 225; 17: 261, 17: 35.
46 Morison, *Christopher Columbus,* 130.
47 "The Decades of the newe worlde of west India," in Eden, *The first Three English books on America,* 189.
48 Hakluyt, *Principal Navigations,* 11: 246; "The Voyage of Sir Francis Alvarez, a Portugall Priest," in Purchas, *Hakluytus Posthumus,* 7: 206.
49 Klein, "Love, Guilt and Reparation," 104.
50 Ralegh, *The discoverie,* 10: 339. Subsequent citations appear in parentheses in the text.
51 Montrose, "The Work of Gender in the Discourse of Discovery," 11.
52 Fuller, "Ralegh's Fugitive Gold," 57.
53 Knapp, *An Empire Nowhere,* 188.
54 For a discussion of Ralegh's relationship to royal patronage, see Tennenhouse, "Sir Walter Ralegh and the Literature of Clientage." For analysis of Elizabethan patronage as it influenced *The discoverie,* see Greenblatt, *Sir Walter Ralegh,* esp. chap. 4; Montrose, "The Work of Gender in the Discourse of Discovery," esp. 8–10; and Fuller, "Ralegh's Fugitive Gold," 57–59.
55 Montaigne, "Of the Caniballes," in *Essayes,* 101.
56 Fuller, "Ralegh's Fugitive Gold," 45–46. Montrose also discusses the relationship between Ralegh's narrative and his experience, describing it as "mutually defeating"; see "The Work of Gender in the Discourse of Discovery," esp. 14–15. For a larger account of the intimate relationship between exploration and writing, and of the expectations, literary and economic, that require narrative to stand in for material findings, see Fuller's introduction to *Voyages in Print,* 1–15.
57 Barbara Herrnstein Smith, *On the Margins of Discourse,* 132.
58 Freud, "The 'Uncanny,' " 17: 244.
59 Knapp, *An Empire Nowhere,* 7, 11.
60 Greenblatt, *Sir Walter Ralegh,* 102–3.
61 Montrose, "The Work of Gender in the Discourse of Discovery," 25. See also his assertion that linking Queen Elizabeth's body to the land "might well serve to aggrandize the sovereign rather than to subordinate the woman" (13).
62 Montaigne, "Of the Caniballes," in *Essayes,* 103.
63 Newman, *Fashioning Femininity,* 18.
64 In their introduction to *Subject and Object in Renaissance Culture,* Margreta de Grazia, Maureen Quilligan, and Peter Stallybrass describe "a dialectic in which subjects and objects reciprocally take and make each other over," and write, "At a time when western Europe had embarked on an extended colonization of the world, such acts of appropriation can be seen as a circulation of objects as well as the oppression of one set of people by another" (8). Ralegh sets up such a circulation by represent-

ing objects of desire and his own desiring subjectivity as interchangeable figures of speech.

65 For discussion of the iconographic tradition linking images of Elizabeth to those of geographical space, see, for example, Helgerson, "The Land Speaks." See also Montrose, "The Work of Gender in the Discourse of Discovery," esp. 28. For a discussion of the equation of land to female bodies more generally, see Parker, *Literary Fat Ladies,* esp. 126–54.

66 Montrose, "The Work of Gender in the Discourse of Discovery," 12.

67 Klein, "Love, Guilt and Reparation," 105.

68 Freud, "The 'Uncanny,'" 17: 245.

69 Fuller, "Ralegh's Fugitive Gold," 58.

2 FEARFUL SIMILE: STEALING THE
BREECH IN SHAKESPEARE'S CHRONICLE PLAYS

1 Candido offers a useful overview of such structural readings in his essay "Getting Loose in the *Henry VI* Plays," esp. 392n; see also Rackin's description of the tetralogy in *Stages of History,* 62–63.

2 For readings of the tetralogy's women as similar to one another, see Bevington, "The Domineering Female," esp. 51; Marcus, *Puzzling Shakespeare,* 89–90; and Rackin, "Anti-Historians," esp. 332.

3 Howard and Rackin, *Engendering a Nation,* 65.

4 Jardine, *Still Harping on Daughters,* 105.

5 Freud, "The 'Uncanny,'" 17: 220.

6 Bevington, "The Domineering Female," 51–58; Rackin, "Anti-Historians," 329; Marcus, *Puzzling Shakespeare,* 75; Gutierrez, "Gender and Value in *1 Henry VI,*" 190; Lee, "Reflections of Power," 214; and Pye, "The Theater, the Market, and the Subject of History," 511.

7 Rackin, "Historical Difference/Sexual Difference," 43. See also Kahn's discussion of Joan's doubly emasculating effect in *Man's Estate,* 55–56.

8 Judith Butler, *Gender Trouble,* 140. Emphasis in original.

9 Quotations from the *Henry VI* plays follow *The Complete Works of William Shakespeare,* ed. Bevington.

10 Brathwait, "Character: A Gentlewoman," epilogue to *The English Gentlewoman,* sig. Gg2v.

11 Lacan, "The Signification of the Phallus," 289.

12 Freedman, *Staging the Gaze,* 3.

13 Kahn, *Man's Estate,* 55.

14 Rackin, "Anti-Historians," 334. For an earlier version of this opposition of the material to the spiritual, see Bevington, "The Domineering Female," 55.

15 Judith Butler, *Bodies That Matter,* 3.

16 Kahn, *Man's Estate,* 47. See also Howard and Rackin, *Engendering a Nation,* 47.

17 Dollimore, *Sexual Dissidence,* 303.

18 See, for example, Gutierrez, "Gender and Value in *1 Henry VI,*" 190.

19 Gabriele Bernhard Jackson, "Topical Ideology," 64–65. See also MacKenzie, "Myth and Anti-Myth in the First Tetralogy," esp. 2–3.

20 See, for example, Hardin, "Chronicles and Mythmaking in Shakespeare's Joan of

Arc," 35; Pye, "The Theater, the Market, and the Subject of History," 511; and Cox, "Devils and Power in Marlowe and Shakespeare," 61.

21 Shaw suggestively calls Joan "the pioneer of rational dressing for women" (*Saint Joan*, 3). On the visual doubleness of her female body and masculine armor, see Marcus, *Puzzling Shakespeare*, 100; Gutierrez, "Gender and Value in *1 Henry VI*," 185; and Gabriele Bernhard Jackson, "Topical Ideology," 54.

22 Rackin, "Anti-Historians," 331. Belsey reads Joan in the context of such "extra-human" figures as Cleopatra and Lady Macbeth; see *The Subject of Tragedy*, 185.

23 Shaw, *Saint Joan*, 3.

24 1.2.51; 1.2.104; 1.4.107; 1.5.6; 1.5.12; 1.6.4; 1.6.4; 1.6.29.

25 Edward Hall, *The Union of the two noble and illustrate famelies of Lancastre and Yorke*, fols. Cvii and Cxiii ᵛ. On the relationship between Shakespeare's portrayal of Joan and the chronicles', see Hardin, "Chronicles and Mythmaking in Shakespeare's Joan of Arc."

26 Agrippa, *Female Pre-eminence*, 66–67.

27 Gibson, *A Womans Woorth*, 12–12v.

28 Newstead, *An Apology for Women*, 17–19.

29 Christine de Pizan, whose *Le Ditié de Jeanne d'Arc* was the first poem praising Joan of Arc and the only one written during Joan's lifetime, also celebrates her martial conquests; for a reading of this poem in the context of Christine de Pizan's life and other writings, see Willard, *Christine de Pizan*, 204–7. For a discussion of the poem in the context of other early literary representations of Joan of Arc, see Fraioli, "The Literary Image of Joan of Arc."

30 Marcus, *Puzzling Shakespeare*, 53.

31 On Joan's confusion of feminine categories, see Jeanne Addison Roberts, "Birth Traumas in Shakespeare," 62.

32 Vives, *The Instruction of a Christen woman*, 15v.

33 For a reading of Joan's feminization as a trope of woman-taming, see Gabriele Bernhard Jackson, "Topical Ideology," 60.

34 Tillyard, *Shakespeare's History Plays*, 162. Shaw suggests that even if the play is Shakespeare's, the intention is not, a possibility that displaces guilt while maintaining authority: "The impression left by it is that the playwright, having begun by an attempt to make Joan a beautiful and romantic figure, was told by his scandalized company that English patriotism would never stand a sympathetic representation of a French conqueror of English troops, and that unless he at once introduced all the old charges against Joan of being a sorceress and harlot, and assumed her to be guilty of all of them, his play could not be produced. As likely as not this is what actually happened" (*Saint Joan*, 24).

35 This conceit, that looking at the beloved object causes a loss of language that nonetheless produces poetry, runs throughout such sonnet sequences as *Astrophil and Stella*. See, for example, the famous concluding lines of Sonnet 1: "Thus great with child to speak, and helpless in my throes,/Biting my truant pen, beating myself for spite,/ 'Fool,' said my Muse to me, 'look in thy heart and write' " (*Sir Philip Sidney: Selected Poems*, ll. 12–14).

36 For historical links between Queen Margaret and Joan of Arc, see Lee, "Reflections of Power," 198–99.

37 For readings of the stage direction and of Suffolk's relationship to Margaret more generally, see Adelman, *Suffocating Mothers*, 8, and Rackin, "Historical Difference," 42.

38 Kahn, *Man's Estate*, 55.

39 MacDonald, " 'Hay for the Daughters!,' " 209.

40 "How king Henry the syxt a vertuous prince, was after many other miseries cruelly murdered in the Tower of London," in *The Mirror for Magistrates*, 216.

41 Heywood, GYNAIKEION, 239–40. It is worth noting that reticence verging on disavowal characterizes the end of Heywood's list of viragoes: Joan la Pucelle, of whom he would prefer to say nothing that others have not already said, is followed by Emma, of whose slaughter of the Danes he says, "Though it after prooved ominous, and was the cause of much miserie and mischiefe, yet it shewed in her a noble and notable resolution" (239); and Emma is followed by Margaret, the last in his catalogue, of whom he would apparently prefer to say nothing at all. Here, as in the *Henry VI* plays, even the encomiasts show a certain ambivalence. For Heywood in particular this ambivalence appears to exercise its own fascination; in his 1640 catalogue of female worthies, *The Exemplary Lives and Memorable Acts of Nine the Most Worthy Women of the World*, he will return to Queen Margaret, making her his second Christian and his penultimate queen, followed only by Queen Elizabeth I.

42 Howard and Rackin, *Engendering a Nation*, 93.

43 Hall, *The Union of the two noble and illustrate famelies of Lancastre and Yorke*, fols. Clij, Cliiij, Clix^{r-v}, Clxvj^v, and Clxx^v. For readings of a possible connection between such descriptions of Margaret and representations of Queen Elizabeth I, see Lee, "Reflections of Power," 214–17, and Marcus, *Puzzling Shakespeare*, 89–93.

44 Hall, *The Union of the two noble and illustrate famelies of Lancastre and Yorke*, fol. Clxxvj^v.

45 Howard and Rackin, *Engendering a Nation*, 84. See also Kahn, *Man's Estate*, 60–61. For a historical view of this issue, see Lee, "Reflections of Power," 192.

46 Heywood, *The Exemplary Lives and Memorable Acts*, 152, 159. Heywood's account of Margaret in this catalogue of worthies, ostensibly a patriotic celebration, is undercut throughout by ambivalence, providing a suggestive footnote to his reticence in the earlier GYNAIKEION.

47 Barckley, *The Felicitie of Man*, 258. This is a popular account of amazonian origins, repeated by several early modern authors. For a more general discussion of its implications, see my reading of Painter's very similar narrative in the introduction.

48 Hall, *The Union of the two noble and illustrate famelies of Lancastre and Yorke*, fol. Clxxxiiij.

49 Judith Butler, *Bodies That Matter*, 2.

50 Brathwait, *The English Gentlewoman*, 123. For a similarly theatrical rhetoric of condemnation, see Rich, *The excellency of good women*, 22.

51 Riviere, "Womanliness as a Masquerade," 101.

52 For a more detailed reading of this slippage in Knox's text, see my discussion in the introduction to this book.

53 On the relationship between male tyranny and female sexual excess, see Bushnell, "Tyranny and Effeminacy in Early Modern England," esp. 343.

54 Diodorus, *Bibliotheca Historica*, 1: 287–88.

55 Images of women who have "stolen the breeches" are an early modern commonplace. Stefans Guazzo writes of domineering wives, "at this daie the race of the *Spartane* women is worne out, and therefore it is best for them to be content, to let their husbands weare the breeches" (*Civile Conversation*, 133). John Ferne, in *The Blazon of Gentrie*,

writes of Semiramis, "She abandoned, all feminine attyre: for shee invented firste, the use of breeches, and betooke her selfe, to the speare and shield" (1: 156). And Robert Burton warns the man who marries a wealthy or noble wife, "Thou shalt be as the Tassell of a gosse-hauk, *she will ride upon thee, domineere as she list,* weare the breeches in her oligarchicall government, and begger thee besides" (*The Anatomy of Melancholy,* 569, emphasis in original).

56 For a particularly symptomatic list of the effects the mother's imagination may produce on the child, see Culpeper, *A Directory for Midwives,* 140. Culpeper recounts the popular story of a woman who looks at a Moor's picture during conception and gives birth to a black child, and also discusses the effects of praying to a picture of John the Baptist and sitting next to a boy with four thumbs.

57 *The Problems of Aristotle,* D8v. This account of children's resemblances to their parents stands in some tension with William Bercher's, which I quoted in the introduction. As the two passages taken together suggest, the question of which parent determines the nature of the child is strongly contested in the early modern period; indeed, the womb is often imagined as a kind of battleground on which mother and father fight for supremacy. For a discussion of the connections between such images and the larger sexual hostilities played out in Amazon myth, see my essay, "Mother Love."

58 Kahn and Adelman have discussed this conviction at length; see Kahn, *Man's Estate,* and Adelman, *Suffocating Mothers.* For readings of the representation of maternal power as a male fantasy, see Gohlke, " 'I wooed thee with my sword,' " and Traub, "Prince Hal's Falstaff."

59 For readings of Margaret's grief as feminization, see Howard and Rackin, *Engendering a Nation,* 97–98, and Dash, *Wooing, Wedding, and Power,* 191.

60 For samples of this debate—Do curses make history or merely take advantage of hindsight?—see Marcus, *Puzzling Shakespeare,* 94, and Rackin, "Anti-Historians," 337. In *Still Harping on Daughters,* Jardine writes, "The politically astute Margaret of the early plays becomes 'poor Margaret . . . prophetess'. The curse of the scold is feared almost as much as the drubbing she supposedly administers to her unfortunate man, as the records of the witch-trials remind us, but it achieves nothing" (118). See also Adelman, *Suffocating Mothers,* 9.

61 Greene, *Greenes Groats-worth of witte,* F1v; emphasis in original.

62 For readings of the relationship between Margaret and Shakespeare as suggested by Greene, see Marcus, *Puzzling Shakespeare,* 96, and Howard and Rackin, *Engendering a Nation,* 95–96.

3 STRANGER IN THE MIRROR: AMAZON
REFLECTIONS IN THE JACOBEAN QUEEN'S MASQUE

1 Wynne-Davies, "The Queen's Masque," 80. See also Lewalski, who describes the Jacobean queen's masque as "a site for contestation about gender, power, and status" (*Writing Women in Jacobean England,* 29).

2 Goldberg, *James I and the Politics of Literature,* 57. Orgel discusses the complementary relationship between masque and king in *The Illusion of Power;* see esp. 37–43. For a similar argument, see Kogan, *The Hieroglyphic King,* 47.

3 Woolf, *A Room of One's Own,* 35.

4 Lindley, *The Court Masque,* 13.

Notes to Chapter Three

5   Lewalski, *Writing Women in Jacobean England*, 28.
6   Daniel, *The Vision of the Twelve Goddesses*, 3:188, in *The Complete Works*. Subsequent citations appear parenthetically, the preface by page, the text by line.
7   Vickers, "Diana Described," 109.
8   Sandys, *Ovid's Metamorphosis Englished*, 132.
9   Dollimore, *Sexual Dissidence*, 287.
10 Qtd. in Spencer, *A Book of Masques in Honour of Alardyce Nicoll*, 41.
11 Gossett, " 'Man-maid, begone!,' " 98.
12 Orgel, *The Jonsonian Masque*, 56.
13 For extensive discussion of the multiple celebratory images attached to Elizabeth I, see Yates, *Astraea*.
14 Jonson, *The Masque of Blackness*, ll. 8–10, in *The Complete Masques*. Subsequent references to Jonson's masques appear parenthetically in the text.
15 The aestheticization of Niger's daughters diverges from the pejorative uses of "Ethiop" in early modern texts; Lysander's command to Hermia, "Away, you Ethiope!" (*A Midsummer Night's Dream*, 3.2.256), like Romeo's image of "A rich jewel in an Ethiop's ear" (*Romeo and Juliet*, 1.5.47), refers to a standardized vocabulary of alienation that becomes both complicated and ambiguous in *Blackness*. For extensive analysis of the aesthetic conventions attached to racial difference, see Kim Hall, *Things of Darkness*. The quotations from Shakespeare follow *The Complete Works*, ed. Bevington.
16 Qtd. in Herford, Simpson, and Simpson, *Ben Jonson*, 10: 448; emphasis in original. I have modernized typography in this and subsequent quotations from this source.
17 Kim Hall, *Things of Darkness*, 134.
18 "The Relation of Nunno di Gusman written to Charles the fift Emperour," in Purchas, *Hakluytus Posthumus*, 18: 60; Morison, *The European Discovery of America*, 620. History, in the case of de Guzmán, translates the amazonian quest object from white to black. In her reading of the amazonian episodes of *Amadis*, Putnam traces this pattern in reverse; Montalvo's Amazons begin as "black women without a single man among them," but later translators often either omit the designation of race or revise it to whiteness. See "California: The Name," 306; 312n.
19 Kim Hall, *Things of Darkness*, 136.
20 For an instance in which anxieties concerning race and gender converge in a more explicit disruption of male power, see Kim Hall's discussion of the 1606 entertainments for King Christian of Denmark (*Things of Darkness*, 138–40).
21 For a discussion of *Blackness* and *Beauty* as antimasque and masque, see Orgel, *The Jonsonian Masque*, 119–20.
22 Gossett, " 'Man-maid, begone!,' " 99.
23 Orgel, "Jonson and the Amazons," 130.
24 Wynne-Davies, "The Queen's Masque," 85. See also Lewalski, *Writing Women in Jacobean England*, 37, and Orgel, *Impersonations*, 110.
25 Sandys, *Ovid's Metamorphosis Englished*, 221.
26 Tyrrell, *Amazons*, 110. For an extended account of the link between Medusa and the Amazons, see my discussion in the introduction to this book.
27 Virgil, *The Aeneid*, l. 469; Spenser, *The Faerie Queene*, 3.4.2.5–6.
28 *Queens*, 542; 543; 545.
29 Orgel, *Impersonations*, 110.
30 Lewalski, *Writing Women in Jacobean England*, 37.

Notes to Chapter Three

31 "Sir Anthony Weldon's Character of King James I," in Ashton, *James I by his Contemporaries*, 13.

32 Lewalski, *Writing Women in Jacobean England*, 38.

33 Heywood, *The Exemplary Lives and Memorable Acts of Nine the Most Worthy Women of the World*, 211.

34 Judith Butler, *Gender Trouble*, 45.

35 Dollimore, *Sexual Dissidence*, 33.

36 Orgel, "Jonson and the Amazons," 134.

37 For a discussion of Prince Henry as an alternative political and representational focus, see, for example, Orgel, "Jonson and the Amazons," 134–36, and Graham Parry, "The Court of Henry, Prince of Wales," chap. 3 in *The Golden Age Restor'd*. Interestingly, Prince Henry was celebrated at least once in an amazonian pageant; Nichols gives this account of his baptism: "Last of all came in three Amazones in women's attire, very sumptuously clad; and these were the Lord of Lendores, the Lord of Barclewech, and the Abbot of Holy-roole-house" (*The Progresses of Elizabeth*, 356). Jonson writes the extensive notes to his *Masque of Queens* at Prince Henry's request, dedicating the text "to the glory of our own, and grief of other nations, my lord Henry, Prince of Great Britain."

38 Lewalski argues that the effective conclusion of Anne's interventions occurs after *Tethys;* for her discussion of *Tethys* as potentially subversive, see *Writing Women in Jacobean England*, 39–40.

39 Daniel, *Tethys Festival: or, The Queenes Wake*, 3: lines 395–96, in *The Complete Works*. Subsequent citations appear in parentheses in the text.

40 Bacon, "Of Masques and Triumphs," 145–46 in *A Selection*.

41 Puttenham, *The Arte of English Poesie*, 148.

42 Plutarch, *The Lives of the Noble Grecians and Romanes Compared*, 1003.

43 Painter, *The Second Tome of The Palace of Pleasure*, Sig. Aiiij. The twenty-eighth novel of the first volume of *The Palace of Pleasure* promises "the straunge and beastlye nature of *Timon of Athenes* enemie to mankinde, with his death, buriall, and Epitaphe" (57v).

44 For the play's stage history, see Charney, "*Timon of Athens* on Stage and Screen," and Gary Jay Williams, "Stage History, 1816–1978."

45 Several scholars have pursued the possibility that Middleton may have written large parts of the play; for examples of the discussion, see MacDonald Jackson, *Studies in Attribution*, and Lake, *The Canon of Thomas Middleton's Plays*.

46 A number of critics contend that Timon lacks the potential for introspection or change that would enable the play to succeed as a tragedy. For an overview of the argument, see Charney's introduction to the Signet edition of the play.

47 See, for example, Bradbrook, *The Tragic Pageant of Timon of Athens;* Charney's introduction; and Harry Levin, "Shakespeare's Misanthrope."

48 Chambers, *William Shakespeare*, 1: 86.

49 Quotations from *Timon of Athens* follow *The Complete Works*, ed. Bevington.

50 Handelman, "*Timon of Athens*," 49. For her discussion of the absence of women as a failure of mediation between men, see esp. 52, 65.

51 Kermode, "Introduction: *Timon of Athens*," 1443.

52 Soellner, *Timon of Athens*, 70. For a reading of Cupid and the Amazons as iconographic figures for the play's negative progress, see Fulton, "Timon, Cupid, and the Amazons."

Notes to Chapter Three

53 Kahn, " 'Magic of Bounty,' " 155–56.

54 For discussion of this correspondence, see ibid., 157–59.

4 DRESSED TO KILL: LOOKING FOR LOVE IN *THE FAERIE QUEENE*

1 Lacan, "The Mirror Stage," 4.

2 Freedman, *Staging the Gaze*, 7.

3 Lacan describes the infant's relationship to his support in these terms: "Unable as yet to walk, or even to stand up, and held tightly as he is by some support, human or artificial (what, in France, we call a '*trotte-bébé*'), he nevertheless overcomes, in a flutter of jubilant activity, the obstructions of his support and, fixing his attitude in a slightly leaning-forward position, in order to hold it in his gaze, brings back an instantaneous aspect of the image" ("The Mirror Stage," 1–2).

4 Rose, "Introduction II," 30; emphasis in original.

5 Paster, *The Body Embarrassed*, 18.

6 Sedgwick, *Between Men*, 1–2.

7 Silberman reads this tension as a symptom of what she terms "problems of representing experience," particularly in Book 4. In her reading, the opposition of homosocial to heterosexual narrative structures critiques homosocial repetition as static and arbitrary, while offering a positive view of the "asymmetric" progress of Britomart's desire. See *Transforming Desire*, esp. 105–9. See also her contrast of Britomart to Marinell, 28–29.

8 Quilligan, "The Comedy of Female Authority in *The Faerie Queene*," 163.

9 Spenser, *The Faerie Queene*, 3.2.23.7–8. Subsequent citations appear in parentheses in the text. For the association of Britomart with excessive sexual desire, see, for example, Leslie's claim that "Britomart is the fitting heroine for a book containing Argante, Ollyphant, and Paridell, not because she is their polar opposite, but because she is so like them. Comparing her with Argante is not merely facetious: both are energetically pursuing men for frankly sexual purposes" (*Spenser's "Fierce Warres and Faithfull Loves*," 83).

10 Suzuki, *Metamorphoses of Helen*, 154. See also Silberman's discussion of the relationship between narcissism and the Hermaphrodite in "The Hermaphrodite and the Metamorphosis of Spenserian Allegory," esp. 216–18.

11 Silberman, "The Hermaphrodite," 216. Readers of *The Faerie Queene* have consistently attempted to attach a redemptive meaning to the potentially grotesque and disruptive hermaphroditic simile; see, for example, Lewis, *The Allegory of Love*, 344; Roche, *The Kindly Flame*, 134–36; and Williams, "Venus and Diana," who argues, like Silberman, for a transition from the image of the actual mythological figure of the hermaphrodite to Britomart's successful synthesis of doubly gendered terms (110).

12 *Shakespeare's Ovid*, 4: 346–481.

13 For analysis of the opposition between idealized androgyny and monstrous hermaphroditism, see Rackin, "Androgyny, Mimesis, and the Marriage of the Boy Heroine," esp. 29. For a reading of Spenser's hermaphrodite in terms of classical and early modern traditions, see Cheney, "Spenser's Hermaphrodite and the 1590 *Faerie Queene*."

14 de Lauretis, "Sexual Indifference and Lesbian Representation," 143. For de Lauretis's discussion of this structure in terms of "the heterosexual social contract by which

Notes to Chapter Four

252

all sexualities, all bodies, and all 'others' are bonded to an ideal/ideological hierarchy of males," see 142–44. In a reading of Shakespeare's *Lucrece*, Vickers traces a conflation of heraldic and rhetorical strategies, and writes, "Read as a martial image, Lucrece's body as shield stands between Tarquin and Collatine to deflect blows, to prevent direct hits; read as a heraldic image, that same body is the medium assuring the passage of Collatium from father to as yet unborn son" ("The Blazon of Sweet Beauty's Best," 105).

15 Suzuki reads Artegall's attraction to both Britomart and Radigund in terms of their likeness to him; see *Metamorphoses of Helen*, 183. See also Villeponteaux's discussion of the sense in which Britomart "becomes" Artegall in her desire for him ("Displacing Feminine Authority in *The Faerie Queene*," 60).

16 Describing the "communal narcissism" shared by heroes in Shakespeare's plays, Bruce Smith writes, "Two conflicting imperatives govern the actions of all these paired heroes: 'fight this man' and 'love this man.' That conflict of impulses helps explain why the violent and the erotic so often coincide" (*Homosexual Desire*, 59).

17 Girard, *Violence and the Sacred*, 144, 146.

18 Sedgwick, *Between Men*, 21.

19 Dollimore, *Sexual Dissidence*, 305. Emphasis in original.

20 Enterline, *The Tears of Narcissus*, 8–9.

21 Silberman, *Transforming Desire*, 106.

22 Davis, "Women on Top," 145.

23 O'Connor, *Amadis de Gaule and Its Influence on Elizabethan Literature*, 33.

24 Stallybrass, "Transvestism and the 'Body Beneath,' " 77.

25 Woods, "Amazonian Tyranny," 59.

26 Villeponteaux, "Displacing Feminine Authority in *The Faerie Queene*," 60. Villeponteaux discusses this constructed masculinity in relation to Queen Elizabeth I, arguing that Spenser displays ambivalence in his representations of martial women.

27 Garber, *Vested Interests*, 119.

28 Burton, *The Anatomy of Melancholy*, 525–6.

29 Anderson, " 'Nor Man It Is,' " 66.

30 Halberstam, *Female Masculinity*, 1–2.

31 Anthony Gibson goes further than Spenser, claiming that men have invented their own heroic history in order to compete with the actual deeds of women. He describes Amazons and other nations under female rule, "who both in common and perticuler, have gotten so much glory by armies of women: as men durst hope no otherwise, but in the meere fables they have written of themselves, boasting of victories gotten over their equalles, and one while against Lions, then Beares, and some Tygers, with other of like strength and violence, wherein women have done as much, or rather more then they" (*A Womans Woorth*, 7–7v).

32 Judith Butler, *Bodies That Matter*, 1–2.

33 For readings that present the opposition between Britomart and Radigund in terms of their potential as doubles, see, for example, Hamilton, *The Structure of Allegory in The Faerie Queene*, 183; Suzuki, *Metamorphoses of Helen*, esp. 181–88; Woods, "Amazon Tyranny," 55; Davis, "Women on Top," 133; Hankins, *Source and Meaning in Spenser's Allegory*, 174; Montrose, " 'Shaping Fantasies,' " 46.

34 *Haec-Vir: Or The Womanish-Man*, sig. C3v.

Notes to Chapter Four

35 Suzuki suggests ways in which Artegall, Radigund, and Britomart are linked by various shared character traits, and argues that these links cause structures of allegorical opposition to break down; see *Metamorphoses of Helen,* esp. 181–86.

36 Gallop, *Reading Lacan,* 80.

37 Jonson, *The Masque of Queens,* 542, in *The Complete Masques.*

38 Sidney, "The Defense of Poesy," 151. Plutarch, in his "Comparison of Demetrius with Antonius," apparently finds nothing to laugh at in this episode, taking it instead as a cautionary tale: "But to conclude, he [Demetrius] never had overthrowe or misfortune through negligence, nor by delaying time to followe his owne pleasure: as we see in painted tables, where *Omphale* secretlie stealeth away *Hercules* clubbe, and tooke his Lyons skinne from him" (*The Lives of the Noble Grecians and Romanes Compared,* 1010).

39 Ralegh, *The discoverie,* 367.

40 Carvajal, *Discovery of the Orellana River,* 222.

41 Painter, *The Second Tome of The Palace of Pleasure,* 2. This narrative of sons who are maimed or killed recurs throughout early modern translations and rewritings of Amazon myth. See for example Barckley, *The Felicitie of Man,* 259; Carvajal, *Discovery of the Orellana River,* 221; Diodorus, *Bibliotheca Historica,* 1: 200; and Thevet, *The Newe Founde Worlde,* 102v.

42 Montaigne, "Of the Lame or Cripple," in *Essayes,* 616.

43 Bushnell argues that female desire in this period is always potentially a form of tyranny: "Woman is represented as framed in nature as what the 'male' tyrant becomes: the principle of the lower and ferocious power of desire usurping the sovereignty of reason" ("Tyranny and Effeminacy in Early Modern England," 342). For an extended discussion of the anxieties displayed in the image of female dominance, see Davis, "Women on Top."

44 Burton, *The Anatomy of Melancholy,* 523. Emphasis in original. For a more optimistic account of the relationship between female and male desires, see Quilligan's analysis of Venus and Adonis in *The Faerie Queene;* Quilligan reads this relationship as "a vision of male sexuality brought safely and creatively under the control of an awesome female power" and links it to Britomart's own generative function ("The Gender of the Reader and the Problem of Sexuality," 141.

45 Quilligan, "The Comedy of Female Authority," 171.

46 Montrose, " 'Shaping Fantasies,' " 36. For a discussion of the relationship between Amazon myth and early modern ideas about maternity, see Schwarz, "Mother Love."

47 Orgel, *Impersonations,* 123, 124.

48 Eggert, " 'Changing all that forme of common weale,' " 269. Eggert goes on to argue that the replacement of "feminine rule" by "masculine poetics" ultimately proves a fantasy (see 284–86). Cavanagh also discusses the pattern of male escapes from female desires in *Wanton Eyes and Chaste Desires;* see esp. 54. See also Parker's discussion of "suspended instruments" in *Literary Fat Ladies,* 54–66.

49 Charles Butler, *The Feminine Monarchie,* 64–65. I have modernized the appearance of "th," "ch," and "wh" throughout.

50 Stephens describes Radigund and the feminized Artegall as "Medusan faces" which, confronting Britomart, circumscribe and finally foreclose her role in the poem. See *The Limits of Eroticism,* esp. 93.

51 For a reading that equates Arthur and Britomart in terms of "love and friendship or knightly brotherhood," see Anderson, " 'Nor Man It is,' " 75. Anderson reads the

Notes to Chapter Four

alliance of Arthur and Artegall as a temporary remedy for Artegall's dual role as knight and as the figure of Justice; the pairing, she argues, enables Artegall to act as an abstraction while Arthur acts as a knight (see esp. 75–78).

52 Cavanagh, *Wanton Eyes and Chaste Desires*, 142.

53 The exception to this rule in Book 4 appears to be the case of Cambell and Triamond, who both marry their ladies and continue their heroic careers. Their ability to do so requires a great deal of magic: three souls condensed into one body, a wound-healing ring, a rod of peace, and a round of nepenthe. Even after all this, the story scarcely merits its nominal place at the book's center, its relatively marginal position reflecting the truncating effect that happy endings have on chivalric narratives.

54 Silberman, *Transforming Desire*, 30. For a further reading of "the *issue* of eroticism between women" in the Malecasta episode, see Stephens, *The Limits of Eroticism*, esp. 78.

55 Stephens, "Into Other Arms," 201.

56 Quilligan, "The Gender of the Reader," 149.

57 Stephens, "Into Other Arms," 202.

58 Schleiner, "Le feu caché," 309.

59 Traub, "The Perversion of 'Lesbian' Desire," 34–35.

60 Recent feminist criticism has offered a variety of readings of Britomart's problematic chastity; see, for example, Cavanagh, *Wanton Eyes and Chaste Desires*, esp. 142, 171, and Suzuki, *Metamorphoses of Helen*, esp. 155. Wofford reads Britomart's complication of allegorical significance in terms of a struggle between male and female perspectives, as well as between allegorical ideal and character; see "Gendering Allegory," esp. 13–16. For a reading that links the text's representational problems to discontent with Elizabeth I's failure to produce an heir, see Villeponteaux, "Displacing Feminine Authority," esp. 54 and 60.

61 Vives, *Instruction of a Christen woman*, 10. Jardine quotes a letter from John Rainoldes to Thomas Thornton, written in 1592, which makes a similar point through a reference to Juvenal's sixth Satire; in Jardine's translation, "What modesty can you expect in a woman who wears a helmet?" (*Still Harping on Daughters*, 14–15).

62 For a reading of the ways in which allegory as a genre complicates the "subject/object split" in *The Faerie Queene*, see Quilligan, "The Comedy of Female Authority," esp. 160–64. See also Silberman's discussion of "subjective participation in the object" (*Transforming Desire*, esp. 22–23).

63 See, for example, Hamilton, *The Structure of Allegory in* The Faerie Queene, 189; Hankins, *Source and Meaning*, 174; Suzuki, *Metamorphoses of Helen*, 186–87.

64 Wofford, "Gendering Allegory," 3.

5 THE PROBABLE IMPOSSIBLE: INVENTING LESBIANS IN ARCADIA

1 *Amazon Quarterly*; Birkby, *Amazon Expedition*; Larkin and Bulkin, *Amazon Poetry*; Covina and Galana, *The Lesbian Reader*.

2 Curb, ed., *Amazon All Stars*.

3 Lynch, *The Amazon Trail*.

4 O'Connor, Amadis de Gaule *and Its Influence on Elizabethan Literature*, 297.

5 Marston, *Antonio and Mellida*, 13, 7.

6 O'Connor, Amadis de Gaule *and Its Influence on Elizabethan Literature*, 104.

7 Carew, "A Lover, in the Disguise of an Amazon, is Dearly Beloved of his Mistress," lines 13–18, in *The Poems and Masque of Thomas Carew*.

Notes to Chapter Five

8 For an analysis of representations of female homoeroticism as potentially obscured or displaced by heterosexual teleologies, see Traub, "The (In)significance of 'Lesbian' Desire."

9 Sidney, *The Countess of Pembroke's Arcadia (The Old Arcadia)*, 18. Subsequent citations appear in parentheses in the text.

10 Kinney, "The Masks of Love," 475.

11 Sidney, *The Countess of Pembroke's Arcadia (The New Arcadia)*, 161. Subsequent citations appear in parentheses in the text.

12 Salzman writes, "The notion that Sidney's revision increased the *Arcadia*'s heroic and epic qualities is now widely accepted" (*English Prose Fiction 1558–1700*, 54). See also Patterson's reference to "the generic shift from pastoral to chivalric romance" (" 'Under . . . Pretty Tales,' " 19), and Shaver, "Woman's Place in the *New Arcadia*," esp. 4, 14–15. But other readers have argued that the revised *Arcadia* fails to produce heroic effects; see, for example, Sinfield, "Power and Ideology," esp. 268; and McCoy, who characterizes the princes as victims of "chaotic conflict, heroic inadequacy, and vulnerable subordination to fortune" (*Sir Philip Sidney*, 161).

13 Sullivan, "Amazons and Aristocrats," 73. For other readings of the revised *Arcadia* as inherently unfinishable, see, for example, McCoy, *Sir Philip Sidney*, esp. 161–63; Helgerson, *The Elizabethan Prodigals*, 147–51; Hunt, "Charactonymic Structures in Sidney's *Arcadias*," esp. 15.

14 Stallybrass, "Transvestism and the 'Body Beneath,' " 77.

15 Garber, *Vested Interests*, 133.

16 For consideration of the anxieties associated with Pyrocles' feminization, see, for example, Lamb, "Exhibiting Class and Displaying the Body in Sidney's *Countess of Pembroke's Arcadia*," esp. 56. Dickson argues for a connection between concerns with "fictional excess" and uneasiness about femininity; see "Sidney's Grotesque Muse," esp. 46–49.

17 Jardine, *Still Harping on Daughters*, 28–29.

18 For an extended discussion of the "one-sex model," see Laqueur, *Making Sex*. Laqueur summarizes the hierarchical assumptions that underlie the idea of a sexual continuum, writing, "Women, in other words, are inverted, and hence less perfect, men" (26).

19 Paré, *On Monsters and Marvels*, 33.

20 Orgel, *Impersonations*, 25.

21 Garber, *Vested Interests*, 117.

22 Richard Levin, "What? How?," 464–65. For a more broadly focused analysis of male and female homoeroticism in romance cross-dressing plots, see Schleiner, "Male Cross-Dressing and Transvestism in Renaissance Romances." Schleiner writes, "While the episodes in question are thus ultimately heterosexually centered, the ambiguity resulting from cross-dressing becomes a vehicle for discussing homosexuality" (619).

23 Orgel, *Impersonations*, 80.

24 See also Musidorus's use of the same figure when he helps Pyrocles to become Cleophila (25). Kinney argues that these Pygmalion references are closely linked to the threat of narcissism; see "The Masks of Love," esp. 477–78.

25 Salzman, *English Prose Fiction 1558–1700*, 53.

26 Paster, *The Body Embarrassed*, 20.

27 *Haec-Vir: Or The Womanish-Man*, sig. A3v. For further discussion of Hercules' prob-lematic status as a point of masculine heroic reference, see my discussion of his relationship to Artegall in chap. 3.

28 Sullivan writes of one heroic act in the revised *Arcadia* that "Zelmane wins praise for Amazonian, rather than Pyroclean, prowess" ("Amazons and Aristocrats," 72). However, in her reading, with its consideration of the relationship between heredi-tary and gendered authority, it is important that we remain aware that Pyrocles is a man; see esp. 71.

29 Adams, *Mystical Bedlam*, 50.

30 Knox, *The First Blast*, 43.

31 Sullivan, "Amazons and Aristocrats," 74.

32 Ariosto, *Sir John Harington's translation of* Orlando Furioso, 20: 2.

33 Kinney, "On the Margins of Romance," 150. For Kinney's reading of the relocated blazon in the revised *Arcadia*, see 145–46.

34 Derrida, ". . . That Dangerous Supplement . . . ," 144–45.

35 Richard Levin, "What? How?," 470.

36 Traub, "The (In)Significance of 'Lesbian' Desire," 68.

37 Park, "The Rediscovery of the Clitoris," 186.

38 Hunt reads the simultaneous identities of Cleophila and Pyrocles structurally, attributing that simultaneity to Sidney's "compositional profusion"; see "Charac-tonymic Structures," esp. 10–12. For a claim that doubled identity constructs and idealizes androgyny, see Celovsky, "Pyrocles' Warlike Peace: Sir Philip Sidney and Androgyny."

39 For recent accounts of *The Arcadia* as a response to or a theory of political power struc-tures, see Tennenhouse, "Arcadian Rhetoric"; Stillman, "The Politics of Sidney's Pastoral"; Patterson, " 'Under . . . Pretty Tales' "; and Sinfield, "Power and Ideology."

40 Garber, *Vested Interests*, 11. Emphasis in original.

41 Lacan, "The Function and Field of Speech and Language," 67.

42 Judith Butler, *Gender Trouble*, 138.

43 Richard Levin, "What? How?"; see esp. 474.

44 *Haec-Vir: Or The Womanish-Man*, sig. C3v–C4.

45 Case, "Toward a Butch-Femme Aesthetic," 304.

46 Traub, "The Perversion of 'Lesbian' Desire," 25.

6 TRAGICAL MIRTH: FRAMING SHAKESPEARE'S HIPPOLYTA

1 Barton, "Introduction," 217.

2 Olson, "*A Midsummer Night's Dream* and the Meaning of Court Marriage," 119.

3 Calderwood, "*A Midsummer Night's Dream:* The Illusion of Drama," 506–7.

4 Young, *Something of Great Constancy*, 8, 4.

5 See also Barton's "Introduction," which concludes via Hippolyta's lines (221).

6 Girard, "Myth and Ritual in Shakespeare," 211; 212.

7 Qtd. in Rolfe, *Shakespeare's Comedy*, 22.

8 Shakespeare, *A Midsummer Night's Dream*, 1.1.7–11. Subsequent citations appear in paren-theses in the text.

9 Qtd. in Rolfe, *Shakespeare's Comedy*, 25.

10 Olson, "*A Midsummer Night's Dream* and the Meaning of Court Marriage," 101.

11 Freedman, *Staging the Gaze*, 164.

Notes to Chapter Six

12 Kavanagh, "Shakespeare in Ideology," 155–56. See also Tennenhouse's discussion of the development of "a more inclusionary order" embodied and controlled by Theseus (*Power on Display*, esp. 73–76; the quote is from 75). In *Literary Fat Ladies*, Patricia Parker writes that the play "ends with the proper marital hierarchy" (19), and points out that in so doing it exposes to question the process through which that hierarchy is constructed. In her reading, Hippolyta is a product of that process, the noun "Amazon" repeatedly modified by the adjectives "chastened" and "defeated" (see esp. 123–25).

13 Montrose, " 'Shaping Fantasies,' " 53.

14 Gohlke, " 'I wooed thee with my sword,' " 171.

15 Plutarch, *The Lives of the Noble Grecians and Romanes Compared*, 14.

16 Marshall, "Exchanging Visions," 555.

17 Bruce Smith, *Homosexual Desire in Shakespeare's England*, 64.

18 Montrose, " 'Shaping Fantasies,' " 39. See also Shirley Nelson Garner's similar point in " 'Jack Shall Have Jill,' " esp. 96.

19 Evans, ed., *The Riverside Shakespeare*, 240 n; Brooks, ed., *A Midsummer Night's Dream*, 93 n; Doran, ed., *A Midsummer Night's Dream*, 89 n.

20 Brooks, ed., *A Midsummer Night's Dream*, 134–35. Ellipses in original.

21 Editors have often been tempted to reinstate the boar, relying on what Brooks describes as "an easy e:o misreading"; for a sense of the debate, see Brooks's defense of his own retention of "bear" ("Introduction," 93 n). See also Brooks's reading of the hunting scene as forming a bond between Theseus and Hippolyta (civ).

22 Freedman, *Staging the Gaze*, 158, 163.

23 Rubin, "The Traffic in Women: Notes on the 'Political Economy' of Sex," 174.

24 Painter, *The Second Tome of The Palace of Pleasure*, 3.

25 Warner, *The First and Second parts of Albions England*, 25–26.

26 Fletcher, *The Purple Island*, 144.

27 Belsey, "Disrupting Sexual Difference," 189.

28 Christine de Pizan, *The Boke of the Cyte of Ladyes*, sig. HHii.

29 Garner argues that this doubleness allows Theseus to satisfy both heterosexual and homoerotic desires, and writes, "If we imagine Hippolyta played by a male actor who, though cast as a woman, dresses and walks like a man ('buskined mistress,' 'bouncing Amazon'), Hippolyta and Theseus must have looked more like homosexual than heterosexual lovers" (" 'Jack Shall Have Jill,' " 90).

30 Woods, "Amazonian Tyranny," 53.

31 Gibson, *A Womans Woorth*, 5.

32 Diodorus, *Bibliotheca Historica*, 1: 200.

33 Painter, *The Second Tome of The Palace of Pleasure*, 3.

34 Strabo, *The Geography*, 5: 237. Lysias makes a similar point, writing, "They were accounted as men for their high courage, rather than as women for their sex; so much more did they seem to excel men in their spirit than to be at a disadvantage in their form" (*Lysias*, 33).

35 Plutarch, *The Lives of the Noble Grecians and Romanes Compared*, 15.

36 Diodorus, *Bibliotheca Historica*, 1: 200.

37 Judith Butler, *Bodies That Matter*, 23.

38 Traub, "The (In)significance of 'Lesbian' Desire," 71. Parker argues that this bond between Helena and Hermia, which she describes as "potentially Amazonian," must

be broken because it threatens a parodic echo of heterosexual marriage; see *Literary Fat Ladies*, esp. 124.

39 Irigaray, *This Sex Which Is Not One*, 25, 30.
40 Adelman, "Male Bonding in Shakespeare's Comedies," 82.
41 Chaucer, *The Knight's Tale*, ll. 8875–85.
42 Lacan, "The Signification of the Phallus," 289.
43 Judith Butler, *Gender Trouble*, 122.
44 [Shirley], *The Accomplished Ladies Rich Closet of Rarities*, 174.
45 Freedman, *Staging the Gaze*, 180.
46 1.1.173; 2.1.190; 2.2.60, 62; 2.2.102; 3.2.251–52.
47 Rambuss, *Closet Devotions*, 1–2. Girard writes of the play's clichés, "The interest of the so-called rhetoric is its frightening pertinence" ("Myth and Ritual in Shakespeare," 196).
48 Levine, "Rape, Repetition, and the Politics of Closure," 216. See also Suzuki's conclusion, "Love is neither an educative nor a civilizing process in *A Midsummer Night's Dream*" ("The Dismemberment of Hippolytus," 108).
49 3.2.65–66; 3.2.67; 3.2.285; 3.2.217; 3.2.151–52.
50 Cullum, *Shake Hands with Shakespeare*, 126. In a section titled "Young Actors Speak," Cullum quotes a former actor: " 'I liked the role of Hermia from *A Midsummer Night's Dream* the best. It was an all boy cast, and I got thrown around quite a bit.' —John Seiffer, sixth-grade Hermia" (131).
51 The battle with the Centaurs is closely linked to Hippolyta's own story; see Tyrrell, *Amazons*, 82.
52 Carla Freccero, "From Amazon to Court Lady," 230.
53 Judith Butler, *Bodies That Matter*, 10.
54 Irigaray, *This Sex Which Is Not One*, 29; Cixous, "The Laugh of the Medusa," 286.
55 duBois argues for a close connection between Centaurs and Amazons, pointing to analogies between the ways in which each figure both poses a threat to men and helps to define "the citizen warrior, who was at the center of the city's discourse, who was the subject of the *logos*" (*Centaurs and Amazons*, 150). Tyrrell describes a comparable association; see *Amazons*, esp. 82.
56 Qtd. in Leonard, *Books of the Brave*, 38.
57 Strabo, *The Geography of Strabo*, 5: 233–35. For early modern accounts of these practices, see, for example, Thevet, *The New found worlde*, 102; and Ralegh, *The discoverie*, 367.
58 Brooks, ed., *A Midsummer Night's Dream*, 27n. Garner describes the contradiction as a product of the tension between "patriarchal and heterosexual values" and bonds between women; see " 'Jack Shall Have Jill,' " esp. 86.
59 Pearson, " 'Unkinde' Theseus," 297. For discussion of the influence of the Hippolytus myth, see Suzuki, who, in "The Dismemberment of Hippolytus," reads *A Midsummer Night's Dream* as a "translation" of Seneca's play. See also Brooks's introduction to the Arden edition, esp. lxii–lxiii.
60 For arguments about thematic doubling, see, for example, Olson, "*A Midsummer Night's Dream* and the Meaning of Court Marriage," 108, and Brooks, introduction, cvi. Chambers connects theatrical doubling to the casting problems caused by a fairy plot; see *William Shakespeare*, esp. 1:82. See also vol. 2, esp. 86–87.
61 Plutarch concludes his account of the siege of Athens by writing, "Afterwards, at the ende of foure monethes, peace was taken betwene them by meanes of one of

the women called *Hyppolita*. For this Historiographer calleth the AMAZONE which Theseus maried, *Hyppolita*, and not *Antiopa*" (*The Lives of the Noble Grecians and Romanes Compared*, 15). For analysis of this nominal multiplicity across the history of the myth, see Tyrrell, *Amazons*, esp. 5.

62 Freud, *The Interpretation of Dreams*, 5: 353.

63 Plutarch, *The Lives of The Noble Grecians and Romanes Compared*, 15.

64 Bercher, *The Nobility of Women*, 103.

65 Brathwait, *The English Gentlewoman*, 133.

66 Ovidius Naso, *The Heroycall Epistles*, 23.

67 Seneca, *Hippolytus*, 169.

68 Montrose, " 'Shaping Fantasies,' " 45. See also Suzuki's discussion of "the still discernable traces of these impulses" in "The Dismemberment of Hippolytus," esp. 106.

69 Qtd. in Rolfe, *Shakespeare's Comedy*, 34.

70 Judith Butler, *Gender Trouble*, 138.

71 Marx, *The Eighteenth Brumaire of Louis Bonaparte*, 15.

72 Marshall, "Exchanging Visions," 548. Through readings of four twentieth-century productions, McGuire argues that Hippolyta's silence requires interpretive choice, and that the implications of that choice shape our perspective on the play's relationships and structures. See "Hippolyta's Silence and the Poet's Pen."

73 Brooks, introduction, lxxxix. See also Olson, "*A Midsummer Night's Dream* and the Meaning of Court Marriage," esp. 117–18, and Calderwood, "*A Midsummer Night's Dream: The Illusion of Drama*," esp. 511.

74 Gibson, *A Womans Woorth*, 37.

EPILOGUE: VIA *THE TWO NOBLE KINSMEN*

1 Shakespeare, *The Two Noble Kinsmen*, 1.1.80–85. Subsequent citations appear in parentheses in the text.

2 Kleinbaum, *The War against the Amazons*, 1.

3 That final "dividual" is a modern substitution for "individuall," the word that originally appeared; for a reading of the significance of "individuall," see Masten, *Textual Intercourse*, esp. 50–51.

4 Ibid., 55.

5 Smith, *Homosexual Desire*, 72.

Bibliography

Adams, Thomas. *Mystical Bedlam, or The World of Mad-Men.* London: Printed by George Purslowe, for Clement Knight, 1615.

Adelman, Janet. "Male Bonding in Shakespeare's Comedies." In *Shakespeare's 'Rough Magic': Renaissance Essays in Honor of C. L. Barber,* edited by Peter Erickson and Coppélia Kahn, 73–103. Newark: University of Delaware Press, 1985.

———. *Suffocating Mothers: Fantasies of Maternal Origin in Shakespeare's Plays, Hamlet to The Tempest.* New York: Routledge, 1992.

Aeschylus. *Prometheus Bound.* Translated by David Grene. In *The Complete Greek Tragedies: Volume 1,* edited by David Grene and Richmond Lattimore, 304–52. Chicago: University of Chicago Press, 1992.

———. *The Suppliant Maidens.* Translated by Seth G. Bernadete. In *The Complete Greek Tragedies: Volume 1,* edited by David Grene and Richmond Lattimore, 174–215. Chicago: University of Chicago Press, 1992.

Agrippa, Heinrich Cornelius. *Female Preeminence: or the Dignity and Excellency of that sex, above the Male.* Translated by H[enry] C[are]. London: Printed by T.R. and M.D. and sold by Henry Million, 1670.

Alvares, Father Francisco. *The Prester John of the Indies: A True Relation of the Lands of the Prester John: being the narrative of the Portuguese Embassy to Ethiopia in 1520, written by Father Francisco Alvarez.* Translated by Lord Stanley of Alderley (1881). Edited by G. F. Beckingham and G. W. B. Huntingford. Cambridge, England: Published for the Hakluyt Society at the University Press, 1961.

Amazon Quarterly: A Lesbian-Feminist Arts Journal. Oakland, CA: Amazon Press, 1972–1975.

Anderson, Judith H. " 'Nor Man It Is': The Knight of Justice in Book V of Spenser's *Faerie Queene.*" *PMLA* 85 (1970): 65–77.

Ariosto, Lodovico. *Sir John Harington's translation of Orlando Furioso, by Lodovico Ariosto* (1591). Edited by Graham Hough. Carbondale: Southern Illinois University Press, 1962.

Ashton, Robert, ed. *James I by his Contemporaries.* London: Hutchinson of London, 1969.

Aylmer, John. *An Harborowe for Faithfull and Trewe Subjectes, agaynst the late blowne Blaste, concerninge the Government of Wemen.* London: John Daye, 1559.

Bacon, Francis. *Francis Bacon: A Selection of His Works.* Edited by Sidney Warhaft. London: Macmillan, 1965.

Barckley, Richard. *A Discourse of The Felicitie of Man: Or, His Summum bonum.* London: Printed for William Ponsonby, 1598.

Barthes, Roland. *Mythologies.* Translated by Annette Lavers. New York: Hill and Wang, 1972.

Barton, Anne. "Introduction: *A Midsummer Night's Dream.*" In *The Riverside Shakespeare,* edited by G. Blakemore Evans, 217–21. Boston: Houghton Mifflin, 1974.

Batman, Stephen. *The Golden Booke of the Leaden Gods* (1577). Reprint New York: Garland, 1976.

Belsey, Catherine. "Disrupting Sexual Difference: Meaning and Gender in the Comedies." In *Alternative Shakespeares,* edited by John Drakakis, 166–90. London: Routledge, 1988.

———. *Shakespeare and the Loss of Eden: The Construction of Family Values in Early Modern Culture.* Houndmills: Macmillan, 1999.

———. *The Subject of Tragedy: Identity and Difference in Renaissance Drama.* London: Methuen, 1985.

Bercher, William. *The Nobility of Women* (1559). Edited by R. Warwick Bond. London: Privately printed, for presentation to the members of the Roxburghe Club, 1904.

Bevington, David. "The Domineering Female in *1 Henry VI.*" *Shakespeare Studies* 2 (1966): 51–58.

Birkby, Phyllis, ed. *Amazon Expedition: A Lesbian Feminist Anthology.* Washington, NJ: Times Change Press, 1973.

Bradbrook, Muriel. *The Tragic Pageant of Timon of Athens.* Cambridge, England: Cambridge University Press, 1966.

Brathwait, Richard. *The English Gentlewoman, drawne out to the full Body.* London: Printed by B. Alsop and T. Fawcet, for Michaell Sparke, 1631.

Bray, Alan. "Homosexuality and the Signs of Male Friendship in Elizabethan England." In *Queering the Renaissance,* edited by Jonathan Goldberg, 40–61. Durham, NC: Duke University Press, 1994.

———. *Homosexuality in Renaissance England.* New York: Columbia University Press, 1982, 1995.

Bredbeck, Gregory W. *Sodomy and Interpretation: Marlowe to Milton.* Ithaca: Cornell University Press, 1991.

Brooks, Harold F. "Introduction" *A Midsummer Night's Dream.* Arden Edition. New York: Routledge, 1979.

Brooks, Harold F., ed. *A Midsummer Night's Dream.* Arden Edition. New York: Routledge, 1979.

Brown, Judith C. *Immodest Acts: The Life of a Lesbian Nun in Renaissance Italy.* New York: Oxford University Press, 1986.

Burton, Robert. *The Anatomy of Melancholy. What it is, With all the kinds, causes, symptomes, prognostickes, and severall cures of it.* The Sixt Edition, corrected and augmented by the Author. Oxford: Printed by Henry Cripps, 1651.

Bushnell, Rebecca. "Tyranny and Effeminacy in Early Modern England." In *Reconsidering the Renaissance,* edited by

Mario A. di Cesare, 339–54. Binghamton, NY: Medieval and Renaissance Texts and Studies, 1992.

Butler, Charles. *The Feminine Monarchie, or, The Histori of Bee's.* Oxford: Printed by William Turner for the Author, 1634.

Butler, Judith. *Bodies That Matter: On the Discursive Limits of "Sex."* New York: Routledge, 1993.

———. *Gender Trouble: Feminism and the Subversion of Identity.* New York: Routledge, 1990.

Calderwood, James L. "*A Midsummer Night's Dream:* The Illusion of Drama." *Modern Language Quarterly* 26, no. 4 (1965): 506–22.

Camden, Carroll. *The Elizabethan Woman.* Houston: Elsevier, 1952.

Candido, Joseph. "Getting Loose in the Henry VI Plays." *Shakespeare Quarterly* 35 (1984): 392–406.

Carew, Thomas. *The Poems and Masque of Thomas Carew.* Edited by Joseph Woodfall Ebsworth. London: Reeves and Turner, 1893.

Cartari, Vincenzo. *Imagini.* Padua, 1571.

Carvajal, Friar Gaspar de. *Discovery of the Orellana River.* In José Toribio Medina, *The Discovery of the Amazon.* Edited by H. C. Heaton. Translated by Bertram T. Lee, 167–242. New York: American Geographical Society, 1934.

Case, Sue-Ellen. "Toward a Butch-Femme Aesthetic." In *The Lesbian and Gay Studies Reader,* edited by Henry Abelove, Michèle Aina Barale, and David M. Halperin, 294–306. New York: Routledge, 1993.

Cavanagh, Sheila. *Wanton Eyes and Chaste Desires: Female Sexuality in* The Faerie Queene. Bloomington: Indiana University Press, 1994.

Celovsky, Lisa. "Pyrocles' Warlike Peace: Sir Philip Sidney and Androgyny." In *Gender Rhetorics: Postures of Dominance and Submission in History,* edited by Richard C. Trexler, 235–44. Bingham-

ton, NY: Medieval and Renaissance
Texts and Studies, 1994.

Chambers, E. K. *William Shakespeare: A Study
of Facts and Problems.* 2 vols. Oxford:
Clarendon, 1930.

Charney, Maurice. Introduction to *The
Life of Timon of Athens.* New York: New
American Library, 1965, 1989.

———. "*Timon of Athens* on Stage and
Screen." In *The Life of Timon of Athens.*
New York: New American Library,
1965, 1989.

Chaucer, Geoffrey. *The Knight's Tale.* In
The Riverside Chaucer, 3d ed. Edited by
Larry D. Benson. Boston: Houghton
Mifflin, 1987.

Cheney, Donald. "Spenser's Hermaphrodite and the 1590 *Faerie Queene.*" *PMLA* 87
(1972): 192–200.

Christine de Pizan. *The Boke of the Cyte of
Ladyes.* Translated by Brian Anslay. In
*Distaves and Dames: Renaissance Treatises for
and about Women,* edited by Diane Born-
stein. Delmar, NY: Scholars' Facsimiles
and Reprints, 1978.

Cixous, Hélène. "The Laugh of the
Medusa." In *The* Signs *Reader: Women,
Gender and Scholarship,* edited by Eliza-
beth Abel, and Emily K. Abel, 279–97.
Chicago: University of Chicago Press,
1983.

Comes, Natalis. *Mythologia.* Edited by
Stephen Orgel. New York: Garland,
1979.

Covina, Gina, and Laurel Galana, eds.
*The Lesbian Reader: An Amazon Quarterly
Anthology.* Oakland, CA: Amazon Press,
1975.

Cox, John D. "Devils and Power in Marlowe and Shakespeare." *The Yearbook
of English Studies: Early Shakespeare Special
Number* 23 (1993): 46–64.

Cuddon, J. A. *A Dictionary of Literary Terms.*
Rev. ed. New York: Penguin Books,
1979.

Cullum, Albert. *Shake Hands with Shakespeare:*

Eight Plays for Elementary Schools. New York:
Citation Press, 1968.

Culpeper, Nicholas. *A Directory for Midwives:
Or, A Guide for Women, In their Conception,
Bearing, and Suckling their Children.* London:
Printed by Peter Cole, 1651.

Curb, Rosemary Keefe, ed. *Amazon All
Stars: Thirteen Lesbian Plays.* New York:
Applause, 1996.

Daniel, Samuel. *The Complete Works in Verse
and Prose of Samuel Daniel.* Edited by
Alexander B. Grosart. 5 vols. London:
Hazell, Watson, and Viney, 188–96.

Dash, Irene G. *Wooing, Wedding, and Power:
Women in Shakespeare's Plays.* New York:
Columbia University Press, 1981.

Davis, Natalie Zemon. "Women on Top."
In *Society and Culture in Early Modern France.*
Stanford: Stanford University Press,
1975.

de Acuña, Father Cristobal. *A New Discovery
of the Great River of the Amazons, A.D. 1639.*
In *Expeditions into the Valley of the Amazons,
1539, 1540, 1639,* edited and translated
by Clements R. Markham. London:
Printed for the Hakluyt Society, 1859.

de Herrera, Antonio. *The Voyage of Francisco
de Orellana Down The River of the Amazons,
A.D. 1540–41.* In *Expeditions into the Valley
of the Amazons, 1539, 1540, 1639,* edited
and translated by Clements R. Markham. London: Printed for the Hakluyt
Society, 1859.

de Grazia, Margreta, Maureen Quilligan,
and Peter Stallybrass. "Introduction."
In *Subject and Object in Renaissance Culture,*
edited by Margreta de Grazia, Maureen
Quilligan, and Peter Stallybrass, 1–
13. Cambridge, England: Cambridge
University Press, 1996.

de Lauretis, Teresa. "Sexual Indifference
and Lesbian Representation." In *The
Lesbian and Gay Studies Reader,* edited by
Henry Abelove, Michèle Aina Barale,
and David M. Halperin, 141–58. New
York: Routledge, 1993.

Bibliography

Derrida, Jacques. ". . . That Dangerous Supplement . . ." In *Of Grammatology.* Translated by Gayatri Chakravorty Spivak. Baltimore: Johns Hopkins University Press, 1974.

Díaz, Bernal. *The Conquest of New Spain.* Edited and translated by J. M. Cohen. New York: Penguin Books, 1963.

Dickson, Lynne. "Sidney's Grotesque Muse: Fictional Excess and the Feminine in the *Arcadia*s." In *Renaissance Papers 1992,* edited by George Walton Williams and Barbara J. Baines, 41–55. Raleigh, NC: Southeastern Renaissance Conference, 1993.

Diodorus Siculus. *The Bibliotheca Historica.* Translated by John Skelton. 2 vols. London: Published for the Early English Text Society by Geoffrey Cumberlege, Oxford University Press, 1956–57.

Dollimore, Jonathan. *Sexual Dissidence: Augustine to Wilde, Freud to Foucault.* Oxford: Clarendon Press, 1991.

Doran, Madeleine, ed. *A Midsummer Night's Dream.* Pelican Shakespeare Edition. New York: Penguin Books, 1971.

Doyle, Sir Arthur Conan. *The Sign of Four.* Edited by Christopher Roden. Oxford: Oxford University Press, 1993.

duBois, Page. *Centaurs and Amazons: Women and the Pre-History of the Great Chain of Being.* Ann Arbor: University of Michigan Press, 1982.

Eaton, Sara J. "Presentations of Women in the English Popular Press." In *Ambiguous Realities: Women in the Middle Ages and Renaissance,* edited by Carole Levin and Jeanie Watson. Detroit: Wayne State University Press, 1987.

Eden, Richard. *The first Three English books on America: Being chiefly Translations, Compilations, &c., by Richard Eden, From the Writings, Maps, &c., of Pietro Martire, of Anghiera (1455–1526), Sebastian Münster, the Cosmographer (1489–1552), and Sebastian Cabot, of Bristol (1474–1557). With Extracts, &c., from the Works of other Spanish, Italian, and Ger-*man Writers of the Time. Edited by Edward Arber. Birmingham, England, 1885.

Eggert, Katherine. " 'Changing all that forme of common weale': Genre and the Repeal of Queenship in *The Faerie Queene,* Book 5." *English Literary Renaissance* 26, no. 2 (1996): 259–90.

Elyot, Sir Thomas. *The Defence of Good Women.* London: In aedibus T. Bertheleti, 1545.

Enterline, Lynn. *The Tears of Narcissus: Melancholia and Masculinity in Early Modern Writing.* Stanford: Stanford University Press, 1995.

Evans, G. Blakemore, ed. *The Riverside Shakespeare.* Boston: Houghton Mifflin, 1974.

Faret, Nicolas. *The Honest Man: Or, The Art to please in Court. Written in French by Sieur Faret.* Translated by E[dward] G[rimestone]. London: Printed by Thomas Harper, for Edward Blount, 1632.

Ferne, John. *The Blazon of* Gentrie: *Devided into two parts.* London: Printed by John Windet, for Toby Cooke, 1586.

Fletcher, Phineas. *The Purple Island, or, the Isle of Man.* Cambridge: Printed by the Printers to the Universitie of Cambridge, 1633.

Foucault, Michel. *The History of Sexuality, Volume I: An Introduction.* Translated by Robert Hurley. New York: Vintage Books/Random House, 1990.

Fradenburg, Louise, and Carla Freccero. Introduction to *Premodern Sexualities,* edited by Louise Fradenburg and Carla Freccero, xiii–xxiv. New York: Routledge, 1996.

Fraioli, Deborah. "The Literary Image of Joan of Arc: Prior Influences." *Speculum* 56 (1981): 811–30.

Fraunce, Abraham. *The Third part of the Countesse of Pembrokes Yuychurch: Entituled, Amintas Dale.* London: Printed for Thomas Woodcocke, 1592.

Freccero, Carla. "From Amazon to Court

Lady: Generic Hybridization in Boccaccio's *Teseida*." *Comparative Literature Studies* 32, no. 2 (1995): 226–43.

Freccero, John. "Medusa: The Letter and the Spirit." *Yearbook of Italian Studies* 2 (1972): 1–18.

Freedman, Barbara. *Staging the Gaze: Postmodernism, Psychoanalysis, and Shakespearean Comedy*. Ithaca, NY: Cornell University Press, 1991.

Freud, Sigmund. "Femininity," in *New Introductory Lectures on Psycho-Analysis*. In *The Standard Edition of the Complete Psychological Works of Sigmund Freud*, volume 22, 112–35. Translated and edited by James Strachey. 24 vols. London: Hogarth Press, 1974.

———. *The Interpretation of Dreams*. In *The Standard Edition*, volume 4, 1–338; volume 5, 339–625.

———. "Medusa's Head." In *The Standard Edition*, 18: 273–74.

———. "On Narcissism: An Introduction." In *The Standard Edition*, 14: 67–104.

———. "The 'Uncanny.' " In *The Standard Edition*, 17: 217–52.

Fuller, Mary C. "Ralegh's Fugitive Gold: Reference and Deferral in *The Discoverie of Guiana*." *Representations* 33 (1991): 42–64.

———. *Voyages in Print: English Travel to America, 1576–1624*. Cambridge, England: Cambridge University Press, 1995.

Fulton, Robert. "Timon, Cupid, and the Amazons." *Shakespeare Studies* 9 (1976): 283–99.

G[ainsford], T[homas]. *The Glory of England, Or A True Description of many excellent prerogatives and remarkeable blessings, whereby She Triumpheth over all the Nations of the World*. London: Printed by Edward Griffin for Th: Norton, 1618.

Gallop, Jane. *Reading Lacan*. Ithaca, NY: Cornell University Press, 1985.

Garber, Marjorie. *Vested Interests: Cross-Dressing and Cultural Anxiety*. New York: Harper Perennial, 1993.

Garcilasso Inca de la Vega. *Expedition of Gonzalo Pizarro to the Land of Cinnamon, A.D. 1539–42*. In *Expeditions into the Valley of the Amazons, 1539, 1540, 1639*, edited and translated by Clements R. Markham. London: Printed for the Hakluyt Society, 1859.

Garner, Shirley Nelson. "*A Midsummer Night's Dream*: 'Jack Shall Have Jill;/Nought Shall Go Ill.' " In *New Casebooks: A Midsummer Night's Dream*, edited by Richard Dutton, 84–100. Houndmills: Macmillan, 1996.

Gibson, Anthony, ed. *A Womans Woorth, defended against all the men in the world*. London: Imprinted by John Wolfe, 1599.

Girard, René. "Myth and Ritual in Shakespeare: *A Midsummer Night's Dream*." In *Textual Strategies: Perspectives in Post-Structuralist Criticism*, edited by Josué V. Harari, 189–212. Ithaca, NY: Cornell University Press, 1979.

———. *Violence and the Sacred*. Translated by Patrick Gregory. Baltimore: Johns Hopkins University Press, 1977.

Gohlke, Madelon. " 'I wooed thee with my sword': Shakespeare's Tragic Paradigms." In *Representing Shakespeare: New Psychoanalytic Essays*, edited by Murray M. Schwartz and Coppélia Kahn, 170–87. Baltimore: Johns Hopkins University Press, 1980.

Goldberg, Jonathan. *James I and the Politics of Literature*. Baltimore: Johns Hopkins University Press, 1983.

———. *Sodometries: Renaissance Texts, Modern Sexualities*. Stanford, CA: Stanford University Press, 1992.

———. *Writing Matter: From the Hands of the English Renaissance*. Stanford, CA: Stanford University Press, 1990.

———, ed. *Queering the Renaissance*. Durham, NC: Duke University Press, 1994.

Gossett, Suzanne. " 'Man-maid, begone!':

Women in Masques." *ELH* 18, no. 1 (1988): 96–113.

Greenblatt, Stephen. *Marvelous Possessions: The Wonder of the New World.* Chicago: University of Chicago Press, 1991.

———. *Sir Walter Ralegh: The Renaissance Man and His Roles.* New Haven: Yale University Press, 1973.

Greene, Robert. *Greenes Groats-worth of witte, bought with a million of Repentance.* London: Imprinted for William Wright, 1592.

Griffiths, Sir Percival. *A Licence to Trade: The History of English Chartered Companies.* London: Ernest Benn, 1974.

Guazzo, Stefano. *The civile Conversation of M. Stephen Guazzo, written first in Italian, divided into foure bookes, the first three translated out of French by G. pettie.* London: Imprinted by Thomas East, 1586.

Gutierrez, Nancy. "Gender and Value in *1 Henry VI:* The Role of Joan de Pucelle." *Theatre Journal* 42 (1990): 183–93.

Haec-Vir: Or The Womanish-Man: Being an Answere to a late Booke intituled Hic-Mulier. London: Printed for J[ohn] T[rundle], 1620.

Hakluyt, Richard. *The Principal Navigations Voyages Traffiques & Discoveries of the English Nation.* 12 vols. Glasgow: James MacLehose and Sons, 1903–1905.

Halberstam, Judith. *Female Masculinity.* Durham, NC: Duke University Press, 1998.

Hall, Edward. *The Union of the two noble and illustrate famelies of Lancastre and Yorke beeyng long in continual discension for the croune of this noble realme.* London, 1548.

Hall, Kim. *Things of Darkness: Economies of Race and Gender in Early Modern England.* Ithaca, NY: Cornell University Press, 1995.

Halperin, David M. "Why Is Diotima a Woman?" In *One Hundred Years of Homosexuality and Other Essays on Greek Love.* New York: Routledge, 1990.

Hamilton, A. C. *The Structure of Allegory in*

The Faerie Queene. Oxford: Clarendon, 1961.

Handelman, Susan. "*Timon of Athens:* The Rage of Disillusion." *American Imago* 36 (1979): 45–68.

Hankins, John Erskine. *Source and Meaning in Spenser's Allegory: A Study of* The Faerie Queene. Oxford: Clarendon, 1971.

Hardin, Richard F. "Chronicles and Mythmaking in Shakespeare's Joan of Arc." *Shakespeare Survey* 42 (1990): 25–35.

H[eale], W[illiam]. *An Apologie for Women. Or An Opposition To Mr. Dr. G. his assertion. Who held in the Act at Oxforde. Anno. 1608. That it was lawfull for husbands to beate their wives.* Oxford: Printed by Joseph Barnes Printer to the Universitie, 1609.

Helgerson, Richard. "The Land Speaks: Cartography, Chorography, and Subversion in Renaissance England." In *Representing the English Renaissance,* edited by Stephen Greenblatt, 327–62. Berkeley: University of California Press, 1988.

———. *The Elizabethan Prodigals.* Berkeley: University of California Press, 1976.

Herford, C. H., Percy Simpson, and Evelyn Simpson, eds. *Ben Jonson.* 11 vols. Oxford: Clarendon, 1925–1952.

Herodotus. *The History.* Translated by David Grene. Chicago: University of Chicago Press, 1987.

Herrmann, Paul. *The Great Age of Discovery.* Translated by Arnold J. Pomerans. Westport, CT: Greenwood, 1958, 1974.

Heywood, Thomas. *The Exemplary Lives And Memorable Acts of Nine The Most Worthy Women Of The World.* London: Printed by Tho. Cotes, for Richard Royston, 1640.

———. GYNAIKEION: *or, Nine Bookes of Various History Concerninge Women.* London: Printed by Adam Islip, 1624.

Hic Mulier: Or, The Man-Woman: Being a Medicine to cure the Coltish disease of the Staggers in the Masculine-Feminines of our Times. London: Printed for J[ohn] T[rundle], 1620.

Horowitz, Maryanne C. "Introduction:

Playing with Gender." In *Playing with Gender: A Renaissance Pursuit*, edited by Jean R. Brink, Maryanne C. Horowitz, and Allison P. Coudert. Urbana: University of Illinois Press, 1991.

Howard, Jean E., and Phyllis Rackin. *Engendering a Nation: A Feminist Account of Shakespeare's English Histories*. New York: Routledge, 1997.

Hunt, Marvin. "Charactonymic Structures in Sidney's *Arcadias*." *SEL* 33 (1993): 1–19.

Irigaray, Luce. *This Sex Which Is Not One*. Translated by Catherine Porter with Carolyn Burke. Ithaca, NY: Cornell University Press, 1985.

Jackson, Gabriele Bernhard. "Topical Ideology: Witches, Amazons, and Shakespeare's Joan of Arc." *English Literary Renaissance* 18 (1988): 40–65.

Jackson, MacDonald P. *Studies in Attribution: Middleton and Shakespeare*. Salzburg, Austria: Institut für Anglistik und Amerikanistik, 1979.

Jardine, Lisa. *Still Harping on Daughters: Women and Drama in the Age of Shakespeare*. Sussex, England: Harvester Press, 1983.

Jonson, Ben. *The Complete Masques*. Edited by Stephen Orgel. New Haven: Yale University Press, 1969.

Kahn, Coppélia. " 'Magic of Bounty': *Timon of Athens*, Jacobean Patronage, and Maternal Power." In *Shakespearean Tragedy and Gender*, edited by Shirley Nelson Garner and Madelon Sprengnether, 135–67. Bloomington: Indiana University Press, 1996.

———. *Man's Estate: Masculine Identity in Shakespeare*. Berkeley: University of California Press, 1981.

Kavanagh, James H. "Shakespeare in Ideology." In *Alternative Shakespeares*, edited by John Drakakis, 144–65. New York: Methuen, 1985.

Kermode, Frank. "Introduction: *Timon of Athens*." In *The Riverside Shakespeare*, edited by G. Blakemore Evans, 1441–1444. Boston: Houghton Mifflin, 1974.

King, Margaret. *Women of the Renaissance*. Chicago: University of Chicago Press, 1991.

Kinney, Clare. "The Masks of Love: Desire and Metamorphosis in Sidney's *New Arcadia*." *Criticism* 33, no. 4 (fall 1991): 461–90.

———. "On the Margins of Romance, at the Heart of the Matter: Revisionary Fabulation in Sidney's *New Arcadia*." *Journal of Narrative Technique* 21, no. 2 (spring 1991): 143–52.

Klein, Melanie. "Love, Guilt and Reparation." In *Love, Hate and Reparation*, by Melanie Klein and Joan Riviere, 57–119. New York: Norton, 1964.

Kleinbaum, Abby Wettan. *The War against the Amazons*. New York: McGraw-Hill, 1983.

Knapp, Jeffrey. *An Empire Nowhere: England, America, and Literature from* Utopia *to* The Tempest. Berkeley: University of California Press, 1992.

Knox, John. *The First Blast of the Trumpet Against the Monstrous Regiment of Women*. In *The Political Writings of John Knox*, edited by Marvin A. Breslow, 37–80. Washington, DC: Folger Shakespeare Library, 1985.

Kogan, Stephen. *The Hieroglyphic King*. Cranbury, NJ: Associated University Presses, 1986.

Lacan, Jacques. "The Agency of the Letter in the Unconscious or Reason Since Freud." In *Écrits: A Selection*. Translated by Alan Sheridan, 146–78. New York: Norton, 1977.

———. "The Function and Field of Speech and Language in Psychoanalysis," in *Écrits*, 30–113.

———. "The Mirror Stage," in *Écrits*, 1–7.

———. "The Signification of the Phallus," in *Écrits*, 281–91.

Lake, D. J. *The Canon of Thomas Middleton's Plays*. London: Cambridge University Press, 1975.

Lamb, Mary Ellen. "Exhibiting Class and Displaying the Body in Sidney's

Bibliography

Countess of Pembroke's Arcadia." *Studies in English Literature 1500–1900* 37, no. 1 (1997): 55–72.

Laqueur, Thomas. *Making Sex: Body and Gender from the Greeks to Freud.* Cambridge, MA: Harvard University Press, 1990.

Larkin, Joan, and Elly Bulkin, eds. *Amazon Poetry: An Anthology of Lesbian Poetry.* Brooklyn: Out and Out Books, 1975.

Lee, Patricia-Ann. "Reflections of Power: Margaret of Anjou and the Dark Side of Queenship." *Renaissance Quarterly* 39 (1986): 183–217.

Leonard, Irving A. *Books of the Brave: Being an Account of Books and of Men in the Spanish Conquest and Settlement of the Sixteenth-Century New World.* Cambridge, MA: Harvard University Press, 1949.

Leslie, Michael. *Spenser's "Fierce Warres and Faithfull Loves": Martial and Chivalric Symbolism in* The Faerie Queene. Cambridge, England: D. S. Brewer, 1983.

Levin, Carole. "Power, Politics, and Sexuality: Images of Elizabeth I." In *The Politics of Gender in Early Modern Europe,* edited by Jean R. Brink, Allison P. Coudert, and Maryanne C. Horowitz, 95–110. Kirksville, MO: Sixteenth Century Journal Publishers, 1989.

Levin, Harry. "Shakespeare's Misanthrope." *Shakespeare Survey* 26 (1973): 89–94.

Levin, Richard A. "What? How? Female-Female Desire in Sidney's *New Arcadia.*" *Criticism* 39, no. 4 (1997): 463–79.

Levine, Laura. "Rape, Repetition, and the Politics of Closure in *A Midsummer Night's Dream.*" In *Feminist Readings of Early Modern Culture: Emerging Subjects,* edited by Valerie Traub, M. Lindsay Kaplan, and Dympna Callaghan, 210–28. Cambridge, England: Cambridge University Press, 1996.

Lewalski, Barbara K. *Writing Women in Jacobean England.* Cambridge, MA: Harvard University Press, 1993.

Lewis, C. S. *The Allegory of Love: A Study in Medieval Tradition.* London: Oxford University Press, 1938.

Lindley, David. *The Court Masque.* Manchester, England: Manchester University Press, 1984.

Lynch, Lee. *The Amazon Trail.* Tallahassee, FL: Naiad Press, 1988.

Lysias. *Lysias.* Translated by W. R. M. Lamb. London: W. Heinemann, 1930.

MacDonald, Joyce Green. " 'Hay for the Daughters!': Gender and Patriarchy in *The Miseries of Civil War* and *Henry VI.*" *Comparative Drama* 24 (1990): 193–216.

MacKenzie, Clayton G. "Myth and Anti-Myth in the First Tetralogy." *Orbis Litterarum* 42 (1987): 1–26.

Maclean, Ian. *The Renaissance Notion of Woman: A Study in the Fortunes of Scholasticism and Medical Science in European Intellectual Life.* Cambridge, England: Cambridge University Press, 1980.

Mandeville, Sir John. *Mandeville's Travels: Texts and Translations.* Edited by Malcolm Letts. 2 vols. London: The Hakluyt Society, 1953.

Marcus, Leah. *Puzzling Shakespeare: Local Reading and Its Discontents.* Berkeley: University of California Press, 1988.

Markham, Clements R., ed. and trans. *Expeditions into the Valley of the Amazons, 1539, 1540, 1639.* London: Printed for the Hakluyt Society, 1859.

Marshall, David. "Exchanging Visions: Reading *A Midsummer Night's Dream.*" *ELH* 49, no. 3 (1982): 543–75.

Marston, John. *Antonio and Mellida and Antonio's Revenge.* London: Printed for the Malone Society by F. Hall at the Oxford University Press, 1922.

Marx, Karl. *The Eighteenth Brumaire of Louis Bonaparte.* New York: International Publishers, 1963, 1991.

Masten, Jeffrey. *Textual Intercourse: Collaboration, Authorship, and Sexualities in Renaissance Drama.* Cambridge, England: Cambridge University Press, 1997.

Mattson, Martha. *Amazons: The Forgotten*

Tribe. San Diego, CA: Amazon Press, 1997.

McCoy, Richard C. *Sir Philip Sidney: Rebellion in Arcadia.* New Brunswick, NJ: Rutgers University Press, 1979.

McGuire, Philip C. "Hippolyta's Silence and the Poet's Pen." In *New Casebooks: A Midsummer Night's Dream,* edited by Richard Dutton, 139–60. Houndmills: Macmillan, 1996.

Medina, José Toribio. *The Discovery of the Amazon.* Edited by H. C. Heaton. Translated by Bertram T. Lee. New York: American Geographical Society, 1934.

The Mirror for Magistrates (1559). Edited by Lily B. Campbell. Cambridge, England: Cambridge University Press, 1938.

Montaigne, Michel de. *The Essayes or Morall, Politike and Millitarie Discourses of Lo: Michaell de Montaigne.* Translated by John Florio. London: Printed by Val. Sims for Edward Blount, 1603.

Montrose, Louis Adrian. " 'Shaping Fantasies': Figurations of Gender and Power in Elizabethan Culture." In *Representing the English Renaissance,* edited by Stephen Greenblatt, 31–64. Berkeley: University of California Press, 1988.

———. "The Work of Gender in the Discourse of Discovery." *Representations* 33 (1991): 1–41.

Morison, Samuel Eliot. *Christopher Columbus, Mariner.* Boston: Little Brown, 1955.

———. *The European Discovery of America: The Southern Voyages, A.D. 1492–1616.* New York: Oxford University Press, 1974.

Muld Sacke: Or The Apologie of Hic Mulier. London: Printed for Richard Meighen, 1620.

Newman, Karen. *Fashioning Femininity and English Renaissance Drama.* Chicago: University of Chicago Press, 1991.

Newstead, Christopher. *An Apology for Women: Or, Womens Defence.* London: Printed by E. G[riffin] for R. Whittakers, 1620.

Nichols, John, ed. *The Progresses and Public Processions of Queen Elizabeth.* London, 1823.

O'Connor, John J. Amadis de Gaule *and Its Influence on Elizabethan Literature.* New Brunswick, NJ: Rutgers University Press, 1970.

Olson, Paul A. "*A Midsummer Night's Dream* and the Meaning of Court Marriage." *English Literary History* 24, no. 2 (1957): 95–119.

Orgel, Stephen. *The Illusion of Power: Political Theater in the English Renaissance.* Berkeley: University of California Press, 1975.

———. *Impersonations: The Performance of Gender in Shakespeare's England.* Cambridge, England: Cambridge University Press, 1996.

———. "Jonson and the Amazons." In *Soliciting Interpretation: Literary Theory and Seventeenth-Century English Poetry,* edited by Elizabeth D. Harvey and Katharine Eisaman Maus, 119–39. Chicago: University of Chicago Press, 1990.

———. *The Jonsonian Masque.* Cambridge, MA: Harvard University Press, 1965.

Osório, Jerónimo. *The Five Bookes of the Famous, learned, and eloquent man, Hieronimus Osorius, contayning a discourse of civill, and Christian Nobilitie.* Translated by William Blandie. London: Thomas Marsh, 1576.

Ovidius Naso, Publius. *The Heroycall Epistles of the Learned Poet Publius Ovidius Naso.* Translated by George Turbervile. London, Imprinted by Henry Derham, 1567.

Painter, William. *The Palace of Pleasure, Beautified, adorned and well furnished, with Pleasaunt Histories and excellent Novelles, selected out of divers good and commendable Authors.* London: Imprinted by Henry Denham, for Richard Tottell and William Jones, 1566.

———. *The Second Tome of The Palace of Pleasure contayning store of goodlye Histories, Tragical matters, and other Morall argumentes, very requisite for delight and profyte.* London: Imprinted by Thomas Marshe, 1575.

Paré, Ambroise. *On Monsters and Marvels* (1573). Translated by Janis L. Pallister. Chicago: University of Chicago Press, 1982.

Park, Katharine. "The Rediscovery of the Clitoris: French Medicine and the Tribade, 1570–1620." In *The Body in Parts: Fantasies of Corporeality in Early Modern Europe*, edited by David Hillman and Carla Mazzio, 171–93. New York: Routledge, 1997.

Parker, Patricia. "Introduction." In *Shakespeare and the Question of Theory*, edited by Patricia Parker and Geoffrey Hartman, vii–xiii. New York: Methuen, 1985.

———. *Literary Fat Ladies: Rhetoric, Gender, Property*. London: Methuen, 1987.

Parry, Graham. *The Golden Age Restor'd*. New York: St. Martin's, 1981.

Parry, J. H. *The Establishment of the European Hegemony, 1415–1715: Trade and Exploration in the Age of the Renaissance*. New York: Harper and Row, 1966.

Paster, Gail Kern. *The Body Embarrassed: Drama and the Disciplines of Shame in Early Modern England*. Ithaca, NY: Cornell University Press, 1993.

Patterson, Annabel. " 'Under . . . Pretty Tales': Intention in Sidney's *Arcadia.*" *Studies in the Literary Imagination* 15, no. 1 (1982): 5–21.

Pearson, D'Orsay W. " 'Unkinde' Theseus: A Study in Renaissance Mythography." *English Literary Renaissance* 4, no. 2 (1974): 276–98.

Penrose, Boies. *Travel and Discovery in the Renaissance, 1420–1620*. Cambridge, MA: Harvard University Press, 1952.

Plutarch. *The Lives of the Noble Grecians and Romanes Compared together by that grave learned Philosopher and Historiographer, Plutarke of Chaeronea*. Translated by Thomas North. London: Imprinted by Thomas Vautroullier and John Wight, 1579.

The Problems of Aristotle, With other Philosophers and Physisians. Wherein are contained divers Questions, with their Answers, touching the estate of mans Bodie. London: Printed by R. R. for R. W., 1647.

Purchas, Samuel. *Hakluytus Posthumus, or Purchas his Pilgrimes: Contayning a History of the World in Sea Voyages and Lande Travells by Englishmen and others*. 20 vols. Glasgow: James MacLehose and Sons, 1905–1907.

———. *Purchas his Pilgrimage. Or Relations Of The World And The Religions Observed In All Ages And places discovered, from the Creation unto this Present*. London: Printed by William Stansby for Henrie Fetherstone, 1613.

Putnam, Ruth. "California: The Name." In *University of California Publications in History* 4: 294–346. Berkeley: University of California Press, 1916.

Puttenham, George. *The Arte of English Poesie*. London: Printed by Richard Field, 1589.

Pye, Christopher. "The Theater, the Market, and the Subject of History." *ELH* 61 (1994): 501–22.

Quilligan, Maureen. "The Comedy of Female Authority in *The Faerie Queene.*" *English Literary Renaissance* 17 (1987): 156–71.

———. "The Gender of the Reader and the Problem of Sexuality [in Books 3 and 4]." In *Critical Essays on Edmund Spenser*, edited by Mihoko Suzuki, 133–51. New York: G. K. Hall, 1995.

Quint, David. "Introduction." In *Literary Theory/Renaissance Texts*, edited by Patricia Parker and David Quint. 1–19. Baltimore: Johns Hopkins University Press, 1986.

Quintus Smyrnaeus. *The Fall of Troy*. Translated by Arthur S. Way. London: William Heinemann, 1913.

Rackin, Phyllis. "Androgyny, Mimesis, and the Marriage of the Boy Heroine on the English Renaissance Stage." *PMLA* 102 (1987): 29–41.

———. "Anti-Historians: Women's Roles in Shakespeare's Histories." *Theatre Journal* 37 (1985): 329–44.

———. "Historical Difference/Sexual Difference." In *Privileging Gender in*

Early Modern England, edited by Jean R. Brink, 37–63. Kirksville, MO: Sixteenth Century Journal Publishers, 1993.

———. *Stages of History: Shakespeare's English Chronicles.* Ithaca, NY: Cornell University Press, 1990.

Ralegh, Sir Walter. *The discoverie of the large, rich, and beautifull Empire of Guiana, with a relation of the great and golden citie of Manoa (which the Spaniards call El Dorado) . . . Performed in the yeere 1595 by Sir Walter Ralegh.* In Richard Hakluyt, *The Principal Navigations Voyages Traffiques & Discoveries of the English Nation,* 10: 338–440. Glasgow: James MacLehose and Sons, 1903–1905.

Rambuss, Richard. *Closet Devotions.* Durham, NC: Duke University Press, 1998.

Rich, Barnabe. *The excellency of good women. The honour and estimation that belongeth unto them. The infallible markes whereby to know them.* London: T. Dawson, 1613.

Riviere, Joan. "Womanliness as a Masquerade." In *The Inner World and Joan Riviere: Collected Papers 1920–1958,* edited by Athol Hughes, 90–101. London: Karnac Books for the Melanie Klein Trust, 1991.

Roberts, Jeanne Addison. "Birth Traumas in Shakespeare." *Renaissance Papers* (1990): 55–65.

Roberts, John Maddox. *Conan and the Amazon.* New York: T. Doherty Associates, 1999.

Roche, Thomas P. Jr. *The Kindly Flame: A Study of the Third and Fourth Books of Spenser's* Faerie Queene. Princeton, NJ: Princeton University Press, 1964.

Rolfe, William J. *Shakespeare's Comedy of A Midsummer Night's Dream.* New York: Harper and Brothers, 1877.

Rose, Jacqueline. "Introduction II," in *Feminine Sexuality: Jacques Lacan and the* école freudienne, edited by Juliet Mitchell and Jacqueline Rose, translated by Jacqueline Rose, 27–57. New York: Norton, 1982.

Rosenthal, Albrecht. "The Isle of the Amazons: A Marvel of Travellers." *Journal of the Warburg Institute* 1, no. 3 (1939): 257–59.

Rothery, Guy Cadogan. *The Amazons in Antiquity and Modern Times.* London: F. Griffiths, 1910.

Rouse, W. H. D., ed. *Shakespeare's Ovid, Being Arthur Golding's Translation of the Metamorphoses.* London: At the De La More Press, 1904.

Rubin, Gayle. "The Traffic in Women: Notes on the 'Political Economy' of Sex." In *Toward an Anthropology of Women,* edited by Rayna R. Reiter, 157–210. New York: Monthly Review Press, 1975.

Salzman, Paul. *English Prose Fiction 1558–1700: A Critical History.* Oxford: Clarendon, 1985.

Sandys, George. *Ovid's Metamorphosis Englished, Mythologiz'd, And Represented in Figures* (1632). Edited by Karl K. Hulley and Stanley T. Vandersall. Lincoln: University of Nebraska Press, 1970.

Schleiner, Winfried. "Divina virago: Queen Elizabeth as an Amazon." *Studies in Philology* 75 (1978): 163–80.

———. "Le feu caché: Homosocial Bonds between Women in a Renaissance Romance." *Renaissance Quarterly* 45, no. 2 (1992): 293–311.

———. "Male Cross-Dressing and Transvestism in Renaissance Romances." *Sixteenth Century Journal* 19, no. 4 (1988): 605–19.

Schwarz, Kathryn. "Missing the Breast: Disease, Desire, and the Singular Effect of Amazons." In *The Body in Parts: Fantasies of Corporeality in Early Modern Europe,* edited by David Hillman and Carla Mazzio, 147–69. New York: Routledge, 1997.

———. "Mother Love: Clichés and Amazons in Early Modern England." In *Maternal Measures: Figuring Caregiving in the Early Modern Period,* edited by Naomi

Miller and Naomi Yavneh. Aldershot, England: Ashgate Publishing, 2000.

Scott, Joan Wallach. *Gender and the Politics of History.* New York: Columbia University Press, 1988.

Sedgwick, Eve Kosofsky. *Between Men: English Literature and Male Homosocial Desire.* New York: Columbia University Press, 1985.

Seneca. *The Fourth, and Most Ruthful Tragedy of L. Annaeus Seneca Entituled Hippolytus.* Translated into Englishe by Jhon [*sic*] Studley. In *Seneca His Tenne Tragedies, Translated into English, Edited by Thomas Newton, Anno 1581, With an Introduction by T. S. Eliot.* London: Constable and Co., 1927.

Shakespeare, William. *The Complete Works of Shakespeare.* Edited by David Bevington, 4th ed. New York: HarperCollins, 1992.

———. *A Midsummer Night's Dream.* Edited by Harold F. Brooks. The Arden Shakespeare. New York: Routledge, 1979.

———. *The Two Noble Kinsmen.* Edited by Lois Potter. The Arden Shakespeare. Surrey, England: Thomas Nelson and Sons, 1997.

Shakespeare's Ovid, Being Arthur Golding's Translation of the Metamorphoses. Edited by W. H. D. Rouse. London: At the De La More Press, 1904.

Shaver, Anne. "Woman's Place in the *New Arcadia.*" *Sidney Newsletter* 10, no. 2 (1989–1990): 3–15.

Shaw, George Bernard. *Saint Joan.* New York: Random House, 1956.

Shepherd, Simon. *Amazons and Warrior Women: Varieties of Feminism in Seventeenth-Century Drama.* New York: St. Martin's, 1981.

[Shirley, John.] *The Accomplished Ladies Rich Closet of Rarities.* 3d ed. London: Printed for N. Bodington and J. Blare, 1691.

Sidney, Sir Philip. *The Countess of Pembroke's Arcadia.* Edited by Maurice Evans. New York: Penguin, 1984.

———. *The Countess of Pembroke's Arcadia (The Old Arcadia).* Edited by Katherine Duncan-Jones. Oxford: Oxford University Press, 1985.

———. "The Defence of Poesy." In *Sir Philip Sidney: Selected Prose and Poetry,* edited by Robert Kimbrough. Madison: University of Wisconsin Press, 1983.

———. *Sir Philip Sidney: Selected Poems.* Edited by Catherine Bates. New York: Penguin, 1994.

Siebers, Tobin. *The Mirror of Medusa.* Berkeley: University of California Press, 1983.

Silberman, Lauren. "The Hermaphrodite and the Metamorphosis of Spenserian Allegory." *English Literary Renaissance* 17, no. 2 (1987): 207–23.

———. *Transforming Desire: Erotic Knowledge in Books III and IV of* The Faerie Queene. Berkeley: University of California Press, 1995.

Sinfield, Alan. "Power and Ideology: An Outline Theory and Sidney's *Arcadia.*" *ELH* 52, no. 2 (1985): 259–77.

Smith, Barbara Herrnstein. *On the Margins of Discourse: The Relation of Literature to Language.* Chicago: University of Chicago Press, 1978.

Smith, Bruce R. *Homosexual Desire in Shakespeare's England: A Cultural Poetics.* Chicago: University of Chicago Press, 1994.

Soellner, Rolf. *Timon of Athens: Shakespeare's Pessimistic Tragedy.* Columbus: Ohio State University Press, 1979.

Spencer, T. J. B. *A Book of Masques in Honour of Allardyce Nicoll.* London: Cambridge University Press, 1967.

Spenser, Edmund. *The Faerie Queene.* Edited by Thomas P. Roche, Jr. New York: Viking Penguin, 1978, 1987.

Stallybrass, Peter. "Patriarchal Territories: The Body Enclosed." In *Rewriting the Renaissance,* edited by Margaret W. Ferguson, Maureen Quilligan, and Nancy J. Vickers, 123–42. Chicago: University of Chicago Press, 1986.

———. "Transvestism and the 'Body Be-

neath': Speculating on the Boy Actor."
In *Erotic Politics: Desire on the Renaissance
Stage*, edited by Susan Zimmerman,
64–83. New York: Routledge, 1992.

Stallybrass, Peter, and Allon White. *The
Politics and Poetics of Transgression*. Ithaca:
Cornell University Press, 1986.

Stephens, Dorothy. "Into Other Arms:
Amoret's Evasion." In *Queering the Renaissance*, edited by Jonathan Goldberg,
190–217. Durham, NC: Duke University
Press, 1994.

———. *The Limits of Eroticism in Post-
Petrarchan Narrative: Conditional Pleasure from
Spenser to Marvell*. Cambridge, England:
Cambridge University Press, 1998.

Stillman, Robert E. "The Politics of
Sidney's Pastoral: Mystification and
Mythology in the *Old Arcadia*." *ELH* 52,
no. 4 (1985): 795–814.

Stoller, Robert J. *Observing the Erotic Imagination*. New Haven: Yale University Press,
1985.

Strabo. *The Geography of Strabo*. Translated
by Horace Leonard Jones. 8 vols. Cambridge, MA: Harvard University Press,
1954–1961.

Sullivan, Margaret M. "Amazons and
Aristocrats: The Function of Pyro-
cles' Amazon Role in Sidney's Revised
Arcadia." In *Playing with Gender: A Renais-
sance Pursuit*, edited by Jean R. Brink,
Maryanne C. Horowitz, and Allison P.
Coudert, 62–81. Urbana: University of
Illinois Press, 1991.

Suzuki, Mihoko. "The Dismemberment
of Hippolytus: Humanist Imitation,
Shakespearean Translation." *Classical
and Modern Literature* 10: 2 (winter 1990):
103–12.

———. *Metamorphoses of Helen: Authority,
Difference, and the Epic*. Ithaca, NY: Cornell University Press, 1989.

Taufer, Alison. "The Only Good Amazon
Is a Converted Amazon: The Woman
Warrior and Christianity in the *Amadís
Cycle*." In *Playing with Gender: A Renais-

sance Pursuit*, edited by Jean R. Brink,
Maryanne C. Horowitz, and Allison P.
Coudert, 35–51. Urbana: University of
Illinois Press, 1991.

Tennenhouse, Leonard. "Arcadian Rhetoric: Sidney and the Politics of Courtship." In *Sir Philip Sidney's Achievements*,
edited by M. J. B. Allen, Dominic
Baker-Smith, Arthur F. Kinney, and
Margaret M. Sullivan, 201–13. New
York: AMS Press, 1990.

———. *Power on Display: The Politics of
Shakespeare's Genres*. New York: Methuen,
1986.

———. "Sir Walter Ralegh and the Literature of Clientage." In *Patronage in the
Renaissance*, edited by Guy Fitch Lytle
and Stephen Orgel, 235–58. Princeton,
NJ: Princeton University Press, 1981.

Tennyson, Alfred, Lord. *Poems of Tennyson,
1829–1868*. London: Oxford University
Press, 1926.

Thevet, André. *The New found worlde, or
Antarctike, wherin is contained wonderful and
strange things*. London: Imprinted by
Henrie Bynneman, for Thomas Hacket,
1568.

Thoreau, Henry David. *Walden*. Edited
by J. Lyndon Shanley. Princeton, NJ:
Princeton University Press, 1971.

Tillyard, E. M. W. *Shakespeare's History Plays*.
London: Chatto and Windus, 1948.

Todorov, Tzvetan. *The Conquest of America:
The Question of the Other*. Translated by
Richard Howard. New York: Harper
and Row, 1984.

Townshend, Aurelian. *Tempe Restored*. In
Aurelian Townshend's Poems and Masks.
Edited by E. K. Chambers. Oxford: At
the Clarendon Press, 1912.

Traub, Valerie. *Desire and Anxiety: Circulations
of Sexuality in Shakespearean Drama*. New
York: Routledge, 1992.

———. "The (In)significance of 'Lesbian' Desire in Early Modern England."
In *Queering the Renaissance*, edited by

Jonathan Goldberg, 62–83. Durham, NC: Duke University Press, 1994.

———. "The Perversion of 'Lesbian' Desire." *History Workshop Journal* 41 (1996): 19–49.

———. "Prince Hal's Falstaff: Positioning Psychoanalysis and the Female Reproductive Body." *Shakespeare Quarterly* 40, no. 4 (1989): 256–74.

Tyrrell, William Blake. *Amazons: A Study in Athenian Mythmaking.* Baltimore: Johns Hopkins University Press, 1984.

Vickers, Nancy. " 'The Blazon of Sweet Beauty's Best': Shakespeare's *Lucrece.*" In *Shakespeare and the Question of Theory,* edited by Patricia Parker and Geoffrey Hartman, 95–115. New York: Methuen, 1985.

———. "Diana Described: Scattered Woman and Scattered Rhyme." In *Writing and Sexual Difference,* edited by Elizabeth Abel, 95–109. Chicago: University of Chicago Press, 1982.

Villeponteaux, Mary. "Displacing Feminine Authority in *The Faerie Queene.*" *SEL* 35, no. 1 (1995): 53–67.

———. " 'Not as Women Wonted Be': Spenser's Amazon Queen." In *Dissing Elizabeth: Negative Representations of Gloriana,* edited by Julia M. Walker, 209–25. Durham, NC: Duke University Press, 1998.

Virgil. *The Aeneid.* Translated by Thomas Phaer and Thomas Twyne. In *The Aeneid of Thomas Phaer and Thomas Twyne: A Critical Edition Introducing Renaissance Metrical Typography,* edited by Steven Lally. New York: Garland, 1987.

Vives, Juan Luis. *A Very Fruteful and Pleasant boke callyd the Instruction of a Christen woman.* Translated by Richard Hyrde. London: in [a]edibus T. Berth[eleti], 1541.

Warner, William. *The First and Second parts of Albions England.* London: Imprinted by Thomas Orwin, for Thomas Cadman, 1589.

Whitney, Geffrey. *A Choice of Emblemes, And Other Devises, For the moste parte gathered out of sundrie writers, Englished and Moralized. And Divers Newly Devised.* Leyden: Imprinted in the house of Christopher Plantyn, by Francis Raphelengius, 1586.

Wilford, John Noble. "Ancient Graves of Armed Women Hint at Amazons." *New York Times,* 25 February 1997.

Willard, Charity Cannon. *Christine de Pizan: Her Life and Works.* New York: Persea Books, 1984.

Williams, Gary Jay. "Stage History, 1816–1978." In *Timon of Athens: Shakespeare's Pessimistic Tragedy,* edited by Rolf Soellner, 161–84. Columbus: Ohio State University Press, 1979.

Williams, Kathleen. "Venus and Diana: Some Uses of Myth in *The Faerie Queene.*" In *Spenser: A Collection of Critical Essays,* edited by Harry Berger Jr., 97–114. Englewood Cliffs, NJ: Prentice-Hall, 1968.

Wither, George. *A Collection of Emblemes, Ancient and Moderne: Quickened with Metricall Illustrations, both Morall and Divine.* London: printed for Robert Milbourne, 1635.

Wofford, Susanne Lindgren. "Gendering Allegory: Spenser's Bold Reader and the Emergence of Character in *The Faerie Queene* III." *Criticism* 30, no. 1 (1988): 1–21.

Woodbridge, Linda. *Women and the English Renaissance: Literature and the Nature of Womankind, 1540–1620.* Urbana: University of Illinois Press, 1984.

Woods, Susanne. "Amazonian Tyranny: Spenser's Radigund and Diachronic Mimesis." In *Playing with Gender: A Renaissance Pursuit,* edited by Jean R. Brink, Maryanne C. Horowitz, and Allison P. Coudert, 52–61. Urbana: University of Illinois Press, 1991.

Woolf, Virginia. *A Room of One's Own.* Edited by Mary Gordon. New York: Harcourt Brace, 1981.

Wright, Celeste Turner. "The Amazons in Elizabethan Literature." *Studies in Philology* 37 (1940): 433–56.

Wroth, Lady Mary. *The First Part of the Countess of Montgomery's Urania.* Edited by Josephine A. Roberts. Binghamton, NY: Medieval and Renaissance Texts and Studies, 1995.

Wynne-Davies, Marion. "The Queen's Masque: Renaissance Women and the Seventeenth-Century Court Masque." In *Gloriana's Face: Women, Public and Private in the English Renaissance,* edited by S. P. Cerasano and Marion Wynne-Davies, 79–104. Detroit: Wayne State University Press, 1992.

Yates, Frances A. *Astraea: The Imperial Theme in the Sixteenth Century.* London: Routledge and Kegan Paul, 1975.

Young, David P. *Something of Great Constancy: The Art of* A Midsummer Night's Dream. New Haven: Yale University Press, 1966.

Index

83, 86, 89, 96, 101, 104, 121, 123, 143, 157,
170–71, 227, 234, 240 n.34, 241 n.53
Exploration narratives, xi, xiii, 15, 37,
50–78, 88, 243 n.6

Faret, Nicolas, 19–21
Female bonding. *See* Homosociality:
female
Feminine masculinity, 183, 188–90, 192–93,
197, 199–200
Femininity, 9–10, 17, 36, 39, 62, 76, 80–82,
94–97, 99–102, 118–19, 126, 152, 158, 161,
183, 190, 192, 198, 200, 204, 207, 217, 219,
220, 234, 256 n.16
Feminization: of land, 37, 71–73, 75–78; of
men, 39, 63, 81, 95, 102, 151, 153, 189, 254
n.50, 256 n.16; of women, 39, 73, 87, 91,
104–5, 146, 153, 217, 249 n.59
Ferne, John, 248 n.55
Fetish, 31–32, 149, 150, 151, 182, 193
Fletcher, John, 236
Fletcher, Phineas, 216
Fool's gold, 60, 70–71
Foucault, Michel, 3
Fradenburg, Louise, 26–27, 43
Fragmentation, 80, 88, 93–96, 105–7, 113–14,
128, 133, 143, 151, 155–56, 191, 227
Fraioli, Deborah, 247 n.29
Frame narrative, 206–10, 218, 221–22, 236,
238
Fraunce, Abraham, 26, 32, 242 n.91
Freccero, Carla, 26–27, 43, 226–27
Freccero, John, 32
Freedman, Barbara, 36, 83–84, 138–39, 207,
214, 223–24
Freud, Sigmund, xiii, 11, 26, 30–33, 38, 66,
76, 81, 138, 148, 231, 242 n.74
Fuller, Mary C., 52, 64, 65–66, 77, 245
nn. 54, 56
Fulton, Robert, 251 n.52

Gainsford, Thomas, 15, 18–19, 21, 52–53
Galatea, 187–88
Galen, 184
Gallop, Jane, 153
Garber, Marjorie, 11, 150, 182, 185, 197

Garcilasso Inca de la Vega, 54
Gargarians, 228–29
Garner, Shirley Nelson, 258 nn. 18, 29, 259
n.58
Gay pride, xii, 176
Gibson, Anthony, 18, 19–20, 89, 217–18,
234–35, 253 n.31
Girard, René, 145–46, 205–6, 259 n.47
Gohlke, Madelon, 208, 249 n.58
Gold, 50–52, 56–57, 59, 66, 68, 69–75
Goldberg, Jonathan, 8, 28, 111, 239 n.2, 243
n.112
Golding, Arthur, 222
Gossett, Suzanne, 116, 121
Greenblatt, Stephen, 54, 56, 58, 69
Greene, Robert, 106–7
Griffiths, Percival, 244 n.21
Guazzo, Stefano, 248 n.55
Gutierrez, Nancy, 246 nn. 6, 18, 247 n.21

Haec-Vir, 152, 176, 188–90, 199–200
Hakluyt, Richard, 15, 63
Halberstam, Judith, 38–39, 151
Hall, Edward, 80, 88, 98–99
Hall, Kim, 118–19, 250 nn. 15, 20
Halperin, David, 25, 145
Hamilton, A. C., 253 n.33, 255 n.63
Handelman, Susan, 131
Hankins, John Erskine, 253 n.33, 255 n.63
Hardin, Richard F., 246 n.20, 247 n.25
Heale, William, 20
Helgerson, Richard, 245 n.65, 256 n.13
Henry, Prince of Wales, 124, 127, 251 n.37
Henry V, 81, 88, 93, 102
Hercules, 17, 122, 150, 153–54, 188–90, 209,
212–13, 215–18, 253 n.38
Hermaphrodites, 142–45, 162, 168, 177, 197,
198, 252 nn. 10, 11, 13
Hermaphroditus, 144–45
Herodotus, xi, 15, 24, 33, 36, 42, 209
Herrmann, Paul, 55, 244 n.37
Heteroeroticism, 8, 36, 159, 161, 162–64, 168,
170, 181–83, 194, 210, 216–17, 220, 224
Heterosexism, 168
Heterosexuality, 3, 5–8, 26–28, 31–33, 40,
42–43, 81–82, 95, 99–100, 104, 140–50,
153–58, 161, 163, 169–71, 176–83, 186, 192–

Index

280

MacDonald, Joyce Green, 95
MacKenzie, Clayton G., 246 n.19
Maclean, Ian, 30, 240 n.39
Magellan, 228
Male bonding. *See* Homosociality: male
Malecasta, 40, 163–67, 173
Mandeville, Sir John, 56–57
Marco Polo, 59
Marcus, Leah, 89–90, 246 nn. 2, 6, 247 n.21, 248 n.43, 249 nn. 60, 62
Margaret of Anjou, 37, 81–84, 92–104
Marriage, 5, 13, 19–20, 24, 27, 36, 39, 41, 53, 54, 60–63, 80, 84, 93–96, 141, 148–49, 152, 154, 157–58, 163, 170, 173–74, 176, 196, 201, 204–35 passim, 236–38, 240 n.52, 242 n.74, 255 n.53, 259 n.38
Marshall, David, 209–10, 234–35
Marston, John, 177–79, 183
Marx, Karl, 234
Masculinity, 20, 33, 35, 36, 38–40, 71, 96, 103, 106, 125–26, 139, 143, 145, 147, 148, 151–53, 160, 161, 167, 180, 183, 190–93, 195, 198–200, 213, 216–17, 220, 222, 234; female, 2–3, 6, 9, 22, 27–29, 33–39, 41–42, 81–87, 99, 101, 103, 118, 123–25, 128, 138–74 passim, 183, 198, 212–13, 217, 253 n.26, 258 n.34; male, 24–26, 35–37, 76, 83, 85–87, 104, 122, 126–27, 146, 149–51, 155–56, 180, 188–89, 199, 204, 211, 215, 230, 238
Masten, Jeffrey, 8, 238, 239 n.2, 260 n.3
Maternity, 10, 21, 63, 76, 80, 82, 90–91, 93, 95, 96–99, 102–4, 120, 131, 141, 155, 228
Matriarchy, 14–15
McCoy, Richard, 256 nn. 12, 13
McGuire, Philip, 260 n.72
Medina, José Toribio, 55, 59, 67, 244 n.19
Medusa, 29–33, 115, 122–23, 128, 147, 188, 242 nn. 83, 91, 92, 250 n.26, 254 n.50
Melancholia, 25, 28, 201
Metalepsis, 128–29
Metaphor, 10, 21–22, 24, 41, 66, 70, 85, 94, 117–18, 126, 151, 193, 208, 214, 216, 224–25, 227, 228, 237
Metonymy, 10, 18, 51–53, 56, 60, 62–63, 65, 66, 69, 71, 77, 83, 89–90, 163, 243 n.6
Middleton, Thomas, 130, 251 n.45

Mirror for Magistrates, 96
Mirroring, 24–29, 36–37, 39, 66–67, 71, 73, 77, 85, 111–15, 117–18, 125–26, 128, 133, 138–43, 145–46, 153, 157, 158, 160, 163, 180, 186, 188, 198, 206, 210, 214, 217
Mirror stage, 11, 83–84, 138–41, 144–45, 153, 155, 188
Misandry, 19
Misogyny, 12, 32, 183, 189, 198, 233
Misrecognition, 24–29, 60–63, 84, 126, 139–42, 145–49, 159, 164–69, 181–82, 186–89, 194–95, 216–17, 224–26
Montaigne, Michel de, 65, 72, 155
Montrose, Louis, 14, 64, 71, 76, 156, 207–8, 233, 240 n.44, 245 nn. 54, 56, 246 n.65, 253 n.33
Morison, Samuel Eliot, 55, 61, 118
Muld Sacke, 22–23

Narcissism, 24–29, 32–34, 38, 39, 44, 111, 114–15, 128, 131, 142–47, 159, 163, 179–80, 200, 214, 216, 242 nn. 74, 83, 253 n.16, 256 n.24
Narcissus, 25–29, 114–15, 128, 142–45, 147, 154, 179
Nationalism, 12, 18–19, 21, 37–38, 72–73, 75–76, 84, 86, 88–89, 91, 93, 96, 99, 101
Newman, Karen, 12, 17, 44–45, 74
Newstead, Christopher, 89
New world, 22, 37–38, 41, 50–78, 112, 118, 153
New York Times, xi-xiii
Nichols, John, 251 n.37
Normativity, xiii, 1–12, 14–15, 27, 36, 44, 99–100, 152, 157, 194–96, 199, 210, 223, 225, 227
North, Thomas, 222

O'Connor, John, 149, 150, 177–78
Oedipal conflict, 11
Olson, Paul, 205–7, 259 n.60, 260 n.73
Orellana, Francisco de, 54–57, 59, 60, 67, 68
Orgel, Stephen, 116, 121–22, 123, 126–27, 156, 160, 185–87, 239 n.2, 249 n.2, 250 n.24, 251 n.37
Origins of Amazons, 22, 98, 124, 248 n.47
Orpheus, 231

Index

282

Schmidel, Ulrich, 57, 61
Scott, Joan Wallach, 4–5, 239 n.8
Scythians, 24, 33, 36, 155, 221
Sedgwick, Eve, 6, 11, 33–34, 41, 140, 145–46
Semiramis, 18, 21, 89, 98
Seneca, 222, 232–33, 259 n.59
Separatism, xi, 14–15, 19, 23, 33, 40, 42, 61, 63, 219–21, 229, 236
Sex toys, 42–43, 96
Sexual difference, 28–29, 36, 42, 44–45, 77, 83, 84–85, 99–100, 118, 141, 145, 147, 152–53, 159, 178–81, 184–85, 189, 195, 197, 200, 218, 222
Sexual identity, 3–8, 83, 100, 183, 195
Sexual orientation, 33, 164–65
Sexual reproduction, 5, 8, 21, 24–25, 27–28, 33, 39, 44, 50, 55, 62, 90–91, 103–4, 111, 141, 143, 145, 152, 176–77, 196, 213, 228–29, 249 n.57, 254 n.44
Shadwell, Thomas, 130
Shakespeare, William, 27, 29, 34, 41, 43, 91, 106–7, 112, 119, 130, 151, 204–6, 209, 211, 213, 220, 222, 229–30, 234, 249 n.62; *1 Henry VI*, 37, 80–92, 107, 119–20; *2 Henry VI*, 80–84, 92–97, 106; *3 Henry VI*, 37, 80–84, 97–107; *A Midsummer Night's Dream*, 5, 39–40, 204–35, 236, 250 n.15; *Richard III*, 81, 105–7; *Romeo and Juliet*, 226, 230, 250 n.15; *Timon of Athens*, 129–33; *The Two Noble Kinsmen*, 236–38
Shaver, Anne, 256 n.12
Shaw, George Bernard, 88, 91, 247 nn. 21, 34
Shepherd, Simon, 240 n.41
Sidney, Sir Philip, 39, 43, 92, 154, 177, 180, 192, 201, 247 n.35; *The (New) Arcadia*, 177, 180, 189, 194, 201; *The (Old) Arcadia*, 5, 39, 176–201
Siebers, Tobin, 242 n.83
Silberman, Lauren, 144, 148, 163, 164, 252 n.7, 253 n.10, 255 n.62
Sinfield, Alan, 256 n.12, 257 n.39
Skelton, John, 218
Skepticism, 13–14, 52–55, 67
Smith, Barbara Herrnstein, 65–66
Smith, Bruce, 8–9, 211, 238, 239 nn. 2, 3, 253 n.16

Socialized desire, 2, 7, 9, 40, 45, 120, 154, 210–11, 222–23, 228, 231, 234
Sodomy, 3–6, 8, 28, 35, 163, 239 nn. 3, 7
Soellner, Rolf, 130–31
Sovereignty, xiii, 53, 63, 69, 92, 98, 106, 117, 208, 234, 254 n.43; female, 12–13, 17–21, 71–78, 89–90, 96–99, 102–3, 123–25, 240 n.43, 241 n.54; male, 81, 93–98, 102–3, 110–15, 118–19, 125–29, 254 n.48
Spenser, Edmund, 17–18, 43, 123, 138, 215; *The Faerie Queene*, 5, 39, 138–74, 216
Stallybrass, Peter, 35, 149, 181–82, 240 n.43, 245 n.64
Stephens, Dorothy, 8, 167–68, 242 n.83, 254 n.50, 255 n.54
Stillman, Robert, 257 n.39
Stoller, Robert, 31
Strabo, 218, 228–29
Sullivan, Margaret, 180, 189–90, 257 n.28
Supplement, 11, 38, 40, 138, 157, 160, 165, 193–95, 197, 220
Suzuki, Mihoko, 142, 253 nn. 15, 33, 254 n.35, 255 nn. 60, 63, 259 nn. 48, 59, 260 n.68
Swetnam the Woman-Hater, 177
Symbolic, 9, 66, 126, 197–98
Synecdoche, 31, 51, 53, 111–14, 124, 128, 155, 243 n.6

Taufer, Alison, 240 n.37
Tennenhouse, Leonard, 245 n.54, 257 n.39, 258 n.12
Thalestris, 16–17
Theatricality, 37–38, 59–60, 82–84, 96–97, 99–102, 104–6, 110–11, 115–21, 124–25, 127–28, 140, 161, 177–78, 181–82, 184, 188, 193–97, 199, 226, 259 n.60, 260 n.72
Theseus, 16, 19, 34–35, 40, 122, 205–35, 236–38
Thevet, André, 29, 52, 68, 254 n.41, 259 n.57
Third term, 11, 25, 36, 111, 182–83, 193, 195, 197, 221
Thisbe, 208, 211, 226, 230–32
Thomiris, 18, 21
Thoreau, Henry David, 176
Tillyard, E. M. W., 91

Index
283

*Kathryn Schwarz is Assistant Professor of
English at Vanderbilt University.*

Library of Congress Cataloging-in-Publication Data
Schwarz, Kathryn, 1966–
Tough love : Amazon encounters in the
English Renaissance / Kathryn Schwarz.
p.   cm. — (Series Q)
Includes bibliographical references and index.
ISBN 0-8223-2602-7 (cloth : alk. paper)
ISBN 0-8223-2599-3 (pbk. : alk. paper)
1. English literature—Early modern, 1500–1700—
History and criticism.   2. Amazons in literature.
3. English literature—Male authors—History and
criticism.   4. Women and literature—England—
History—16th century.   5. Women and literature—
England—History—17th century.   6. Gender
identity in literature.   7. Women soldiers
in literature.   8. Sex role in literature.
9. Renaissance—England.   10. Love in literature.
I. Title.   II. Series.
PR428.A47 S39   2000
820.9'352—dc21
00-030866